Gender, Conservatism and Political Representation

Edited by
Karen Celis and Sarah Childs

© K. Celis and S. Childs 2014

Cover Image: © 'Dummy' by Fraser King

First published by the ECPR Press in 2014

The ECPR Press is the publishing imprint of the European Consortium for Political Research (ECPR), a scholarly association, which supports and encourages the training, research and cross-national cooperation of political scientists in institutions throughout Europe and beyond.

ECPR Press
Harbour House
Hythe Quay
Colchester
CO2 8FJ
United Kingdom

Typeset by ECPR Press

Printed and bound by Lightning Source

British Library Cataloguing in Publication Data

A catalogue record for this book is available from the British Library

Hardback ISBN: 978-1-907301-71-1
PDF ISBN: 978-1-910259-57-3
EPUB ISBN: 978-1-910259-56-6
KINDLE ISBN: 978-1-910259-55-9

www.ecpr.eu/ecprpress

ECPR – *Studies in European Political Science* is a series of high-quality edited volumes on topics at the cutting edge of current political science and political thought. All volumes are research-based offering new perspectives in the study of politics with contributions from leading scholars working in the relevant fields. Most of the volumes originate from ECPR events including the Joint Sessions of Workshops, the Research Sessions, and the General Conferences.
Books in this series:

Personal Representation: The Neglected Dimension of Electoral Systems
ISBN: 9781907301162
Edited by Josep Colomer

The Political Ecology of the Metropolis
ISBN: 9781907301377
*Edited by Jefferey M. Sellers, Daniel Kübler, R. Alan Walks
and Melanie Walter-Rogg*

Political Participation in France and Germany
ISBN: 9781907301315
Oscar Gabriel, Silke Keil, and Eric Kerrouche

A Political Sociology of Transnational Europe
ISBN: 9781907301346
Edited by Niilo Kauppi

Political Trust: Why Context Matters
ISBN: 9781907301230
Edited by Sonja Zmerli and Marc Hooghe

**Practices of Interparliamentary Coordination in International Politics:
The European Union and Beyond**
ISBN: 9781907301308
Edited by Ben Crum and John Erik Fossum

Spreading Protest: Social Movements in Times of Crisis
ISBN: 9781910259207
Edited by Donatella della Porta and Alice Mattoni

Please visit www.ecpr.eu/ecprpress for up-to-date information about new publications.

Contents

List of Figures and Tables

List of Abbreviations

AN	*Alleanza Nazionale* (National Alliance, Italy)
AWNL	Australian Women's National League
BBB	Bulgarian Business Bloc
BES	British Election Study
BNS	Bulgarian National Union
BSP	Bulgarian Socialist Party
BZNS	*Balgarski Zemedelski Naroden Sayuz* (Agrarian Party, Bulgaria)
CBLPI	Clare Booth Luce Policy Institute (USA)
CD&V	*Christen-Democratisch en Vlaams* (Flemish Christian Democratic Party, Belgium)
CDU	Christian Democratic Union (Germany)
CEDAW	Convention on the Elimination of all kinds of Discrimination against Women
CIF	*Centro Italiano Femminile* (Italian Women's Centre)
CSU	Christian Social Union (Bavaria)
CWA	Concerned Women for America (USA)
DC	*Democrazia Cristiana* (Christian Democratic Party, Italy)
DPJ	Democratic Party of Japan
DRW	Descriptive representation of women
DSB	Democrats for Strong Bulgaria
EELV	*Europe Écologie – Les Verts* (Green Party, France)
EF	Eagle Forum (USA)
FDP	*Freie Demokratische Partei* (Free Democratic Party, Germany)
FN	*Front National* (National Front, France)
GERB	*Grazhdani za evropeysko razvitie na Balgariya* (Citizens for European Development of Bulgaria)
GOP	'Grand Old Party' or Republican Party (USA)
IWF	Independent Women's Forum (USA)
JDP	*Adalet ve Kalkinma Partisi* (Justice and Development Party, Turkey)
JSP	Japanese Socialist Party
LDP	Liberal Democratic Party (Japan)
LGBT	Lesbian, gay, bisexual and transgender
MMD	Multi-member district (Japan)
MoDem	*Mouvement Démocratique* (France)
MRF	Movement for Rights and Freedoms (Bulgaria)
NAP	*Milliyetci Hareket Partisi* (Nationalist Action Party, Turkey)

NeW	Network of enlightened Women (USA)
NDSV	*Nacionalno Dvizhenie Simeon Vtori* (National Movement Simeon Second, Bulgaria)
NOW	National Organization for Women (USA)
N-VA	*Nieuw-Vlaamse Alliantie* (Flemish Regionalist Party, Belgium)
NYTKIS	Coalition of Finnish Women's Associations
ODIHR	Office for Democratic Institutions and Human Rights
ODS	United Democratic Forces (Bulgaria)
Open VLD	*Open Vlaamse Liberalen en Democraten* (Flemish Liberal Democratic Party, Belgium)
OSCE	Organisation for Security and Co-operation in Europe
PARC	Policy Affairs Research Council (Germany)
PBW	Party of Bulgarian Women
PCI	Italian Communist Party
PdL	*Popolo della Libertà* (People of Freedom, Italy)
PDP	*Baris ve Demokrasi Partisi* (Peace and Democracy Party (Kurdish Nationalist), Turkey)
PDS	Party of Democratic Socialism (Germany)
PJ	*Partido Justicialista* (Peronist Party, Argentina)
PJD	Party for Justice and Development (Morocco)
PPI	*Partito Popolare Italiano*
PR	Proportional representation
PRO	*Propuesta Republicana* (Argentina)
PSL	Personal status legislation
PTA	Parent-Teacher Association (USA)
RPP	Republican People's Party (*Cumhuriyet Halk Partisi*, Turkey)
RZS	*Red, zakonnost i spravedlivost* ((party of) Law, Order and Justice, Bulgaria)
SDP	Social Democratic Party (Finland)
SGP	Smart Girl Politics (USA)
SMIC	*Salaire minimum de croissance* (minimum wage, France)
SNTV	Single non-transferable vote
SP.A	*Socialistische Partij Anders* (Flemish Social Democratic Party, Belgium)
SPD	Social Democratic Party (Germany)
SRW	Substantive representation of women
TGNA	*Türkiye Büyük Millet Meclisi* (Turkish Grand National Assembly)
UCR	*Unión Cívica Radical* (Argentina)
UDC	Union of Christian and Centre Democrats (Italy)
UDF	Union of Democratic Forces (Bulgaria; essentially the same as ODS)
UMP	*Union pour un Mouvement Populaire* (Union for a Popular Movement, France)

Contributors

DIDIER CALUWAERTS is a postdoctoral researcher from the Research Foundation Flanders (FWO) at the Vrije Universiteit Brussel, and a Fulbright Democracy Fellow at the Harvard Ash Center for Democratic Governance and Innovations. His research focuses on deliberative and participatory democracy.

ROSIE CAMPBELL PhD is a Senior Lecturer in Politics at Birkbeck University of London. Rosie has research interests in British politics, particularly voting behaviour, political participation, representation, political careers and women and politics. Her book *Gender and the Vote in Britain* was published in 2006 and she has recently written on the politics of diversity, women voters and what voters want from their parliamentary candidates. She is co-investigator of the Leverhulme-funded project 'The new political class? The changing socio-economic profile of PPCs and MPs in Britain, 1945–2015' with Jennifer Hudson (UCL).

FRANCESCO CAVATORTA is Associate Professor at the Department of Political Science, Laval University, Quebec. His research focuses on processes of regime change in the Arab world, Islamist movements and civil society activism. He has previously published on these topics in *Democratization, Journal of Modern African Studies, Government and Opposition, Totalitarian Movements and Political Religions, Contemporary Arab Affairs, Mediterranean Politics* and *British Journal of Middle Eastern Studies,* among others.

KAREN CELIS is research professor at the Department of Political Science of the Vrije Universiteit Brussel, and affiliated to RHEA (Centre for Gender and Diversity). She conducts theoretical and empirical research (qualitative, comparative) on political representation of groups (women, ethnic minorities, class, age groups, LGBT), equality policies and state feminism. She is co-editor of *The Oxford Handbook on Gender and Politics* (OUP, 2013, with Georgina Waylen, Johanna Kantola and Laurel Weldon).

SARAH CHILDS is Professor of Politics and Gender at the University of Bristol, UK. She has published widely on women, representation and party politics and Parliament over the last decade or so. Key articles on new Labour's women MPs, descriptive and substantive representation, the concept of critical mass, and conservatism, gender and representation, have been published in *Political Studies, Politics and Gender, Government and Parliamentary Affairs* and *Party Politics.* Her latest book, *Sex, Gender and the Conservative Party: From Iron Lady to Kitten Heels,* with Paul Webb, was published in 2012.

JENNIFER CURTIN is an Associate Professor in Politics and International Relations at the University of Auckland in New Zealand. Her research spans the fields of comparative politics and public policy, with a focus on Australia and New Zealand, and women in politics. She has published widely on these topics including, most recently, articles on the status of women in the discipline (*Political Science* 2013), and on how federalism matters to domestic violence policy (co-authored in *Publius* 2013). In 2011, she co-edited a special issue on Coalition Formation in the journal *Political Science*.

EMANUELA DALMASSO is a postdoctoral Researcher at the University of Amsterdam. Her research focuses on Moroccan civil society actors and how they interact with the regime, and also on the role of Islamist parties and movements activism in Morocco. She has previously published on these topics in the *Journal of Modern African Studies*, *Totalitarian Movements and Political Religions*, *Contemporary Arab Affairs* and *Mediterranean Politics*.

SILVIA ERZEEL is an FRS–FNRS postdoctoral researcher (*chargée de recherches*) at the Institut de sciences politiques Louvain-Europe of the Université catholique de Louvain. Her research focuses on political representation, political parties and gender, and diversity politics in Europe.

ALISA GAUNDER is professor of political science at Southwestern University in Georgetown, Texas. Her research interests include comparative political leadership, campaign finance reform, and women and politics in Japan. She is the author of *Political Reform in Japan: Leadership Looming Large* (Routledge 2007) and editor of the *Routledge Handbook of Japanese Politics* (Routledge 2011).

ROBERTA GUERRINA is Reader in Politics and Head of the School at the University of Surrey. She is a European policy analyst with a particular interest in European social policy, citizenship policy and gender equality. She has published in the area of women's human rights, work-life balance, identity politics and the idea of Europe. She is author of *Mothering the Union* (Manchester University Press, 2005) and *Europe: History, Ideas and Ideologies* (Arnold, 2002).

JOSEF HIEN is a postdoctoral researcher at the Collegio Carlo Alberto in Turin. He was a postdoctoral fellow at the Max Planck Institute for the Study of Societies in Cologne and holds a PhD from the European University Institute in Florence. Hien is interested in the connection between political economy and religion. His thesis analysed the role of religiously informed doctrines in the formation of the German and Italian welfare states.

JOHANNA KANTOLA is Academy Research Fellow in Gender Studies in the University of Helsinki, where she also holds a permanent position as a Senior Lecturer in Gender Studies. She has published extensively on gender, politics and the state, and her monographs include *Gender and the European Union* (Palgrave 2010) and *Feminists Theorize the State* (Palgrave 2006). She is co-editor of the *Oxford Handbook on Gender and Politics* (OUP 2013, with Georgina Waylen, Karen Celis and Laurel Weldon) and co-editor of the Palgrave *Gender and Politics Book Series* (with Judith Squires).

ZEYNEP ŞAHIN-MENCÜTEK is Assistant Professor of International Relations at Gediz University, Turkey. Her research focuses on women's political activism in relation to democratisation, socio-political movements, international migration, and representation, with an emphasis on Turkey and the Middle East. She is currently examining the factors influencing women's representation in conservative and ethno-nationalist parties. Based on her dissertation study, she is preparing a book addressing gender politics in Turkey.

RAINBOW MURRAY is Reader in Politics at Queen Mary University of London. She researches political representation, with particular interests in gender, French politics, and political institutions. Current projects include the impact of gender quotas on parliament, and challenging existing notions of 'meritocracy'. She has published widely in journals such as *Party Politics, Political Research Quarterly, Politics & Gender* and *West European Politics*.

DANIELA R. PICCIO holds a PhD from the European University Institute, Florence. Since 2010 she has been a postdoctoral Research Associate at Leiden University. Her work has appeared in *South European Society and Politics*, *Representation*, and *International Political Science Review*, as well as in several edited book volumes. Her main research interests include political parties, political representation, social movements, and party (finance) regulation.

JENNIFER M. PISCOPO is Assistant Professor of Politics at Occidental College in Los Angeles, California. She has published widely on representation, gender quotas, and legislative institutions in Latin America, and she co-edited *The Impact of Gender Quotas* (Oxford University Press, 2012). She holds a PhD in Political Science from the University of California, San Diego (2011) and an MPhil in Latin American Studies from the University of Cambridge (2003), where she was a Gates Cambridge Scholar.

EKATERINA R. RASHKOVA is an Assistant Professor of Comparative Politics at the University of Innsbruck. Her research interests lie in electoral and party systems and the strategic behaviour of political actors, institutions, party system development, party regulation and gender representation. Her work compares new and established democracies and has appeared in *Comparative European Politics, Party Politics* and *Political Studies*, as well as in several edited book volumes.

MILJA SAARI is an Early Stage Researcher in the University of Helsinki, in the Department of Political and Economic Studies. The working title of her PhD dissertation is 'Equal pay – a negotiated human right'. Her main academic fields of expertise are equal pay and gender mainstreaming. She also trains and consults organisations, especially trade unions, in conducting gender equality plans and pay surveys.

RONNEE SCHREIBER is Professor of Political Science at San Diego State University. Her book, *Righting Feminism: Conservative Women and American Politics*, was published by Oxford University Press and examines how conservative women's organisations represent women in national politics. She has also published in *Journal of Women, Politics and Policy*, *Journal of Urban Affairs*, *New Political Science*, *Political Communication*, *Politics & Gender*, *Queries*, *Sex Roles*, *Social History* and several edited volumes. Her current research explores how women political leaders construct and represent mothers' interests.

RÉJANE SÉNAC is a CNRS Research Fellow at the Centre for Political Research at Sciences Po (CEVIPOF) and teaches in the gender studies programme of Sciences Po (PRESAGE). Her research challenges the relationships between norms and rules, justice and public policy, with particular interest in republican equality. She has published in journals such as *French Politics*, *Modern and Contemporary France* and *Revue française de science politique*, and her books include *L'invention de la diversité* (Paris, PUF 2012).

SARAH ELISE WILIARTY is an Associate Professor of Government at Wesleyan University in Connecticut. She is the author of *The CDU and the Politics of Gender in Germany: Bringing Women to the Party* (2010). Her research focuses on women and politics, political parties, Christian Democracy and energy policy. Her new project investigates gender differences in media coverage of politicians in Europe.

EMILIA ZANKINA is an Assistant Professor in Political Science at the American University in Bulgaria. Her research examines democratisation and elite transformation in Eastern Europe, populism, civil service reform, and gender political representation. In the past, Zankina has served as Associate Director of the Center for Russian and East European Studies at the University of Pittsburgh, Managing Editor of *East European Politics and Societies*, and Editor-in-Chief of the *Newsletter* of the Bulgarian Studies Association. She is the recipient of a number of national grants from IREX, ACLS, American Councils, Wilson Center, and more.

Acknowledgements

For our pioneering feminist foremothers of political science on whose shoulders we stand, who opened up the space for us and later generations to study sex, gender and politics. To *Les Grandes Dames*, thank you!

Karen Celis and Sarah Childs
November 2014

Introduction: The 'Puzzle' of Gender, Conservatism and Representation

Karen Celis and Sarah Childs

In a good number of countries, the number of conservative women participating in democratic politics appears to be increasing. Conservative women leaders like Michelle Bachmann and Sarah Palin in the US, and the German Chancellor, Angela Merkel, are notable on the world political stage; in the 2010 US primaries a record number of conservative women featured; three out of the ten Canadian governors in 2012 were representatives of the Conservative Party; the UK's Westminster Parliament witnessed more than a doubling in the number of conservative women MPs at its general election in 2010; and (young) women's participation in Islamist movements and parties was highly visible during the Arab Uprisings of 2011–12.

In recognising such changes in women's political participation and representation in recent years, gender and politics scholars have been increasingly aware of the importance of doing something more than the 'simple counting' of women's presence in electoral politics. In addition to documenting the overall numbers of biological females elected to our parliaments or participating in democratic politics and movements, there is appreciation of the necessity of attending to women political actors' particular characteristics. Amongst other background differences such as race and class, party and ideological identities are deemed increasingly salient to understandings of women's political representation.

The academic study of women's political representation, over the last two decades or so (largely following Pitkin's classic typology), has investigated women's (1) descriptive, (2) symbolic and (3) substantive ('acting for') representation.[1] Descriptive representation refers to a notion of correspondence between a representative's characteristics and the represented: the representative 'stands for' them, by virtue of a correspondence or connection between them (Pitkin 1967: 61). In symbolic representation, symbols represent something or someone because they 'stand for' and 'evoke' their referent. Substantive representation, in everyday language, points to the notion that representatives act 'on behalf of others' and 'in their interest' (Pitkin 1969: 17). In this, the represented is 'logically prior'; the representative must be 'responsive to' the represented (Pitkin 1967: 140). Of these types of representation, 'acting for' or substantive representation is considered the true meaning of representation: the representative

---

1. Pitkin's formalistic representation type has rarely been taken up by gender and politics scholars. Whilst it helps identify the basis of authorisation or accountability of this conception, as she points out, it fails to permit an evaluation of the activity of representation – the relationship between the represented and the representative – as it occurs (*see* Childs 2008, Chapter Four).

system must look after and be responsive to public opinion, except insofar as non-responsiveness can be justified in terms of the public interest (Pitkin 1967: 224). However, Pitkin's confidence in substantive representation as the true definition of representation has not gone unchallenged by representation theorists (Birch 1971; Judge 1999). And when feminist scholars have added sex and gender into the mix, the limitations of Pitkin's conceptualisations has become increasingly clear (*see* Childs and Lovenduski 2013 for an overview).

The attention of gender and politics scholars has only recently been paid to symbolic representation (*see* for instance, Lombardo and Meier 2014). This is not to say that the implication of Pitkin's position has been accepted (Childs 2008), namely, that if symbols can be arbitrary it should not matter if our political representatives are all – or even disproportionately – male. Similarly, a conclusion that women are symbolically represented only when women believe they are represented is surely as unconvincing now as the general principle was for Pitkin in the late 1960s. Instead, gender and politics research suggests that, as symbols, women political representatives have the potential to act as role models; to signify women's political equality as participants in politics; and to enhance the legitimacy of political institutions and engender women's mass engagement with formal politics (Campbell and Wolbrecht 2006; Wolbrecht and Campbell 2007; Zetterberg 2008).

Studying women's descriptive representation – sometimes referred to as numerical or microcosmic representation – was the focus of the earliest gender and politics research. This has generated extensive studies of women's recruitment into politics across the globe as well as consideration of what interventions can be undertaken to increase their presence (Krook 2009; Kittilson 2006; Norris and Lovenduski 1995). Given that only in two countries in the world, as of Spring 2014, do women reach fifty-plus per cent of representatives (namely Rwanda and Andorra[2]), documenting the numbers of women standing for selection and election, and most importantly, being elected, remains a constant task for researchers – and is addressed in Part I in this volume. Similarly, academic and activist efforts regarding the identification of the various factors that inhibit, and the (multiple) interventions that can enhance, women's recruitment remain important political projects. The latter might include reforms to electoral systems and party regulations, including the introduction of sex quotas (Childs 2013; Krook and Norris 2014; Celis *et al.* 2011).

Once women enter elected political institutions, historians and gender and politics scholars have looked to see whether there were any gendered effects (Dahlerup 1988; *see* Childs and Lovenduski 2013 for an overview). Would the presence of women correspondingly lead to the feminisation of politics – the inclusion both of women's bodies and women's concerns and perspectives? (Lovenduski 2005, *see also* below)[3] – the subject of Part II of this book. Researchers often questioned

---

2.   *See* http://www.ipu.org (accessed 5 May 2014).

3.   We largely sidestep debates about critical mass in this Introduction (*see* Childs and Krook 2006,

Pitkin's dismissal of descriptive representation and both theorised and empirically studied the relationship between this and substantive representation. In the work of Anne Phillips (1995), Jane Mansbridge (1999), amongst others, there is a healthy scepticism of Pitkin's take on the link between representatives' characteristics and their actions. A man, she wrote, can 'only be held to account for what he has done' and 'not for what he is', and there may be 'no simple correlation' (Pitkin 1967: 89) between descriptive and substantive representation. That said, gender and politics theory and empirical observations suggested something a little different: that there may well be a complicated, mediated, and probabalistic relationship between women's descriptive and substantive representation (Childs 2004; Lovenduski 2005; Reingold 2000; Swers 2002; Beckwith 2007). Phillips' (1995) 'shot in the dark' phrase has resonated with many academics and, indeed, activists.

The basis for such a feminist argument linking women's descriptive and substantive representation has rarely been biological – that is, underpinned by notions of sex difference. Black feminist thought and post-structuralist gender theory had already warned us of the dangers of essentialism and of presuming that women were a homogeneous category (Hill Collins 1990; Hooks 1994; Butler 1990). And subsequent discussions of intersectionality would confirm this (*see* Hill Collins and Chepp 2013).[4] Rather, scholars have favoured grounding the relationship between the two dimensions of representation in women and men's differently gendered experiences. As Phillips' explicitly admitted: there is no 'empirical or theoretical plausibility' to the idea that women share experiences, or that women's shared experiences translate into shared beliefs or goals. Neither does she consider it likely that women will organise themselves into a group with group opinions and goals (Phillips 1995: 53–5). Mansbridge (1999: 644) puts it like this: when there are contexts of (1) mistrust between disadvantaged and advantaged groups; (2) uncrystallised, not fully articulated, interests; (3) where the social meaning of 'ability to rule' has been seriously questioned for members of disadvantaged groups; and (4) past discrimination against disadvantaged groups, descriptive representation is necessary. As issues arise, the woman representative is more likely than the non-descriptive representative to 'react more or less the way' the represented would have were they present. This is because women representatives share 'the outward signs of having lived through' the same experiences giving them 'communicative and informational advantages' and enabling women representatives to 'forge bonds of trust' and vertical communication with the women they represent (Mansbridge 1999: 641). Critics might still query the assumption of shared gendered experiences. What would the 'content' of women's substantive representation in this case be: what would women representatives seek to act in respect of, as they 'acted for' women?

2008; Dahlerup in Campbell and Childs 2014, forthcoming). For discussions of feminist institutionalism *see* Krook and Mackay 2011.

4. *See* also issue on 'Recent Developments in Intersectionality Research: Expanding beyond Race and Gender' in *Politics & Gender*, 8 (3), September 2012.

We have, with colleagues, written elsewhere that theories of women's substantive representation must come to terms with the empirical fact that whilst there may be some universal *women's issues* (the broad policy category of issues that concern women), shared by all women, it is unlikely that there are universal women's interests (the content given to particular issues) (Celis *et al.* 2014; cf. Schwindt-Bayer and Taylor-Robinson 2011; Reingold and Swers 2011; Baldez 2011).[5] Accordingly, identifying a priori a set of 'women's issues' and evaluating the actions of representatives against these can – in our view – only present a partial account of women's substantive representation. And when combined with a feminist take (however defined) on what is in the interests of women (Celis and Childs 2013), scholars risk reducing the substantive representation of women to the feminist substantive representation of women in a context when non- and anti-feminist women may well be articulating competing gendered representative claims 'for' women. Gendered representative claims can be considered those that frame the claim as first, directly of importance to women; second, only affecting women; third, discussed in terms of gender difference; fourth, spoken of in terms of gendered effects; and finally framed in terms of equality between women and men (Celis *et al.* 2014; Severs 2012; Celis 2006). In more concrete terms we can say in the West that acting for women, in the existing literature, has frequently been equated – and operationalised in empirical studies – with the demands of the second wave of women's movements. Issues such as violence against women, childcare, reproductive rights, equal pay and equal rights are usually named. Yet gendered representation claims that stand in opposition to these widely recognised second-wave western feminist representative claims have also been identified by some scholars. These claims are likely underpinned by notions of maternal feminism (Offen 2000), emphasis on women's private roles (Carroll 1992), social (Schreiber 2008), and liberal conservative views of 'the individual', equality and the market (Schreiber 2008; Celis and Erzeel 2013; Childs and Webb 2012), and/ or Islamic feminism (Ahmed 1992; Badran 2009; Karam 1998). Accordingly, we have concluded that the presumption of a universal and feminist set of women's issues and concept of women's interests can only ever be a myth: as a heterogeneous category women are likely to have at least some different interests, both within the same location and over time (Celis *et al.* 2014). Newer research – addressed in Part III of this book – moreover explores the concepts of accountability and attitudinal congruency between women representatives and the represented; between women at the mass and the elite levels.

So, what of the conservative woman representative? What is her potential to 'act for' women? Much of the research on women's substantive representation has focused – as hinted at above – on the actions of leftist women, in part because they were (at least in many established democracies) present in higher numbers. It was also a reflection of the aforementioned equation of the substantive representation

---

5.   *See* Celis (2014) for a more extensive debate on the concept and operationalisation of women's issues in gender and politics research.

of women with a feminist substantive representation of women by leftist feminist women (Childs and Krook 2006, 2008). However, imagine once again the Michelle Bachman and Sarah Palin's of US politics; or Germany's Angela Merkel; or the Islamic women on the streets in the Middle East. These conservative women seem – at least at first blush – to challenge rather than 'fit' the dominant claims made in the gender and politics literature about women's substantive representation. But given the refinement to conceptions of women's substantive representation evident in more recent research, the contribution of these and other conservative women might well be better captured – empirically and conceptually.[6]

Existing empirical research on gender, conservatism and representation is, unfortunately limited. This is, in part, again and as just noted, a reflection of the lesser number of conservative women representatives that have been hitherto elected to many political institutions. But it is also because conservatives' claims and actions for women have frequently been judged against feminist criteria – and found wanting in those terms (Celis and Childs 2013). If we turn to the comparative parties and civil society literature, we also see a limitation in the literature: a failure to gender its analysis of conservative politics, although recent exceptions include Wiliarty's (2010) study of the German Christian Democratic Union (CDU), and Childs and Webb's study of the UK Conservative Party (2012) in respect of the former, and Schreiber's (2008) analysis of US conservative women's movements in respect of the latter.

This book aims then, to provide a much-needed contribution to the study of women's political presentation by bringing together leading and younger politics and gender experts in this emergent area of research,[7] and presenting conceptually and empirically rich scholarship at the intersection of gender, conservatism, conservative parties and organisations, and representation. Collectively, the volume provides wide geographic coverage, with case studies from Europe and the US, but also from Argentina, Australia, New Zealand, Japan, Turkey and Morocco. Individual chapters employ a range of qualitative and quantitative research methods and are informed by an overarching conceptual framework for studying conservative gendered representation. Key to this are: the already noted concept of feminisation (the inclusion of women and their women's concerns and perspectives), following Lovenduski (2005); attention to the discursive struggles and strategies associated with conservative women's political participation and representation; acknowledgement of the complex relationship between women's descriptive and substantive representation; conceptual distinctions between women's issues and interests; and notions of responsiveness in the citizen-representative relationship. By exploring different types of conservative actors, parties, organisations over time, and in different locations, and subjecting their

---

6. Later in this Introduction we expand on a distinction between gendered claims – Type I and Type II claims – that informed the research in this edited collection.

7. The chapters are based on the papers presented at the ECPR Joint Sessions Workshop 'Conservatism, Conservative Parties and Women's Political Representation' in 2012.

actions to systematic analysis, this edited volume offers new initial insights as well as suggesting a future comparative research terrain.

Taken together, the chapters establish that women are occupying spaces within conservative politics and parties, and are frequently articulating explicitly gendered discourses on women and gender relations. Without exception, the chapters speak to the uneasy coexistence of party feminisation and gendered representation on the one hand, and rightist ideologies on the other hand. In other words, they observe that the space available for conservative women in political parties and parliaments is often limited and constrained. Constraints include for example, the male breadwinner model dominant in European Christian Democratic parties, and the formal and informal rules about women's appropriate behaviour as adhered to by Muslim parties.

Part I opens with a series of chapters on legislative recruitments. It asks questions about the enhanced presence of women in conservative parties and their ambition to establish feminist and/or gendered change. Chapters explore the issue of the position and power women have within in their parties – as individual members, as elected representatives, and collectively in terms of parties' women's sections – and the conditions under which conservative women acquire greater influence.

Part II provides more fulsome analysis of the gendered changes required to enable the entrance of conservative women into the political arena, and the resultant changes their participation and representation bring about. This part of the book, reflecting the current strengths of politics and gender research, focuses on women's substantive representation. The chapters examine the struggles over the definition of women's interests and gender equality, and explore the renegotiation of gender roles that conservative women grapple with. Key questions include whether conservative women (and men) in government, parliaments and parties represent women's issues and interests (and what that might mean in practice), and whether they thereby challenge and, or, broaden the scope of what counts as women's substantive representation. Conservative women's descriptive representation as a source for substantive representation of women – a relationship touched upon in Part I and addressed more systematically Part II – turns out to be highly conditional and does not depend on the numbers of women alone (as is true also for leftist women). Even when there is agreement about what is in the interests of women – and we would argue this is rarely likely to be the case – the presence of influential women or high numbers of elected women from conservative parties in parliaments and governments, is no guarantee of action 'for women'.

The final part of the book, Part III, explores the roles of citizens and voters in the analysis of gender, conservatism and representation. Chapters address whether there is such an entity as a feminist conservative female citizen, and if so, what she is like, what her issues and interests are, and how we might best understand the representational relationship between her and those who claim to represent her, in this instance, conservative political parties and elected representatives.

It is worth stating baldly at this point, that conservatism means different things in different places and times. For example, European Christian Democratic parties and Muslim parties likely look and act very differently from non-religious conservative ones. As the chapters investigating such parties and movements indicate, religious values underpinning specific gender roles mould women's descriptive as well as substantive representation. And, even amongst European Christian Democratic parties for example, one should have an eye for differences, namely, whether they are premised upon Protestantism or Catholicism. Furthermore, differences between social/moral conservatism and economic liberalism/conservatism immediately suggest a dualism playing out within and between different conservative parties. Rightist, conservative, religious and nationalist parties, frequently have what might be widely recognised as a traditional take on women's roles in society, whereas rightist liberal parties might be morally progressive, even as they reject at the same time the idea of structural discrimination – and the state's role in actively enhancing women's status – that arguably hinder women's equal political representation and women's equality more generally. Conservatism and conservative parties in non-Western democracies likely mean something different yet again; notions of left/right may simply not travel easily, if at all. In post-communist countries the key political cleavage is communist versus non-communist rather than the classic left/right divide. Similarly, the distinction between Islamist and non-Islamist conservatism might make more sense in countries where the majority of the citizens are Muslim. In these cases left/secular stands for the status quo, and conservatism/Islam for change, albeit within traditional/religious values.

Part I: Feminising conservative parties: Women's participation and descriptive representation

As noted already, it has almost become commonplace over the last few years when looking at the composition of the worlds' parliaments to comment on the increased number of conservative women representatives. There appears to be a new pattern emerging in women's descriptive representation: leftist dominance, at least as evidenced in long standing democracies from the 1970s and 1980s onwards, is being, albeit to varying degrees, rebalanced as conservative parties select and elect greater numbers of women representatives. Indeed, in some countries, such as Turkey, as discussed in Chapter Four, the number of women in rightist parties equals the numbers elected by leftist parties.

As would-be conservative women representatives seek to gain access to legislative office they routinely have to negotiate many of the same barriers faced by women in leftist parties. Women of both parties are affected by the classic demand- and supply-side factors of political recruitment; the effects of electoral systems and inter-party competition; and the presence and influence, or the absence, of women's sections within political parties (*see* for example, Norris and Lovenduski 1995; Kittilson 2006; Celis *et al.* 2011). Besides these general contextual factors and dynamics, conservative women have additionally to negotiate the conservatism (ideology and practices) that is specific to their parties, party systems, and wider political contexts (*see* for example, Young 2000; Wiliarty 2010; Childs and Webb 2012; Bryson and Heppell 2010; Dillard 2005).

To illuminate the determinants of conservative women's descriptive representation, the chapters in Part I explore specifically the patterns of women gaining access to, and power across, a range of conservative parties around the globe. In their analyses, chapter authors recognise and give considerable weight to the importance of institutions and agency in mediating the emergence and consolidation of conservative women's political presence. The gendered formal structures and informal norms of particular institutions – such as the historical form that a particular political party takes at a specific moment – as well as the capacity of individuals to deploy and gain power therein, are given considered attention. In this way the chapters pay particular attention to party structure and organisation as well as to individual women, as conservative women address, and sometimes challenge or transform, the existing gender regime within conservative parties and the wider society.

Taken together the chapters in Part I tell a complex and nuanced story about the feminisation of conservative parties; how, when and why conservative women are able to achieve presence within individual conservative political parties, and build capacity to represent women substantively from within their conservative parties, as well as in political and policy making in legislatures and governments. In so doing, they further illuminate understandings of feminisation: revealing how women are integrated into political parties and in what ways, and to what extent, women's concerns are correspondingly integrated. In other words, they throw new light on the links between women's descriptive and substantive representation, respectively, and show how the relationship between the two operates within conservative parties. Notably, they collectively suggest the importance of sensitivity to specific historical and ideological legacies, alongside an appreciation of contemporary contexts, in gaining a better understanding of the relationship between conservatism, feminism, and political recruitment and participation. Only by recognising this can we explain the very different conclusions regarding the inclusion of women within conservative parties: 'presence without real power', as in Italy, Japan and Turkey, for example, and conservative parties as the 'most promising site' for women's representation, as in the Bulgarian case.

The first chapter 'The Supply and Demand of Conservative Female Candidates in Germany and Japan', by Sarah Elise Wiliarty and Alisa Gaunder, explores the reasons for varying levels of women's descriptive representation in conservative parties with very similar ideological profiles: the CDU in Germany and the Liberal Democratic Party (LDP) in Japan. In Germany, women have found real power in terms of government personnel; in Japan in contrast, conservative women largely remain tokens. Williarty and Gaunder argue that differences in party organisation are the dominant explanation. In particular, as a corporatist catch-all party the CDU is able to represent diverse interests in the party, which allow for a positive response to the challenges from the left in ways that helped it win votes and survive – and gender had a role to play here.

The subsequent chapter, 'Christian Democratic Party Feminisation: The German CDU and the Male Breadwinner Model' by Josef Hien, extends the analysis of Germany by contending that the type of Christianity matters, as does party closeness to the Church as an 'outsider' organisation. Hien shows that it was with the dealignment of the party from its predominantly Catholic heritage, and a shift to a neo-Protestant party, itself a result of German reunification, that the male breadwinner bias could begin to be overhauled. German family policy was subsequently remodelled; not only through a reinvention and struggle of conservative feminism, but also as a result of a heated interdenominational clash between the ideas and material interests of the Churches.

Whilst we might frequently consider conservative parties as actors for women's representation they should also be understood *as sites* for women's and gendered representation. In other words, women and women's organisations frequently strive for better representation within their political party. Only after achieving some success internally, might they be more effective in moving to act externally to further a women's political agenda. This point is developed in the next three chapters.

Daniela Piccio's chapter, 'A Complex Mediation of Interests: Party Feminisation Processes in the Italian Christian Democratic Party', shows how the Italian party *Democrazia Cristiana* (DC) and its organisation Christian Democratic Women framed 'women's issues' during the 1970s–80s. She argues that in order to understand the DC's public discourse regarding women, a wide range of representational claims need to be considered. Whilst the official discourse of the party predominantly framed women within traditional family and domestic roles, Christian Democratic Women articulated a discourse favouring the reconciliation of the party's traditional position and the changing perceptions of women and their social roles in the 1970s.

'Gender Politics of the Justice and Development Party in Turkey' by Zeynep Şahin-Mencütek is premised upon the observation that women's political representation in Turkey is dramatically low, overall. That said, the conservative Justice and Development Party (JDP) has experienced increasing numbers of women acting as both supporters of, and mobilisers for, the party. Yet despite such increases in women's descriptive representation in the JDP, Şahin-Mencütek concludes that the promotion of gender equality therein remains limited: women's sections are the main platform for conservative women's participation in electoral politics. It is also the case that the JDP's female representatives' claims to substantively represent women are limited by conservative ideology.

The final chapter of Part I, 'When Less Means More: Influential Women of the Right – the Case of Bulgaria' by Ekaterina R. Rashkova and Emilia Zankina, contends that the historical legacy of communism in Bulgaria – in which large numbers of women were present in the communist party but lacked substantive power and voice – distorts the traditional meaning of left and right regarding gender equality. After the fall of the communist regime rightist parties, whilst not including as many women representatives as the former communist party, have been home to several influential female politicians. Critically, Rashkova and Zankina hold that it is precisely in these parties that Bulgarian women have real political influence in the post-communist era.

The chapters in Part I draw attention, collectively, to a wide variety of factors that need to be taken into account in research trying to explain *why* and *when* a feminisation of conservative parties occurs. With regard to the *why* question, it is clear that changes in women's gender roles in society at large have incentivised right-wing parties –just like leftist ones, albeit often later – to modify traditional gender views and attune them to the more modern, progressive women's movement agenda (as in the Italian, German and Japanese cases). However, greater equality between women and men in wider society is not a necessary condition, as the Bulgarian case shows. One might go so far as to claim that women's emancipation was reversed in this case at precisely the moment that a formal feminisation of conservative parties in parliaments (descriptive representation) occurred. It might well be, too, that the Bulgarian case is representative of post-communist states more generally: that the transition to post-communism and the rejection of state-driven emancipation for women ensures that conservative parties are the most promising site for enhancing women's status in such societies.

If major societal evolutions as well as drastic regime change both seem able to explain *why* the feminisation of conservative parties takes place, more ad hoc events, domestic and international, seem to determine *when* it occurs. The Italian case, for instance, points at a very specific domestic cocktail of events: the anti-divorce referendum, electoral gains by leftist parties, and the feminist women's movement reaching its peak in the mid 1970s. Similarly, the German case points at changed relationships between the CDU and the Church in explaining the moment when feminisation occurred. The integration of women into conservative parties might also happen because conservative parties experience a need to look modern (Italy), secular (Turkey), or European (Bulgaria).

Evidently, electoral instrumentalism drives conservative parties, just like other parties, when it comes to party feminisation (*see* Kittilson 2006). Right-wing parties' vulnerability to an electoral threat from the left championing a women-friendly label can indeed urge parties on the right to formulate proposals to present female candidates and enhance (or claim to enhance) women's substantive representation. But once again, the Bulgarian case reminds us that inter-party competition over feminisation is not a necessary condition: Conservative Party feminisation can occur when the left has lost all credibility in respect of women's interests and gender equality.

Electoral 'top-down'-driven feminisation can be augmented by a 'bottom-up' feminisation: via party's women's organisation and the actions of key party women. The importance of the former for women's descriptive and substantive representation is identified in a number of the cases studies presented here, not least in the German case. Nevertheless, in comparison to inter-party competition, the intra-party push by women's sections seems less of a necessary condition in and of itself. Comparison of the Italian, German, Japanese and Turkish cases suggests that the women's sections need not only to exist, but also to be strong and well-embedded within the party structures that hold real power. If not, they are likely to remain without real impact (as in the Japanese and Italian cases, for instance), and might even harm women's representation, both descriptive and substantive.

The Turkish case makes the point well, that women's sections can contribute to marginalisation through segregation rather than having an empowering effect through agency, as in the German case.

Part II: Conservatives renegotiating gender roles and equality: Women's interests and substantive representation

Existing accounts of women's substantive representation frequently take this concept to refer to the notion that the greater presence of women representatives (women's descriptive representation) will engender, even if it cannot guarantee, the greater (read: feminist) substantive representation of women. In everyday words, elected women representatives are widely considered more likely to act for women in a feminist fashion than male elected representatives. According to the concept of 'critical mass', politics will be re-gendered once the 'tipping point' has been met – when women reach, say, 15–30 per cent of representatives. Criticism of critical mass theory has, however, taken hold amongst many gender and politics scholars on the grounds that it gives little or no attention to who our representatives are, what attitudes they hold, and what kind of behaviour they engage in, as well as ignoring the context and institutions within which they operate (Childs and Krook 2006, 2008; Dahlerup 2014). Furthermore, and as noted in the opening to this introduction, too little space is given to asking what the substantive representation of women equates to on the ground. Is it always and necessarily by definition feminist/leftist, however both are defined?

In the context of such debates, the greater presence of conservative women political actors coupled with conservative claims to act for women constitute something of a discombobulating intervention for some feminist activists and scholars. In short, we contend that much feminist scholarship is unsure – perhaps even suspicious – of the nature of conservative women's representational contribution (Celis and Childs 2012). Having undertaken an extensive review of the literature published to date, it is evident that conservative women representatives sometimes make explicitly anti-feminist claims; at other times they make recognisably feminist ones, what we term here *Type I claims*; and yet at other times still, they make gendered claims, what we term *Type II claims*. These latter claims are those that address women's concerns and perspectives but do so in ways distinct from traditionally understood (even liberal) feminism. Type II claims might well be underpinned by a commitment to women's traditional roles and experiences, not least as mothers, care givers, and victims of violence. They may also reflect associations with traditional organisations that value women's difference, or that see women's public role as a manifestation of their private role. Type II claims will, moreover, be framed in terms of improving women's lives within traditional terms, rather than in feminist ones that seek to transform existing gender roles and norms. This claims framework suggests that when conservative representatives act in an anti-feminist fashion, feminists will find it easy to critique them; when they act like their leftist feminist sisters, the tendency might be to praise them, as 'good' representatives of women; but when they act on issues of particular concern to women, or when they privilege a conception of femininity that some feminists would contest or disapprove of, there is likely to be a reluctance to see what they are doing as constituting the substantive representation of women. This is because of the aforementioned tendency to conflate women's and feminist substantive representation.

Whilst a feminist definition of substantive representation might be attractive for those (of us) who want a feminist transformation of politics it is, in our view, an ultimately untenable scholarly approach. This is because different groups of women may very well have different opinions about the particular issues that affect women; may see different solutions to these; and may prioritise competing issues as politically salient for women. Drawing a distinction between (1) women's issues (broad policy areas) and (2) women's interests (the content given to these) is useful here: whilst there may be some universal women's issues, it is more likely that what counts as 'women's interests' will be contested. In such a context, Type II gendered claims articulated by conservative representatives present – we argue – a peculiarly conservative view of women's roles, and importantly, one that is additional to, and, or may compete with, feminist claims. When voiced by women representatives, this surely constitutes a conservative form of women's politics of presence. It is just one that might not be frequently recognised or legitimated. At the same time, such representative claims and acts may appeal to women who did not identify themselves as conservatives originally. It may very well, moreover, change conservatives' stances on gender and gender relations by stretching and bending conservative gender ideology. All of the chapters in Part II of this book are informed by this overarching analytic approach to gender, conservatism and representation.

The first chapter by Ronnee Schreiber, 'Motherhood, Representation and Politics: Conservative Women's Groups Negotiate Ideology and Strategy', analyses how conservative women leaders manage the tension between traditional views of motherhood and their desire to engage in formal politics. This dilemma was exposed in the US when Sarah Palin, a mother of five, was nominated in 2008 to be John McCain's running mate for President. In June 2011 another conservative mother of five, Congresswoman Michele Bachmann, announced her candidacy for President. Both women's gender and maternal status influenced their campaigns and generated extensive public debate about whether or not mothers should seek high office. Despite widespread traditional views, legions of conservative women and men supported both candidates: Schreiber's chapter investigates precisely how conservative women negotiate and reconcile theologically and ideologically traditional views about motherhood with the seemingly incompatible desire of some conservative women to engage in politics.

Women leaders are also the subject of Jennifer Curtin's chapter, 'Conservative Women and Executive Office in Australia and New Zealand', in which she analyses the descriptive and substantive representation of, and by, women from Australia's Liberal Party and New Zealand's National Party. In this she extends the limited literature on women and executive office, which in many instances focuses on women in leftist parties in government. In both her cases women are found to constitute at least one-quarter of the centre-right parliamentary caucus. Yet it is only in New Zealand that women from the centre-right are selected to cabinet in proportion to their party's parliamentary representation. In addressing women's substantive representation by these conservative women, Curtin analyses the first or maiden speeches of conservative women who later became cabinet ministers alongside a review of legislative and policy decisions taken by these women as ministers. She finds early evidence of Type 1 feminist claims by these women but suggests that in recent times these have become muted if not replaced by neo-liberal and anti-feminist claims. She further claims that diversity amongst conservative women representatives may be more significant than amongst leftist feminist representatives, further complicating considerations of conservatism, gender and representation.

'(Re)Presenting Women: Gender and the Politics of Sex in Contemporary Italy', by Roberta Guerrina, examines the position of women in the Berlusconi IV government. By the time Berlusconi resigned as Prime Minister in November 2011, there were five women in the cabinet, holding largely marginal portfolios, and much criticised for simply augmenting his masculinity. Unpacking the idiosyncrasies of conservative values as appropriated by the *Popolo della Libertà*, Guerrina evaluates whether at this particular historical moment, women of the centre-right could meaningfully appropriate a 'feminist agenda' based on the politics of emancipation. In so doing she assesses the nature and quality of women's substantive representation provided by women in positions of leadership in Italy since 2008.

Johanna Kantola and Milja Saari's chapter, 'Conservative Women MPs' Constructions of Gender Equality in Finland', explores constructions of gender equality. Whilst leftist parties have traditionally been more aligned with feminist discourses on women's interests and issues, and have had higher descriptive representation in parliament, the authors contend that conservative women MPs have nonetheless played a crucial role as shapers of feminist and gendered claims. The political process that surrounded Finland's first ever government 'Report on Gender Equality' published in 2010, is subject to close scrutiny; three debates addressed by the government Report are examined, on work and family, equal pay, and gender violence. What is of particular note in the associated parliamentary debates are the specific controversies that surrounded the policy-making process and the constructions of feminist and gendered claims made in the Report.

Jennifer M. Piscopo's chapter, 'Feminist Proposals and Conservative Voices: The Substantive Representation of Women in Argentina', examines 'acting for women' in the Argentine case between 2005 and 2011. By classifying bills into three constituent categories: feminist claims (Type I), gendered claims (Type II), and claims about children, Piscopo establishes that male legislators introduce fewer feminist bills, but more children's bills when compared to female legislators, and that across leftist and rightist political parties, feminist proposals predominate. Socially conservative legislators – both male and female – do constitute a vocal minority, however. Competing views of gender are also readily identifiable: in bills allocating state assistance to pregnant women and to families, feminist claims emphasise the importance of women's autonomy, whilst gendered claims frame mothers as needing state tutelage and protection. Finally, and despite their greater numerical strength, feminist and leftist legislators face challenges from men and from social conservatives when seeking policies that distance women from their maternal roles.

In 'Mapping "Feminist" Demands Across the French Political Spectrum', Rainbow Murray and Réjane Sénac hold that feminism does not map easily onto a left-right spatial model of political beliefs. Analysing the different programmes in the 2012 French presidential election campaign alongside a survey conducted amongst members of the French National Assembly, this chapter offers an original analysis of conservative representatives claims, both in political party programmes and in parliamentary practice. Differing levels of importance accorded to gender by interviewees are revealed and critical actors for women are identified. In particular, a comparison of attitudes towards the law on parity is undertaken, showing how different actors have embraced, rejected, or grudgingly accepted gender parity.

When looking closely at what conservative women representatives say and do – as in the chapters in Part II – it becomes apparent that a good number of conservative women representatives are making explicit claims to act for women. They may not be talking about the same things as their leftist feminist sisters, as what counts as women's issues may differ between conservative and leftist women political actors. And even where there is agreement over the identity and/ or saliency of particular women's issues, there may well still be differences in how conservative and leftist women define what is in the interests of women. Strong evidence for the distinction between women's issues and interests and for recognising Type I (feminist) and Type II (gendered) claims are found across the chapters, most notably in the French and Argentinean cases. The Finnish case points out that identifying Type I and Type II claims may be harder to capture in some instances, as notions of gender neutrality and gender harmony are in play; and that socially conservative ideology may be hidden behind neo-liberal critiques. Nevertheless, the chapters in this Section reinforce earlier studies of leftist women representatives, who confirm that the sex of our representatives matters, but they also add empirical evidence that the party of our women representatives matters too. In short, the substantive representation of women does not equate in practice – at least in the case addressed here –with the feminist substantive representation of women.

In representing women, conservative women political actors are themselves challenging gendered notions of what is appropriate for women to do and be – in this instance, participants in the political sphere. Accordingly they both confront and need to negotiate the traditional public/private distinction. Maintaining – or rather claiming to maintain – a traditional marriage may be one way in which conservative women seek to reconcile such tensions on the ground; articulating a defence of traditional women's concerns and values may well be another, as the US and Argentinean cases suggest, respectively. And as the US case further demonstrates, claiming one's motherhood as the basis for one's participation in politics is another. Motherhood, moreover, permits the articulation of a conservative-inspired set of women's interests, as Bachmann's and Palin's 'conservative supermoms' contribution to US politics exemplifies. The analysis of Italian politics under Berlusconi prompts further consideration of the constraints that face conservative women, as conservative notions of women's sexuality, mothering and religiousness curtails the political agency of individual women in government. The Australian and New Zealand cases, again, point to a particular conservative content to women's substantive representation. Notwithstanding conservative women's presence in each country's government, the issue of women's equality is pre-empted by a neo-liberal turn in politics. The trends identified in the Finnish case also acknowledge such a shift in discourse, with gender equality framed as a matter of numbers; defined in terms of productivity and efficiency; and achievable only at some (un)economic cost.

Part III: Gender, feminism and conservatism at the mass level

If the substantive representation of women is taken to refer only to feminist substantive representation, then conservative representative claims – their particular take on women's interests – are by definition excluded from the political debate and, in turn, academic study. Once included however, competition amongst political representatives – conservative and other – about what constitutes the interests of women is revealed. Establishing differences in conservative women representatives' understandings and actions in respect of women's issues and competing conceptions of women's interests in our view deepens, rather than undermines, conceptions of substantive representation. Such competition, we contend, delivers better accountability and responsiveness to women. Put another way, once a conservative women's politics of presence is acknowledged then the question can be posed regarding the quality of representational congruency and responsiveness by conservative representatives. This might be operationalised as congruency between mass/elite attitudes and policy preferences but might also look at the quality of relationships on the ground between representatives and those they claim to act for. This line of reasoning demands a shift of focus towards the mass level: the conservative member, voter and supporter. Is there a group of women conservative members, voters or identifiers with specific views – for instance feminist attitudes – that political elites should be responsive to and ally with?

The first chapter in this part of the book, by Rosie Campbell and Sarah Childs 'Representing Women's Interests and the UK Conservative Party: "To the Left, To the Right", Party Members, Voters and Representatives', jumps off from a previous study of UK Conservative Party members that finds that on left/right attitudes women are more often 'wet' and men more likely to be 'dry'. This chapter assesses whether this gender gap mirrors differences amongst conservatives in the general public – finding that conservative women party supporters and identifiers are also to the left of men on economic issues. This finding has important implications for Conservative Party strategy when issues of taxation and spending dominate the political terrain, as is the case in the UK at this time. Routinely since 2010, conservatives have been accused of failing to act in women's interests because their austerity politics are said to disproportionately and negatively impact women. The media suggest that this is putting women off voting for the party. In such a context, and noting that there is also a sex gap amongst conservative MPs, Campbell and Childs conclude that the Conservative Party may well need higher levels of women's descriptive representation to ensure that its platform represents conservative women supporters' views.

The chapter by Silvia Erzeel, Karen Celis and Didier Caluwaerts, 'Are Conservatism and Feminism Mutually Exclusive? A Study of "Feminist Conservative" Voters in Belgium', indicates that feminism and conservatism are in fact not mutually exclusive. This study of voters' attitudes and behaviour at the time of the 2009 regional elections in Flanders, Belgium, contradicts the idea that conservatism and feminism do not abide well together. Nearly one-quarter of Flemish voters combine feminist and conservative attitudes. This combination furthermore steers voting behaviour and directs voters to the right end of the political spectrum. The chapter concludes that the relatively large number of voters combining feminist and conservative views constitutes an important pool of potential voters for parties on the right, although they might not always manage to capitalise on this potential.

The final chapter by Emanuela Dalmasso and Francesco Cavatorta, 'Islamist Women Leadership in Morocco', seeks to explain the participation of women in the Moroccan Islamist Party for Justice and Development (PJD), traditionally known for its social conservatism on gender issues. In fact, such women clearly operate against the liberal feminist framework. The reasons for such participation, the chapter argues, are very similar to the ones that men have: socio-economic grievances and Arab–Muslim identity. Furthermore, women who become active in politics join and/or support Islamist parties in part, because they can remain true to the traditional values they hold, even whilst challenging traditional gender roles.

In sum, the chapters in Part III do identify a group of women conservative citizens that are distinct from conservative men in their views with regard to salient political topics (as in the UK case). They even identify a feminist conservative electorate (as in the Belgian case). These women and feminist conservative voters and identifiers might furthermore be of great electoral importance in the future. Put simply, conservative political parties should be aware of potential electoral risks when alienating themselves from their female electorate and supporters, and should be aware of a potential electoral group that they have not have yet tapped into. Nevertheless, as the Moroccan case highlights, it cannot be assumed that all conservative women's political participation is per se driven by gendered or feminist concerns. Indeed, the similarities between men and women conservatives might be more important to acknowledge than the differences. Taken together, the chapters in this part of the book thus call for more research about gender and feminism at the conservative mass level, to better understand the reasons and political implications of feminist and women's conservative attitudes and political participation.

Overall this edited collection suggests that the study of conservatism and representation has significant empirical and theoretical value in and of itself. But, most importantly, the additive case study of a relatively new set of actors on the political scene – as undertaken in this edited volume – feeds into current efforts to better theorise the concept of representation. More precisely, gender and politics scholarship on conservatism and representation speaks to contemporary concerns within mainstream theoretical scholarship about how representation theory and practice 'cope with' diversity and intersectionality: inter alia, multiple and intersecting identities of representatives, voters and citizens; diverse and competing representation claims; and various ways of establishing descriptive, substantive and symbolic linkage between citizens, on the one hand, and political actors and institutions, on the other hand.

Bibliography

Ahmed, L. (1992) *Politics and Gender in Islam*, New Haven, CT: Yale University Press.

Badran, M. (2009) *Feminism in Islam*, Oxford: Oneworld.

Baldez, L. (2011) 'The UN Convention to Eliminate All Forms of Discrimination Against Women (CEDAW): a new way to measure women's interests', *Politics and Gender*, 7 (3): 419–23.

Beckwith, K. (2007) 'Numbers and newness: the descriptive and substantive representation of women', *Canadian Journal of Political Science*, 40 (1): 27–49.

Birch, A. H. (1971) *Representation*, Basingstoke: Macmillan.

Bryson, V. and Heppell, T. (2010) 'Conservatism and feminism: the case of the British Conservative Party', *Journal of Political Ideologies*, 15 (1): 31–50.

Butler, J. (1990) *Gender Trouble: Feminism and the Subversion of Identity*, London, New York: Routledge.

Campbell, D. E. and Wolbrecht, C. (2006) 'See Jane run: women politicians as role models for adolescents', *Journal of Politics* 68 (2): 233–47.

Carroll, S. (1992) 'Women state legislators, women's organizations, and the representation of women's culture in the United States', in Bystydzienski, J. (ed.) *Women Transforming Politics: Worldwide Strategies for Empowerment*, Bloomington, IN: Indiana University Press, pp. 24–40.

Celis, K. (2006) 'Substantive representation of women and the impact of descriptive representation. Case: the Belgian Lower House 1900–1979', *Journal of Women, Politics and Policy*, 28 (2): 85–114.

— (2014) 'Representation', in Campbell, R. and Childs, S. (eds) *Deeds and Words: Gendering Politics*, Essex: ECPR Press.

Celis, K. and Childs, S. (2012) 'The substantive representation of women: what to do with Conservative's claims?, *Political Studies*, 60 (2): 213–25.

— (2013) 'Good representation as a democratic economy of claims', paper presented at the Third European Conference on Gender and Politics, 21–3 March, Barcelona.

Celis, K. and Erzeel, S. (2013) 'Beyond the usual suspects: non-left, male and non-feminist MPs and the substantive representation of women', *Government and Opposition*. DOI: http://dx.doi.org/10/1017/gov.2013.42.

Celis, K., Childs, S., Kantola, J. and Krook, M. L. (2014) 'Constituting women's interests through representative claims', *Politics & Gender*, forthcoming.

Celis, K., Krook, M. L. and Meier, P. (2011) 'The rise of gender quota laws: expanding the spectrum of determinants for electoral reform', *West European Politics*, 34 (3): 514–30.

Childs, S. (2004) *New Labour's Women MPs*, London: Routledge.

— (2008) *Women and British Party Politics*, London: Routledge.

— (2013) 'Intra party democracy: a gendered critique and a feminist agenda', in Katz, R. and Cross, W. (eds) *Intra Party Democracy*, New York: Oxford University Press.

Childs, S. and Krook, M. L. (2006) 'Should feminists give up on critical mass? A contingent yes', *Politics & Gender*, 2 (4): 203–5.

—   (2008) 'Critical mass theory and women's political representation', *Political Studies*, 56 (3): 725–36.

Childs, S. and Lovenduski, J. (2013) 'Political representation', in: Waylen, G., Celis, K., Kantola J. and Weldon, L. (eds) *The Oxford Handbook of Gender and Politics*, Oxford, New York: Oxford University Press.

Childs, S. and Webb, P. (2012) *Sex, Gender and the Conservative Party: From Iron Lady to Kitten Heels*, Palgrave Macmillan.

Dahlerup, D. (1988) 'From a small to a large minority: women in Scandinavian politics', *Scandinavian Political Studies*, 11 (4), 275–98.

—   (2014) 'The story of critical mass', in Campbell, R. and Childs. S. (eds) *Deeds and Words: Gendering Politics*, Essex: ECPR Press, forthcoming.

Dillard, A. D. (2005) 'Adventures in conservative feminism', *Society*, 42 (3): 25–7.

Hill Collins, P. (1990) *Black Feminist Thought*, London: Routledge.

Hill Collins, P. and Chepp, V. (2013) 'Intersectionality', in Waylen, G., Celis, K., Kantola, J. and Weldon, L. (eds) *The Oxford Handbook of Gender and Politics*, Oxford and New York: Oxford University Press.

Hooks, B. (1994) *Feminist Theory: From Margin to Center*, Cambridge: South End Press.

Judge, D. (1999) *Representation*, London: Routledge.

Karam, A. (ed.) (1998) *Women in Parliament: Beyond Numbers*, Stockholm: International Institute for Democracy and Electoral Assistance.

Kittilson, M. (2006) *Challenging Parties, Changing Parliaments*, Columbus, OH: Ohio State University Press.

Krook, M. L. (2009) *Quotas for Women in Politics: Gender and Candidate Selection Reform Worldwide*, USA: Oxford University Press.

Krook, M. L. and Mackay, F. (2011) *Gender, Politics, and Institutions: Towards a Feminist Institutionalism*, New York: Palgrave.

Krook, M. L. and Norris, P. (2014) 'Beyond quotas: strategies to promote gender equality in elected office', *Political Studies*, 62 (1): 2–20.

Lombardo, E. and Meier, P. (2014) *The Symbolic Representation of Gender: A Discursive Approach*, Surrey: Ashgate.

Lovenduski, J. (2005) *Feminizing Politics*, Cambridge: Polity.

Mansbridge, J. (1999) 'Should blacks represent blacks and women represent women? A contingent "yes"', *Journal of Politics*, 61 (3): 628–57.

Norris, P. and Lovenduski, J. (1995) *Political Recruitment: Gender, Race and Class in the British Parliament*, Cambridge: Cambridge University Press.

Offen, K. (2000) *European Feminisms 1700–1950: A Political History*, Stanford, CA: Stanford University Press.

Phillips, A. (1995) *The Politics of Presence*, Oxford: Clarendon Press.

Pitkin, H. F. (1967) *The Concept of Representation*, Berkeley, CA: University of California Press.

—   (1969) *Representation*, New York: Atherton Press.

Reingold, B. (2000) *Representing Women*, Chapel Hill: University of North Carolina Press.

Reingold, B. and Swers, M. (2011) 'An endogenous approach to women's interests: when interests are interesting in and of themselves', *Politics & Gender*, 7 (3): 429–35.

—   (2008) *Legislative Women, Getting Elected, Getting Ahead*, Colorado, CO: Reiner.

Schreiber, R. (2008) *Righting Feminism*, Oxford, New York: Oxford University Press.

Schwindt-Bayer, L.A. and Taylor-Robinson, M. M. (2011) 'Critical perspectives: the meaning and measurement of women's interest', *Politics & Gender*, 7 (3): 417–46.

Severs, E. (2012) 'Substantive representation through a claims-making lens: a strategy for the identification and analysis of substantive claims', *Representation*, 48 (2): 169–181, published online, June.

Swers, M. L. (2002) *The Difference Women Make: The Policy Impact of Women in Congress*, Chicago: University of Chicago Press.

Wolbrecht, C. and Campbell, D. E. (2007) 'Leading by example: female Members of Parliament as political role models', *American Journal of Political Science*, 51 (4): 921–39.

Wiliarty, S. (2010) *The CDU and the Politics of Gender in Germany. Bringing Women to the Party*, New York: Cambridge University Press.

Young, L. (2000) *Feminists and Party Politics*, Ann Arbor, MI: University of Michigan Press.

Zetterberg, P. (2008) 'Do gender quotas foster women's political engagement? Lessons from Latin America', *Political Research Quarterly*, 62: 715–30.

Chapter One

Conservative Female Candidates in Germany and Japan: Supply and Demand

Sarah Elise Wiliarty and Alisa Gaunder

Introduction

Conservative parties in Germany and Japan have behaved very differently in descriptively representing women. In Germany, the largest party of the right, the Christian Democratic Union (CDU), dramatically increased its descriptive representation of women in response to both internal and external pressure. Germany has had one of the highest rates of women in parliament worldwide for over two decades. In Japan, on the other hand, lack of pressure, either internal or external, has meant that the Conservative Party (the Liberal Democratic Party) neglects women's descriptive representation and Japan's rate of descriptive representation of women remains extremely low. While these two countries are rarely compared, studying them in tandem reveals insights that have implications not just for the gender and politics literature, but also more generally for scholars of comparative democracies.

After a discussion of case selection, the analysis proceeds by examining the supply of and demand for female candidates.[1] On the supply side, we look at the eligibility pool, including women's education, women's career tracks and labour force participation, and also the women's movement. On the demand side, we consider the role of party competition, party organisation, and gender quotas. Ultimately we conclude that while supply side factors in Germany and Japan are quite similar, demand side factors can help explain the difference in rates of female representation.

Case selection

Germany and Japan are rarely compared by scholars of comparative politics because they are located in different regions. Upon closer inspection, however, the countries are quite similar. They both had limited, often unsuccessful experiences with democracy prior to World War II, yet they emerged from the war as strong

---

1. The supply and demand approach to women's representation is used by many scholars, including Randall 1987; Norris 1997; Paxton 1997.

parliamentary democracies.[2] They also both experienced the 'economic miracle' of the 1950s, with very strong economies that should be considered coordinated market economies rather than liberal market economies (Yamamura and Streeck 2003). A conservative party has dominated politics in each country and partly because of this dominance these welfare states have followed the male breadwinner model. Finally, in both countries, the women's movements were slow to push for female suffrage (though women gained the vote earlier in Germany than in Japan). This analysis of both the CDU in Germany and the Liberal Democratic Party (LDP) in Japan follows, then, a similar systems approach.

Germany and Japan experimented with democratic government in the early twentieth century. The Weimar Republic (1919–33) and Taisho Democracy (1912–26) were both parliamentary democracies and both eventually had universal male suffrage, with universal female suffrage as well under Weimar. In each country, these institutions marked a significant change from imperial rule. Yet the democracies were flawed and both systems broke down by the 1930s (Fulbrook 2009; Reischauer 1991). The post-war transition to democracy after World War II was facilitated by the United States in each case. The advent of the Cold War clarified any lingering doubts about West Germany's and Japan's international position and both countries were integrated into the Western security alliance (Berger 1998). These commitments to democracy at home and cooperation with the West internationally were not at all to be taken for granted, yet neither country has wavered from them in the post-World War II era. (Fulbrook 2009; Duus 1998).

The economic systems of (West) Germany and Japan also have many similarities. Germany and Japan experienced dramatic economic growth in the 1950s. Both countries have coordinated market economies rather than liberal market economies (Hall and Soskice 2001). Rather than trusting the market to regulate the economy in a satisfactory manner, Germany and Japan have relied on various coordination mechanisms, such as collective bargaining or bureaucratic oversight. Both have focused on high-end manufacturing and the export market (Dower 1999; Hall 1986).

The conservative parties in (West) Germany and Japan also have much in common. The mainstream conservative parties – the German CDU and the Japanese LDP – dominated post-war politics and oversaw the transition, as each country became a stable democracy and an economic powerhouse. Both the CDU and the LDP have been in government more than any other party in their respective countries. The CDU has been in the governing coalition for a total of forty-four years since 1949 and the LDP for fifty-four years since 1955. The long tenures in office allowed these two parties to shape the post-war political and economic systems more than any other political party. Moreover, both parties

---

2.   This research focuses primarily on West Germany though it includes some historical factors from the pre-World War II era and also continues into the post-unification era.

favour industry and big business and prioritise regulations that favour economic growth. The parties also have conservative notions of family and view women as mothers rather than as workers.[3]

The varieties of conservatism do, nonetheless, feature some key differences. Most notably religion informs Christian Democracy (*see also* Chapter Two in this volume by Hien) while it plays no role in the LDP's party ideology or support base. Christian Democracy is a political movement that emerged in Western Europe following World War II (Irving 1979; Hanley 1996; Gehler and Kaiser 2004). It has its roots in political Catholicism, but in Germany it combined Catholics and Protestants from the start (Uertz 1981; Mitchell 2012). In the early decades of the Federal Republic of Germany, the Catholic Church and Christian Democratic politicians agreed that mothers should stay home with their children and that fathers should earn a 'just wage', enough to support their families. This set of beliefs meshed well with the male breadwinner model of the welfare state (*see* below). Christian Democracy promotes capitalism moderated by a strong safety net for the less fortunate, which is partially motivated by Christian doctrine (Pridham 1977; van Kersbergen 1995). The CDU has worked closely with both Protestant and Catholic organisations to implement welfare state policies (Hien, Chapter Two in this volume). The CDU is sometimes criticised (by both insiders and outsiders) for paying insufficient attention to the 'C' in the party's name, but the assumption is that the ideas of Christianity will provide some guidance to party policy.

In contrast, Occupation officials in Japan prioritised separating Shintoism from the state. The emperor had been viewed as a descendent of the sun goddess with direct connections to Shintoism. This separation of church and state was seen as critical in weakening the role of the Emperor, a driving force behind fascism (Toyoda and Tanaka 2002). Separation of church and state did not necessarily preclude the emergence of religious parties. The Komeito (Clean Government Party) is the political arm of the Soka Gakkai, a Buddhist sect that emerged to serve this active but small segment of the population in the 1960s. More relevant perhaps is the fact that religion simply plays a different role in Japan. Very few people define themselves as having one religion (Earhart 2004: 214–15). Instead, the Japanese incorporate aspects of Shintoism, Buddhism, and Confucianism into different aspects of their lives. These beliefs and practices do not neatly fit a conservative/progressive dichotomy.

The welfare state regimes in (West) Germany and Japan can be categorised as belonging to the strong male breadwinner model (Lewis 1992; Ostner and Lewis 1995; Gottfried and O'Reilly 2002). In this type of welfare state regime, welfare benefits encourage families to have one adult, generally the father, participate

---

3.   For more background on the CDU, *see* Pridham (1977); Bösch (2001, 2002); Granieri (2003); Wiliarty (2010). For more on the LDP, *see* Curtis (1988, 1999); Krauss and Pekkanen (2011).

in paid labour, while the other adult, generally the mother, stays home to care for the children. Germany is a core example of what Esping-Andersen (1999) calls the conservative cluster of welfare state regimes. In *Social Foundations of Postindustrial Economies*, Esping-Andersen notes that Japan could easily be included in his conservative cluster along with Germany. The only way in which Japan differs significantly from other countries in this cluster is that in Japan, many welfare benefits come from the employer rather than the state (Esping-Andersen 1999: 82). In Japan, Confucianism can be seen as a 'functional equivalent' of Catholic familialism, and Japan also has a strong male breadwinner welfare state regime (Esping-Andersen 1999: 82).

Neither Germany nor Japan should be seen as a leader in advocating for women's political rights. Both countries have women's movements dating back to the nineteenth century, but these movements were divided (often by class) and frequently did not represent a unified position on women's suffrage. In both countries, women were legally permitted to attend political gatherings only in the late nineteenth century. German women were allowed to vote first, after World War I, but this timing had more to do with the European context than any particular action or demand from German women's groups. Japanese women were granted suffrage after World War II as part of the new democratic constitution imposed by the occupying powers (Hannam *et al.* 2000).

Despite these similarities, women have been represented at very different rates in the German and Japanese parliaments. The German Bundestag is approximately 36.5 per cent female while the Japanese Diet is approximately 8.1 per cent female (Inter-Parliamentary Union 2014). One explanation for this difference is the stronger presence of the major party of the left in Germany (the Social Democratic Party, or SPD). Parties of the left tend to represent women at higher rates, so a system with a stronger party of the left will probably have more women in parliament (Duverger 1955; Lovenduski and Norris 1993; Rule 1987; Caul 1999). Indeed, we can see that the Japanese Socialist Party (JSP) represents women at quite high rates, but the party itself is very small. When we compare only women in the conservative parties, however, a large difference remains. The parliamentary delegation of the German CDU is currently 22 per cent female while the parliamentary delegation of the Japanese LDP is 7.8 per cent female. Tables 1.1 and 1.2 show the number and percentage of women in parliament in Germany and Japan, both by party and overall.

In summary, Germany and Japan share many social, economic and political characteristics. They both transitioned successfully to democracy after World War II. Their economic systems are of similar structure. They have similar welfare state regimes, conservative parties, and women's movements. The significant difference in female representation remains to be explained.

Table 1.1: Number of female members of the Bundestag (Percentage of Women in Party Caucus)

	CDU/CSU	CDU	CSU	SPD	FDP	Greens	PDS (Linke after 2005)	Total
1987–1990	18 (8%)	15 (9%)	3 (6%)	31 (16%)	6 (13%)	25 (57%)	–	80 (15%)
1990–1994	44 (14%)	39 (15%)	5 (10%)	65 (27%)	16 (20%)	3 (38%)	8 (47%)	136 (21%)
1994–1998	41 (14%)	35 (14%)	6 (12%)	86 (34%)	8 (17%)	29 (59%)	13 (43%)	177 (26%)
1998–2002	45 (18%)	39 (20%)	6 (13%)	105 (35%)	9 (20%)	27 (57%)	21 (60%)	207 (31%)
2002–2005	57 (23%)	43 (23%)	12 (21%)	95 (38%)	10 (21%)	32 (58%)	2 (100%)	195 (32%)
2005–2009	44 (20%)	38 (21%)	7 (15%)	80 (36%)	15 (25%)	29 (57%)	26 (46%)	193 (31%)
2009–2013	48 (20%)	42 (22%)	6 (13%)	56 (38%)	23 (25%)	37 (54%)	40 (53%)	204 (33%)

Information calculated from Ritter and Niehuss (1991); Frauen-Union der CSU (1997); Schindler (1999); Von Schwartzenberg (2002); McKay (2004); Statistisches Bundesamt (2005, 2009).

Table 1.2: Number of female members of the Japanese Diet (Percentage of Women in Party Caucus)

	LDP	DPJ	Komeito	Socialists	JCP	Total
1996	4 (1.7%)	3 (5.8%)	n/a	3 (20%)	4 (15%)	23 (4.6%)
2000	8 (3.4%)	6 (4.7%)	3 (9.68%)	10 (53%)	4 (20%)	35 (7.3%)
2003	9 (3.8%)	15 (8.5%)	4 (11.8%)	3 (50%)	2 (22%)	34 (7.1%)
2005	26 (8.8%)	7 (6.2%)	4 (12.9%)	4 (57%)	2 (22%)	43 (9%)
2009	8 (6.7%)	40 (13%)	3 (14.3%)	2 (29%)	1 (11%)	54 (11.3%)
2012	23 (7.9%)	3 (5.2%)	3 (9.6%)	0 (0%)	1 (12.5%)	39 (8.1%)

Source: Ministry of Internal Affairs and Communications (MIC). http://www.soumu.go.jp/ senkyo/senkyo_s/data/ (accessed August 16, 2012).

Supply factors

As other chapters in this book outline, one way of thinking about how many women end up represented in parliament is to consider the 'supply' of eligible candidates. Certain educational paths and professions are more likely to lead to political careers for both women and men (Norris 1996: 188–90; Burns et al. 2001). If few women are on these tracks, a political system is unlikely to end up with very many female politicians (Conway et al. 1997; Darcy et al. 1994; Duerst-Lahti 1998; Thomas 1998). This situation is sometimes referred to as a 'pipeline' problem (Clark 1994).[4] The results of cross-national scholarship in determining the importance of women's educational attainment and labour force participation for women's representation in parliament have been indeterminate.[5] Some of the problem in determining the importance of these variables may have to do with measurement difficulties, particularly in different national contexts. Yet there is little reason to expect that women's education and labour force participation would play different roles in Germany and in Japan.

Another factor that may affect the supply of potential female candidates is the strength and orientation of the women's movement (Katzenstein and Mueller 1987; Lovenduski and Norris 1993; Rule 1994; Young 2000; Paxton et al. 2006). The women's movement is likely to call attention to differences between women and men and also to the ways in which women suffer discrimination. A stronger movement might bring greater societal focus to these issues. If the women's movement recognises discrimination against women, it might (or might not) see women's political participation as a possible solution to that problem.

In terms of the eligibility pool, women in Japan and Germany are similar. As Table 1.3 reveals, recent education and labour statistics paint compatible pictures. The percentage of women who receive at least a secondary education is extremely high in both Germany (91.3 per cent) and Japan (80 per cent) (United Nations 2011: 139). A large proportion of women also attend college, although again the rate is higher in Germany. Women in both countries are very well educated. Although women are educated at slightly higher rates in Germany, this difference is not large enough to explain the difference in women's parliamentary representation.

Despite these high levels of education, and as noted above, both countries have maintained a male breadwinner model of the welfare state for most of the post-war period. This model is reflected in the labour statistics, which show women working at much lower rates than men (Esping-Andersen 1990, 1997, 1999;

---

4. The eligibility pool is not the only factor contributing to the supply of female candidates. In the United States context, an extensive literature analyses how political ambition contributes to the likelihood that an individual woman will decide to run for office. See especially Fox and Lawless (2010) and Lawless (2012). Davidson-Schmich explores how ambition plays a role in Germany, but there is very little research on this topic in Japan so comparisons are not possible (Davidson-Schmich forthcoming).

5. Rule (1987) found that women's educational levels mattered for women's representation, while Norris (1985), Paxton (1997) and Matland (1998) found that they did not. Rule (1987) and Matland (1998) found that women's labour force participation rate mattered for women's representation while Norris (1985) and Paxton (1997) found that it did not.

Table 1.3: A comparison of education and employment for women in Germany and Japan

	Germany	Japan
Secondary education completion	91.3% women (92.8% men)	80% women (82.3% men)
Percentage college education	131.3 per 100 men (Eurostat)***	94.2 per 100 men (Eurostat)***
Female employment rate	66.2% in 2009 (75.6% men)	59.8% in 2009 (80.2% men)
Part-time adult employment	37.9% women (7.9% men)	33.9% women (10.4% men)
Female professional technical positions	50%	46%

Sources: United Nations (2011, 139); Eurostat; The World Bank; United Nations Statistics Division.

Osawa 2007). The employment rate for women in Germany stands at 66.2 per cent and 59.8 per cent in Japan (Eurostat). In Germany women make up 37.9 per cent of employed adults while the rate for Japan is 33.9 per cent (United Nations Statistics Division, n.d.). Furthermore, women in both Germany and Japan are employed in professional and technical positions at fairly high rates. From these statistics, it is clear that the eligibility pool in Germany is somewhat larger, albeit not significantly larger. Both countries show a similar pattern: women are educated at very high rates, but employed at significantly lower rates. Thus, they have similar eligibility pools so this factor cannot explain differential rates of female representation.

Turning to the women's movements in Germany and Japan, Weldon ranks them as having similar strength (Weldon 2002). Some differences exist, but one similarity stands out – neither movement has historically advocated political activism as a remedy for improving women's disadvantaged position in society. In Germany, the feminist movement historically focused on issues of autonomy. By working to carve out separate female-only areas of life (cafés, bookstores, even summer universities), activists hoped to both create both a feminist haven and a source of gender role transformation. The movement did not work much with political parties until the advent of the Green Party in the 1980s (Ferree 1987, 2012).[6]

---

6. The role of political parties will be discussed further under demand factors.

The women's movement in Japan has historically been weak (Mackie 2003; Murase 2006; Shin 2011). It has worked mainly through bureaucracy and advisory councils to provide expertise for policies such as the Equal Employment Opportunity Law. It is more active on the local level and has not made electing female politicians or cooperating with political parties a priority. Lack of political input from women's organisations has made it difficult for policy makers to discern what women (especially working mothers) might want (Schoppa 2006). Therefore, until quite recently, neither Germany nor Japan had women's movements that were engaged with formal/electoral politics.

Neither the eligibility pool nor the structure of the women's movements can provide a clear explanation for the difference in female representation in the two cases. Germany has a slightly greater eligibility pool, but the CDU's parliamentary delegation is almost three times greater (in terms of percentages) than the LDP's (22 per cent versus 7.9 per cent).

Demand factors

Supply factors in Germany and Japan are too similar to explain differences in women's descriptive representation, but demand factors are likely to offer greater explanatory value. Three major sources of 'demand' for conservative parties to promote female politicians are considered: (1) the electoral system; (2) the threat from parties on the left; and (3) internal party mechanisms, such as party organisation and quotas. Despite the importance of the electoral system in facilitating female representation in many extant studies, in these cases the latter two factors prove critical.

Several researchers have found strong evidence that proportional representation systems are more likely to facilitate women's representation than majoritarian systems. Proportional representation systems can create an innate sense of pressure for political parties to present a diverse slate of candidates, including women. Majoritarian systems, on the other hand, force parties to pick a single candidate and often that person is a male (Rule 1987, 1994; Matland 1998, 2006; Norris 1985, 1987, 1997, 2004; Lovenduski and Norris 1993; Darcy et al. 1994).

Germany has a mixed electoral system called personalised proportional representation. Half of the seats are elected through proportional representation and the other half through a majoritarian single-member district system. Female candidates have often been shown to fare better in the proportional representation component of the electoral system (Davidson-Schmich 2010). For Germany at least, it seems clear that proportional representation helps elect women. Japan used a multiple-member district/single non-transferable vote (MMD/SNTV) electoral system from 1955 to 1993. Research on the gendered effects of this system has been inconclusive. Under MMD/SNTV, voters cast one ballot and each district elected two to six representatives to serve in the Japanese Diet. Because voters select individual candidates, parties felt pressure to choose candidates with the greatest potential to win and party leaders often considered men to have more viable candidacies. The MMD/SNTV system does not appear to have benefited women (Hickman 1997) but this system was also changed soon after parties became more interested in electing women in the late 1980s (Eto 2010).

Larger parties (and particularly the LDP) consistently ran more than one candidate per district under MMD/SNTV. Therefore, the logic of proportional representation – that it might be seen as advantageous to run a diverse slate of candidates – could easily apply to Japan's single non-transferable vote system as well. The LDP did in fact seek to run a range of candidates specialising in different policy and geographic areas, but pressure to present a diverse slate of candidates does not on its own require political parties to use sex as a method to illustrate the diversity of their candidate pool. Under the 1955 system, Japanese parties apparently felt no such pressure to represent women. From 1952 until 1990, the percentage of total women in the lower house remained below 2 (Cabinet Office 2005: 20). The MMD/SNTV system might have facilitated the election of women if party leaders had wanted to pursue that option. In Japan under the 1955 system, they did not.

In 1994 Japan adopted a new electoral system, which is very similar to Germany's. Under the new system 180 candidates are elected through proportional representation and 300 are elected through single-member districts. Parties did show a greater propensity to select female candidates after electoral reform, as would be expected by the inclusion of the proportional representation component of the system (Moser and Scheiner 2012). The increase also appeared to come initially from parties on the left, in keeping with cross-national evidence about left-wing parties supporting women representatives at greater rates than right-wing parties (Duverger 1955; Lovenduski and Norris 1993; Rule 1987; Caul 1999). In Japan, however, female representation actually declined after an initial increase. In 2005 LDP President (and Japanese Prime Minister) Junichiro Koizumi put women at the top of 7 of 11 PR blocs. This electoral strategy was leader-driven and not institutionalised. After Koizumi retired, this policy was abandoned. The proportional representation component of the electoral system did not therefore lead to persistent pressure to increase female representation. Since 1994, Germany and Japan have had very similar electoral systems yet Japan is still electing very few women.

Although the electoral system seems to have made only a minor contribution to the different levels of female representation in Japan and Germany, another systemic difference matters more. The party systems in Japan and Germany are quite different. Unlike the LDP, the CDU faced a significant threat from a party of the left, especially from the 1950s. In Germany, the major party of the left is the Social Democratic Party (SPD). The SPD has been an important actor in the German party system since the late nineteenth century. Social Democratic Chancellors led Germany from 1969 to 1982 and again from 1998 to 2005. The SPD remains the most serious threat to Christian Democratic rule. As we shall see, the different roles of parties of the left in the two countries partially explain the different approaches of the CDU and LDP to incorporating women.

In contrast, the LDP in Japan did not face a significant threat from a party of the left after the 1950s. The JSP posed a real threat to conservative rule from the late

1940s to the mid-1950s, but by the 1960s, this threat had been contained (Duus 1998). The 1955 system of LDP dominance is characterised as a 'one and a half party system'; the Socialists never commanded the resources and organisational support to overthrow the LDP from 1955 to 1993. The JSP did win the upper house in 1989 but this vote is often considered an anti-LDP not a pro-JSP election. The JSP lost strength and support following the first Gulf War. When the LDP did fall from power in 1993, it was due to an internal party split.

The CDU experienced a greater threat from the SPD than the LDP experienced from the JSP. In the 1970s, female voters in (West) Germany began to shift their allegiance from the Christian Democrats to parties on the left, both the Social Democrats and, in the 1980s, the Greens. The Social Democrats initially picked up the cause of the women's movement and the Greens followed suit shortly afterward and more vigorously. This strong left-wing challenge forced the CDU to respond by accommodating the demands of the women's movement in a variety of ways (Wiliarty 2010). The Christian Democratic response was successful enough to slow the emergence of the 'modern gender gap' in Germany (a gender gap in which women favour parties of the left) (Inglehart and Norris 2003). Part of the explanation for why women are better represented in the CDU is that the CDU did a better job than most conservative parties at responding to changing demands from female voters, for example by increasing female representation within the party.

In Japan the situation is somewhat more complicated. The LDP has had an average gender gap in voting of around 8 per cent, but with men consistently favouring the party more than women (Burden 2009). In Inglehart and Norris's terms, we do not see a 'traditional gender gap' (in which women favour the party of the right) in the immediate post-war era. Instead, Japan consistently exhibits a 'modern gender gap' even prior to the arrival of second wave feminism. However, this gendered appeal did not provoke the LDP to respond by selecting more women as candidates because its main rival, the JSP, was not coming close to overall victory at the polls. In other words, the importance of the threat from a party of the left is not just about the distribution of men's and women's votes. It is also – perhaps more importantly – about whether the gendered nature of that distribution might make a difference in the electoral outcome. In Germany, it seemed that it might. In Japan, it clearly did not.

The lack of a challenge from the left in Japan is partially a story of missed opportunity. The JSP went into the election of 1989 billing itself partially as a women's party. Party leaders selected many female candidates (the so-called 'Madonnas') and the party gained a majority in the upper house for the first time. Under a female leader, Doi Takako, the JSP saw unprecedented success. However, while the JSP had a strong performance in the 1990 lower house election, it struggled to find quality candidates (Stockwin 2000). After Doi resigned in 1991 to take responsibility for the JSP's loss in the local unified election, her so-called 'women changing politics' policy was abandoned. The JSP suffered a devastating defeat in the 1993 Lower House election due to its outdated ideology. Thus, while the JSP had the potential to provide a challenge from a left-wing party on women's participation, the timing was less than propitious.

In addition to pressure created by electoral systems or by competition from other parties, political parties might create demand for female candidates by adopting their own mechanisms to increase women's representation. Gender quotas are certainly one technique parties can adopt that would create a demand for female candidates. The CDU has a gender quota (or 'quorum' as the party calls its own, fairly weak, voluntary quota) but the party also has an internal structure that facilitates female representation (Wiliarty 2010). Although neither of these mechanisms is very strong when compared with the SPD, a comparison of the CDU's representation of women with the LDP's representation of women reveals the importance of party organisation in creating a demand for female candidates.

Party organisation affects party behaviour. Both the CDU and the LDP are catch-all parties, in that they attempt to appeal to many different kinds of voters, but they manage the challenges of appealing to a diverse range of interests in ways that affect how the parties represent women differently.[7] The CDU is best described as a corporatist catch-all party rather than a classic or standard catch-all party (Wiliarty 2010). Corporatist catch-all parties are divided into leaders and members, but also into internal party interest groups. Recognised groups have institutionalised representation on the party's decision-making bodies and participate in policy making.

The CDU's women's organisation, the Women's Union, was integrated into the CDU's structure of internal representation at the founding of the party. In the 1950s and 1960s, a single woman on a committee was often seen as sufficient representation. As the rise of the second-wave feminist movement in Germany contributed to a decline in CDU support from women at the polls, the Women's Union responded by demanding more influence and policy adjustments. The CDU largely accommodated their demands, at least in the 1970s and 1980s (Wiliarty 2010). The Women's Union was an organised voice, ready to object if women were inadequately represented. Even prior to the adoption of the quota, the CDU's internal organisation encouraged the presence of at least some women in the parliamentary delegation, as well as on other decision-making bodies within the party.

The CDU's move to adopt a gender quota was influenced by left-wing parties in Germany. In the 1980s, both the Greens and the SPD adopted gender quotas, increasing the presence of female candidates on the left. In the 1990s, the Women's Union pushed for the CDU to adopt its own gender quota. After significant internal party debate, the CDU implemented a modified gender quota, which it called a 'quorum' (Leslie and Wiliarty 2009; Wiliarty 2010). The quorum stipulates that one-third of elected and party offices held by the CDU go to women. The sanctions for non-compliance are weak; if the CDU fails to meet its goal of electing one-third women in an internal party election the first time around, the party simply holds a second election. For the second election, there is no target for electing

---

7.   There is a significant literature on catch-all parties, starting with the seminal article by Kirch-heimer (1966). Wolinetz (1979) and Dittrich (1983) both analyse Kirchheimer's argument in detail.

women. Despite the weakness of this mechanism, it has significantly increased women's representation within the Bundestag and at the upper levels of the party hierarchy (Wiliarty 2013).

The corporatist, catch-all party organisation of the German CDU is moreover leading to greater female representation throughout the party. Its Women's Union is not a mere social club, but rather a powerful actor within the party, at times able to influence both policy and personnel decisions. It means that women within the party have a foothold from which to operate when lobbying their party for change.

Unlike the CDU, the Japanese LDP is a classic catch-all party rather than a corporatist catch-all party. Since its inception, it has been a large party that has reached out to cross-cutting interests. While the CDU mobilised interests through internal representation on party decision-making bodies, the LDP never felt the pressure to engage its membership base in such a manner. One way, then, in which the LDP managed the centrifugal force of its various support bases is by not allowing them much influence over the party. The LDP has used two main organisational structures for maintaining internal balance: factions and the Policy Affairs Research Council (PARC). Unlike the CDU, neither of the LDP's structures for incorporating groups has focused on women. The LDP's factions have not been ideologically based. Instead, they have focused on raising and distributing funds to support candidates for office in return for the faction member's support in the party presidential election. Factions have also served as an important mechanism for distributing party and Diet positions. Factions receive representation within the party and the cabinet in proportion to their numerical strength (Kohno 1997).

Factions present obstacles to women who seek LDP endorsement. The same constraints to recruitment and nomination hold under both the new and the old electoral systems. Factions fight to receive party endorsement when open seats become available, because such openings provide an opportunity for a faction to increase its overall strength in the LDP (Park 2001: 438). No faction has adopted the cause of women's representation or been willing to risk gaining party endorsement for open seats by consistently proposing female candidates.

The PARC is the other structure within the LDP that organises interests. It parallels the Diet committee structure and served as the main forum for policy debate under the 1955 system of LDP dominance. During the period of LDP dominance this body was responsible for national policy formulation. Participation on the PARC committees provided opportunities for claiming credit and fundraising as politicians could pursue the interests of their district and key interest groups. Until recently, female politicians in the LDP have had little to no influence on the PARC. Prior to electoral reform, no women served as chairs, vice chairs, or acting chairs of the PARC divisions (Krauss and Pekkanen 2011: 192). After reform (from 1996 to 2008), a handful of women have been tapped to these positions, illustrating some increased influence.[8]

---

8. One woman served as chair of a PARC committee in the 43rd legislative session and two women served as chair in the 44th session. Between one and four women have chaired Lower House

A third method of structuring interests – external to the LDP, but important to candidate selection – are *kōenkai* or personal support networks. *Kōenkai* are difficult for all politicians to build, but women face even greater obstacles because they often are excluded from the old boys' networks that are crucial to the creation of these organisations. These connections come from education, work, and family. Moreover, due to the personal allegiances that *kōenkai* foster, these organisations are often passed from a retiring politician to a family member or a former political assistant. Daughters and wives have occasionally inherited a *kōenkai*, but the norm has been to pass these personal support groups on to a male representative of the family or a male political assistant.[9]

Under both the old and new electoral systems, factions, the PARC and *kōenkai* have played a key role in the recruitment and nomination process. Women faced barriers to entry in all three areas. Recruitment and nomination in Japan is largely a local affair and local branch offices are patriarchal. Iwamoto notes that one of the largest obstacles potential women candidates face is 'the aged male gatekeepers who select candidates in almost all the districts' (2001: 226). Very few women have the type of experience that is rewarded by local party gatekeepers and/or factions, such as local and prefectural assembly members, or political assistants to politicians (Ogai 2001: 208).

Since electoral reform, factional balancing and seniority have not been strictly adhered to for cabinet level appointments, especially under Koizumi; however, these norms continue to govern appointments for the PARC and legislative positions below the cabinet level (Krauss and Pekkanen 2011: 199). Women have benefited from the recent trend away from seniority and factional balancing norms governing high-level appointments. Owing to the incentives of the electoral system, electoral contests have become more party/leader focused. Party leaders have found appointing well-known, popular female politicians an effective tool for winning votes (Krauss and Pekkanen 2011: 143–4; Gaunder 2009). These appointments of female candidates and female cabinet or party officials have been closely tied to the personal priorities of the party leader (Gaunder 2009). The lack of institutionalisation has resulted in inconsistent female representation and limited progress.

Conclusion

Germany and Japan should be seen as mostly similar systems. Both countries were late developers with similar experiences with flawed democracies prior to World War II. Both countries experienced significant economic success following the war. Because of a history of conservative dominance, Germany and Japan share a

---

committees in the Diet at any given time since 1996 and between one and two women have chaired standing committees in most sessions of the lower house during the same time period (Ellis Krauss, personal correspondence, 3 March 2012).

9. Still, of the three main paths most likely to lead to recruitment in the LDP, women had fared best as second-generation politicians, inheriting a personal support network (Ogai 2001: 209).

historic commitment to the male breadwinner model welfare state. Furthermore, neither country has been home to a strong women's movement. When women have organised, they have not targeted the state as a source of potential political benefits. Given these similarities, the varying levels of women's descriptive representation in the key conservative parties, in contrast to left-wing parties, is intriguing.

Both supply and demand factors potentially influence women's representation in conservative parties. The supply of potential female candidates in Germany and Japan is quite similar and therefore cannot explain different rates of representation. Demand factors created by both the political system and the conservative parties themselves offer the best explanation for differing rates of female representation in the CDU and the LDP. The greater role for proportional representation in the German electoral system has likely facilitated increased female representation in that country. When Japan changed its electoral system to one with greater proportionality, the number of women in the Diet increased. Furthermore, the German CDU experienced a greater threat from the SPD than the Japanese LDP has felt from the JSP. The presence of a left-wing party that came close to or even won elections led the CDU to make adjustments to attempt to win back female voters. The CDU knew what adjustments to make partly because of its internal organisation for women, the Women's Union. The Japanese LDP, on the other hand, lacks a women's organisation and sometimes appears unable to respond to women's demands. Furthermore, the LDP's standard recruitment pathways for candidates act as barriers to female candidates.

The 2009 victory of the Democratic Party of Japan (DPJ) in the lower house might have been expected to serve as a threat that would cause a response from the LDP. However, women do not appear to have gained in terms of governance or policy under the DPJ for several reasons (Gaunder 2012). Most significantly, the DPJ's shift from a centre-left to a centrist party has enhanced its electoral performance, but has not allowed it to champion issues of concern to women (Kabashima and Steel 2006; Köllner 2011; Miura *et al.* 2005). Moreover, Ozawa, like Koizumi before him, has used women as symbols of change to enhance the party's electoral appeal (Gaunder 2009, 2012). Neither the LDP nor the DPJ has moved to enhance women's real power. Given the poor performance of the DPJ in office and the LDP's victory in the December 2012 elections, further adjustments to enhance women's representation in the LDP seem unlikely at this time.

References

Berger, T. (1998) 'From swords into plowshares and back', in *Cultures of Antimiliatarism: National Security in Germany and Japan*, Baltimore, MD: Johns Hopkins University Press, pp. 22–54.

Bösch, F. (2001) *Die Adenauer-CDU: Gründung, Aufstieg und Krise einer Erfolgspartei, 1945–1969*. Stuttgart: Deutsche Verlags-Anstalt.

—— (2002) *Macht und Machverlust: Die Geschichte der CDU*, Stuttgart: Deutsche Verlags-Anstalt.

Burden, B. (2009) 'The puzzle of the Japanese gender gap in Liberal Democratic Party support', in Reed, S., Mori, K., and Shimizu, K., (eds) *Political Change in Japan: Electoral Behavior, Party Realignment and the Koizumi Reforms*, Washington, DC: Brookings Institution Press, pp. 221–37.

Burns, N., Schlozman, K. and Verba, S. (2001) *The Private Roots of Public Action: Gender, Equality and Political Participation*, Cambridge, MA: Harvard University Press.

Cabinet Office (2005) FY 2004 Annual Report on the State of Formation of a Gender Equal Society, available at http://www.gender.go.jp/english_contents/category/pub/whitepaper/pdf/ewp2005.pdf (accessed 22 March 2012).

Caul, M. (1999) 'Women's representation in parliament: the role of political parties', *Party Politics*, 5 (1): 79–98.

Clark, J. (1994) 'Getting there: women in political office', in Githens, M., Norris, P. and Lovenduski, J. (eds) *Different Roles, Different Voices*, New York: HarperCollins, pp. 99–110.

Conway, M. M., Steuernagel, G. and Ahren, D. W. (1997) *Women and Political Participation*, Washington, DC: Congressional Quarterly Press.

Curtis, G. L. (1988) *The Japanese Way of Politics*, New York: Columbia University Press.

—— (1999) *The Logic of Japanese Politics: Leaders, Institutions, and the Limits of Change*, New York: Columbia University Press.

Darcy, R., Welch, S. and Clark, J. (1994) *Women, Elections, and Representation*, 2nd edn, Lincoln, NE: University of Nebraska Press.

Davidson-Schmich, L. (2010) 'Gender quota compliance in the 2009 Bundestag election', *German Politics and Society*, 28 (3): 133–55.

—— (forthcoming) *A Glass Half Full: Gender Quotas and Political Recruitment* (working title), unpublished monograph.

Duerst-Lahti, G. (1998) 'The bottleneck: women as candidates', in S. Thomas and C. Wilcox (eds) *Women and Elective Office*, New York: Oxford University Press, pp. 15–25.

Dittrich, K. (1983) 'Testing the catch-all thesis: some difficulties and problems', in Daalder, H. and Mair, P. (eds) *Western European Party Systems, Continuity and Change*, London: Sage, pp. 257–66.

Dower, J. W. (1999) 'Engineering growth', in *Embracing Defeat: Japan in the Wake of World War II*, New York: W. W. Norton & Company, pp. 525–46.

Duus, P. (1998) 'The politics of confrontation', in *Modern Japan*, 2nd edn, Boston: Houghton Mifflin Company, pp. 274–90.

Duverger, M. (1955) *The Political Role of Women*, Paris: UNESCO.

Earhart, H. B. (2004) *Japanese Religion: Unity and Diversity*, 4th edn, Belmont, CA: Wadsworth Cengage Learning.

Esping-Andersen, G. (1990) *Three Worlds of Welfare Capitalism*, Princeton, NJ: Princeton University Press.

— (1997) 'Hybrid or unique? The Japanese welfare state between Europe and America', *Journal of European Social Policy*, 7 (3): 179–89.

— (1999) *Social Foundations of Postindustrial Economies*, Oxford: Oxford University Press.

Eto, M. (2010) 'Women and representation in Japan: the causes of political inequality', *International Feminist Journal of Politics*, 12 (2): 177–201.

Eurostat (n.d.) 'Employment rate by gender, 2012', available at http://epp.eurostat. ec.europa.eu/tgm/table.do?tab=table&init=1&plugin=1&language=en& pcode=tsdec420 (accessed 30 June 2014).

Ferree, M. M. (1987) 'Equality and autonomy: feminist politics in the United States and West Germany', in Katzenstein, M. and Mueller, C. (eds) *The Women's Movements of the United States and Western Europe: Consciousness, Political Opportunity, and Public Policy*, Philadelphia: Temple University Press, pp. 171–95.

— (2012) *Varieties of Feminism: German Gender Politics in Global Perspective*, Stanford, CA: Stanford University Press.

Fox, R. L. and Lawless, J. L. (2010) 'If only they'd ask: gender, recruitment, and political ambition', *Journal of Politics*, 72 (2): 310–36.

Frauen-Union der CSU (ed.) (1997) *50 Jahre Frauen-Union in Bayern*, Augsburg: Hofmann-Druck GmbH.

Fulbrook, M. (2009) *A History of Germany 1918–2008: The Divided Nation*, 3rd edn, Chichester: Wiley-Blackwell.

Gaunder, A. (2009) 'Running for national office in Japan: are Koizumi's female "children" a short-term anomaly or a long-term phenomenon?', in Reed, S., Mori, K. and Shimizu, K. (eds) *Political Change in Japan: Electoral Behavior, Party Realignment and the Koizumi Reforms*, Washington, DC: Brookings Institution Press, pp. 239–59.

— (2012) 'The DPJ and women: the limited impact of the 2009 alternation of power on policy and governance', *Journal of East Asian Studies*, 12 (3): 441–66.

Gehler, M. and Kaiser, W. (2004) *Christian Democracy in Europe since 1945: Volume 2*, New York: Routledge.

Gottfried, H. and O'Reilly, J. (2002) 'Re-regulating bread winner models in socially conservative welfare regimes: comparing Germany and Japan', *Social Politics*, 9 (1): 29–59.

Granieri, R. J. (2003) *The Ambivalent Alliance: Konrad Adenauer, The CDU/CSU, and the West, 1949–1966*, New York: Berghahn Books.

Hall, P. (1986) 'The institutional logic of comparative political economy', in *Governing the Economy: The Politics of State Intervention in Britain and France*, New York: Oxford University Press, pp. 229–42.

Hall, P. and Soskice, D. (eds) (2001) *Varieties of Capitalism: The Institutional Foundations of Comparative Advantage*, Oxford: Oxford University Press.

Hanley, D. (1996) *Christian Democracy in Europe: A Comparative Perspective*, Pinter: London.

Hannam, J., Holden, K. and Auchterlonie, M. (2000) *International Encyclopedia of Women's Suffrage*, Santa Barbara, CA: ABC-Clio.

Hickman, J. C. (1997) 'The candidacy and election of women in Japanese SNTV electoral systems', *Women and Politics*, 18 (2): 1–26.

Inglehart, R. and Norris, P. (2003) *Rising Tide: Gender Equality and Cultural Change Around the World*, Cambridge: Cambridge University Press.

Inter-Parliamentary Union (2014) 'Women in national parliaments', http://www.ipu.org/wmn-e/world.htm, accessed 30 June 2013.

Irving, R. E. M. (1979) *The Christian Democratic Parties of Western Europe*, London: George Allen & Unwin.

Iwamoto, M. (2001) 'The Madonna boom: the progress of Japanese women into politics in the 1980s', *PS: Political Science & Politics*, 34 (2): 225–6.

Kabashima, I. and Steel, G. (2006) 'How the LDP survives', *Japan Echo*, 7–15 June.

Katzenstein, M. F. and Mueller, C. M. (eds) (1987) *The Women's Movements of the United States and Western Europe: Consciousness, Political Opportunity, and Public Policy*, Philadelphia, PA: Temple University Press.

Kirchheimer, O. (1966) 'The transformation of the Western European party systems', in La Palombara, J. and Wiener, M. (eds) *Political Parties and Political Development*, Princeton, NJ: Princeton University Press, pp. 177–200.

Kohno, M. (1997) *Japan's Postwar Party Politics*, Princeton, NJ: Princeton University Press.

Köllner, P. (2011) 'The Democratic Party of Japan: development, organization and programmatic profile', in Gaunder, A. (ed.) *The Routledge Handbook of Japanese Politics*, London: Routledge, pp. 24–35.

Krauss, E., and Pekkanen, R. (2011) *The Rise and Fall of Japan's LDP: Political Party Organizations as Historical Institutions*, Ithaca: Cornell University Press.

Lawless, J. L. (2012) *Becoming a Candidate: Political Ambition and the Decision to Run for Office*, Cambridge: Cambridge University Press.

Leslie, J. and Wiliarty, S. E. (2009) 'Gate crashers and engraved invitations: integrating women activists in the SPD and CDU from the 1960s to the 1980s', in McLeay, E., Macmillan, K. and Leslie, J. (eds) *Women and Politics in New Zealand*, Wellington, New Zealand: Victoria University Press, pp. 218–46.

Lewis, J. (1992) 'Gender and the development of welfare regimes', *Journal of European Social Policy*, 2 (3): 159–73.

Lovenduski, J. and Norris, P. (eds) (1993) *Gender and Party Politics*, London: Sage.

Mackie, V. (2003) *Feminism in Modern Japan*, Cambridge: Cambridge University Press.

Matland, R. E. (1998) 'Women's representation in national legislatures: developed and developing countries', *Legislative Studies Quarterly*, 23 (1): 109–25.

— (2006) 'Enhancing women's political participation: legislative recruitment and electoral systems', in International Institute for Democracy and Electoral Assistance, *Women in Parliament – Beyond Numbers*, Stockholm: International Idea, pp. 93–111.

McKay, J. (2004) 'Women in German politics: still jobs for the boys?', *German Politics*, 13 (1): 56–80.

Ministry of Internal Affairs and Communications (MIC) (n.d.), 'Political Party by Gender, 2012 Lower House Election' (translation from Japanese), available at http://www.soumu.go.jp/main_content/000194169.xls, accessed 30 June 2014.

Mitchell, M. (2012) *The Origins of Christian Democracy: Politics and Confession in Modern Germany*, Ann Arbor: University of Michigan Press.

Miura, M., Lee, K. Y. and Weiner, R. (2005) 'Who are the DPJ? Policy positioning and recruitment strategy', *Asian Perspective*, 29 (1): 49–77.

Moser, R. G. and Scheiner, E. (2012) *Electoral Systems And Political Context: How the Effects of Rules Vary across New and Established Democracies*, Cambridge: Cambridge University Press.

Murase, M. (2006) *Cooperation Over Conflict: The Women's Movement and the State in Postwar Japan*, London: Routledge.

Norris, P. (1985) 'Women's legislative participation in Western Europe', *West European Politics*, 8 (4): 90–101.

— (1987) *Politics and Sexual Equality: The Comparative Position of Women in Western Democracies*, Sussex: Lynne Reinner.

— (1996) 'Legislative recruitment', in LeDuc, L., Niemi, R. and Norris, P. (eds) *Comparing Democracies*, London: Sage, pp. 184–215.

— (1997) 'Conclusions: comparing passages to power', in Norris, P. (ed.) *Legislative Recruitment in Advanced Democracies*, Cambridge: Cambridge University Press, pp. 209–31.

— (2004) *Electoral Engineering: Voting Rules and Political Behavior*, Cambridge: Cambridge University Press.

Ogai, T. (2001) 'Japanese women and political institutions: why are women politically underrepresented?', *PS: Political Science and Politics*, 34 (2): 207–10.

Osawa, M. (2007) *Gendai nihon no seikatsu hoshō shisutemu: zahyō to yukue* [The Livelihood Security System in Contemporary Japan: Its Coordinate and Future], Tokyo: Iwanami Shoten.

Ostner, I. and Lewis, J. (1995) 'Gender and the evolution of European social policies', in Leibfried, S. and Pierson, P. (eds) *European Social Policy: Between Fragmentation and Integration*, Washington, DC: Brookings Institution Press, pp. 159–93.

Park, C. H. (2001) 'Factional dynamics in Japan's LDP since political reform: continuity and change', *Asian Survey*, 41 (3): 428–61.

Paxton, P. (1997) 'Women in national legislatures: a cross-national analysis', *Social Science Research*, 26 (4): 442–64.

Paxton, P., Hughes, M. M. and Green, J. L. (2006) 'The international women's movement and women's political representation, 1893–2003', *American Sociological Review*, 71 (6): 898–920.

Pridham, G. (1977) *Christian Democracy in Western Germany: The CDU/CSU in Government and Opposition, 1945–1976*, London: Croom Helm.

Randall, V. (1987) *Women and Politics: An International Perspective*. Basingstoke: Macmillan Educational.

Reischauer, E. O. (1991) *Japan: The Story of a Nation*, 4th edn, New York: McGraw-Hill, pp. 139–43.

Ritter, G. A. and Niehuss, M. (1991) *Wahlen in Deutschland, 1946–1991: Ein Handbuch*, Munich: Verlag C. H. Beck.

Rule, W. (1987) 'Electoral systems, contextual factors and women's opportunity for election to parliament in twenty-three democracies', *Western Political Quarterly*, 50 (3): 477–98.

— (1994) 'Women's underrepresentation and electoral systems', *PS: Political Science and Politics*, 27 (4): 689–92.

Schindler, P. (1999) *Datenhandbuch zur Geschichte des Deutschen Bundestages 1949 bis 1999*, Baden-Baden: Nomos Verlagsgesellschaft.

Schoppa, L. (2006) *Race for the Exits: The Unraveling of Japan's System of Social Protection*, Ithaca, NY: Cornell University Press.

Shin, K.-Y. (2011) 'The women's movements', in Gaunder, A. (ed.) *The Routledge Handbook of Japanese Politics*, London: Routledge, pp. 175–86.

Statistisches Bundesamt (2005) *Wahl zum 16. Deutschen Bundestag am 18. September 2005*, Wiesbaden: Statistisches Bundesamt.

— (2009) *Wahl zum 17. Deutschen Bundestag am 27. September 2009*, Wiesbaden: Statistisches Bundesamt.

Stockwin, J. A. A. (2000) 'The Social Democratic Party (formerly Japan Socialist Party): a turbulent odyssey', in Hrebenar, R. J. (ed.) *Japan's New Party System*, 3rd edn, Boulder, CO: Westview Press, pp. 209–51.

Thomas, S. (1998) 'Introduction: women and elective office: past, present, and future', in Thomas, S. and Wilcox, C. (eds) *Women and Elective Office*, New York: Oxford University Press, pp. 1–14.

Toyoda, M. A. and Tanaka, A. (2002) 'Religion and politics in Japan', in Jelen, T. G. and Wilcox, C. (eds) *Religion and Politics in Comparative Perspective: The One, the Few, the Many*, New York: Cambridge, pp. 269–86.

Uertz, R. (1981) *Christentum und Sozialismus in der frühen CDU: Grundlagen und Wirkungen der christlich-sozialen Ideen in der Union, 1945–1949*, Stuttgart: Deutsche-Verlags-Anstalt.

United Nations (2011) 'Gender inequality index and other related indications', In *Human Development Report 2011*, available at http://hdr.undp.org/en/media/HDR_2011_EN_Table4.pdf (accessed 22 March 2012).

United Nations Statistics Division (n.d.) 'Statistics and Indicators on Women and Men', available at http://unstats.un.org/unsd/demographic/products/indwm/default.htm (accessed 1 May 2014).

van Kersbergen, K. (1995) *Social Capitalism: A Study of Christian Democracy and the Welfare State*, London and New York: Routledge.

von Schwartzenberg, M. (2002) *Wirtschaft und Statistik,* Wiesbaden: Statistisches Bundesamt.

Weldon, S. L. (2002) *Protest, Policy, and the Problem of Violence against Women: A Cross-National Comparison*, Pittsburgh: University of Pittsburgh Press.

Wiliarty, S. E. (2010) *The CDU and the Politics of Gender in Germany: Bringing Women to the Party*, Cambridge: Cambridge University Press.

— (2013) 'Gender as a modernising force in the German CDU', *German Politics*, 22 (1–2): 172–90.

Wolinetz, S. B. (1979) 'The transformation of Western European Party systems revisited', *West European Politics*, 2 (1): 4–28.

World Bank (n.d.) Fertility rate, total (births per woman), available at http://data.worldbank.org/indicator/SP.DYN.TFRT.IN (accessed 27 March 2012).

Yamamura, K. and Streeck, W. (eds) (2003) *The End of Diversity? Prospects for German and Japanese Capitalism*, Ithaca: Cornell University Press, pp. 183–211.

Young, L. (2000) Feminists and Party Politics. Ann Arbor, MI: University of Michigan Press.

Chapter Two

Christian Democratic Party Feminisation: The German Christian Democratic Union and the Male Breadwinner Model

Josef Hien

Introduction

In 2006 Germany saw a substantive change in its family policy. After sixty years of a male-breadwinner-centred family policy, a government coalition, headed by Christian Democrats, enacted a shift towards a dual earner/caretaker regime.[1] Commentators were surprised: had not the German welfare state usually been described as the archetypal conservative welfare state (Esping-Andersen 1990, 1999; Sainsbury 1999)? How could the Christian Democrats, commonly perceived as the constructors and guardians of the male breadwinner model (van Kersbergen 1995), be at the forefront when it came to dismantling it?

The answer lies in the phenomenon of party feminisation (Lovenduski 2005). Since the slow breakup of the classic continental European electoral cleavages (Bartolini and Mair 1990), Christian Democratic parties could no longer count on a fixed core of religiously informed female votes (Manow and Emmenegger 2012). Instead, they would have to compete for them. Like other parties (Childs and Webb 2012b), Christian Democracy has reacted to this trend with strategies of party feminisation (Wiliarty 2010). Hence, they tried to incorporate the representation of women and of women's concerns into their programmes (Childs *et al.* 2009). However, the male breadwinner model, for decades at the heart of male-centred Christian Democratic programmes, seemed to be especially resilient to reform.

Adopting a historical perspective, the analysis traces how the male breadwinner model originated in Catholic thought and was subsequently implemented by Catholic Christian Democrats in post-World War II Germany, until it was abandoned as part of the family policy reforms of the mid-2000s.

History shows that party feminisation is especially hard for Christian Democratic parties due to the strong attachment between these parties and religious ideology and institutions. However, the chapter also finds that the extent to which

---

1. For accounts describing the reform: Fleckenstein (2010, 2011); Fleckenstein and Seeleib-Kaiser (2011); Henninger *et al.* (2008); Seeleib-Kaiser (2010); von Wahl (2011).

Christian Democratic parties can be feminised, and the ease with which this is implemented, varies not only with the degree of religious attachment but also with the type of Christian denomination that forms the basis of the party's ideology. While Catholicism has a restricting effect on party feminisation, Protestantism allows for easier feminisation.

The feminisation of the German Christian Democrats only became possible once the party realigned from a Catholic to a liberal Protestant constituency during the 2000s. This realignment was facilitated by the German reunification process, which provided the possibility of adding a new East German electorate, which was both more Protestant and more liberal than the West German population, to the Christian Democratic constituency. As a consequence, the party could reduce its reliance on Catholic voters and was therefore less vulnerable to threats from the Catholic Church to withdraw its electoral support. However, the softening of the connection between the Christian Democratic party, Catholic voters and the Catholic Church did not alone pave the way to reform. Rather, the ever deeper entanglement of the Catholic Church in the market of care and welfare provision in Germany since the 1970s also played a role. This was important because the Christian Democratic leadership was able to secure Catholic consent to its reform of the male breadwinner model in 2006 by guaranteeing that the welfare providers of the Catholic Church would not be sidelined in the successive expansion of child care provision.

Christian Democracy and party feminisation

Conservative Parties have, as other chapters in this volume attest, become increasingly feminised in recent years. This also holds for the Christian Democratic continental parties, which differ from their conservative counterparts owing to their stronger attachment to Christian values and religious authorities. While there is some analysis that scrutinizes the feminisation of conservative parties (for example: Childs and Webb 2012a, 2012b; Celis and Erzeel 2011), there are only very few accounts looking to the feminisation of continental European Christian Democratic parties (notable exceptions: Davidson-Schmich 2011; von Wahl 2011; Wiliarty 2010, 2011). This follows a general trend in political science of neglecting the study of Christian Democracy (Kitschelt 1994: 1; Kaiser 2004: 129; Kalyvas and van Kersbergen 2010: 184).

Christian Democracy has its roots in the church–state conflicts of late nineteenth century continental Europe. When Christian denominations came under pressure from liberal–secularising (e.g. Italy, France) or conservative (e.g. Germany) nation building elites in the nineteenth century, parties of religious defence were formed (Kalyvas 1996, 1998). These 'religious interest groups' (Warner 2000) were marked by their strong attachment to national (or international) clerical hierarchies and had a political programme that was firmly rooted in the doctrine of the corresponding Christian denomination (Catholic, Protestant, Lutheran). After WWII, these parties transformed into Christian Democratic parties, which were more inclusive than their predecessors (Kselman and Buttigieg 2003). Post-war Christian Democrats aspired to build people's parties. By forming the Christian Democratic Union (CDU), German Christian Democracy abandoned the Catholic Centre party and founded an inter-religious party designed to attract both Catholics and Protestants. However, for post-war Christian Democracy, the effect of their legacies as former parties of religious defence persisted. Their strong ties with church hierarchies (Bösch 2001), their continuous reliance on religious voters (Arzheimer 2006; Arzheimer and Schoen 2007; Elff and Roßteutscher 2011) and their specific socio-economic doctrine of Social Capitalism, which tries to forge a third way between Socialism and Liberalism, still strongly distinguished them from classic conservative parties (van Kersbergen 1995, 1999).

Despite being inter-religious parties, the concept of Social Capitalism preferred by Christian Democracy originates largely in Catholic economic thinking. Central to its development were the two papal encyclicals, Rerum Novarum (1891) and Quadragesimo Anno (1932), which emerged as reactions to the capitalist crisis in the nineteenth and twentieth centuries and presented a Catholic alternative to the secular socio-economic ideologies of liberalism and socialism (Misner 1992). The core element of Social Capitalism is the male breadwinner model. This family-centred doctrine offers well protected and well paid jobs for men that compensate for the unpaid domestic labour of women within a family household. Neither the Protestant church nor the Protestant parts within the Christian Democratic party was ever closely associated with the concept. Even today, Protestants within the Christian Democratic party, as well as their Protestant voters, express views that are more compatible with a dual earner/caretaker model than a male breadwinner family policy (Neu 2012).

The male breadwinner model and the prospects of party feminisation

Today, the male breadwinner model is held accountable for the declining birth rates, which are now, in most continental European countries, well beneath the reproduction rate. It is a commonly held assumption by policymakers, policy advisors (see the publication series 'Babies and bosses': OECD 2008) and the public, that the solution to declining birth rates lies in the provision of services that allow women to reconcile their working and family lives by de-burdening them from their caretaker role at home (Esping-Andersen 1996).

The male breadwinner model is also perceived by the public as a symbol of a conservative and antiquated gender role model. It has been increasingly depicted as the root cause of the declining electoral fortunes of Christian Democratic parties among women voters. Although these parties enjoyed a net surplus in female votes until the end of the 1960s, the situation reversed thereafter (Wiliarty 2010: 21). Party competition over the abolition of the male breadwinner model and the introduction of its counterpart, the dual earner/caretaker regime, has considerably increased in most continental European countries over the past two decades (Manow and Emmenegger 2012). In this respect, the abolition of the male breadwinner model has become a central component of party feminisation strategies.[2]

According to the original definition, party feminisation requires the integration of women's concerns into the party (and the integration of women into politics) (Lovenduski 2005). However, identifying women's concerns in the sphere of family policy is complicated. The preferences of female conservative politicians and voters often stand in sharp contrast to feminist claims on women's preferences which are often taken as the benchmark for women's concerns (Celis and Childs 2012: 12). The problem can be defused – arguably – if one does not automatically attribute fixed interests to women, but rather analyses women's interests through a constructivist lens (Berman 1998; Blyth 2002). Fundamental to this is an acceptance that 'what constitutes the interests of women cannot be assumed' (Celis and Childs 2012: 12). Instead, one has to carefully empirically reconstruct what women's interests mean to different women in different times and different places. The interests of different groups of women have, then, to be assessed, contextualised and embedded in their cultural and historical context.

The following analysis follows the interests of the Christian Democratic Party and the women it represents, in the debate over federal German family policy from the foundation of the party until today. German Christian Democratic family policy is an especially interesting case as it reveals how complex party feminisation can be for Christian Democratic parties and how it is contingent not only on the changes in the attitude of conservative women themselves but also on the constraints that outside actors pose to these parties – namely, in the case of Christian Democracy, the churches and their auxiliary organisations.

The male breadwinner model and German Christian Democracy

The male breadwinner model was not the traditional model of German society but largely a creation of the first half of the twentieth century and especially of the post-World War II period (Pfau-Effinger 2004). Before the twentieth century, Germany was based on a society of dual-income households (Gerlach 2010). In the Kaiserreich (1871–1918) and the Weimar Republic (1918–33), the male breadwinner model was a 'vision' (Naumann 2005: 51), rather than a social reality. The vast majority of families could not afford to rely on one breadwinner only.

---

2. While some scholars herald the emancipatory effects of the family policy of Nordic welfare states, which stem from its compatibility of child bearing and work for women through the provision of ample state-driven day care provision, others criticise such arrangements as being nothing more than paternalism on a larger scale (Jenson 1997; Sasson 1997). Jane Lewis and others have repeatedly pointed out that, since the 1970s, 'greater numbers of women have entered the labor market', however, 'all the evidence suggests that the division of unpaid work has changed little' (Lewis 1997: 162; for a non-feminist critique see Streeck 2011).

One of the first institutions that explicitly incorporated the male breadwinner model into its worldview was the Catholic Church (Morgan 2006). Rerum Novarum, the first papal social encyclical (1891), stated that '[p]aternal authority can neither be abolished nor be absorbed by the State' (Rerum Novarum 1891, para. 14) and added that it was sinful for 'mothers on account of the father's low wage to be forced to engage in gainful occupations outside the home to the neglect of their proper cares and duties, especially the training of children' (Rerum Novarum 1891, para. 71). Quadragesimo Anno, the second social encyclical (1932), advanced a theory of the 'just wage' (Quadragesimo Anno 1932, para. 72). The just wage should be allocated to the 'authority of the father' (Rerum Novarum 1891, para. 13) and must be sufficient to maintain the entire family.

After WWII, the newly founded CDU picked up the male breadwinner model and firmly anchored it into its programmes. In the early Christian Democratic party manifestos, the family is constituted as 'the foundation of social life' and 'holy' (CDU 1945a: 10). Christian Democratic programmes of the 1940s stated that any 'adult and working human has the right to a salary that will make it possible for him to found and sustain a family' (CDU 1945a: 12). The Frankfurter Leitsätze (CDU 1945b), set out that 'men must […] be the head of the family' and that the 'state must, by its economic and social policy, give him the opportunity to nurture his family in honour' (CDU 1945b: 4–5). These provisions are very close to the papal encyclicals of 1891 and 1932.

Such statements about the patriarchal family were not mere catchphrases. In order to further secure the support of the Catholic Church, the Christian Democrats built the male breadwinner model firmly into the early family policy arrangements of the Federal Republic (Naumann 2005: 51; Moeller 1993: 1–7). Adenauer (then German Chancellor) founded the first Family Ministry in 1953 and made the Catholic Josef Würmeling the responsible minister.

Würmeling opened his first parliamentary speech with the claim that 'the Church was his best and most important comrade-in-arms' (Würmeling cited in Gerlach 2010: 179). His policy was built on the confinement of women to the home and on the promotion of marriage in order to counter the increasing divorce rates of the 1950s that, according to Würmeling, would create moral havoc and increase the number of 'stray kids' (Würmeling cited in Gerlach 2010: 180). The second family minister, the Catholic Bruno Heck, also had close ties to the Catholic Church (Gerlach 2010). Both ministers engineered the first institutions of the Federal Republic in a way that made 'the housewife model of the male breadwinner family […] the basis of West German family culture' (Pfau-Effinger 2004: 384). The tax break for married couples with children from 1949 (*Kinderfreibetrag*); the tax advantage for married couples from 1951 (*Ehegattensplitting*); the house ownership promotion laws and the family allowance law (*Kindergeld*) from 1954, were all part of this strategy. Even in light of the labour shortage of the early 1960s, the Christian Democrats did not alter their strategy. When industry demanded the entry of women into the job market the Christian Democrats opted for wooing foreign *Gastarbeiter* instead of women's paid employment. Day care and the dual earner model was essentially a moral taboo (Moeller 1993: 219).

The male breadwinner model was, furthermore, a decommodifying welfare policy aiming at reducing the family's exposure to the forces of the market. It was put into the party programmes as a central claim of the Catholics and the employees' wing of the party. Protestants in the CDU, organised within the employers' and Ordoliberal wings of the party (Bösch 2001; Zolleis 2008), were either indifferent or opposed to the policies that pushed the male breadwinner idea. In contrast, the Catholic Church and the Catholic Unions urged its followers to gratify the CDU for these policies on election day.

The German Christian Democratic female electorate appreciated the support of the church and the decommodifying effects of the male breadwinner model. 'Less a political party than a protective institution, which adhere(d) to comfortable values, shelter(ed) marriage and the family, and live(d) in peace with the churches', as Pridham observes (cited in Rusciano 1992: 348), the party had a continuous advantage among female voters. '[U]ntil 1972, the CDU regularly received 8 per cent to 10 per cent more [support] from female voters than from male voters' (Wiliarty 2010: 20). According to Rusciano the 'CSU[Christian Social Union]/CDU outpolled the SPD [Social Democratic Party] by fifteen percentage points or more of the female vote between 1949 and 1965 and by ten percentage points in 1969' (Rusciano 1992: 339).

However, this pro-woman gender gap did not last forever. The (revolutionary) social changes of the 1960s and 1970s brought ever more women into full- or part-time employment (1960: 0.5 mio; 1970: 1.6 mio, Bertram 2009: 35–7; *see also* Naumann 2005: 32). Female enrolment in tertiary education in West Germany rose from 23.1 per cent in 1960 to 34.8 per cent in 1978. Church attendance started to decline and the birth rate started to fall. *Kinder, Küche, Kirche* (children, church, kitchen), the (in)famous three Ks that were so strongly associated with the role of women in West German post-war society, had started to crumble. This was reflected in a decline in traditional patriarchal family values. The share of women who wanted to be 'only housewives declined from 57 per cent in 1961 to 29 per cent in 1973' (Rusciano 1992: 351), which led to what Jane Lewis coined 'the erosion of the male breadwinner model at the behavioral level' (Lewis 2001: 153).

The Christian Democrats did not adapt to this transformation of society. Instead, as Naumann notes, 'there was a strong antifeministic "coalition" between the Christian Democratic parties and the churches, as well as the experts from various fields (family policy, child development, medicine) ready to ward off feminist demands' (Naumann 2005: 58). For Christian Democrats, the problem was that the 'feminist representation of "women" as [...] independent and autonomous being[s] without automatic family obligations was antithetical to the role envisaged for women in the social Catholic family ideal' (Naumann 2005: 58).

In contrast, the Social Democrats increasingly engaged programmatically with the changes in women's attitudes and behaviours of the 1960s. For example, proposed legal regulations for part-time employment that were designed to be favourable for women were included in the Social Democratic programme for the 1966 and 1969 elections. This was a wake up call for the Christian Democrats, who experienced their first loss of power in 1969 to a Social Democratic/Liberal coalition headed by Chancellor Brandt. The party's reaction was a mild attempt at party feminisation.

The Berliner Programme of 1971 and the 1973 Düsseldorf manifesto introduced the concept of 'free choice' (CDU 1971: 77). It recognised that 'a woman must be able to decide freely whether she wants solely to dedicate herself to the tasks in family and household or also wants to be full or halftime employed in addition to that' (CDU 1971: 77). However, the manifesto makes clear that 'the position of the housewife and mother is in every aspect equal to the one of the employed woman' (CDU 1971: 77).

From the mid-1970s onwards, the Catholic Church started to raise concerns about the new family policy of the Social Democratic/Liberal coalition. The *Frankfurter Allgemeine Zeitung* wrote that the issue was a source of 'continuous trouble between Catholics and SPD/FDP' (FAZ 1978a: 3). To build up political pressure on the government, the Catholic Church lobbied the opposition Christian Democratic party. It made its influence felt through a series of meetings during the 1970s between key Christian Democratic party officials and Catholic bishops (FAZ 1978b: 3). This push bore its first fruit in the form of the CDU's Mannheimer Programme, which paints the Social Democratic/Liberal government's family policy as leading to the dismantling of the family (CDU 1971: 77). Social Democratic plans to introduce day care and all-day schools were criticised as being 'dangerous experiments' in 'socialist schooling' on the 'back of our children' (CDU 1978: 3, 10). Such policies are presented as connected with 'an increase in mental and physical disturbances of children, teenagers and adults' (CDU 1975, point 2.2), as well as with the increase in alcoholism, drug consumption and criminality (CDU 1975, point 2.2). In 1978, the new party leader Kohl called the government's family policy a 'social policy scandal' (FAZ 1978c: 2). The CDU's Ludwigshafen Programme of 1978 states that 'devotion can usually only be given to the child if the mother abstains in the first years of her child's life from her employment' (CDU 1978, point 47). During the fall of 1980, the Catholic bishops started to plan the release of a letter from the pulpit (*Hirtenbrief*) that would heavily criticise the family policy of the Social Democratic/Liberal government. The Social Democrats retorted that the Catholic Church should not degrade itself to being a mere electoral tool of the Christian Democratic parties (FAZ 1980: 1).

In 1982, the Christian Democrat Helmut Kohl succeeded the Social Democrat Schmidt as Chancellor. Kohl won the elections on the platform of a 'moral and intellectual rebound' (CDU 1982; *see also* Bösch 2002: 44), which also included a return to male breadwinner-centred provisions in family policy. However, plummeting fertility rates became an ever more vexing issue in public discourse during the 1980s. Much to the applause of the Catholic Church, the Christian Democrats tried to counter this by calling for a renaissance of traditional male breadwinner family values. Regarding all-day schooling, the 1984 Stuttgart Programme emphasises that the CDU stands 'in opposition to a society in which children get alienated from their parents and pressed through "school fabrics"'

Figure 2.1: Female vote bonus, Christian Democratic Party, Germany, 1953–2005

Sources: Figure by the author. Data from Wilarty (2010: 21).
Note: The 0-line represents the male vote.

(CDU 1984). The head of the CDU workers' organisation, Norbert Blüm, demanded 'more motherhood' (Blüm, in *Der Spiegel* 1985: 26) and Helmut Kohl warned that 'without the sacrifice of our mothers our nation will have no future' (Kohl, in *Der Spiegel* 1985: 28).

Nevertheless, the value changes that the 1960s and 1970s had brought to West German society could not simply be undone. Ever more women defected from the Christian Democratic electorate (in 1980, for the first time since 1949, more men than women voted Christian Democrat, *see* Figure 2.1)

The divergence between the attitudes of West German women and the programmatic position of the Christian Democratic party became increasingly obvious through the systematic inclusion of public opinion surveys into the strategic reasoning of the Christian Democratic electoral strategists. Elisabeth Noelle-Neumann, head of the Allensbach (public opinion) Institute (which was closely tied to the Christian Democratic party), was declared by *Der Spiegel* to be 'arguably the most influential woman' in politics (*Der Spiegel* 1985: 24–35). In an editorial for the conservative *Frankfurter Allgemeine Zeitung* in 1985, she suggested that children would not suffer any detrimental effects in dual earner/ caretaker family models. She added that the Christian Democratic party had continuously lost ground among female voters since the 1960s and that other political contenders, such as the Green Party, were strongly capitalising on this by explicitly targeting female issues (Noelle-Neumann 1985: 11). Later that year, the Christian Democrats reacted with a second attempt to feminise the party. Heiner Geissler, the new party secretary, organised an explicitly gendered party congregation in Essen where 500 female delegates would discuss new family proposals. The outcome was the Essen manifesto of 1985 with the title 'For a new partnership between men and women' (CDU 1985). The proclaimed aim of the programme was that 'equality between men and women should be achieved before the end of the century in all essential aspects of life' (CDU 1985: 1). The weekly *Der Spiegel* made it its cover story and commented that the proposal for the new party manifesto read like an editorial in *Emma*, a prominent German feminist magazine. A first attempt to abandon the male breadwinner concept, the programme proclaims that 'it is an expression of outdated thinking to confine the tasks of the woman to those of mother and housewife and the task of the man to that of the breadwinner' (CDU 1985: 2). The re-entry of parents into their jobs after rearing should, consequently, be codified and facilitated through retraining programmes. The programme further confesses that in Germany 'the legal and social requirements for a better reconciliation of job and family are missing' (CDU 1985), and that 'parents should choose freely who stays at home and gets the family allowance' (CDU 1985, para. 10). Even though the proposal was hammered out by the 500 female delegates, it was however, voted on by the male-dominated general party assembly. As consequence, the manifesto also features ambiguous if not contradictory statements, including: 'the CDU rejects a policy that confines women or men to certain roles or which does not want to acknowledge the differences between men and women', and: '[i]t is a mistake of radical feminists to withdraw into a male free shelter and to dream of the matriarchy' (CDU 1985, para. 2).

A year prior to such official attempts to feminise family policy, the Catholic Church had been wary about the liberal forces that were at work within the Christian Democratic party. In 1984, the main congregation of the German Catholic bishops urged in an official statement that '[n]owhere do we need a more urgent turn than in the fields of family and family policy' (Schilder 1984: 5). The critique reached its peak with the appointment of Rita Süßmuth as the new Christian Democratic family minister. Seeking to accelerate the feminisation of the party, she was met with strong criticism from the Catholic camp. In a letter to the editor of the *Frankfurter Allgemeine Zeitung*, a reader complained that the minister's plans on family policy and abortion were 'stabbing us [Catholics] in our back' and that 'my family and I no longer feel represented by Ms Süßmuth' (Geppert-Rahm 1985: 10). Catholic resistance within the party grew and ultimately stalled any further party feminisation. Bösch, perhaps the most prominent historian working on the CDU, comments that 'Rita Süßmuth was therefore becoming a politician that found ever more consent in public than in her own party' (Bösch 2002: 253). In 1988 Süßmuth had to leave her post as family minister, officially in order to become President of the Bundestag, and unofficially because of the Catholic resistance to her family policy (Gerlach 2010). The Catholic Church was pleased. Alois Glück from the Bavarian Christian Democrats, who is today at the head of the largest German Catholic lay organisation, summarised the new Christian Democratic family policy by suggesting in 1989 that a 'comprehensive coverage with day care facilities would be a meander to the disservice of children, the family and society as a whole' (Glück, cited in SZ 2005: 8). For most of the second half of the 1980s and the 1990s, any attempt to further feminise the CDU and German family policy was halted and no legislative reform of the male breadwinner model was enacted under the Christian Democratic/Liberal government coalition during that time.

While the late 1980s saw some recovery in the female Christian Democratic vote, the female electoral fortunes of the party started to crumble again with reunification. Some 2.9 per cent more women than men voted for the Christian Democratic party in 1990, but this number fell to 1.6 in 1994 and by 1998 it had shrunk to 0.1 (Wiliarty 2010: 21). This year also marked the first time in sixteen years when the Christian Democrats lost their government majority. Chancellor Kohl was succeeded by the Social Democrat Gerhard Schröder, who headed a coalition between the Social Democrats and the Green Party until 2005.

Party feminisation after reunification

The electoral defeat of Chancellor Kohl in 1998 was attributed not only to his jaded appeal after sixteen years in office but also to the old-fashioned party platform that he represented within the CDU. During the 1990s, Germany had faced substantial difficulties in coping with the enormous task of reunification and seemed incapable of keeping up with the challenges of globalisation. It was even labelled by commentators as the 'sick man of Europe' (Kitschelt and Streeck 2003). Its Bismarckian welfare institutions, and with it the male breadwinner model, were internationally and nationally criticised as outdated in a decade ripe with neo-liberal thought and policy prescriptions (Esping-Andersen 1996, 1999). Much of the blame was put on the Christian Democrats, the party that had ruled Germany for the preceding sixteen years.

At this point Angela Merkel became CDU party secretary and promised to make the CDU 'one of the most modern parties of Europe' (CDU 1999: 3). To Merkel, as an East German Protestant, the Catholic (West German) male breadwinner regime was alien. Party feminisation quickly became one of her first projects. For Von Wahl, Merkel, as a 'child from a Protestant home', who grew up 'in the context of the East German socialist regime, [was] likely to support a moderately progressive view on gender equality embedded in a Protestant worldview' (von Wahl 2011: 394).

Reunification brought not only the Protestant Angela Merkel into the party but also changed the electoral map of Germany. The result was not necessarily the strengthening of the Protestant electorate but the re-inclusion of a part of Germany that had a strong Protestant cultural and political history. In 1950, 80 per cent of the East German population had been Protestant. After the secularisation efforts of the Socialist regime the figures had dropped to 30 per cent in 1989. Nominally, reunification contributed to an increase in the secularised segment of German society – however, it was one that originated from a strong Protestant heritage. Indeed, Protestants in Germany and Protestants in the Christian Democratic party differ considerably from their Catholic counterparts. The segment of Protestants that go to church on a regular basis is much smaller than among Catholics (5 per cent of Protestants attend mass on a regular basis, compared to 12 per cent of Catholics). Protestant Christian Democrats also have far fewer problems with secular values than Catholics (Neu 2012: 10, 12, 13). Such characteristics reinforced the secular trends in wider German society. While in 1987 only 11.4 per cent of the West German population indicated that they were secular or that they belonged to a non-Christian religion, this figure had increased to 38.8 per cent of the West and East German population in 2011. Around 30.8 per cent indicated that they were Catholic while 30.3 per cent were Protestant (Zensus 2013).

By feminising family policy, Merkel tried to detach the CDU's family policy from its Catholic heritage. By making it more compatible with liberal and Protestant values, Merkel tried to turn the family policy of the CDU from a negative asset into an attraction. The first result of her strategy of party feminisation was the *Lust auf Familie* ('Desire for Families') manifesto of 1999 (CDU 1999). The party congregation in Berlin, from which it originated, was portrayed as a Christian Democratic 'cultural revolution' (SZ 1999a: 4). A female journalist remarked in an editorial in the *Süddeutsche Zeitung* that 'the proposal is almost too good to be true' (SZ 1999b: 10). The programme opens with an assessment of the socio-economic gender realities in Germany and puts forward that '[f]ewer and fewer men can or want to be the sole male breadwinner of the family' (CDU 1999: 3). It recognises that 'the simultaneous occupation of both partners is nowadays the life model aspired to by the majority' (CDU 1999: 3). The manifesto postulates that '[a] modern family policy cannot lead to a state supported institutionalisation of one sided gender patterns that lead to a work division between men and women' (CDU 1999: 13). So tangible was the feminisation of the Christian Democratic party programme that the Green Party accused the Christian Democrats of stealing from their programmes (*Der Spiegel* 1999).

In the 2002 elections, the Bavarian Edmund Stoiber from the CSU ran as a joint candidate for CDU and CSU. To counter his conservative image and the defection of female voters, Stoiber declared that modern (feminised) family policy would become a major topic in his 2002 campaign (SZ 2002: 6; Höll 2002a: 8). Day care should be expanded in order to reconcile work and family (CDU 2002) and he made a gesture in favour of Protestantism and East German values by nominating Katherina Reiche as his designated family policy minister. Reiche was a young unmarried mother, as well as being a Protestant from East Germany (Kahlweit 2002a).

Reaction to the nomination of the Protestant Reiche in the Catholic Church was extremely critical. Cardinal Meisner from Cologne advised the Christian Democrats to scrap the 'C' from their name (Daenzer-Vanotti 2002: 50; Augstein 2002a: 13). Yet many Catholics saw in Meisner's reaction to the nomination of Reiche 'one of the nails in the coffin of the electoral victory of the Christian Democrats' (Daenzer-Vanotti 2002: 50). The Catholic Church openly blackmailed the Christian Democrats by releasing an unfavourable election recommendation through a letter from the pulpit (*Hirtenbrief*) (Schwilk 2002; Dobrinski 2002). Against this backdrop, pollsters predicted losses in the Catholic core vote for the party (Schwilk 2002). Cardinal Ratzinger, then the chief of the Catholic congregation in Rome but later to become Pope Benedict, was cited as having 'great concern regarding the developments of German Christian Democracy' (Ratzinger, cited in Schwilk 2002). The Christian Democrats' fear of losing parts of their Catholic core electorate was so strong that Ms Reiche had to publicly announce her own marriage, and renounce all her liberal views on partnership outside wedlock and homosexual partnership (Kahlweit 2002b: 5; Höll 2002b: 6). Stoiber himself had to water down his feminised family policy platform, and lost the elections.

Most newspaper editorials pointed to the negative effect of the Christian Democrats' orthodox family position on the 2002 election results. The *Süddeutsche Zeitung* commented that '[t] he Union claims to stand in the middle of life. That's right. It stands in the middle of life, however of a past century' (Höll 2002c: 3). Rita Süßmuth pointed out that '[t]he party gives itself a new perception of women but, when it comes down to it, it retracts' (Süßmuth cited in Augstein 2002b).

The differences in how the electoral defeat was interpreted by Christian Democratic progressives and conservatives were mirrored in the programmatic discussion that followed their electoral defeat. Conservative Catholics, like Teufel and Vogel, argued that changing the stance in family policy had boiled down 'to hawking the conservative silverware' (Heuwagen 2002: 5) and to 'driving the Union into its nemesis' (Höll 2002a: 8; SZ 2006a: 4). In other words, they interpreted the defeat as a loss of the Catholic core electorate. In contrast, the reformers around Merkel argued that it was the failed feminisation of the party that had contributed to the electoral defeat by not appealing to the female electorate sufficiently. Merkel herself commented that a new family policy must not merely pay lip service but rather has to be credible in order to win elections (Heuwagen 2002: 5). The *Süddeutsche Zeitung* remarked that: '[a]fter the electoral defeat [of 1998], Schäuble, Merkel and some others had started to guide the parties into the contemporary. However, it seems that many of the Christian Democrats do not want to arrive there' (Höll 2002a: 8). In fact, opinion poll data and electoral statistics point out that the interpretation of Merkel's camp was correct. The election of 2002 marks the height of the negative trend of female votes for the Christian Democrats. Some 1.4 per cent fewer women than men voted for the Christian Democrats in 2002, while the governing Social Democrats made (together with the 1998 election) their greatest inroads into the female electorate (1998: 41 per cent; 2002: 40.2 per cent of the total female vote; *see* Deutscher Bundestag 2013).

The Christian Democratic manifesto for the next federal election, in 2005, shows that the party feminisers around Merkel had gained the upper hand. When von der Leyen, the designated family minister, presented her family policy plans, the *Süddeutsche Zeitung* commented that it is 'striking that the traditional family picture is not granted a central place anymore' (Schneider 2006). The plan foresaw a strong shift away from the male breadwinner-centred family policy towards a dual earner/caretaker regime in the federal family policy through the introduction of a parental leave scheme and the expansion of day care facilities.

As with the Christian Democratic party's previous attempts at feminisation, the Catholic Church and the conservative Catholic party establishment protested fiercely. Bishop Reinhardt Marx commented, in an interview with *Der Spiegel*, that 'politics is erring if it wants to make citizens believe that one can have everything at the same time: career, high income and children' (Marx 2010: 22). Cardinal Meisner criticised the Christian Democratic family policy plans as 'pay-check politics', and suggested that the equation '[t]he more day care facilities, the more children' was wrong (FAZ 2007a). Bishop Walter Mixa called von der Leyen's family policy 'ideologically fatuous' and held that 'her concept was degrading women to birth machines' (FAZ 2007b). The idea to give a two-month leave bonus to each couple as soon as the father went on parental leave came, particularly, under fire. Older conservative state prime ministers expressed concerns (SZ 2006b: 1). Peter Ramsauer from the Bavarian Christian Democrats sarcastically called the new arrangement a 'traineeship for changing nappies' (Fleckenstein 2011: 559). In contrast, the Protestant Bishop and later head of the main congregation of the German Protestant Bishops, Margot Käßmann, stated that she 'could not understand the [Catholic] critique at all' (FAZ 2007b). In an interview with *Der Spiegel*, the Catholic Bishop Marx complained that '[d]ue to East Germany and through Angela Merkel the Union has become more Protestant'. He also criticised what he called the 'strong position of the Protestants in the Christian Democratic leadership' (Marx 2010: 22).

The positive reaction of the Protestant church enabled Merkel, along with her family minister von der Leyen, to overcome the resistance of the Catholic Church and the traditional Catholic party establishment. However, this did not happen, exclusively because of the strength of the Protestants in the Christian Democratic leadership as Bishop Marx suspected.

Merkel and her followers were concerned that, if they failed to come to terms with the Catholic Church, they would risk facing a major protest campaign from the Catholic Church and would lose the Church's support for the next election. Despite the realignment of the CDU under Merkel towards liberal Protestantism, the Christian Democratic core electorate in West Germany remained mainly Catholic (in 2009: 44 per cent of Catholics voted Christian Democrat; Deutscher Bundestag 2013). Therefore the Catholic Church could not simply be sidelined during the feminisation efforts.

The way out of this dilemma was to take advantage of a phenomenon that has remained largely unnoticed by students of the welfare state: the role of the churches as welfare providers, which has drastically increased since the 1970s. Both the Catholic and Protestant churches have become considerably entangled in the field of welfare service provision. Today the Catholic and Protestant churches, through their welfare-providing auxiliary organisations, are the second largest employer in Germany. Figure 2.2 shows the development of the employees of the German Caritas, the welfare service provider of the Catholic Church in Germany. The Catholic Church alone employs roughly 600,000 people in Germany. The

Figure 2.2: Employees of Caritas Germany, 1950–2005

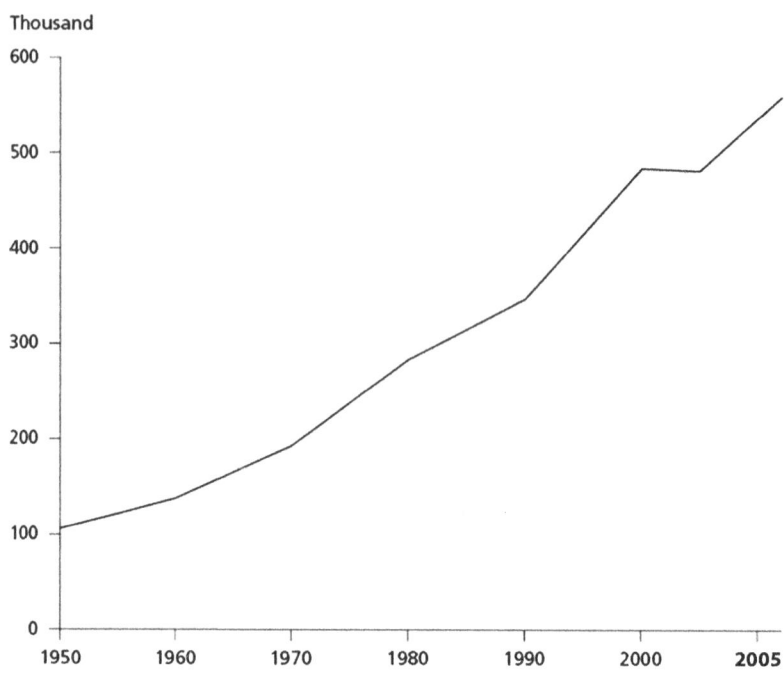

Source: Data from Lührs (2006) and Caritas (2012).

Catholic Church's economic interest in the provision of day care has therefore increased substantially since the 1970s.

A senior female member of the Christian Democrats, long-term member of the committee on family affairs and board member of the Catholic women's organisation, described the situation in the following fashion:

> We knew that if we wanted to get this thing through, we had to get to terms with the churches. The Protestants were easy. When von der Leyen sent me instead for the first time to present our new plans to the Catholic bishops it seemed to me as if I was speaking to a wall of stone. The thirteen bishops sat in front of me and unanimously told me that what we wanted to do was witches brew. When I met them the second time and confronted them with the possibility of losing the 4 billion Euros of federal funding for their day care facilities the situation changed. The hardliners did, of course, not change their mind but it was enough to get a majority with the moderates in favour of the reform.[3]

---

3.   Interview 1: interview at *Deutscher Bundestag*, 10 February 2011.

Angela Merkel's party feminisation in the field of family policy became possible, then, because the Catholic Church could be coerced into supporting it by threatening its economic interest in the field of welfare provision.

Merkel's strategy of party feminisation paid off. Seeleib-Kaiser remarks that '[i]n the 2005 elections the Christian Democrats were able to narrow the gender gap and significantly improve their perceived competency in the field of family policy' (Seeleib-Kaiser 2010: 421). Neu reaches a similar conclusion (Neu 2009) and the federal returning officer (*Bundeswahlleiter*) writes, in his report on the 2009 elections, that the Christian Democrats have become once again 'like in the 1950s to 1970s, a party preferred by women' (Bundeswahlleiter 2010: 85). With a 4.8-point difference between the male and female vote in 2009, the CDU was the party with by far highest female vote bonus in the electorate (Bundeswahlleiter 2010: 85). The strategy of feminising the party through a dual earner/caretaker model also led to another piece of electoral fortune: after a long exodus since 1990, the party was able to stabilise its share in Protestant votes in 2005 and subsequently significantly outpace all other parties in attracting the Protestant vote in the 2009 federal elections (Deutscher Bundestag 2013). The Christian Democrats were able to gain a remarkable surplus among East German women (plus 8 per cent, *see* Neu 2009: 82) – in other words, precisely those voters targeted by Anglea Merkel's party feminisation in the field of family policy.

Conclusion

Historical analysis has shown that there were four attempts to feminise the German Christian Democratic Union in the period since the 1970s, a move designed to recover the loss of its female voters. The first three attempts failed due to protests from the Catholic Church, an institution influential within the Christian Democratic party. Only with the advent of German reunification was there a window of opportunity for party strategists to push for feminisation. Under the stewardship of the Protestant Angela Merkel, reunification allowed for the realignment of the party, which since WWII had been dominated by Catholics, towards a stronger anchoring in a secularised Protestant electorate. The realignment furthermore allowed the CDU to credibly threaten the Catholic Church with the loss of their state-financed day care provisions by positioning itself to prioritise federal funding for Protestant caretaker organisations. Confronted with this possibility, the Catholic Church had to agree to the abolition of the male breadwinner model in both the Christian Democratic party programme and the German federal family policy. The result was telling: for the first time since the 1970s the CDU was able to gain a surplus of female votes in the 2009 elections.

The historical approach has additionally revealed that the feminisation of Christian Democratic parties is not determined solely by inter- and intra-party competition – but, rather, outside actors were also of crucial importance. In the case of the West German Christian Democrats, these outside actors are the churches. That said, not all religions and churches acted in the same way regarding family policy. For many decades, the Catholic Church held a de-facto veto position over the feminisation of the Christian Democratic party in Germany such that it overruled the opinion and efforts of party strategists and leadership. Future research on Christian Democratic party feminisation should take this conclusion further: the German case suggests that similar patterns might well be found in other continental Christian Democratic parties where Catholicism plays a major role.

References

Arzheimer, K. (2006) '"Dead men walking?" Party identification in Germany, 1977–2002', *Electoral Studies*, 25: 791–807.

Arzheimer, K. and Schoen, H. (2007) 'Mehr als eine Erinnerung an das 19. Jahrhundert? Das sozio-ökonomische und das religiös konfessionelle Cleavage und Wählerverhalten 1994–2005', in Rattinger, H., Gabriel, O. W. and Falter, J. W. (eds) *Der gesamtdeutsche Wähler: Stabilität und Wandel des Wählerverhaltens im wiedervereinigten Deutschland*, Baden-Baden: Nomos.

Augstein, F. (2002a) 'Weiße Kaninchen', *Süddeutsche Zeitung*, 17 July, p. 13.

—— (2002b), *Süddeutsche Zeitung*, 17 July.

Bartolini, S. and Mair, P. (1990) *Identity, Competition, and Electoral Availability: the Stabilization of European Electorates 1885–1985*, Cambridge: Cambridge University Press.

Berman, S. (1998) *The Social Democratic Moment: Ideas and Politics in the Making of Interwar Europe*, Cambridge, MA: Harvard University Press.

Bertram, H. (2009) 'Familienforschung und Familienpolitik: Themen, Felder und familiale Lebenslagen', in Mertens, G., Frost, U. and Böhm, W. V. (eds) *Handbuch der Erziehungswissenschaft Band III, Im Auftrag der Görres-Gesellschaft zur Pflege der Wissenschaft*, Ladenthin Verlag Ferdinand Schöningh: Paderborn.

Blyth, M. (2002) *Great Transformations: Economic Ideas and Institutional Change in the Twentieth Century*, Cambridge: Cambridge University Press.

Bösch, F. (2001) *Die Adenauer CDU*, Stuttgart: Deutsche Verlags-Anstalt.

—— (2002) *Macht und Machtverlust: Die Geschichte der CDU*, Stuttgart: Deutsche Verlags Anstalt.

Bundeswahlleiter (2010) 'Wahl zum 17. Deutschen Bundestag am 27. September 2009: Heft 5, Textliche Auswertung der Wahlergebnisse', Wiesbaden, p. 85. Available from: http://www.bundeswahlleiter.de/de/bundestagswahlen/BTW_BUND_09/veroeffentlichungen/BTW09_Heft1_Gesamt_Internet.pdf (accessed 14 August 2013).

CDU (1945a) *Kölner Leitsätze*, CDU, June.

—— (1945b) *Frankfurter Leitsätze: Politische Leitsätze der Christlich Demokratischen Union, Stadtkreis Frankfurt am Main*, CDU, September.

—— (1971) 'Berliner Programm: In der Form der zweiten Fassung vom 18. Bundesparteitag, 25–27.1.1971, Düsseldorf mit der Ergänzung vom 22. Bundesparteitag, 18–20.11.1973, Hamburg', in Hintze, P. (1995) *Die CDU Parteiprogramme: Eine Dokumentation der Ziele und Aufgaben*, Bonn: Bouvier.

—— (1975) *'Unsere Politik für Deutschland', Mannheimer Erklärung, 23. Bundesparteitag*, 23–25 June, Mannheim: CDU.

—— (1978) *Grundsatzprogramm 'Freiheit, Solidarität, Gerechtigkeit' Grundsatzprogramm 26. Bundesparteitag*, 23–25 October, Ludwigshafen: CDU.

— (1982) Helmuth Kohl, Regierungserklärung, 13 October, Bonn: CDU.

— (1984) *Stuttgarter Leitsätze für die 80er Jahre: Deutschlands Zukunft als moderne und humane Industrienation, 32. Bundesparteitag*, 9–11 May, Stuttgart: CDU.

— (1985) *Leitsätze der CDU für eine neue Partnerschaft zwischen Mann und Frau, 33. Bundesparteitag*, 20–22 March, Essen: CDU.

— (1999) *Lust auf Familie – Lust auf Verantwortung. Beschluss des 'kleinen Parteitages' der CDU Deutschlands*, 13 December, Berlin: CDU.

— (2002) *Leistung und Sicherheit – Zeit für Taten – Regierungsprogramm 2002/2006 von CDU und CSU*, Berlin: CDU and CSU.

Celis, K. and Childs, S. (2012) 'Diversity and substantive representation: conservatives representatives representing women', paper prepared for ECPR Joint Sessions Workshop, 2012, Antwerp.

Celis, K. and Erzeel, S. (2011) 'Beyond the usual suspects: the role of non-left, male and non-feminist MPs in the substantive representation of women', paper presented at the ECPR General Conference, 2011, Reykjavik.

Childs, S. and Webb, P. (2012a) 'Have the Conservatives been feminized?', *Sociology Review*, 22 (1): 16–20.

— (2012b) *Sex, Gender and The Conservative Party: From Iron Lady to Kitten Heels*, Basingstoke: Palgrave Macmillian.

Childs, S., Webb, P. and Sally, M. (2009) 'The feminization of the Conservative parliamentary party: party member's attitudes', *Political Quarterly*, 80 (2): 204–13.

Daenzer-Vanotti, I. (2002) Wider die Normabweichung, *Süddeutsche Zeitung*, NRW Teil, 21 December, p. 50.

Davison-Schmich, L. (2011) 'Gender, intersectionality, and the executive branch: the case of Angela Merkel', *German Politics*, 20 (3): 325–41.

Der Spiegel (1985) 'Bonn Reizt die Frauen', *Der Spiegel*, 25 March/13: pp. 24–35.

— (1999) 'Lust auf Familie', *Der Spiegel*, 12 October (n.p.).

Deutscher Bundestag (2013) *Datenhandbuch zur Geschichte des Deutschen Bundestages 1990 bis 2010*, Berlin, forthcoming. Early access available from: http://www.bundestag.de/dokumente/datenhandbuch/index.html (accessed 14 August 2013).

Dobrinski, M. (2002) 'Ein Hirtenbrief gegen Katherina Reiche, wie es ein Gerücht besagte?', *Süddeutsche Zeitung*, 5 October, p. 1.

Elff, M. and Roßteutscher, S. (2011) 'Stability or decline? Class, religion and the vote in Germany', *German Politics*, 20: 107–27.

Esping-Andersen, G. (1990) *The Three Worlds of Welfare Capitalism*, Princeton: Princeton University Press.

— (1996) 'After the golden age? Welfare state dilemmas in a global economy', in Esping-Andersen, G. (ed.) *Welfare States in Transition*, London: Sage.

— (1999) *The Social Foundations of Postindustrial Economies*, Oxford: Oxford University Press.

FAZ (1978a) 'Bundeskanzler und katholische Bischöfe sprechen miteinander', *Frankfurter Allgemeine Zeitung*, 21 February, p. 3.

—   (1978b) 'Katholische Bischöfe sprechen mit CDU Vertretern', *Frankfurter Allgemeine Zeitung*, 11 April, p. 3.

—   (1978c) 'Die Unionsparteien machen sich zum Anwalt der Familie', *Frankfurter Allgemeine Zeitung*, 18 April, p. 2.

—   (1980) 'Vogel: Die Bischöfe greifen "Stichworte" der Union auf', *Frankfurter Allgemeine Zeitung*, 13 September, p. 1.

—   (2007a) 'Kardinal Meisner zur Familienpolitik', *Frankfurter Allgemeine Zeitung*, 24 March.

—   (2007b) 'Bischof Mixa lässt nicht locker', *Frankfurter Allgemeine Zeitung*, 23 February.

Fleckenstein, T. (2010) 'Party politics and childcare: comparing the expansion of service provision in England and Germany', *Social Policy & Administration*, 44, 789–807.

—   (2011) 'The politics of ideas in welfare state transformation: Christian Democracy and the reform of family policy in Germany', *Social Politics*, 18 (4): 543–71.

Fleckenstein, T. and Seeleib-Kaiser, M. (2011) 'Business, skills and the welfare state: the political economy of employment oriented family policy in Britain and Germany', *Journal of European Social Policy*, 21 (2): 136–49.

Geppert-Rahm, M. (1985) 'Das Dehnbare "C" der CDU', *Frankfurter Allgemeine Zeitung*, 26 October, 10.

Gerlach, I. (2010) *Familienpolitik*, Wiesbaden: Opladen.

Henninger, A., Wimbauer, C. and Dombrowski, R. (2008) 'Demography as a push toward gender equality? Current reforms of German family policy', *Social Politics*, 15 (3): 287–314.

Heuwagen, M. (2002) 'Union über Richtige Strategie zerstritten', *Süddeutsche Zeitung*, 7 October, p. 5.

Höll, S. (2002a) 'Familien Treffen auf der Edel Alm', *Süddeutsche Zeitung*, 12.October, p. 8.

—   (2002b) 'Reiche ist nun doch Familienexpertin Stoibers', *Süddeutsche Zeitung*, 4 July, p. 6.

—   (2002c) 'Familienbild von Anno Dunnemals', *Süddeutsche Zeitung*, 3 July, p. 3.

Jenson, J. (1997) 'Who cares? Gender and welfare regimes', *Social Politics*, 4 (2): 182–87.

Kahlweit, C. (2002a) 'Die doppelte Frau', *Süddeutsche Zeitung*, 23 July.

—   (2002b) 'Reiche will Segen der Kirche', *Süddeutsche Zeitung*, 17 June, p. 5.

Kaiser, W. (2004) 'Christian democracy in twentieth century Europe', *Journal of Contemporary History*, 39, 128–31.

Kalyvas, S. (1996) *The Rise of Christian Democracy in Europe*, Ithaca, NY: Cornell University Press.

—   (1998) 'From pulpit to party: party formation and the Christian Democratic phenomenon', *Comparative Politics*, 30 (3): 293–312.

Kalyvas, S. and Van Kersbergen, K. (2010) 'Christian Democracy', *Annual Review of Political Science*, 13, 183–209.

Kitschelt, H. (1994) *The Transformation of European Social Democracy*, Cambridge: Cambridge University Press.

Kitschelt, H. and Streeck, W. (2003) 'From stability to stagnation: Germany at the beginning of the twenty-first century', in Streeck, W. and Kitschelt, H. (2003) 'Germany: beyond the stable state', *West European Politics, Special Issue*, 26 (4): 1–34.

Kselman, T. A. and Buttigieg, J. A. (2003) *European Christian Democracy: Historical Legacies and Comparative Perspectives*, Notre Dame: University of Notre Dame Press.

Lewis, J. (1997) 'Gender and welfare regimes: further thoughts', *Social Politics*, 4 (2): 160–77.

— (2001) 'The decline of the male breadwinner model: implications for work and care', *Social Politics*, 8 (2): 152–69.

Lovenduski, J. (2005) *Feminizing Politics*, Cambridge: Polity Press.

Lührs, H. (2006) 'Kirchliche Arbeitsbeziehungen: Die Entwicklung der Beschäftigungsverhältnisse in den beiden großen Kirchen und ihren Wohlfahrtsverbänden', WiP Working Paper, 33.

Manow, P. and Emmenegger, P (2012) 'Religion and the gender vote gap – women's changed political preferences from 1970s to 2010', *Arbeitspapiere des Zentrums für Sozialpolitik*, 1, Bremen: Zentrum für Sozialpolitik.

Marx, R. (2010) 'Bishop Reinhardt Marx interview by R. Pfister', *Der Spiegel*, 11 January, p. 22.

Misner, P. (1992) 'Social Catholicism in nineteenth-century Europe: a review of recent historiography', *Catholic Historical Review*, 78 (4): 581–600.

Moeller, R. G. (1993) *Protecting Motherhood: Women and the Family in the Politics of Postwar West Germany*, Berkeley: University of California Press.

Morgan, K. (2006) *Working Mothers and the Welfare State: Religion and the Politics of Work–Family Policy in Western Europe and the United States*, Stanford: Stanford University Press.

Naumann, I. (2005) 'Child care and feminism in West Germany and Sweden in the 1960s and 1970s', *Journal of European Social Policy*, 15 (1): 47–63.

Neu, V. (2009) 'Bundestagswahl in Deutschland am 27. September 2009: Wahlanalyse', Berlin: Konrad Adenauer Stiftung, available from: http://www.kas.de/wf/doc/kas_18443-544–1–30.pdf (accessed 15 August 2013).

— (2012) 'Religion, Kirche und Gesellschaft: Ergebnisse einer Umfrage der Konrad Adenauer Stiftung', Sankt Augustin, available from: http://www.kas.de/wf/doc/kas_31750-544–1–30.pdf?120801142955 (accessed 14 August 2013).

Noelle-Neumann, E. (1985) 'Frauen in Beruf und Politik', *Frankfurter Allgemeine Zeitung*, 19 March, p. 11.

OECD (2008) 'Babies and bosses: balancing work and family life', OECD Policy Brief, July, available from: http://www.oecd.org/els/family/34566853.pdf (accessed 1 September 2013).

Pfau-Effinger, B. (2004) 'Socio-historical paths to male breadwinner model: an explanation of cross-national differences', *British Journal for Sociology*, 55, 377–99.

Rusciano, L. (1992) 'Rethinking the gender gap: the case of West German elections, 1949–1987', *Comparative Politics*, 24 (3): 335–57.

Sainsbury, D. (1999) *Gender and Welfare State Regimes*, Oxford: Oxford University Press.

Sasson, A. S. (1997) 'Comment on Jane Lewis: gender and welfare regimes: further thoughts', *Social Politics*, 4 (2): 178–81.

Schilder, P. (1984) 'Kritik an der Bonner Familienpolitik', *Frankfurter Allgemeine Zeitung*, 16 March, p. 5.

Schneider, J. (2006) 'CDU soll ihr Familienbild modernisieren', *Süddeutsche Zeitung*, 26 October.

Schwilk, H. (2002) 'Katholische Bischöfe drohen Stoiber mit *Hirtenbrief*', *Die Welt*, 14 July.

Seeleib-Kaiser, M. (2010) 'Socio-economic change, party competition and intra-party conflict: the family policy of the grand coalition', *German Politics*, 19 (3–4): 416–28.

Streeck, W. (2011) 'Volksheim oder Shopping Mall? Die Reproduktion der Gesellschaft im Dreieck von Markt, Sozialstruktur und Politik', MPIfG Working Paper, 11/5.

SZ (1999a) 'Die Kulturrevolution der CDU', *Süddeutsche Zeitung*, 21 October, p. 4.

—   (1999b) 'Abschied vom Heimchen am Herd', *Süddeutsche Zeitung*, 11 December, p. 10.

—   (2002) 'Die Familie als Thema entdeckt', *Süddeutsche Zeitung*, 25 March, p. 6.

—   (2005) *Süddeutsche Zeitung*, 9 August, p. 8.

—   (2006a) 'Abschied von Gestern', *Süddeutsche Zeitung*, 24 October, 4.

—   (2006b) *Süddeutsche Zeitung*, 21 April, p. 1.

van Kersbergen, K. (1995) *Social Capitalism*, London: Routledge.

—   (1999) 'Contemporary Christian Democracy and the demise of the politics of mediation', in Kitschelt, H., Lange, P., Marks, G. and Stephens, J. D. (eds), *Continuity and Change in Contemporary Capitalism*, Cambridge: Cambridge University Press.

von Wahl, A. (2011) 'A women's revolution from above? Female leadership, intersectionality, and public policy under the Merkel government', *German Politics*, 20 (3): 392–409.

Warner, C. M. (2000) *Confessions of an Interest Group*, Princeton: Princeton University Press.

Wiliarty, S. (2010) *The CDU and the Politics of Gender in Germany: Bringing Women to the Party*, New York: Cambridge University Press.

—   (2011) 'Gender and energy policy making under the first Merkel government', *German Politics*, 20 (3): 449–63.

Zensus (2013) 'Bevölkerung im regionalem Vergleich nach Religion – in %', *Statistische Ämter des Bundes und der Länder*, available from: http://www.destatis.de/DE/PresseService/Praaesse/Pressekonferenzen/2013/Zensus2011/bevoelkerung_zensus2011.pdf?__blob=publicationFile (accessed 14 August 2013).

Zolleis, U. (2008) *Die CDU: Das Politische Leitbild im Wandel der Zeit*, Wiesbaden: VS Verlag für Sozialwissenschaften.

Chapter Three

A Complex Mediation of Interests: Party Feminisation Processes in the Italian Christian Democratic Party

Daniela R. Piccio

Introduction

Either because, traditionally, they have brought the greatest number of women into parliaments (Wängnerud 2009; Caul 2010), or because they have supported, to varying degrees, the feminist movement's cause (Lovenduski and Norris 1993; Banaszak *et al.* 2003), the literature on party feminisation processes has typically focused on leftist political parties. Indeed, they are often considered the 'natural allies' of the women's cause, both for integrating women into their organisational structures and for bringing women's concerns and perspectives into party and political debates (Childs and Webb 2012).

More recently, however, several limits to this approach have been observed in the literature. First, scholars have noticed a bias on behalf of researchers towards progressive policies and towards the representation of an overly specific section of women actors, thus overshadowing the possibility that women's interests are various and not reducible to feminist interests (Dovi 2007; Celis 2009). Second, such an approach fails to recognise empirical reality, in which rightist parties also claim to act for women; nor does it offer a means by which to interpret the type of representation currently advanced by the party family that has, in recent years, dominated the governments of a number of Western democracies: conservative parties (Celis and Childs 2012; Childs and Webb 2012). Research on feminisation in Italian political parties is no exception to the 'left-leaning' bias in gender and politics scholarship mentioned above, and scholars have focused largely on the Italian Communist Party (PCI). The PCI was the most important political party on the left of the Italian party system during the so-called 'first' Italian Republic; it was also the party that brought more women into parliament than any other from the end of the 1940s to the early 1990s, and as a result it became the major institutional reference for the Italian feminist movement during the 1970s. Scholars have analysed the PCI's co-option of feminist activists, the descriptive representation of women, and the party's substantive representation of women's/ feminist concerns (Ergas 1982; Beckwith 1985; Guadagnini 1993; Beccalli 1994; Della Porta 2003; Piccio 2011). Less studied, despite its attention to women's issues, are the party feminisation processes of the Italian Christian Democratic Party (*Democrazia Cristiana*, hereafter DC).

Although the DC effectively disappeared from the Italian political landscape in the early 1990s, its supremacy and centrality within the party system (1948–93), its relations with the Catholic Church, its links with Catholic women's organisations, and, not least, the fact that it underwent one of the largest feminist mobilisations to have taken place in Europe during the 1970s, makes women's representation by the DC particularly interesting. But what did the party stand for in terms of the integration of women's concerns into the political debate? What type of claims did the DC articulate, and did the party's claims for women, change over time? And finally, what was the position of women within the party? This chapter addresses these questions in the light of the complex and multi-faceted notion of the substantive political representation of women, and of the more recent literature on women's representation in conservative parties.

The Italian Christian Democratic Party: An overview

The Italian Christian Democratic Party – the DC – was founded between 1942 and 1943 with the convergence of different Catholic groups and personalities who had been part of the pre-fascist *Partito Popolare Italiano* (PPI). It exited the Italian political stage in 1992, following anti-corruption investigations.[1] Yet from the first legislature in 1948 until 1992, the DC was the largest political party of the Italian party system, securing the relative majority of the vote in all political elections. This numerical supremacy was further reinforced by the so-called *convention ad excludendum* (Galli 1966), an agreement that excluded the Italian Communist Party, Italy's second largest party, from the government arena. Hence, all governing majorities formed between 1948 and 1992 contained the DC. The DC was, then, a political party that played a fundamental role for four decades, from the introduction of universal suffrage – ratified in the Italian Constitution of 1948 – until the early 1990s, a period that covers the feminist mobilisation of Italian women in the 1970s.

Caciagli defines the DC as 'the conservative party *par excellence* of the Italian party system' (Caciagli 1992: 11). From the moment of its establishment, the DC received legitimation and support from the Catholic Church, and hence presented itself to the electorate as *the* Catholic party. The consequences of this endorsement were numerous. First, it guaranteed permeation throughout Italian civil society via Catholic organisations – which Farneti described as the 'indirect party' (Farneti 1983). Secondly, the support of the Church ensured an immediate 'nominal' hold on the Italian electorate. By presenting itself as the only party with the *imprimatur* of the Church, it catalysed votes from the Catholic population – the majority of

---

1. The anti-corruption investigations that began in 1992 are often taken as the benchmark of the collapse of the Italian party system that developed after the Second World War (Morlino 1996). In the parliamentary elections of 1994, none of the previously existing political parties campaigned with the same name or symbol.

the Italian citizenry – both conservatives and moderates. The bulk of the Christian Democratic constituency was, moreover, composed of women. Indeed, analyses of electoral participation reveal that from the first elections in 1948, women have accounted for more than 60 per cent of the party's electoral strength (Galli and Prandi 1970: 56–7; Wertman 1979).

From its establishment, the DC supported (with financial and logistical aid) the *Centro Italiano Femminile* (CIF) – an organisation of Catholic women, first established in 1945 (Taricone 2001). In addition, within its party organisation, it formed the *Movimento Femminile* (Female Movement). Despite being seen as a 'corporatist catch-all party' (Wiliarty 2010), a condition said to enhance the likelihood of female political activists having their agenda adopted, the DC Female Movement was a weak player within the party's internal organisation. Indeed, the Female Movement of the DC had the typical characteristics of auxiliary, insulated women's sections (cf. Norris and Krook 2011; Childs and Webb 2012) that have often been criticised in gender and politics research – as well as by inter-governmental organisations:[2] it constituted as a separate organ, and was far from being fully integrated into the party's factional distribution of power and policymaking.

Despite remaining marginal in the party organisation and lacking power, the Female Movement constituted the main recruitment reservoir of the (few) DC female political representatives, and it helped stimulate political participation and political debate among women, becoming crucial for conservative women's political activism in the decades following the Second World War (Noce 2003; Gaiotti 2004). Nevertheless, the Female Movement's insularity remained a key factor explaining the low representation of women within the DC (Cattaneo and D'Amato 1990; Guadagnini 1993).

A politics of absence: Women's descriptive representation in the DC

If there exists a link between descriptive and substantive representation (Phillips 1998), we should expect very little from the Italian Christian Democratic Party. Italian women have, historically, been seriously under-represented in the national parliament (Guadagnini 1987). Among the Italian political parties the Italian Christian Democratic Party ranked second after the Italian Communist Party, in terms of its numerical representation of women. And even if the DC was the second of the largest parties in terms of women's representation, the average percentage of women elected in parliament by the DC for the political elections between 1948 and 1987 (3.8 per cent) stands ten percentage points lower than the figures of the first ranking party, the PCI.[3] As Table 3.1 shows, throughout the entire history

---

2. The fact of women's internal sections hampering – rather than favouring – the internal processes of representation has also been recognised, for instance, by the OSCE/ODHIR's *Handbook for Monitoring Women's Participation in Elections*, 2004, p. 31.

3. The average proportion of women represented in parliament by the PCI, for the same period (1948 to 1987), was 13.7 per cent (Piccio 2011).

of the Italian Christian Democratic Party (1948 to 1987), the number of women in the DC's parliamentary group remained essentially stable with no significant increases occurring over time.

Scholars have observed a significant difference between the number of DC women standing as candidates and the number of women actually elected to parliament. Guadagnini explains this pattern by the limited tendency of the DC electorate to vote for female candidates, which in turn could be seen as indicative of the factional and clientelistic nature of the party itself (Guadagnini 1993). A second, more critical, interpretation of the difference between the number of female candidates and the number of women elected to parliament was raised by Cattaneo and D'Amato (1990). They argue that in all the Italian political parties: 'a two-fold phenomenon can be traced, on one hand an often exaggerated search for women to add to the electoral lists, on the other hand the tendency to elect as few women as possible' (Cattaneo and D'Amato 1990: 48). Thus, by nominating female candidates, parties could appear women-friendly and innovative, without any guarantee that those candidates would be elected. Figures for women's representation in the DC's internal party structures do seem to confirm a rather strategic placement of female candidates.

If very few DC women actually entered parliament, even fewer were represented in the DC's internal decision-making organs. Observing the presence of women in the main national decision-making organs of the party (the National Council, the Direction, and the party Secretary), not only are women markedly under-represented but, again, no increase took place over time. Table 3.2 shows the number of women elected to the DC National Council from 1946 to 1989.

In the National Council of the party, women constituted an average of 2.12 per cent, with no increase over time. It was specifically to counterbalance the persistent under-representation of women in one of the highest internal party organs that the Female Movement of the party demanded (first in 1981 and later in 1986)[4] the establishment of a quota of reserved seats for women in the National Council. From the single seat previously established, the number of reserved seats was increased to eleven in 1983, and to twenty in 1989. The DC's central decision-making organ, the National Executive Committee (or Direction), was composed entirely of men for over four decades,[5] as were the party secretaries.

Women's interests and substantive representation

Research into the substantive representation of women by political parties has often started from an implicit feminist perspective (Childs and Krook 2006; Saward 2008; Celis 2009). Assuming this perspective is valid, political actors

---

4.   The demands made by the Female Movement for a greater number of reserved seats in the National Council are reported in the party's journal *La Discussione*, on 23 September 1981 and 16 June 1986, respectively.

5.   From 1974, a seat was assigned to the national representative of the party's Female Movement (Guadagnini 1995).

Table 3.1: Women's representation in the DC party group (Chamber of Deputies), 1948–87

Election year	1948	1953	1958	1963	1968	1972	1976	1979	1983	1987
Elected women	18	12	11	11	8	7	9	10	7	12
Elected deputies	323	276	285	271	275	273	269	274	237	251
% of women	5.57	4.35	3.86	4.06	2.9	2.56	3.35	3.65	2.95	4.78

Source: Chamber of Deputies of the Italian Parliament (http://storia.camera.it/, accessed 14 May 2014) (author's elaboration).

Table 3.2: Women representatives elected to the DC's National Council, 1946–89

Year	1946	1947	1949	1952	1954	1956	1959	1962	1964	1967	1969	1973	1976	1980	1982	1984	1986	1989
Elected women	3	1	2	2	2	2	3	3	3	2	1	2	3	4	2	2	3	1
Elected members	58	51	61	62	63	89	121	150	153	119	125	130	124	169	193	160	160	163
% of women	5.1	1.9	3.2	3.2	3.1	2.2	2.4	2.0	1.9	1.6	0.8	1.5	2.4	2.3	1.0	1.2	1.8	0.6

Note: 'N' indicates the number of women elected; 'Total', the total number of members within the National Council.

Source: Malgeri 1987 (author's elaboration).

are 'substantively acting for' women if they promote acts in line with feminist discourse. This approach has, however, been criticised as 'elitist', for ascribing women's interests in a top-down fashion, and as 'essentialist', for viewing women as fixed categories (Wängnerud 2009: 53). Others have argued that political parties may *act for women* even if they fail to live up to particular feminist standards. Recent critical work on the substantive representation of women and the women's movement contends that it is important for gender scholars to go beyond an analysis of exclusively feminist concerns, and integrate a broader set of claims 'for women' that are not assigned *a priori* along the feminist agenda (Celis and Childs 2012; Beckwith 2000). As underscored in the introduction to this book, women's claims may be framed in terms of addressing women's issues or improving women's lives – even if they reject existing feminist accounts of what constitutes women's interests. Indeed, different actors may provide different content to women's issues depending on their perception of what constitutes women's interests (Celis *et al.* 2008). Focusing on how conservative representatives can and do make claims 'for women' presents an important opportunity to shed light on the role of other actors in the substantive representation of women, as well as to understand the representative relationship between conservative representatives and conservative women in society, and to capture the broader processes of responsiveness towards women. Moreover, the distinction between women's issues and women's interests allows us to observe the wider 'economy of gendered representation' (Saward 2006; Celis and Childs 2012), including gendered claims that would not necessarily or routinely be considered feminist.

Such an approach is particularly useful as it provides analytical space for understanding the claims and actions for women of traditional conservative parties, such as the Italian Christian Democratic Party. As we will see, despite failing to integrate women into the party structures, and despite the fact that the DC's attention to women has always been interpreted as strategic – aimed at securing the female vote while not actually representing women's actual interests (Beckwith 1985; Ergas 1982) – an in-depth analysis of the party's claims for women reveal that the DC has addressed women's issues to a far greater extent than the literature has traditionally acknowledged. Moreover, the space given to women's issues in the party's public discourse changed in the mid-1970s, not least as a consequence of the emergence in Italy during that time of the largest feminist mobilisation in Western Europe. Yet more fundamental changes in the perception of women's interests are found at the level of the conservative female representatives within the party.

Women's substantive representation in the DC

The Christian Democratic Party developed a political discourse on women's issues at its establishment in the early 1940s. It was on the initiative of the DC Secretary Alcide de Gasperi that universal suffrage was introduced in Italy in January 1945. The literature has often highlighted the fact that the Christian Democratic Party was the party with the most to gain from universal suffrage. This has led to an interpretation of de Gasperi's actions as strategic, aimed at capturing the votes of women who were historically anchored to the domestic and traditional spheres of Italian society and who would thus, it was assumed, naturally vote for a conservative Church-based party (Beckwith 1985; Ergas 1982). Yet, even if women, the majority of the Italian population, undoubtedly constituted a crucial electoral category for the DC, other scholars argue that a cynical interpretation of de Gasperi's initiative is misguided. With their participation in the Resistance during the War and their mobilisation in aid initiatives during its aftermath, Italian women had acquired an important social and political visibility that could not simply be ignored in the constitutional process of the new democratic system.[6]

Moreover, and consistent with the introduction of universal suffrage, the DC leader opened a discourse that appeared to appreciate the social and cultural obstacles that women in Italian society had to face. The party Secretary's speech to the First National Assembly of the Female Movement of the DC in 1946 is an apt example:

> Since I was young I have always been concerned about the condition of women. [...] Now that we are in a phase of our political organisation of the party, we have to face a number of objections, difficulties and strong prejudices, which need to be overcome.[7]

Apart from the introduction of universal suffrage and the principles of equality between the sexes approved in the Italian Constitution,[8] the DC was also among those promoting the actual legal implementation of these principles – to a greater extent than is commonly assumed. In fact, at the policy level, the DC sponsored important legislation that favoured women by facilitating their entrance into the labour market and public sphere. These legislative proposals were often brought forward on the initiative of Christian Democratic MPs, and were strongly supported by the party's internal Female Movement (Cattaneo and D'Amato 1990; Piccio 2011).[9] Yet, while recognising their formal equality in the social and public spheres and promoting egalitarian legislation, the way in which the DC framed women and their role in Italian society remained strongly tethered to specific traditional family roles, that is, as wives and mothers. The following extract comes from the speech made by the DC Secretary to the first national meeting of the CIF:

---

6. It should be noted, moreover, that women's suffrage had already been proposed by the PPI (the DC's predecessor) at its first Congress in 1919 (Dalla Torre 2010).

7. Cited in Gaiotti 1996, p. 161.

8. These principles are found in Arts 3, 37, 48, and 51 of the Italian Constitution.

9. Examples of legislation supported by the DC favouring women's equality are: a law for the physical and economical protection of working mothers (l.860/1950); a law for the participation of women in the Popular Courts (l.1441/1956); a law for the establishment of a female police corps (l.66/1963); a law for the prohibition of dismissing women after marriage (l.7/1963); a law for the admission of women to public offices and professions (l.66/1963); a law for the protection of working mothers (l.1204/1971); a law establishing equality between wives and husbands (l.151/1975); and a law establishing equality between men and women in the labour market (L.903/1977).

We men need you and your contribution, we need your active participation in meetings, congresses, and parliaments; we need you especially for the following reason: that you will be able to teach us and anticipate us on the road of sacrifice. We need you especially as wives and mothers, or future wives and mothers, because real politics [...] is the defence of morality, and the defence of Christianity. [...] I therefore welcome your contribution to our battle, as I am aware that instinctively with your maternal heart, you will never forget those duties that concern our children, the family and future generations.[10]

The Secretary's speech neatly encapsulates the general conception of women within the DC, which anchored them to private and domestic spheres by stressing the importance of their nurturing and reproductive roles. The DC, strongly characterised by 'traditional conservatism', focused on social cohesion, the defence of tradition, and the importance of traditional family arrangements (Bryson and Heppell 2010). The defence of the traditional role of the family also implied that the participation of women in the labour market was more often perceived as a necessity deriving from economic needs (to compensate the husband's salary), rather than as a positive outcome of female emancipation. The type of claims that the party made for women, and the DC's perception of what constituted women's interests, were aimed mainly to improve women's lives on these terms, along the 'type II' gendered claims (*see* the introduction to this volume).

A qualitative analysis of the DC's official documents (e.g. election manifestos and party secretaries' opening speeches to the party congresses) from 1969 to 1987 reveals that until the mid-1970s the DC's discourse on women hardly changed. In its 1969 manifesto, the party still referred to women within the context of the family and their 'household responsibilities':

Women have their essential and irreplaceable function within the family.[11]

In the mid-1970s, however, attention to women's issues in the DC's political discourse increased considerably. An analysis of the frequency of references to women's issues in the party's election manifestos, and in the speeches delivered to the congresses by the party secretaries, from 1969 to 1987, clearly shows that the figures in the mid-1970s stand out.

For the political elections of 1976, there were seventeen references to women's issues in the DC political manifesto, a significant increase when compared to the DC manifesto of 1972 which included only seven references; and the number of positive references made by the DC Secretary in his speeches to Congress rose to ten, as opposed to the two references made in the Secretary's speech of 1973. Conversely, from the 1980s onwards attention to women's issues in the party's public discourse decreased.

---

10. De Gasperi, from a speech given at the first national meeting of the CIF (cited in Gaiotti 1996: 164).

11. DC manifesto, 1969.

Table 3.3: *Women's issues in the DC election manifestos and Congresses, 1969–87*

Women's Issues	(M) 1969	(C) 1969	(M) 1972	(C) 1973	(M) 1976	(C) 1976	(M) 1979	(C) 1980	(M) 1983	(C) 1982	(M) 1986	(C) 1987
Women's equality principle[a]	6	–	4	1	9	9	–	3	–	3	1	1
Equality in the familial sphere[b]	2	–	2	1	1	–	–	–	–	–	–	1
Equality in the labour market[c]	4	–	1	–	2	–	–	–	1	–	–	3
State services for women[d]	–	–	–	–	5	1	–	–	–	–	–	3
Women's representation[e]	–	–	–	–	–	–	–	–	–	–	2	–
Frequency per document	*12*	*0*	*7*	*2*	*17*	*10*	*0*	*3*	*1*	*3*	*3*	*8*

Note: A score was assigned for each reference to any of the five equality issues found across the documents. (M) = Election manifesto; (C) = Party Secretary's speeches to the Congress.

[a] Includes statements referring to the general principles of women's equality, women's emancipation, and equal dignity.

[b] Includes statements referring to reform in the Family Right law (regulating the juridical relationship between husband and wife), and/or statements supporting equality in the familial sphere more generally.

[c] Includes statements referring to women and the labour market, such as equal treatment, equal opportunity of access, equal salary, defence and promotion of women's employment, and the protection of working mothers.

[d] Includes statements referring to State assistance beneficial to women, such as nurseries, centres providing medical or psychological aid to women, and centres providing assistance/care for the elderly.

[e] Includes statements referring to women's representation in the political sphere.

Three main factors led to the DC's surge in attention to women's issues in the mid-1970s. First, the failure of the 1974 anti-divorce referendum, promoted by the DC, constituted a severe blow to the party.[12] The outcome showed – for the first time – that Italian voters, including female voters, could no longer be defined *a priori* as traditional, conservative, and loyal to the Christian Democrats. Second, the electoral gains of the Italian Communist Party at the local elections of 1975 (the PCI were only two percentage points lower than the DC) challenged – again for the first time in the country's political history – Christian Democratic numerical supremacy over the Italian party system.[13] Third, from 1974, the feminist movement gathered pace and entered the phase of its greatest social and political visibility, managing to place women's issues higher on the public, media and political agenda than ever before. Combined, these factors forced the DC to pay more attention to women in its public discourse and, most importantly, to change the quality of the party's claims for women.

Qualitative changes emerge most prominently in the party's manifesto for the 1976 elections, arguably the most 'sensitive' elections in the history of the Italian Republic as far as women's representation is concerned, and in the DC Congress that took place in the same year. In this, women's issues were said to be at the core of the DC's political vision. The DC now emphasised strongly the fact that, since the introduction of universal suffrage, the party had always actively promoted legislation that favoured women's equality and admission to all sectors of society. Even though the defence of the family – as the 'core social community' – remained central, women were treated less within the context of the family than before, and the importance of public social services (nurseries, part-time work, services for elderly people, family allowances) was emphasised as the fundamental means by which to facilitate women's full participation in the public sphere. Moreover, at the fourteenth DC Congress in 1980, the party Secretary addressed themes that had been introduced to the public agenda by the feminist movement itself, such as women's personal autonomy and women's empowerment.[14] Far from endorsing feminists' representative claims, and without challenging the party's core ideological position regarding the importance of the family and of women's traditional nurturing and reproductive roles, the DC incorporated additional content to its claims for women, reflecting an adaptation to the social transformations that were taking place in Italian society.

Yet the centrality of women that was so evident in the second half of the 1970s, and had the potential to herald a change in the party's conception of women and

---

12. The divorce law was adopted in 1970 (1.898/1970) and was voted in by all parties with the exception of the DC and the post-fascist party, the MSI (Italian Social Movement). Anti-divorce committees, with the support of the Catholic Church and the DC, started a collection of signatures to promote a referendum. The referendum, held in 1974, resulted in a striking victory for the pro-divorce front (59.3 per cent of citizens voted against the repeal).

13. These elections, described as 'the earthquake of 15th of June', caused a sensation, as this was the lowest electoral percentage that the DC had ever obtained (Caciagli 1985; Ghini 1976).

14. *Atti del XIV Congresso nazionale della Democrazia Cristiana*, Edizioni Cinque Lune, Roma 1982.

Table 3.4: Speeches of women delegates to DC Congresses, 1973–1986

Congress Year	1973	1976	1980	1982	1986
Women's speeches on representation	1 (33.3)	4 (44.4)	3 (50.0)	5 (55.6)	7 (77.7)
Number of speeches by women	3 (3.37)	9 (4.22)	6 (4.02)	9 (6.82)	9 (6.92)
Total number of speeches	89	166	149	132	130

Note: Raw count reported; per cent from the larger category in parenthesis.
Source: *Atti del XIII Congresso nazionale della Democrazia Cristiana* (1973–1986).

their role in the society, was ultimately short-lived. While the feminist movement was entering its latent phase, the DC's official documents show not only a decrease in the party's attention to women's issues, as previously mentioned, but also a qualitative return to the party's older, traditional conception of women. Indeed, the party's claims for women's personal autonomy, self-determination, and political participation, and the issues concerning a cultural reorientation of society around women, disappeared from the 1980s onwards. Women's issues were marginalised once more and revolved around the family sphere, and the party primarily stressed women's reproductive roles (DC manifesto 1987), or made brief mentions to women's issues as typical 'subcategories' along with youths and the elderly (Seventeenth Congress of 1986).

In general, then, claims for women by the Italian Christian Democratic Party remained centred on women's traditional roles. In the mid-1970s, simultaneously with the peak of the feminist movement's visibility, and at a time of unprecedented attention to women's issues in Italian society more broadly, the DC seemed to adapt its discourse on women, expanding its perception of women's interests beyond the traditional roles that the party had been advancing. This was, as previously discussed, a political and tactical necessity, as the changes that the party introduced proved to be short-lived, with no real impact on the party's broader conception of women, or on women's actual integration within the party. The Christian Democratic women were no longer willing to toe the line.

Voices from within the party: Christian Democratic women

For many years, DC women had remained silent, rather than voice their right to play an active role in the internal life of the party and make their own claims on women's issues and interests. For many decades, the party and its Female Movement framed women within the private and domestic spheres. The Female Movement perceived the defence of the importance of the family as essential and a precondition for women's justice (Dau Novelli 1988; Gaiotti 1981). Family and motherhood were conceived as the fundamental vocation of women, and their main sphere of realisation. Women's participation in the public and political spheres was regarded as an extension of this natural 'vocation', from the family to society as a whole, rather than the right of women to self-realisation (Noce 2003). This vision significantly changed during the second half of the 1970s. A conception of women framed mainly around motherhood and family responsibilities did not sit well with the changes taking place in Italian society from the mid-1960s, which significantly altered the material, social and cultural conditions of women. Modernisation, the arrival of household appliances, increasing levels of education, and the increasing number of employed women – albeit limited to certain sectors – had the outcome of reducing familial duties and the traditional role of women, on the one hand, and encouraging women to reflect upon the distribution of domestic labour, paid work, and their own personal time, on the other hand (Giannuli 1998). Moreover, the feminist experience had radically touched the cultural perception of women's issues in Italian society (Gaiotti 1996). In particular, the feminist experience touched the perception of the DC women participating actively – although marginally – in the party's political life through the Female Movement and the Catholic women's organisations. As Noce argues, the emergence of the feminist movement 'disoriented the cultural parameters of the Catholic female militancy' (Noce 2003: 452). DC women had to reconcile the changes that were taking place in society with respect to women, with their traditional understanding of the role of women. This reconciliation was stated as a necessary priority, precisely in order to avoid women's issues becoming the exclusive property of the 1970s feminist movement – a 'radical–bourgeois group of women', as one of the leading Christian Democratic women described it.[15]

Women's political participation and autonomy are vital notions in the discourse of DC women from the 1970s. According to Gaiotti, the focus on participation was already present in the party's Female Movement, as well as the CIF, from the very beginning of the 1970s:

> The Female Movement of the DC and the CIF identified in participation the model of the new role of women in society. Participation means the exaltation of the social role of women and their taking part in the realm of competences and responsibilities [...] so as to fight their isolation, designing a new social figure of women that united the public and the private (Gaiotti 1996).

During the early 1970s, this remained a minority discourse with a very limited audience even within the Female Movement. From the second half of the 1970s, however, political participation became a key reference in Congress speeches, and in the articles published by DC women in the party's weekly journal *La Discussione*.[16] Observing the women's speeches at the DC Congresses from 1973 to 1986, we see an increase in not only the number of women's speeches, but also in the number of speeches raising the issue of women's representation.

---

15. Speech by Maria Eletta Martini to the Thirteenth DC Congress (*Atti del XIII Congresso della Democrazia Cristiana*).

16. Since 1977, a specific page dedicated to women's issues was published in the party's weekly journal *La Discussione*. This page was headed 'Partito Donna' (literally 'Woman Party') and appeared for the first time in issue number 1192 of 1977.

Although women's speeches accounted for a striking minority overall, ranging from 3.37 to 6.92 per cent of the total number of speeches at the DC Congresses, Table 3.4 shows that the number of women's speeches referring to the need for the integration of women into the party structures had more than doubled in the period from 1973 (33.3 per cent) to 1986 (77.7 per cent).[17] During the Thirteenth Congress of 1976, female delegates criticised the party for the first time for the ways in which women's participation had been handled by the party's internal workings. The following two examples are illustrative:

> We [women] have been treated as a reservoir of votes more than as actors in political life.

> I ask myself and ask you what is the relationship between the DC's majority female electorate and the appointments that women receive within the party's internal structures [...]. There is an absence of political will to insert women in the local, regional, and national direction.[18]

Female delegates within the DC pushed the party management to bring women's issues to the core of the party's political action and initiate a politics of the recognition of women within the party. This pattern continued throughout women's speeches during the 1980s. Not only did the women of the DC stress this subject greatly but, unsurprisingly, their tone became increasingly bitter over the years, given that, in spite of its rhetoric, the DC had been persistently inattentive to the internal representation of women. Instead, women in the DC became increasingly aware of about this issue and explicitly critical of their own party. The following excerpts offer further examples of their frustration:

> There's a great discussion about the DC's renewal, but if this party will not include women as a leading part of its renewal, not only will it not be able to follow and truly understand the transformations in society, but it will soon be short of breath.

> It's useless to say we are clever and capable, if so little space is given to us. What is expected from us [i.e. from the DC] is a truly Christian space. We say this because we want it to be put on the record: we want political responses to this issue.[19]

---

17. Note that the 1973 speech claiming support for women's representation was given by a non-party member, Baroness Diana Elles.

18. Speeches by Viola Zalaffi, representative of the Female Movement, and Maria Bianca Pallini to the Thirteenth DC Congress (*Atti del XIII Congresso della Democrazia Cristiana*).

19. Speeches by Lucia Pigno and Maria Luisa Cassamagnago to the Fifteenth DC Congress (*Atti del XV Congresso della Democrazia Cristiana*).

As no responses were given, the tones of the DC women became even more bitter, to the extent that even the PCI's Seventeenth Congress of 1986 (in which the PCI remarkably opened up to women) was used as an opportunity to highlight that the DC should give women a central role in its upcoming Congress.[20]

In addition to the issue of political participation, many interventions seemed to indicate an openness to a different conception of women than that traditionally proclaimed by the party's public discourse. Women in the DC become more centred on women's autonomy and on women's self-realisation as individuals. First, there was a lack of reference to what were previously conceived as women's 'ancient duties' (as wives and mothers) in any of the speeches. On the contrary, the notion of women as operating mainly within the family sphere was explicitly criticised:

> Despite changes that have occurred in the recognition of the right of women to fully participate in social life, the habit of saddling women with all the needs and problems related to family life have not changed.[21]

Second, from the end of the 1970s DC women adopted many elements of the feminist movement's discourse, attempting to appropriate and reinterpret it by eradicating its more radical components. If certain issues brought up by the feminist movement were difficult for a traditional Catholic women's organisation to debate – for example, sexual liberation, the family as the structure at the core of women's oppression, the self-determination of women and other feminist conflicts of the 1970s – DC women sought to solve this problem by adapting the feminist discourse to suit their own agenda.

Accordingly, the terms (women's) 'self-determination' and 'women's liberation' appear in many articles published in the DC party journal *La Discussione*. It is in this journal, edited by the DC's Female Movement, that we find the greatest evidence of how the women of the party perceived women's interests and how they dealt with the feminist movement's emergent claims. Just as the official discourse of the party appropriated themes linked to women's emancipation, so the discourse of DC women from the mid-1970s adopted feminist themes, filtering the feminist discourse through their own ideological identity, as the following examples show:

> Women's issues today should be considered as a matter of liberation [...] within a context in which greater consciousness is being acquired on the personal individuality of human beings.

---

20. *La Discussione*, 17 March 1986.

21. Speech delivered to the DC Congress by Ines Boffardi (*Atti del XIV Congresso Nazionale della Democrazia Cristiana*).

Women's liberation is positive when it means that women acquire greater consciousness of their potential; women's self-determination, also of their own body, is positive when it means that women are no longer objects but subjects.

We agree on a notion of liberation that implies the full freedom of human potential. And we need policies that help women to be freed from their isolation within the family.[22]

Particular emphasis was given to women's autonomy and to the self-realisation of women as individuals; the importance of extra-domestic work for women as fundamental for the realisation of their full personality; and the importance of women's free time for their personal, cultural and social 'interests' (another catchword of the feminist movement). With respect to the feminist movement itself, while DC women considered it wrong in many of its premises, and criticised it in particular for its conception of the family, its focus on sexual liberation, its separatist practices and not least its views about abortion,[23] it was, nonetheless, recognised positively for having brought to the fore the 'profound willingness of women [...] to be protagonists of change'.[24]

All in all, while the party's official discourse remained anchored to the formal recognition of women's equality but was unprepared to really support women's political participation and autonomy as individuals, some Christian Democratic women were no longer willing to toe the line. Although they opposed what they interpreted to be the individualistic and libertarian drives within feminism, they opened themselves up to the language of the feminist movement and their slogans (such as 'women's self-determination' or 'women's liberation') by adapting their meanings to their own ideological cultural and identity frameworks. Christian Democratic women consequently broadened the agenda on women's issues, offering a particular take on women's interests, by advancing a discourse that sought to keep pace with the social transformations taking place in Italian society, albeit in a way that was compatible with their conservative stance.

---

22. *La Discussione*, 27 December 1976, 11 May 1981 and 12 January 1985.

23. The DC's position on abortion – that it constituted murder and 'the most absolute negation of the sacred' (*La Discussione*, 13 April 1981) – did not change, even after the implementation of abortion legislation in 1978, and following the defeat of the referendum that aimed to repeal this legislation in 1981. Not only is the defence of life a Christian and civic value, but abortion is also defined as a 'false trap' for women, as it actually represents a further victory of male chauvinism: 'instead of recalling men to their own responsibilities and sense of control they now discharge on women's shoulders the weight of common responsibilities' (*La Discussione*, 11 November 1981).

24. Speech to the DC Congress by Francesca Meneghin (*Atti del XIII Congresso Nazionale della Democrazia Cristiana*).

Conclusion

With respect to the descriptive representation of women, the DC has returned very low figures in terms of female representatives, both in parliament and in its internal structures. This pattern of under-representation did not change over time and women remained seriously under-represented throughout the party's history. Yet, even though it failed to integrate women in its party structures, the DC's public discourse on women can by no means be considered indifferent to women's issues and interests. In order to really understand the DC's representation of women, and to recognise the DC's public discourse with respect to women, a wider range of claims constituting the interests of women need to be considered, beyond the feminist criteria.

Indeed, the DC stimulated the principle of formal equality between men and women by pushing for the introduction of universal suffrage, and later it pressed actively for the implementation of legislation that favoured women's participation in the public sphere. Despite its recognition of the formal equality of women, however, the party framed women predominantly within traditional family and domestic roles. This changed to some extent during the second half of the 1970s. Influenced by the social transformation that Italian society was going through, and in particular by the feminist mobilisation, which drew unprecedented attention to women's issues, the DC appeared willing to endorse a different public discourse for women, partially unyoking women from the family roles traditionally attributed to them, and recognising the importance of women's social and political autonomy. This 'feminist twist' was, however, short-lived. With the waning of the feminist movement as a visible social actor, the DC underwent a qualitative return to the party's older conception of women.

The women within the party, conversely, took a different line. DC women brought up own their demands for greater representation within the party and articulated a discourse favouring the recognition of women's need for personal autonomy, freedom and empowerment, reinterpreting the feminist slogans through their own cultural, partisan and Catholic identity.

The traditional conservative ideas about women's issues and women' interests held by the Italian Christian Democrats were difficult to reconcile with feminist claims. Yet, compared to the official political discourse of the party, the DC female representatives were much more attentive to the need to reconcile the party's traditional position with the changing perceptions of women and of their social roles in the 1970s. Ultimately these women were not granted the hearing within the party that they hoped for. The DC Female Movement remained a powerless minority within the party, and ultimately the Christian Democratic women's claims for women did not reach a wider audience. The Christian Democratic women were, then, defeated in their struggle, and thus the history of women's political representation in the DC can only be a history of partial feminisation.

Party documents

DC election manifestos

1968: 'Il programma della DC a servizio del paese', *Il Popolo*, 19 April 1968.

1972: 'Gli impegni programmatici della *Democrazia Cristiana*', *Il Popolo*, 1 April 1972.

1979: 'La DC chiede maggiori consensi per un'Italia libera e stabile', *Il Popolo*, 12 May 1979.

1983: 'Un programma per garantire lo sviluppo', *Il Popolo*, 5–6 May 1983.

1987: 'Un programma per l'Italia', *Il Popolo*, 24–5 April 1987.

DC Congress Acts

Atti del [XI ... XVII] Congresso nazionale della Democrazia Cristiana, Roma: Edizioni Cinque Lune, 1972–88.

References

Banaszak, L. A., Beckwith, K. and Rucht, D. (eds) (2003) *Women's Movements Facing the Reconfigured State*, Cambridge: Cambridge University Press.

Beccalli, B. (1994) 'The modern women's movement in Italy', *New Left Review*, 1 (204): 86–112.

Beckwith, K. (1985) 'Feminism and leftist politics in Italy: the case of UDI–PCI relations', *West European Politics*, 8 (4): 19–37.

— (2000) 'Beyond compare? Women's movements in comparative perspective', *European Journal of Political Research*, 37 (4): 431–68.

Bryson, V. and Heppell, T. (2010) 'Conservatism and feminism: the case of the British Conservative Party', *Journal of Political Ideologies*, 15 (1): 31–50.

Caciagli, M. (1985) 'Il resistibile declino della Democrazia cristiana', in Pasquino, G. (ed.), *Il sistema politico italiano*, Bari: Laterza, pp. 101–27.

— (1992) 'Doomed to govern? Christian Democracy in the Italian political system', in Caciagli, M. and Institut de Ciencies Politiques i Socials (eds), *DC, Christian democracy in Europe*, Barcelona: ICPS, pp. 7–27.

Cattaneo, A. and D'Amato, M. (1990) *La politica della differenza*, Rome: Franco Angeli.

Caul, M. (2010) 'Women's representation in parliament: the role of political parties', in Krook, M. L. and Childs, S. (eds) *Women, Gender, and Politics: A Reader*, Oxford: Oxford University Press, pp. 159–66.

Celis, K. (2009) 'Substantive representation of women (and improving it): what it is and should be about?', *Comparative European Politics*, 7, 95–113.

Celis, K. and Childs, S. (2012) 'The substantive representation of women: what to do with conservative claims?', *Political Studies*, 60 (1): 213–25.

Celis, K., Childs, S., Kantola, J. and Krook, M. L. (2008) 'Rethinking women's substantive representation', *Representation*, 44 (2): 99–110.

Childs, S. and Krook, M. L. (2006) 'Gender and politics: the state of the art', *Politics*, 26 (1): 18–28.

Childs, S. and Webb, P. (2012) *Sex, Gender and the Conservative Party: From Iron Lady to Kitten Heels*, Basingstoke: Palgrave Macmillan.

Dalla Torre, G. (2010) 'Il Partito popolare, Sturzo e il voto alle donne', in Bonacchi, G. and Dau Novelli, C. (eds) *Culture politiche e dimensioni del femminile nell'Italia del Novecento*, Soveria Mannelli: Rubbettino, pp. 75–102.

Dau Novelli, C. (1988) 'Il movimento femminile della democrazia cristiana dal 1944 al 1964', in Malgeri, F. (ed.), *Storia della Democrazia Cristiana, Vol. III, Gli anni di transizione: da Fanfani a Moro (1954–1962)*, Rome: Cinque Lune, pp. 331–68.

Della Porta, D. (2003) 'The women's movement, the left, and the state: continuities and changes in the Italian case', in Banaszak, L. A., Beckwith, K. and Rucht, D. (eds), *Women's Movements Facing the Reconfigured State*, Cambridge: Cambridge University Press, pp. 48–68.

Dovi, S. (2007) 'Theorizing women's representation in the United States', *Politics & Gender*, 3, 297–319.

Ergas, Y. (1982) '1968–79: Feminism in the Italian party system: women's politics in a decade of turmoil', *Comparative Politics*, 14 (3): 252–75.

Farneti, P. (1983) *Il sistema dei partiti in Italia 1946–1979*, Bologna: Il Mulino.

Gaiotti, P. (1981) 'Movimento Cattolico e questione femminile', in Traniello, F. and Campanini, G. (eds), *Dizionario storico del movmimento cattolico in italia 1860–1980*, Vol. I/II, Turin: Marietti, pp. 96–111.

— (1996) 'Il voto alle donne nel 1945', in Gaiotti, P. (ed.) *I cattolici e il voto alle donne*, Turin: Società Editrice Internazionale.

— (2004) 'Cattoliche e cattolici di fronte all'aborto e il mutamento degli equilibri della Repubblica', *Genesis*, 3 (1): 57–86.

Galli, G. (1966) *Dal bipartitismo imperfetto alla possibile alternativa*, Bologna: Il Mulino.

Galli, G. and Prandi, A. (1970) *Patterns of Political Participation in Italy*, London: Yale University Press.

Ghini, C. (1976) *Il terremoto del 15 giugno*, Milan: Feltrinelli Editore.

Giannuli, A. (1988) *Il sessantotto. La stagione dei movimenti (1960–1979)*, Rome: Edizioni Associate.

Guadagnini, M. (1987) 'Una rappresentanza limitata: Le donne nel Parlamento italiano dal 1948 ad oggi', *Quaderni di Sociologia*, 8, 130–57.

— (1993) 'A Partitocrazia without women: the case of the Italian party system', in Lovenduski, J. and Norris, P. (eds), *Gender and Party Politics*, London: Sage Publications, pp. 168–204.

— (1995) 'The latecomers: Italy's equal status and equal opportunities agencies', in Stetson, D. (ed.), *Comparative State Feminism*, Thousand Oaks, CA: Sage, pp. 150–67.

Lovenduski, J. and Norris, P. (eds) (1993) *Gender and Party Politics*, London: Sage Publications.

Malgeri, F. (1987) *Storia della Democrazia cristiana*, Rome: Cinque Lune.

Morlino, L. (1996) 'Crisis of parties and change of party system in Italy', *Party Politics*, 2 (1): 5–30.

Noce, T. (2003) 'La militanza politica delle cattoliche. Appunti per una ricerca', in Lussana, F. and Marramao, G. (eds) *L'Italia repubblicana nella crisi degli anni settanta. III. Culture, nuovi soggetti, identità*, Soveria Mannelli: Rubbettino, pp. 433–66.

Norris, P. and Krook, M. L. (2011) *Gender Equality in Elected Office: A Six-Step Action Plan*, Warsaw: OSCE, Office for Democratic Institutions and Human Rights (ODIHR).

Phillips, A. (1998) 'Democracy and representation: or, why should it matter who our representatives are?', in Phillips, A. (ed.) *Feminism and Politics*, Oxford: Oxford University Press, pp. 224–40.

Piccio, D. R. (2011) 'Party responses to social movements: a comparative analysis of Italy and the Netherlands in the 1970s and 1980s', Doctoral dissertation. Florence: European University Institute.

Saward, M. (2006) 'The representative claim', *Contemporary Political Theory*, 5 (3): 297–318.

— (2008) 'The subject of representation', *Representation*, 44 (2): 93–7.

Taricone, F. (2001) *Il Centro Italiano Femminile. Dalle origini agli anni settanta*, Milano: Franco Angeli.

Wängnerud, L. (2009) 'Women in parliaments: descriptive and substantive representation', *Annual Review of Political Science*, 12: 51–69.

Wertman, D. (1979). 'La partecipazione intermittente. Gli iscritti e la vita di partito', in Parisi, A. (ed.) *Democristiani*, Bologna: Cattaneo/Il Mulino, pp. 61–84.

Wiliarty, S. E. (2010) *The CDU and the Politics of Gender in Germany: Bringing Women to the Party*, Cambridge: Cambridge University Press.

Chapter Four

Gender Politics of the Justice and Development Party in Turkey

Zeynep Şahin-Mencütek

Introduction

Scholars of gender and politics have paid considerable attention to mechanisms that advance women's descriptive and substantive representation (*see* Childs and Lovenduski 2013). They have addressed the role of institutions in women's integration in electoral politics and found that political parties notably influence women's engagement with politics. Parties are often characterised both as *gendered* organisations, reflecting the gender ideology of their membership and leaders in their internal culture and practices, and as *gendering* institutions, shaping women's political agency as supporters, activists, leaders, candidates, and representatives (Lovenduski and Campbell 2005). As political parties are clearly important actors in determining representation, a salient question to ask is under what circumstances do parties promote gender-balanced approaches in their policies and practices? Or, put another way, how and when do parties integrate women in their ranks and in their parliamentary delegation?

Many studies have found that external conditions – such as the presence of a proportional representation system, an egalitarian political culture and certain socio-economic factors – are preconditions for a better representation of women in politics (Baldez 2008; Dahlerup 2006; Leyenaar 2004; Lovenduski, and Norris 2003; Mackay 2004, Matland and Studlar 1996; Norris and Lovenduski 1995; Rule and Zimmerman 1994). Other studies have reported that intra-party factors like party ideology, candidate selection procedures, party size, party institutionalisation, and intra-party relations influence the descriptive representation of women (Kittilson 2006; Kunovich and Paxton 2005; Lawless and Fox 2005; Macaulay 2006; Saint-Germain and Metoyer 2008; Sanbonmatsu 2006). In particular, party ideology is one of the major factors influencing policies on women's representation. Thus, parties that are on the left in their political leanings typically demonstrate more balanced gender politics compared to rightist, conservative, religious, and nationalist parties, which have a traditional take on women's roles in society (Caul 1999; Leyenaar 2004; Paxton *et al.* 2007).

Interest in the gender politics of conservative parties, in particular, has grown in light of recent studies addressing women's representation in conservative parties in Western European democracies and the involvement of women in conservative politics in the United States (Childs 2008; Childs and Webb 2012; Schreiber 2008; Wiliarty 2010). While conservative parties assume many forms, they commonly espouse conservative gender ideologies and place significance on the role of the family in maintaining social cohesion. Conservatives are characterised by a strong belief in traditional, complementary gender roles, emphasising women's nurturing and reproductive roles, rather than gender equality. Unsurprisingly, women have historically been under-represented in these parties (Leyenaar 2004; Paxton and Kunovich 2003; Paxton *et al.* 2007). On the other hand, conservative women have been increasing their involvement in politics, as supporters, participants and representatives. Despite growing academic interest, there are still many unexplored issues relating to descriptive and substantive representation of women in conservative parties, the gender dimension of conservative politics, claims of conservative representatives on women, and political involvement of conservative women. Investigation of these issues necessitates knowledge of different types of conservative parties and actors over time and across locations. So, country-specific and/or comparative research on the status of women in conservative and religious parties of Muslim-populated countries may provide some insights for a discussion on how various types of differences mediate women's political representation. Such an analysis will also contribute to the limited literature on women and political representation in these countries.

The conservative parties in Muslim-populated countries take various forms and are usually closely related to parties with Islamic discourse. There are several reasons to think that Muslim conservative/Islamic parties tend to exclude women from representation. First, the culture of these parties is typically more patriarchal than the centrist or leftist parties of that country. Second, they have a poor record of women's representation in positions of power. These reasons stem from the fact that Islamic parties are historically and/or currently tied to religious movements and authorities that maintain inegalitarian values and are resistant to change, as traditional gender relations remain at the core of their ideology (Diederich 2009; Blaydes and El Tarouty 2009; Abdel-Latif and Ottaway 2007; Abdel-Latif 2008).

As a Muslim-majority country, and one that has had a conservative governing party known for its Islamic roots since 2002, Turkey offers an ideal subject for addressing questions regarding women's representation within Muslim conservative politics. In Turkey, women's political representation has traditionally been very low. Between 2002 and 2011, the percentage of women in the Turkish parliament increased from 4 to 14 per cent; and no quotas or reserved seats were introduced. In this period, the conservative Justice and Development Party (JDP: Adalet ve Kalkınma Partisi), known as a party for espousing traditional views about gender roles, has been the government party, holding more than two-thirds of parliamentary seats. However, its party ideology did not hinder its progress electorally, and importantly it does not differ from the other three parties in the parliament with regards to women's descriptive representation. The party has, even so, experienced increasing presence of conservative women as supporters and mobilisers. So, an analysis of the JDP's position in women's descriptive representation is important in gaining a more general understanding of why, and under what conditions, women have come to play an active role within conservative Islamic parties.

The Turkish case

Turkey has a multi-party system in which parties are the main vehicle of political participation and representation. A party list proportional representation system is used to elect 550 deputies directly to the parliament, called the Turkish Grand National Assembly (TGNA: *Türkiye Büyük Millet Meclisi*) for a four-year tenure. There are eighty-one multi-member constituencies corresponding to the country's provinces. Candidates who run in the general elections for the TGNA seats can be nominated by parties or enter as independent candidates. Parties need to win over 10 per cent of the votes in the province where they stand for election in order to send a deputy to the parliament; smaller parties are not expected to meet this threshold for election and are more likely to participate in elections using independent candidates. The parties represented in the TGNA since 2002, are the JDP (conservative, neoliberalist, right-wing), the Republican People's Party (RPP) (social democratic, Kemalist, left-wing), the Nationalist Action Party (NAP) (Turkish nationalist, right-wing), and the Peace and Democracy Party (PDP) (Kurdish nationalist, left-wing).[1]

Despite Turkey's secular state system, which is protected by the constitution and several other institutional mechanisms, religious parties have emerged alongside rightist/centrist parties, with discourses emphasising traditionalist and Islamic values (Altunisik and Tur 2005; Tuncay 1981). The JDP, coming from an Islamic party tradition, became the governing party as a result of victories in each the last three general elections – in 2002, 2007 and 2011 – and in local elections in 2004 and 2009.[2] The JDP presents itself as 'a centrist conservative democratic party', thus aligning itself with the European Christian Democratic party tradition. In this regard, many analysts avoid defining the JDP as an Islamist party; they argue that the party discourse centres on a political style that is free from the politicisation of religion by acknowledging the importance of secularism in politics (Akdogan 2006; Çakır 2004; Dagı 2004; Yılmaz 2004). However, it has in common with more overtly Islamist parties the promotion of an understanding and tolerance of Islamic life. Its leadership cadres and a substantial part of its electorate are pious or religious people.

---

1. Its forerunners, the People's Democracy Party (*Demokratik Halk Partisi*) participated in the 2002 election and the Democratic Society Party (*Demokratik Toplum Partisi*) participated in the 2007 election. They were banned by the Constitutional Court in 2003 and 2009 respectively, due to their alleged support for Kurdish separatism.

2. In the 2002 general election, the JDP received 34.2 per cent of the popular vote and gained 363 out of the 550 parliamentary seats. In 2007, it received 47 per cent of the vote, resulting in 341 seats, and in 2011 it received 49.8 per cent of the vote and took 327 seats.

The processes through which the JDP puts women forward for election to national office, and through which its gender policies are transformed, were identified on the basis of personal interviews, participant observation, and archival and documentary research, focusing on the 2007–11 period. (It was in this period that the Turkish parliament saw the highest percentage of women since 1935, the year women made their road to the parliament.) Interview data were obtained between May and September 2009 by conducting a total of thirty-four interviews in three metropolitan cities: Ankara, Istanbul and Diyarbakır. Semi-structured interviewees include fourteen women JDP Members of Parliament (MPs) who held office between 2007 and 2011, representing half of the women MPs from the party at that time; twelve representatives of the JDP women's branches; and eight members of opposition parties (*see* Appendix for details of interviews). Interviews lasted between forty-five minutes and two hours at offices, or at locations recommended by the interviewees. Instead of videotaping, extensive notes were taken, according to the preferences of interviewees. All interviews were semi-structured, with closed and open-ended questions that asked about interviewees' political socialisation, their ideas about their role in the party and the parliament, and questions on their opinion of gender-based violence, gender quotas and democratisation.

Participant observation of weekly meetings, gatherings, and picnics[3] was undertaken in 2009. Moreover, the election campaign in Istanbul was observed between April and June 2011 to better capture women's candidate selection processes and campaign activities. For the documentary research, sources included party platforms, election programmes, brochures, activity reports, official statements of the JDP and its women's sections. In January and February 2013, the Turkish parliament's online archives were reviewed to identify by-laws, bills, oral/written parliamentary questions, and parliamentary debates on women's issues that took place in 2011 and 2012.

Gender equality discourse and the policies of the JDP governments

The JDP has separate sections relating to women and family in its party programme. In this way, it differs from its predecessor Islamic parties' programmes, which rarely mentioned women separately, and usually did so only as part of family issues. The JDP programme addresses women's political agency by highlighting their motherhood role:

Not [only] because women make up half of our population, they should be considered as individuals before everything else [because they are] primarily effective for the raising of healthy generations. Our Party shall pay attention to all kinds of women's problems, which have been neglected for years. All

---

3. Picnics are often used by the JDP to attract female voters. Participants, usually housewives, are able to socialise and eat together with their neighbours and other party women in a relaxed/informal environment, while the party women are able to make election propaganda.

necessary measures shall be taken to encourage women to participate in public life. Women shall be encouraged to enrol as members of our Party and to play an active role in politics[...] (Party Programme 2013).

In common with other conservative parties in the Muslim world, the JDP promotes the belief that 'family constitutes the foundation of society and is an institution which plays an important role in the formation of social solidarity' (Party Programme 2013); the family needs protection from dissolution and social degeneration (Akdogan 2006: 67). The party assigns priority to 'family-centred policies': 'to work out arrangements to support family members in order to preserve family peace and [the] spiritual health of children from disturbances due to the intensity of the work environment'. It stresses the well-being of the family for the sake of societal good. The family-centred policy approach is, moreover, allied with a gender-based division of labour, in which women are seen the caretakers of the family. By emphasising the complementary roles of men and women and a division of labour in both family and society, the JDP frames gender equality differently from secular and feminist women groups in Turkey.

Some progress was made in the first term of the JDP government (2002–7) in terms of legal and institutional reforms for improving gender equality as a result of (1) European Union conditionality; (2) the long-term efforts of the women's movement and (3) the JDP's moderation claims – which aim to prove that the party does not pose a threat to the secular character of the state (Ayata and Tütüncü 2008; Sözen 2008; Gender Inequality Report 2008). For example, unlike its forerunner Islamic parties, the JDP did not place a headscarved candidate in its party election lists in three elections, despite popular demand and intense campaigning by Islamic women's groups.

The most important legal reform during this time was the amendment of more than forty articles, particularly those related crimes about honour killings and rape in the Turkish Penal Code in 2004. It abolished the supremacy of men in the family, provided equal rights for men and women on family abode, marital property, divorce, child custody, inheritance and rights to work and travel. The Turkish women's movements played a substantial role in drafting and advocating the legal changes in the Penal Code. The parliament, led by the JDP government, ultimately passed the Penal Code despite the amendments in some articles contradicting the conservative values of the JDP. For instance, the issue of adultery sparked heated parliamentary discussions in September 2004. The JDP party leader and Prime Minister Tayyip Erdoğan claimed to be protecting women by proposing an article in which adultery was defined as a crime for which both men and women have to be punished. This reflected the JDP's conservative ideology and its intention to intervene in the private sphere (Arat 2009; Ilkkaracan 2005). As a result of pressure from feminist groups and the EU, however, Erdoğan was forced to withdraw the proposal.

Other legislative changes relating to women's rights also took place in 2004, with constitutional amendments to Articles 10 and 90. The amendment to Article 90 promoted the Convention on Elimination of all kinds of Discrimination against

Women (CEDAW), which Turkey ratified in 1985, to primary law, i.e. higher than national law. Article 10, known as the equality article, states that women and men have equal rights and that the state must ensure that this equality exists *in practice*. This article was amended further in a 2010 draft with the following sentence: 'Measures taken for this purpose shall not be interpreted as contrary to the principle of equality'. This addition is used by the government to legitimise or 'mask' its policy choices, for example, by arguing that a gender-based quotas system would be a violation of this principle. Similarly, demands from women's groups and LGBT groups to include ethnic origin, sexual orientation, gender identity, marital status, age, and disability in the equality article were rejected before the 2010 amendment on the basis that such a move would compromise the principle of equality, a position that critics argue is another example of the conservative values of the government (Birdal 2013). Although constitutional amendments partially strengthened the principle of gender equality in Turkey, they also failed to provide an adequate basis for further reforms.

After 2007, the conservative ideology of the JDP in respect of gender equality issues became more apparent at discursive, legislative and policy levels (Acar and Altunok 2012; Arat 2009; Ilkkaracan 2005). At the discursive level, on many occasions, the Prime Minister and the JDP elites reaffirmed the notion that 'men and women are not equal, they are complementary'. On numerous occasions the Prime Minister asks for newly-weds to have at least three children. The JDP advocates typical pro-natal approaches despite the existence of an anti-natal population planning policy in Turkey since the 1960s. On the subject of abortion rights, the Prime Minister denounced abortion as 'murder' and the government has been working on a new law that would restrict the right of women to have an abortion. Through these policies, the government has sought to use moral judgements in politics and has demonstrated a strongly conservative attitude in what is a key area for women's rights (Acar and Altunok 2012: 2).

At the institutional level, the problematic nature of the government's approach to gender was apparent in the establishment of women's state machinery, namely the Parliamentary Commission on Equal Opportunities for Men and Women in 2009, and the Ministry of Family and Social Policies in 2011. The process of naming the Commission was controversial, with women's movements demanding it be called the Commission on Equality of Men and Women; but government approved the name 'Equal Opportunities'. Women's groups and opposition parties argued that this does not embrace total equality between men and women, further reflecting the government's belief in the complementary nature of men and women, rather than their equality. A similar situation evolved with the naming of the Ministry of Family and Social Policies: many felt that 'women' should be included in the name, but the government instead placed 'women's issues' as a subgroup of family and social policy issues by including women as a vulnerable group (RPP Legislative Proposal 2013, Personal communication).

A review of the policies and parliamentary discussions in 2011 further demonstrates that the JDP prioritises the needs of the family and market in explaining and proposing solutions to gender inequalities. At the same time, the party consistently fails to emphasise the state's role in providing the necessary services to enable women to participate in the labour market, and pays limited attention to economic equality and the rights of working mothers. Where there is an attempt to produce a solution, it is often driven by government desire to appease critics, because the current government has been questioned widely by opposition parties in parliamentary questions and the reports of international organisations.

Political participation: Women's branches

Despite the evidence presented above of the JDP's conservative approach to gender equality, reflected in its discourse and policies, large numbers of women are interested in the party as a vehicle for political participation and representation. Women have been very actively involved in propaganda activities and election campaigns, and it is widely believed that women's votes played a significant role in elevating the JDP into government. Indeed, since the JDP's establishment in 2001, women have shown a notable interest in voting for the party, with a 5 per cent sex gap in women's favour. Compare, with the main opposition party RPP, where the percentage of men supporting the party is one per cent higher than women: men 14 per cent, women 13 per cent (Turan 2004).

Women's participation is not limited to voting. In the JDP, many women are also actively involved in party activities, specifically through women's branches (WBs), which have three-and-a-half million recorded members. WBs are well established, with its headquarters in Ankara, and sub-organisations in the eighty-one provinces and 896 districts, as well as villages and neighbourhoods, wherever the number of female members is sufficient to carry out party activities. Such a high level of institutionalisation has not been observed in women's sections of other Turkish parties. The WBs used to be an auxiliary organisation that did not have a voice in decision making and was under the control of the male party elites in the respective provinces or districts. Especially in small provinces and districts, women's sections could be considered to reinforce the subordination of women and gender segregation within the party bodies. After 2007, some important steps were taken to include the WBs in the decision-making process. The WBs were given equal representation rights with nineteen other party organisations in the JDP's highest decision-making body, the Central Executive Committee. Another regulation granted the right for the head of WB to vote on the party's provincial boards. According to a 2009 regulation, the impeding of WBs' activities by male members is a 'disciplinary offence', punishment for which is temporary dismissal.

WBs play several roles: recruiting new female members into the party; providing political training to women; propagating the party's policies; helping mobilisation at party events such as annual congresses and public meetings; collecting data about local needs and feedback on the party's current and prospective electorate; building networks with local, national, and international organisations to disseminate the idea that the party has a progressive perspective about women; and developing projects to further women's education, health, and employment opportunities. The WBs generate many benefits for the party, particularly in mobilisation. Two members of the WBs stated that 'women constitute the backbone of the JDP, the WBs are the backbone of the party organisations… The party cannot be successful without women' (Personal communication 22 June 2009). Widespread mobilisation efforts of members of WBs in the 2011 election campaign in Istanbul were evident. Women ensured that rallies and meetings were crowded by inviting their friends and neighbours, and by arranging accommodation for them. WBs were also in charge of recruiting new members to the JDP in small portable offices opened in front of children's playgrounds, bus stations, malls and public squares.

It is clear, then, that the party benefits from the activities of members of WBs. But what are the benefits of these activities to women? Female activists of the party have approached the WBs as a civil society organisation and these activists consider their participation as a form of civic engagement. They participate in WBs in order to serve the public and to contribute to solving the country's problems, and to be able to say that 'they do something good' (Arat 2005; personal communication). Such motivations help to increase the capacity of the WBs, because conservative, Muslim women have perceived the WBs as the most salient venue for their political and civic engagement, as well as their training, that contributes to their Islamic and personal cause. Thus, women put extraordinary effort into making these organisations effective and strong.

Turning to political recruitment: until the 2007 national election, the party was not eager to include women as candidates. And activist women were hesitant to ask for it because this demand might be regarded as 'inappropriate' and might harm their voluntary participation. However, since 2007, JDP women have begun to make representation demands. Rather than being assertive and vocal in asking for more representation, they have aimed to change the sex composition of the party in favour of women by avoiding confrontation with men. Safiye Seymenoglu and Fatma Şahin, two female deputies 'raised' in the WBs, stated that in the early years their efforts were aimed at demonstrating their political presence to male counterparts who dominated the political domain (Personal communication, 17 and 19 June 2009). Similarly, Serpil Çakır, the head of Diyarbakır Province's WB, explained that although their suggestions and their efforts were sometimes disregarded by Central Provincial Party organisations, the WBs continued and even intensified their activities in order to demonstrate the importance of women's presence. Such statements, as well as the emphasis on the political training of women in the WB, have demonstrated female party members' willingness to be present in party politics, to develop their political abilities and capacities, enhance their effectiveness, and ultimately enforce their demands regarding representation. More recently, women of the WBs have felt motivated to pursue stronger representation, aimed at increasing their effectiveness and ability in negotiating for power, particularly in the selection of candidates, as discussed below.

Descriptive representation in the JDP

Compared to previous Islamic parties, the JDP has demonstrated more 'women-friendly' attitudes in terms of women's descriptive representation. The party invited thirteen women to be among its sixty-four founders in 2001, signalling its intention to further women's advancement in party politics. In terms of intra-party positions, the highest decision-making body is the Central Executive Council, which has three women (15 per cent) out of twenty members. The percentage of women holding high positions in the Central Executive Council, the Central Division and Executive Council, and the Discipline Council rose from 19 per cent in 2007 to 23 per cent in 2011,[4] compared to a national average of 18 per cent across parties. However, the party has not had any women among its eighty-one provincial heads.[5]

Contrary to expectations stemming from the JDP's religious conservative party ideology, women's descriptive representation in candidate lists and parliamentary delegations has increased slightly over time, in line with its electoral victories. Table 4.1 demonstrates the changes in women's descriptive representation in comparison with other Turkish parties.

Table 4.1 shows that the JDP doubled the number of woman candidates between the elections of 2002 and 2007, representing an increase from 5.6 per cent to 11.6 per cent of their total candidates, and increased a further 2.5 per cent in the 2011 elections. In addition to the number of candidates, the placement of candidates on party lists is important given the proportional representational system used in Turkey. The first four places from each party list are generally considered to be the electable positions. In 2011, the JDP placed only one woman in first place, in the largest district in Istanbul, whereas the social democratic left-wing RPP and the nationalist right-wing NAP came fourth and second, respectively. In the top ten places, the JDP had 35 women candidates, the RPP had 36 and the NAP had 23. Confirming the findings of literature on gender and politics about the reluctance of parties to select women for the most winnable list positions, the JDP placed more women candidates in larger districts. In smaller districts, where only two to three MPs are elected, there were almost no women JDP candidates. The number of women being nominated as candidates overall shows the JDP on a par or doing better than other parties: in the JDP, this was around 22 per cent in 2011 (compared with 14 per cent in the RPP and 20 per cent in the DSP). However, due to their list position, the rate of JDP women being elected after being nominated is low, around 18 per cent (2011), and this compares unfavourably with a rate of 48 per cent in the RPP and 89 per cent in the DSP. The explanation for this is a lack of confidence on behalf of the JDP to place women in the more electable ranks,

---

4. The percentage of women is relatively higher both in the Central Division and Executive Council (25 per cent) and in the Discipline Council (27 per cent). There are no data available on the number of women in JDP committees in 2002, or on other parties, making a comparison difficult.

5. The opposition parties RPP had two women out of eighty-one provincial heads, the PDP had twenty-two out of twenty-six, and the NAP had no women.

Table 4.1: Number and percentage of women candidates and MPs by party

Election years	Party name	Women candidates		Elected women	
		Number	%	Number	%
2002 election	Justice and Development Party	31	5.6	11	3.01
	Republican People's Party	42	7.6	11	6.2
	Democratic People's Party	103	18.7	No seats	No seats
2007 election	Justice and Development Party	64	11.6	30	8.7
	Republican People's Party	50	9.1	9	8.0
	Democratic Society Party	9	15.0	8	36.3
	Nationalist Action Party	Not known	Not known	2	2.8
2011 election	Justice and Development Party	78	14.1	45	13.8
	Republican People's Party	99	18	19	14.0
	Nationalist Action Party	61	11	3	5.6
	Peace and Democracy Party	13	20.3	11	34.3

despite Matland and Tezcur's study (2011), which found that the sex of candidates is not important in voting, even among religiously observant voters in Turkey (Gender Inequality Report 2008). In short, although it could take positive steps for better representation of women, on the back of its election victories and high party support among women the JDP prefers to take a moderate stance in terms of the number of both woman candidates and elected representatives.

At the executive level, during its three tenures, the JDP have tended to have one or two female ministers, of which one has been appointed to the Ministry on Family and Social Policies. Typically it is senior MPs who have served in the parliament more than once who are selected as ministers. Appointments to the Parliamentary Commission seem gendered but there is no systematic pattern when comparing 2007–11 and post-2011, with the exception of the Women and Men Equal Opportunity Commission, which is dominated by women. As of 2012, it includes twenty-six women and only five men, with two-thirds of the women coming from the JDP, reflecting their parliamentary composition.

The increase in the descriptive representation of women in the JDP over time might seem puzzling given the party's conservative ideology. A number of scholars have explained this in terms of the party presenting a more moderate image and or to reduce or deflect criticism by secular groups; that the increases mask the party's traditional gender ideology (Ayata and Tütüncü 2008; Tur and Çıtak 2009). Critics contend that the JDP uses women to garner votes and manipulate women's religious motivations, but that this does not translate into valuing women's political activism. In other words, increases in the number of JDP women in the parliament are regarded as tokenism.

Portraying the increases in women's political participation in the JDP as mere tokenism arguably underestimates the agency of JDP women, and fails to recognise the negotiations that take place among various actors inside and outside the party for increasing descriptive representation. It is plausible to suggest that top-down (party leadership) and bottom-up (WBs) mechanisms have interacted in such a way that numerical increases in women's political presence have taken place both within the party and within its parliamentary delegation. From the bottom, the WBs act as a platform for increasing descriptive representation, and had a voice in the selection of women candidates in the 2007 and 2011 parliamentary elections, as well as in the 2009 local election. All prospective women candidates were interviewed by a selection committee from the WBs and importance was given to the duration of experience in the WBs' various ranks, so that some of the prospective candidates were chosen from among the section's senior and experienced members. The heads of provincial women's sections were chosen as candidates if they did not wear a headscarf, because headscarved women would not be approved as an MP, in line with related regulation.[6] Ultimately, the party selection committee prepared a list of prospective candidates, which was combined with a list of women who had been recruited personally by party leader Erdoğan on the recommendation of his wife, Emine Erdoğan, constituting the preliminary female candidate pool. Selected candidates were placed in safe seats on the party list and thus constituted the parliament's female composition. In the 2007 elections, seven out of thirty women MPs came from WB cadres. For the 2011 elections, all candidates went through the approval of the WBs. In explaining these party processes, women's laborious contributions to party mobilisation, their dissemination and their work in election campaigns could no longer be ignored by the party leadership, and this brought them negotiating power and some gains in candidate selection. Nevertheless, the number of women candidates who were selected for electable ranks was ultimately decided by the male party leader.

The role of the party leadership in top-down feminisation is also relevant to the Turkish case (*see also* Kittilson 2006, Clark and Swedler 2003). The JDP is often

---

6.   Regulation on the Clothes of Officers Working in Public Institutions, 16 July 1982, No. 8/5105. Published in the *Official Gazette* on 25 October 1982, No. 17849 5, Volume 21, No. 2879. Retrieved from http://www.mevzuat.gov.tr/Metin.Aspx?MevzuatKod=3.5.85105&MevzuatIliski=0 &sourceXmlSearch, 4 October 2013.

defined as a party of the leader, with more limited intra-party democracy compared with other Turkish parties (Tezcur 2010). Party leader Erdoğan controls the party's policy-making agenda and nominations for elected offices. He can dominate party bodies, imposing his preferences on both party members and party representatives. A review of speeches made by Erdoğan to members of WBs, personal interviews conducted with female political activists and interviews published in the print media, together indicate that Erdoğan promotes women's descriptive representation and seems to have a great deal of ongoing influence on female politicians and activists. He uses a paternalist tone, which is welcomed by JDP women working in the WBs and elected MPs. Interviewees reported that Erdoğan personally convinced them and others to become candidates. In some instances, paradoxically, he encouraged women to make claims regarding representation and to fight against male-dominated politics within the party, although he himself has the power to push further changes if he wants. He also backed the WBs when there was a backlash from male party members. It seems that Erdoğan is very aware that much of the hard work of party organisation, including mobilisation in mass organisations, has fallen to JDP women, particularly during election campaigns; accordingly, such a contribution from WBs forces him and party elites to acknowledge women's labour in order to prove its authenticity.

Substantive representation in the JDP

It is widely expected in the literature on gender and politics that women will have a distinct group identity based upon shared common interests on women's issues. Hence, it is frequently assumed that women's presence in political institutions will likely translate into substantive public policy that promotes women's social, economic, and political well-being (Phillips 1995). Thus we can ask, what has been the JDP women's impact on legislative agenda setting and on adopting laws and policies empowering women?

An initial way of assessing female deputies' willingness and capacity for substantial representation is to examine whether they approach women as a social category with which they feel obliged to deal, and if they consider that the unequal balance of power between the sexes is a problem, often called the 'woman question' (Ayata and Tütüncü 2008). When elected women representatives were asked to list the top three problems in Turkey, none of them listed gender inequality or women's empowerment. Instead they cited issues such as unemployment, security, and education. Issues such as girls' education, the dramatic gender gap in the labour force, and gender-based violence were ranked as less important. Those MPs who considered gender inequality as a problem chose to frame it either within the context of human rights or the family. According to one line of reasoning coming from the interviews, when democracy is consolidated and human rights violations decrease, problems pertinent to gender inequality will be solved. A second line of reasoning suggested that when female deputies develop education and social policies addressing the well-being of children and elderly people in the family, they will be contributing to women's empowerment. Many female MPs did not, moreover, accept sole responsibility for addressing women's issues at the policy-making level and instead advocated for the inclusion of male deputies in the process. They also pointed to civil society organisations as platforms for advancing solutions to the woman question. At the same time party loyalty is very strong, and it is almost impossible to find evidence of a female JDP deputy in a personal confrontation with the party. They have avoided negotiating or collaborating with women of other parties represented in the parliament, or women in civil society organisations, so as not to come into conflict with their own party (Turam 2008). None of the deputies reported having had to confront double standards or gender stereotyping in the party.[7]

Alternative women's perspectives recognising the existence of problems relating to gender equality in Turkey and elected officials' responsibilities in addressing the problems were articulated by individual women.[8] For example, Aşkın Aşan, who served in the parliament between 2007 and 2011, stated that the problems around women's issues in Turkey are very important. She regarded herself as responsible for contributing to their resolution by providing opportunities for women, particularly opportunities for them to become involved in public life, to participate in politics, and to be represented in the parliament. Aşan and another MP Alev Dedegil, both of whom identify themselves as feminists, developed projects addressing polygamy and the sexual abuse of children, problems that politicians have often been silent about. Dedegil, along with deputies of opposition parties, also put women's poverty and violence against women on the parliamentary agenda.

Although, as noted above, women's representation has gradually increased since 2002, both national and international reports have cited this as one of the most prominent dimensions of gender inequality in Turkey. JDP interviewees stated that the reasons for women's limited participation in politics include lower levels of education, economic dependence, meagre financial resources for political campaigns, and a lack of role models. Cultural values prioritising the domestic role of women, along with women's inexperience in politics, have also influenced the political involvement of women negatively. Many deputies also stated that women in general tend to avoid politics. Women, they claim, are not confident about being candidates and they often leave politics if they are not elected, whereas men are more persistent. Personal communications with politicians and party women identify a lack of solidarity among women as the main impediment to women's advancement in party ranks.

As with the party leadership, JDP women in general seem to oppose a gender quota system for parliamentary candidates. During interviews many JDP women argued that quotas might hamper what they considered the merit-based candidacy

---

7. According to their reporting, these attitudes were not prevalent even among their electorate. I find this unconvincing.

8. 'Women's perspectives' refer to women's views on all political matters. It is widely believed that women may perceive some issues, particularly women's issues, differently from men.

process. For example, a senior female JDP deputy, Guldal Aksit, who served as the minister responsible for Family and Social Policies, said that they (as a party) oppose quotas. She believes that women deserving of political office will be successful. Aksit also considers that as long as women's interest in politics increases and party elites support them, women's representation will improve and there is no need for a change in election law (Personal communication 25 June 2009). Other party women agreed, and expressed the belief that women should come to power by proving their quality and that if a quota system is adopted, the quality of the female deputies would decline. They held that, as women are less experienced compared to their male counterparts, they should wait before making claims for better representation. The importance of role models and political learning was highlighted. The anti-quotas discourse of these women is also partially due to the deputies' loyalty to the party leadership and their dependence for re-election on party male elites.

A review of parliamentary debates in 2011 and 2012 shows that women MPs from the JDP rarely participate in parliamentary discussions or ask the chair for permission to give a speech, except on Women's Day. Compared to women from opposition parties, they tend to be less active in parliamentary debates and rarely act across parties, except on the issue of violence against women. As they are part of the ruling party, they neither sponsor bills nor propose oral or written parliamentary questions.[9] Questions about women's issues are answered by the relevant minister, regardless of sex. Nevertheless, women MPs of the JDP are 'very grateful' to the party and believe that women's status has improved substantially during their party's tenure. MP Ayse Turkmenoglu stated that 'a new era started, women found opportunities to prove themselves and to be represented in the parliament, politics, and administration' (TGNA 2013). Although women said that legislative changes are not enough to achieve gender equality, on each occasion they referenced these reforms rather than discussing ongoing problems. On the other hand, they tended to frame women's issues by referring to conservative democratic ideals with which the party identities. For example, one deputy who rose through the party ranks stated that women are expected to be conservative in both their dress and their attitudes. A number of deputies framed their concerns about identity issues by highlighting the party's 'conservative democratic' ideals. For example, Halide İncekara, a JDP deputy elected in the 2002, 2007, and 2011 national elections, stated:

---

9. According to my review of the 82 oral and written parliamentary questions posed in 2012, the nature of parliamentary questions and the gender of MPs vary across parties. For example, the PDP women MPs questioned the number and the conditions of women prisoners and women's suicides in the eastern provinces; RPP women questioned women's employment, shelters, and women's representation in the decision-making positions; NAP women raised issues related to the health of mothers and children. Domestic violence was a topic addressed by members of different parties, both women and men.

I am a member of the party that identifies itself as conservative democratic. I am not supposed to think either as a social democrat or a liberal … I cannot propose policies like liberals do. No one can criticise me for embracing a conservative identity, traditional values, and faith. I develop policies with respect to my identity, values, and faith (JDP Women's Branch Conference Proceedings 2005, 36–7, 39).

Like male elites in the party, women JDP MPs emphasised the need to preserve cultural and family values. Selma Kavaf, an MP and Minister of State for Women and Family Affairs between 2009 and 2011, maintained:

We believe that women may become involved in politics as women and mothers in an environment in which globalisation threatens families. Because of that, we may develop close relations with and support individuals and organisations that have worked to keep alive conservative values. (p. 8)

Similarly, in her comments to the party's monthly journal, *Turkiye Bulletin*, in August 2006, Fatma Şahin, who was elected to the parliament in 2007 and led the WBs until 2011, stated, 'We are a conservative society in which families are a very important part of its fabric. Violence against children and women does not fit into our faith and culture' (p. 53).

Conclusion

Gender and politics scholarship acknowledges that within the country inter-party differences are identifiable in the descriptive and substantive representation of women. The high level of women's participation and relatively lower level of representation within conservative parties necessitate an examination of these parties' gender ideology as well as their stances toward descriptive representation. Conservative Muslim parties are an important aspect of the wider picture on gender and conservative politics. This article finds that the gender ideology of the JDP in Turkey is similar to many conservative parties as it emphasises the complementary roles of men and women, as well as the division of labour in family and in society. Although some of the evidence presented here suggests that the JDP has increased women's descriptive representation, their promotion of gender equality is limited. Women's sections, which are outdated in many European countries, appear as the main platform for conservative women's participation in electoral politics. Women's mobilisation in these organisations benefits the parties, as women members garner substantial votes for the parties during elections. Women's participation in these sections has also ultimately translated over time into some gains in women's descriptive representation. Women have become influential actors in preparing candidate lists, and some were nominated and later elected. The women's sections appear then to constitute an opportunity structure for conservative women in lobbying the party leader, and gradually participating in decision making and facilitating their integration into mainstream party channels.

In terms of substantive representation, as in many parties, the JDP's female representatives claim to represent women substantively, and to have diverse and contested conceptions of women's interests. While some tend to frame women's issues by referring to conservative democratic ideals with which the party used to identify itself – particularly referring to the salience of family – a limited number of them also see women's issues in terms of gender inequality: domestic violence, early marriages, sexual abuse of children, the education of girls, and women's health. Overall, women MPs of the party seem to be more concerned with women's issues than their male colleagues, reflecting the findings in the literature.

As parties are very important to feminist activitists and gender politics, it might be useful in subsequent research to analyse: (1) similarities and differences between motivations of women joining the conservative parties and those joining other parties; (2) variations in the forms of activities; and (3) variations in the benefits of participation. Furthermore, comparing Muslim conservative party's gender ideology and policies in different countries may provide important insights for understanding the dynamics of gender and politics. Although it is difficult to fully extrapolate from the situation in the JDP to that of other conservative/Islamic parties more broadly, the JDP's stances regarding women's representation might provide some insights in other Islamic conservative parties in other countries such as Tunisia, Malaysia and Morocco.

Annex: List of interviews

1. Edibe Sözen, JDP MP, 16 June 2009, Ankara
2. Güldal Akşit, JDP MP, 16 June 2009, Ankara
3. AnkaraNursuna Memecan, JDP MP, 17 June 2009, Ankara
4. Birnur Şahinoğlu, JDP MP, 17 June 2009, Ankara
5. Gönül Şahkulubey-Bekin, JDP MP, 17 June 2009, Ankara
6. Safiye Seymenoğlu, JDP MP, 17 June 2009, Ankara
7. Kemalettin Aydin, JDP male MP, 17 June 2009, Ankara
8. Özlem Türköne-Piltanoğlu, JDP MP, 17 June 2009, Ankara
9. Fatma Kotan-Salman, JDP MP, 18 June 2009, Ankara
10. Esra Şeker, JDP WB Provincial Branch, 20 June 2009, Ankara
11. Tülay Selamoğlu, JDP WB Provincial Branch, elected as MP in 2011, 20 June 2009, Ankara
12. Nimet Cubukcu, JDP MP, 23 June 2009, Ankara
13. Gülşen Orhan, 23 June and 25 June 2009, Ankara
14. Özlem Müftüoğlu, JDP MP, 24 June 2009, Ankara
15. Alev Dedegil, JDP MP, 24 June 2009, Ankara
16. Abdulkadir Aksu, JDP male MP, 24 June 2009, Ankara
17. Betul Keskin, JDP WB Headquarters, 24 June 2009, Ankara
18. Fatma Kurtulan, Opposition party MP, 24 June 2009, Ankara
19. Ayse Kesir, JDP WB Headquarters, 24 June 2009 and 10 June 2010, Ankara
20. Fatma Şahin, JDP MP, president of Women's Branch, 25 June 2009, Ankara
21. Naci Orhan, former male mayor and father of Gulsen Orhan, 25 June 2009, Ankara
22. Ayşe Jale Ağırbaş, Opposition party MP, 25 June 2009, Ankara
23. Fatma Nur Serter, Opposition party MP, 25 June 2009, Ankara
24. Nesrin Baytok, Opposition party MP, 25 June 2009, Ankara
25. Askin Asan, JDP MP, 30 June 2009, Ankara
26. Şenol Bal, Opposition party MP, 30 June 2009, Ankara
27. Canan Aritman, Opposition party MP, 30 June 2009, Ankara
28. Bihlun Tamaylıgil, JDP MP, 2 July 2009, Ankara
29. Ayla Akat, Opposition party MP, 10 July 2009, Ankara
30. Süheyla Ulak, JDP, WB Provincial Branch, 20 July 2009, Diyarbakir
31. Serpil Cakir, WB Provincial Branch, 20 July 2009, Diyarbakir
32. Deniz Ayaşlı, WB Provincial Branch, 20 July 2009, Diyarbakir

References

Abdel-Latif, O. (2008) 'In the shadow of the Brothers: the women of the Egyptian Muslim Brotherhood', *Carnegie Endowment for International Peace*, 13, October.

Abdel-Latif, O. and Ottaway, M. (2007) 'Women in Islamist movements: toward an Islamist model of women's activism', *Carnegie Endowment for International Peace*, 2, June.

Acar, F. and Altunok, G. (2012) 'The "politics of intimate" at the intersection of neo-liberalism and neo-conservatism in contemporary Turkey', Women's International Forum, Vol. 41, Part 2, November–December 2013, pp. 14–23.

Akdogan, Y. (2006) 'The meaning of conservative democratic political identity', in Yavuz, H. (ed.), *The Emergence of a New Turkey: Democracy and the AK Parti*, Utah: University of Utah Press, pp. 49–66.

Altunisik, M. and Tur, O. (2005) *Turkey: Challenges of Continuity and Change*, New York and London: Routledge.

Arat, Y. (2005) *Rethinking Islam and Liberal Democracy: Islamist Women in Turkish Politics*, New York: State University of New York Press.

— (2009) *Religion, Politics and Gender Equality: Implications of a Democratic Paradox*, United Nations Research Institute for Social Development, final research report prepared for its project on Religion, Politics and Gender Equality, available at http://www.unrisd.org/unrisd/website/document.nsf/(httpPublications)/13142DE24D017133C1257505004B7E70?OpenDocument (accessed 14 May 2014).

Ayata, A. G. and Tütüncü, F. (2008) 'Critical acts without a critical mass: the substantive representation of women in the Turkish Parliament', *Parliamentary Affairs*, 61 (3): 461–75.

Baldez, L. (2008) 'Political women in comparative democracies', in Wolbrecht, C., Beckwith, K. and Baldez, L. (eds), *Political Women and American Democracy*, Cambridge: Cambridge University Press, pp. 167–180.

Birdal, S. (2013) 'Queering conservative democracy', *Turkish Politics Quarterly*, 11 (4): 119–29.

Blaydes, L. and El Tarouty, S. (2009) 'Women's electoral participation in Egypt: the implications of gender for voter recruitment and mobilization', *Middle East Journal*, 63 (3): 364–380.

Çakır, R. (2004) 'Milli Görüş Hareketi', in *Modern Turkiye'de Siyasi Dusunce: Islamcılık* [Encyclopaedia of Political Thought in Contemporary Turkey] (Vol. 6),. Istanbul: Iletisim Yayinlari.

Caul Kittilson, M. (1999) 'Women, parties, and platforms in post-industrial democracies', *Party Politics*, 17, 66–92.

Childs, S. (2008) *Women and British Party Politics: Descriptive, Substantive, and Symbolic Representation*, New York: Routledge.

Childs, S. and Lovenduski, J. (2013) 'Political representation', in Waylen, G., Celis, K., Kantola, J. and Laurel W. (eds) *The Oxford Handbook of Gender and Politics*, Oxford: Oxford University Press.

Childs, S. and Webb, P. (2012) *Sex, Gender and the Conservative Party: From Iron Lady to Kitten Heels*, Palgrave Macmillan.

Clark, J. A. and Swedler, J. (2003) 'Who opened the window? Women's activism in Islamist parties', *Comparative Politics*, 35 (3): 293–312.

Dagı, I. (2004) 'Rethinking human rights, democracy, and the West: post-Islamist intellectuals in Turkey', *Critique Critical Middle Eastern Studies*, 13 (2): 135–51.

Dahlerup, D. (2006) *Women, Quotas and Politics*, New York: Routledge.

Diederich, M. (2009) 'Islamic parties in Indonesia's political landscape and their respective stances on women and minorities', in Salih, M. A. M. (ed.) *Interpreting Islamic Political Parties*, Houndmills: Palgrave Macmillan, pp.83–103.

Gender Inequality Report (2008) 'Gender inequality in Turkey: problems, priorities and suggestions for solutions' (Türkiye'de Toplumsal Cinsiyet Eşitsizliği: Sorunlar, Öncelikler ve Çözüm Önerileri), Ankara: TÜSIAD and KAGİDER.

Ilkkaracan, P. (2005) *Turkish Civil and Penal Code Reforms from a Gender Perspective*, Istanbul: WWHR-New Ways.

JDP Women's Branch (2005) Conference Proceedings, 8 May.

Kittilson, M. C. (2006) *Challenging Parties, Changing Parliaments: Women and Elected Office in Contemporary Western Europe*, Columbus, OH: Ohio State University Press.

Kunovich, S. and Paxton, P. (2005) 'Pathways to power: the role of political parties in women's national political representation', *American Journal of Sociology*, 111 (2): 505–52.

Lawless, L. J. and Fox, R. L. (2005). *It Takes a Candidate: Why Women Don't Run for Office*, New York: Cambridge University Press.

Leyenaar, M. (2004) *Political Empowerment of Women: The Netherlands and Other Countries*, Leiden, NLD: Martinus Nijhoff Publishers.

Lovenduski, J. and Campbell, R. (2005) 'Winning women's votes: the incremental track to equality', *Parliamentary Affairs*, 58 (4): 837–53.

Lovenduski, J. and Norris, P. (2003) 'Westminster women: the politics of presence', *Political Studies*, 51 (1): 84–102.

Macaulay, F. (2004) 'Gender and political representation in the UK: the state of the "discipline"', *British Journal of Politics & International Relations*, 6 (1): 99–120.

— (2006) *Gender Politics in Brazil and Chile: The Role of Parties in National and Local Policymaking*, Houndmills: Palgrave Macmillan.

Matland, R. E. and Studlar, D. T. (1996) 'The contagion of women candidates in single-member district and proportional representation electoral systems: Canada and Norway', *Journal of Politics*, 58, 707–33.

Matland, R. and Tezcur, M. (2011) 'Women as candidates', *Politics & Gender*, 7, 365–90.

Norris, P. and Lovenduski, J. (1995) *Political Recruitment: Gender, Race, Class in the British Parliament*, Cambridge: Cambridge University Press.

Party Programme of JDP, Family and Social Policies Section (2013), 1 April, retrieved from http://www.akparti.org.tr/english/akparti/parti-programme#bolum (accessed 5 May 2014).

Paxton, P. and Kunovich, S. (2003) 'Women's political representation: the importance of ideology', *Social Forces*, 82 (1): 87–113.

Paxton, P., Kunovich, S. and Hughes, M. M. (2007) 'Gender in politics', *Annual Review of Sociology*, 33, 263–84.

Phillips, A. (1995) *The Politics of Presence*, Oxford, New York: Clarendon Press.

RPP Legislative proposal (27 March 2013), retrieved from http://www.tbmm. gov.tr/develop/owa/tasari_teklif_sd.onerge_bilgileri?kanunlar_sira_no=103752, 10 April 2013.

Rule, W. and Zimmerman, J. F. (1994) *Electoral Systems in Comparative Perspective: Their Impact on Women and Minorities*, Westport, CT: Greenwood Publication Group.

Saint-Germain, M. A. and Metoyer, C. C. (2008) *Women Legislators in Central America: Politics, Democracy, and Policy*, Austin, TX: University of Texas Press.

Sanbonmatsu, K. (2006) *Where Women Run: Gender and Party in the American States*, Ann Arbor, MI: University of Michigan Press.

Schreiber, R. (2008) *Righting Feminism: Conservative Women and American Politics*, Oxford: Oxford University Press.

Sözen, E. (2006) 'Gender politics of the JDP', in Yavuz, H. (ed.) *The Emergence of a New Turkey: Democracy and the AK Parti*, Salt Lake City, UT: University of Utah Press, pp. 258–81.

Tezcur, G. M. (2010) *The Paradox of Moderation*, Austin, TX: University of Texas Press.

TGNA (2013) Plenary section minutes, 24th period, 3rd legislative year, 75th meeting, 7 March. Retrieved from http://www.tbmm.gov.tr/develop/owa/ tutanak_sd.birlesim_baslangic?P4=21908&P5=H&page1=6&page2=6 &web_user_id=11062402, 12 April 2013.

Tuncay, M. (1981) *Türkiye Cumhuriyeti'nde Tek-parti Yönetimi'nin Kurulması (1923–1931)*, İstanbul: Türkiye Ekonomik ve Toplumsal Tarih Vakfı Yayınları.

Tur, O. and Çıtak, Z. (2009) 'AKP ve Kadin: Teskilatlanma, Muhafazakarlik ve Turban', in Uzgel, I. and Duru, B. (eds) *AKP Kitabı – Bir Dönüşümün Bilançosu*, Ankara: Phoenix Kitabevi (n.p.)

Turam, B. (2008) 'Turkish women divided by politics: secularist activism versus pious non-resistance', *International Feminist Journal of Politics*, 10 (4): 475–94.

Turan, A. E. (2004) *Türkiye'de Seçmen Davranışı*, Istanbul Bilgi University Publications.

Wiliarty, S. E. (2010) *The CDU and the Politics of Gender in Germany: Bringing Women to the Party*, New York: Cambridge University Press.

Yılmaz, N. (2004) 'Islamcilik, AKP, Siyaset', in Modern Turkiye'de Siyasi Dusunce: Islamcılık [Encyclopaedia of Political Thought in Contemporary Turkey] (Vol. 6), Istanbul: Iletisim Yayinlari.

Chapter Five

When Less Means More: Influential Women of the Right – the Case of Bulgaria

Ekaterina R. Rashkova and Emilia Zankina

Introduction

A longstanding agreement in the gender and politics literature posits that female legislators are more likely than male legislators to represent women's interests and support legislation beneficial to women, although this is by no means guaranteed (Jones 1998; Phillips 1995). In addition to studies of the descriptive and substantive representation of women, and the link between the two, more recent debates have focused on the diverging interests of women as voiced by various sections of the political spectrum. In particular, there is greater acknowledgement of the presence of conservative female politicians and their claims to act for women. This chapter contributes to these recent debates by examining the case of Bulgaria. While there is no true conservatism in Bulgaria (a claim we discuss below) and the discourse on gender equality is still limited at best, the Bulgarian case offers new insights into the discussions of the substantive representation of women (SRW) in more than one way. First, it presents a different meaning of *conservatism*, describing the altered implication of the political Left and Right within the East European context, and, second, it shows that it is mostly non-Left political parties that promote women more actively in Bulgaria, especially when it comes to evaluating what these women do while in office. Furthermore, we explain how the legacy of communism and its forced gender equality project led to a rejection of feminism, and of any attempts on the part of the state to promote gender equality. We offer an account of a case showing a declining trend in descriptive representation, yet one where women are nonetheless involved in politics, and also, unlike under the communist era, where they have influenced important political decisions. Studying women's descriptive and substantive representation, as well as examining the regulatory framework within which gender equality is supposed to be established and preserved, we find that while voicing women's needs has not been a priority in Bulgaria's political agenda in the last twenty years, the presence of powerful female politicians has served as an important step in striving towards gender equality in a country where the feminist agenda has been affected strongly by the negative connotation that the term 'equality' carries from its political past. We call this presence 'substantive presence', and we argue that it is a condition that is necessary to the achievement of a real substantive representation of women, as SRW is understood in the West.

The principal argument of this chapter is that although women representatives have decreased in number since the abolition of the communist-era gender quotas, the post-communist presence of women in parliament has been more significant than women's 'symbolic' inclusion prior to 1989. In evaluating the SRW in Bulgaria we argue that albeit few, women on the Right have been more politically influential than any of their female predecessors during communism, or their counterparts on the Left. Our account clearly shows that although the number of politically active women in the post-communist years is generally smaller than that before the change of the regime, more women have been promoted and elected to high offices, mostly by right-of-centre political parties. We conclude that while SRW in the true sense of the term is still in the making, in the context of post-communist reality conservative women, or at least women of the Right, can and are more likely to act for women and for political change more broadly than their female colleagues from the Left – perhaps the most valuable new insight that our study can bring to gender scholars of the West.

The declining descriptive representation of women in Bulgaria: From communism to post-communism

With the establishment of communist regimes across Eastern Europe following World War II, women's status and their role in society were to be irreversibly changed. Marxist ideology demanded – at least in theory – the eradication of class differences and social inequalities, including those of gender. Hence, women's emancipation became an official goal of state policy, centring on the political and economic imperative of integrating the female population into paid work and into positions of state socialist authority (Fodor 2004: 783).

The collection of policies aimed at reaching gender parity, termed the 'socialist emancipation project', focused on fully engaging women in the labour force by introducing childcare facilities, maternity provisions and protection, and ensuring a range of domestic services such as laundry and semi-prepared food (Linkova 2007: 3). The policy produced mixed results, yet there were some undeniable improvements in women's social status. Female participation in the labour force steadily increased, even surpassing figures in Western countries, and so did the nature of female labour with more women occupying jobs in industry and state administration. Women were making headway in managerial positions, occupying 32 per cent of such positions in Bulgaria by 1990, and the number of women with university education in Bulgaria increased fifteen-fold between 1946 and 1991 (Kostova 1998: 207).

These figures are misleading, however, when assessing the success of the socialist emancipation project. Although women reached equal status as a proportion of the labour force, they occupied less prestigious, lower-level and lower-paid jobs. Women were more welcome in professions that required less education and more commitment, leading to the feminisation of entire sectors. It is in these feminised professions that women enjoyed greater access to managerial positions. Furthermore, women's share in managerial jobs did not correspond to their employment levels or to their level of educational and professional training (Kostova 1998: 208). Ultimately, East European women came to detest the state-sponsored emancipation, which, in the eyes of many, was driven by ulterior motives of achieving economic and demographic targets (Harvey 2002: 30). In addition to being given the additional role of workers, women were still expected to carry out most household chores and the bases of the unequal gender order were never contested (Popa 2003: 69).

Regarding the political sphere, the communist regimes showed great commitment to opening up channels for women's participation. Women were granted voting rights and access to political positions (those that had not been gained in the interwar period); women's mass organisations were formed to mobilise the female population; gender quotas for state legislatures were introduced, raising the proportion of women in parliaments to over 25 per cent by the 1980s (Forest 2011: 4); and efforts were made to recruit women to the Communist Party. For the first time women entered executive positions – between 1945 and 1950, fifteen women were appointed to government offices (eleven at the rank of minister) in Bulgaria, Czechoslovakia, Hungary and Romania, in the Slovenian and Croatian provinces of Yugoslavia and the Soviet Republic of Estonia. No women had achieved such a position before 1945 (Forest 2011: 3).

Despite such formal gains, women played only a marginal role in political decision making. While rubber-stamp parliaments with no real power welcomed female representatives, women's participation in bodies with real political power, especially at the party level, was extremely limited: the more powerful the political body or industry, the lower the representation of women (Graham and Regulska 1997). Indeed, women did not exceed 10 per cent of party central committees, and hardly featured at all in Politburos. When women were allowed access to political office, it was primarily at the lower and/or local level. Women's organisations were also deprived of real autonomy. They became an instrument of party control rather than propagators and defenders of women's rights. In this way, political equality came to be associated with women's meaningless presence in political bodies and a hollow commitment to women's emancipation.

The Bulgarian case provides a good example of the questionable success of the communist regime in promoting women's political representation. Bulgarian women were enfranchised in 1937, but it was not until 1945 that they were able to compete for parliamentary seats. The introduction of gender quotas (ranging from 20 to 30 per cent) led to female representation of 21.8 per cent in the last communist parliament (Kostadinova 2003: 304). In the 1980s, women constituted 50.5 per cent of the membership of the Fatherland Front (the largest mass organisation in the communist period subservient to the Communist Party), 50 per cent of the Communist Youth Organisation, and 46.4 per cent of the trade unions, while at the same time 35.4 per cent of women held leadership positions in political organisations, and 34 per cent of the members of local government bodies were women (Kostova 1998: 212). However, women's political involvement was limited to local and lower-level positions, with very limited female presence in national decision- making bodies.[1] For example, there were a total of five women cabinet members in all governments between 1946 and 1989, with no more than two women ever present in a single government and a number of cabinets with no female representation at all.[2] And women's involvement was limited to what were considered the less important ministries, such as culture, light industry, and justice.[3] The supreme body of the Communist Party, the Politburo, accepted only two women for the duration of its existence, one of whom was Lyudmila Zhivkova, the daughter of the communist dictator Todor Zhivkov.

Following the collapse of the communist regime and the abolition of legislative gender quotas, the number of women involved in politics declined significantly, especially during the first ten years of the transition (*see* Table 5.1).

Between 1991 and 2000, there were on average 12.3 per cent women in parliament, most of whom were part of the Bulgarian Socialist Party, the successor of the Bulgarian Communist Party. After 2001, however, Centre– right and Right parties began to send female politicians to parliament. The peak was undeniably achieved by the National Movement Simeon Second (NDSV), whose MPs were 40.5 per cent female in 2001. This achievement was due largely to the fact that NDSV, first established as a movement, used the mandate of the Party of Bulgarian Women (PBW) to register for the parliamentary election.[4] Other parties of the Right followed suit with the Bulgarian National Union (BNS), the United Democratic Forces (ODS), the Democrats for Strong Bulgaria (DSB), and later the Blue Coalition, returning a significant number of female legislators. Even the extreme nationalist party, Ataka, included a significant amount of female candidates on its party lists, a relatively large percentage of whom were elected. The fact that in the last decade not only Left parties have seen women elected to parliament, may signify that the feminisation of parties is taking place across the board, along with more awareness about gender and gender equality. Yet, despite such gains, the increase in the descriptive representation of women (DRW) has still not achieved gender parity.

A significant push in that direction – and on placing gender equality high on Bulgaria's political agenda – was made with the adoption of multiple amendments to national legislation under the guidance of the EU (Anderson 2006). During the

---

1. Women constituted 25 per cent of the Communist party leadership at the local level, but only 5.6 per cent at the national level (Kostova 1998: 213).

2. During that time, the Bulgarian Council of Ministers numbered between twenty-five and thirty people – hence women's representation in government during the entire communist period remained in the single digits.

3. The judicial system in communist societies was not independent, being completely subservient to the Communist party. Thus, judicial positions were not considered to be among the top leadership positions. Lacking real clout, the judicial branch was highly feminised.

4. Under Bulgaria's electoral law at the time, only registered political parties could enter the electoral process. Being formed less than three months before the 2001 election, NDSV was not registered as a political party.

Table 5.1: Women's representation in Bulgarian politics, 1991–2009

Political Party	1990	1991	1994	1997	2001	2005	2009
BSP/	11.4	19.8	16.8	12.1			
Coalition for Bulgaria (L)					10.4	18.3	17.5
BBB (R)	–	–	7.7	0.0	–	–	–
People's Union/BZNS+ (C)	6.3	–	5.6	12.5	–	–	–
Euroleft (L)	–	–	–	13.3	–	–	–
NDSV (C-R)	–	–	–	–	40.5	37.7	–
BNS/BZNS+ (C)	–	–	–	–	–	7.7	–
UDF/ ODS (R)	6.2	8.2	8.7				
				14.5	17.6	20.0	–
DSB (R)	–	–	–	–	–	23.5	–
Blue Coalition (R)	–	–	–	–	–	–	13.3
RZS (C-R)	–	–	–	–	–	–	20.0
MRF (C)	0.0	12.5	0.0	6.3	5.0	8.8	7.9
ATAKA (N)	–	–	–	–	–	4.8	14.3
GERB (R)	–	–	–	–	–	–	27.6
Parliament (total)	8.5	13.8	12.1	12.1	26.7	20.0	20.4
Government	*	6.7	5.6	17.6	11.8	16.7	23.5

Sources: Kostadinova (2003) and own calculations.
Notes: *Appointed, not elected government. L = Left, R = Right, C = Center, N= Nationalist.

harmonisation process, for example, national norms on gender equality and equal treatment were made congruent with EU norms (NSEGE 2009: 8). However, and despite the existence of legal rules on the equal treatment of men and women in various laws, the conditions that guarantee such equality are not yet present in every sphere of public life, and specific legislation for the achievement of gender equality is yet to be enacted (NSEGE 2009: 12). This is certainly still true in political parties, as there is little in the Party Law, Electoral Law, or the Constitution that pertains to women and gender balance *per se*. While clauses that could allow 'gendered' interpretation do exist, they are dubious at best. For example, the fairly limited barriers to formation – according to Bulgaria's Party Law, the initiative of fifty citizens with voting rights and a constituent meeting with 500 supporters is sufficient to establish a political party (Arts 10. 1, 12 and 13, Party Law 2009) – make it easy, on the one hand, for small parties, such as gender-based or minority parties to form. Yet on the other hand, the low formation costs make it easier for larger parties or parties with broader scope to exclude women and minorities, since the base needed to start and maintain a party is set low and can easily be fulfilled. Another such example is the provision encouraging political parties to create their own youth and women's organisations (Art. 20.2) – a right exercised by most Bulgarian political parties which, coupled with the low barriers to entry, can explain the short-lived PBW and the lack of other attempts to mobilise solely around women's representation since. Furthermore, Bulgarian political parties enjoy a substantial amount of public funding – each political party with more than 1 per cent of the popular electoral vote is entitled to state money (Art. 27.1). Such money is independent of the party's characteristics and the number of party members, the gender balance of the leadership body or its MPs, and in this way it may also disadvantage women.

The representation of women in Right and Left political parties compared

If the story of DRW from communist times to the present day remains one of declining numbers, one of the most interesting aspects of the Bulgarian case is the representation of women (both descriptive and substantive) in Right and Left parties, and their almost reversed positions when it comes to promoting women's interests compared to parties in the West. This paradox is related to the legacy of the communist past and the specific meaning of Right in the East European post-communist context, as well as the lack of real *conservatism*, as understood in the West.

If *conservatism* is generally understood to refer to the promotion of traditional values, roles and institutions, there is no conservatism in post-communist Bulgaria as yet. The meaning of Left and Right also differs from what these terms traditionally stand for in the West. Since the Left is represented by the former Communist Party, which has come to dominate almost exclusively the Left of the political spectrum (in Bulgaria and other East European countries), it stands for the status quo, ties with the old regime, and is perceived, at least initially, as anti-democratic. The Right, initially associated with the anti-communist opposition, which included parties and organisations from the entire political spectrum, stands for change, acceptance, tolerance and human rights, albeit also for *laissez-faire* economics, competition, less taxation and fewer benefits. Thus, in Bulgaria, as well as in other Eastern European countries, the political space (at least initially) is divided among communists and anti-communists (Enyedi 2006), which is a much more meaningful cleavage than the Left-Right division.

The notion of (gender) equality in Bulgaria is also burdened by the communist legacy (*see* discussion on womanism vs feminism below), as a result of which the Left (given the failure of the socialist emancipation project) is discredited as a promoter of parity, and the Right (associated with anti-communism and standing in opposition to communist-era policies) is seen as a more legitimate actor for equality. Given these specificities of the Bulgarian case, it is not surprising that it is Right and Centre-right parties that are more active in staging women, as we demonstrate here.

Table 5.2: Women's status in parliamentary political parties

Political Party	Political Orientation	Women's Organisation	Women in Parliament as of Feb 2013	Women-related Clauses in the Platform
GERB	Right	Yes	37/117	No
BSP	Left	Yes	8/40	No
UDF/Blue Coalition	Right	Yes		Yes
Agrarian Party (BAPU)/ Blue Coalition	Center-Right	Yes	1/14	Yes
DSB/Blue Coalition	Right	No		No
RZS	Center-Right	No	3/10	No
MRF	Center	Yes	4/35	No
ATAKA	Extreme Right	No	1/10	No

Source: Data collected by authors.

Before comparing Right and Left parties in terms of women's representation, we need to keep in mind that, despite the slightly better figures more recently in terms of the numbers of female legislators in parliament, women are still far from being equally represented (either in a descriptive or a substantive manner) at either end of the political spectrum. This is evident not only in the fact that Bulgaria has neither specific gender equality legislation, nor has it adopted gender quotas, be they on a national or an intra-party level, but also in the fact that there are very few parties with women-related clauses in their party programmes (*see* Table 5.2).

Although, as the data in Table 5.2 suggest, women's issues rarely figure on party platforms (and it is Centre and Right parties that do include such clauses in their platforms), a number of parties in the last parliament (2009–13) have women's organisations. The Union of Women Socialists for Parity and Solidarity of the Bulgarian Socialist Party (BSP) is among the most active among the party's women's organisations. The successor of the Communist Party's women's organisation, the Union holds regular meetings, issues a bulletin, takes positions on the party programme, and articulates women's interests. At the opposite end of the political spectrum, the 2009–13 ruling party *Grazhdani za evropeysko razvitie na Balgariya* (Citizens for European Development of Bulgaria, or GERB) is no less active in mobilising its female members. GERB-Women has a platform that promotes equality of opportunities, family values, civil rights, Europeanisation and prosperity. It holds regular forums that discuss women-related issues such as education, healthcare and employment. Furthermore, GERB's parliamentary group includes some proactive women such as Maria Gabriel, vice-president of the women's organisation of the European People's Party, and Tzveta Karayancheva, the only Bulgarian invited to the International Women's Summit 'Partnership for Change – Empowering Women', which took place in 2012 in Kosovo. Other

Centre and Right parties (the *Balgarski Zemedelski Naroden Sayuz* or Agrarian Party (BZNS), the ethnic Turkish Party Movement for Rights and Freedoms (MRF), and the UDF) also have women's organisations that mobilise women and promote women's issues. Hence, Right parties are just as likely to have proactive women organisations as Left parties, making it hard to argue for a link between the Left and greater substantive representation for women.

The DRW in Right and Left parties shows similar trends, as is further confirmed by an examination of electoral party lists: it is Centre and Right parties that include the largest number and percentage of women on their lists (Table 5.3), as well as the most women in the top five positions on the lists (Table 5.4). Furthermore, Centre and Right parties have more women in their leadership bodies, as the data in Table 5.5 show. This confirms that in Bulgaria, descriptive representation is no higher in Left parties than in Right parties.

The substantive representation of women in Bulgaria

The SRW under communism in Bulgaria was nominal and limited. While the share of women who participated in political life was large, those women had no substantive power. As indicated above, although the number of women in state legislatures was higher than in Western countries, women's political involvement in the Communist era gave them little or no actual voice in politics. Given the low social status of most female MPs, they were hardly viewed as capable of changing the political agenda and influencing political outcomes.[5] Ultimately, women's presence in political decision-making bodies did not result in significant action for women. Rather, the political agenda in communist countries was dictated by the overwhelmingly male party leadership. Women's issues were present on the agenda only when they were related to other higher priority goals. The generous welfare provisions for which communist regimes are known, for example, were guided primarily by pro-natalist policy, which tied a growing population to industrial growth and increased production.

The communist experience left a legacy of high-level, yet passive, political involvement by women. As Kostadinova points out, this has had a dubious effect on access to power in the post-communist period. While women became skilful and knowledgeable in the public arena, they have remained relatively passive with regard to competing for and winning public office (Kostadinova 2003: 318). Such passivity can be explained by an all-dominant state that encouraged, in fact commanded, political participation, yet choked and persecuted any independent initiative. The centralisation of the decision-making process under socialism was a strong mechanism for creating such passivity (Ilonszki and Kostova 2003: 670).

---

5. Many of the women in the Bulgarian National Assembly, for example, were weavers, seam-stresses, heroes of socialist labour, and women with low-status jobs. The fact that these women did not have the experience to be taken seriously in important decision making, was the reason they were chosen (Kostova 1998: 213).

Table 5.3: Women in electoral party lists for the 2005 parliamentary elections

Political Party	Total	Women	% Women
BSP/Coalition for Bulgaria (L)	458	100	22
NDSV (C)	408	106	26
Coalition of the Rose (L)	227	59	26
DSB (R)	413	130	31
ODS (R)	415	76	18
BNS (C)	437	104	24
New Time (C)	444	174	39
ATAKA (N)	252	42	17
MRF (C)	450	92	20
Total (all parties and all electoral districts)	6681	1784	27

Sources: Center of Women's Studies and Policies, 2005.
Notes: Only major political parties included in the list. The total includes all parties running in the elections.

Table 5.4: Number and per cent of women from 1st to 5th place in the electoral party lists of the major political parties

Position in the electoral party list	BSP (L)	NDSV (C-R)	ODS (R)	MRF (C)	DSB (R)	BNS/ BZNS + (C)	New Time (C)	Coalition of the Rose (L)
1st	2	8	3	4	6	4	7	4
	6.5%	25.8%	9.7%	12.9%	19.4%	12.9%	22.6%	12.9%
2nd	7	13	4	1	6	3	12	2
	22.6%	41.9%	12.9%	3.2%	19.4%	12.9%	38.7%	6.5%
3rd	10	11	4	7	7	5	10	2
	32.3%	35.5%	12.9%	22.6%	22.6%	16.1%	32.3%	6.5%
4th	8	12	4	5	15	5	9	8
	25.8%	38.7%	12.9%	16.1%	48.4%	16.1%	29.0%	25.8%
5th	5	14	6	5	6	8	8	13
	16.1%	45.2%	19.4%	16.1%	19.4%	25.8%	25.8%	41.9%
Total number of women	32	58	21	22	40	25	46	29
	20.6%	37.4%	13.5%	14.2%	25.8%	16.1%	29.7%	18.7%

Sources: Center of Women's Studies and Policies, 2005.
Notes: Data is up to 5th place for multimember districts for the parties which (according the opinion polls published in the media) were expected to pass the 4% threshold. L = Left, R = Right, C = Center.

Table 5.5: Women and men in party leadership bodies

Political Party	Leading body	Total	Women	Leader
BSP	Executive Bureau	15	2	male
NDSV	Political Council	25	7	male
PBW	n/a	n/a	n/a	female
MRF	Central Operations Bureau	15	3	male
ATAKA	n/a	n/a	n/a	male
UDF	National Executive Council	10	1	male
New Time	Executive Bureau	21	6	male
DSB	National Leadership	12	3	male
BZNS-People's Union	Permanent Presence	11	2	male

Sources: Center of Women's Studies and Policies, 2005.

Another legacy of communism is 'womanism', a term Harvey employs to contrast Western feminism and its Eastern European counterpart (Harvey 2002).[6] Originally applied to the unique experiences of black women facing racial discrimination, womanism, as Harvey suggests, can successfully travel as a concept to describe the distinct experience of East European women who viewed the state, and not men, as the source of oppression and who, similarly to women of colour, find white Western feminist rhetoric to be alien and irrelevant to their experiences and concerns. Womanism further challenges the feminist distinction between (male) public and (female) private. In a country where the public sphere was monopolised by the state, the private sphere provided freedom and independence. Hence, East European women viewed the family and the private sphere as a shelter from the all-intrusive state. Finally, womanism opposed communist women's organisations which it saw as yet another instrument of state oppression. Women's independent grassroots organisations never emerged (at least not on the scale witnessed in Western societies), as women activists were attracted and absorbed by dissident organisations. Indeed, women played a prominent part in dissident activity throughout the region.[7]

---

6. Womanism celebrates womanhood and the strength of women. It is a term coined by Alice Walker (1983) and is associated with the distinct experiences of African–American women and, more broadly, women of colour. Also known as black feminism, womanism rejects 'white' feminist thought which ignores and silences the voice of women of colour. For womanists, racial discrimination and exclusion poses a far greater problem than gender inequality. Thus, feminism, viewed as the voice of white women, speaks a language that is irrelevant to the women of colour, who see their men not as oppressors but fellow victims in a society dominated by the white race.

7. Notable example in the Bulgarian case is the 'Committee for the Defense of Ruse', a dissident organisation founded by mothers who opposed pollution from a Romanian factory across the Danube river.

The legacies of womanism and passivity were ultimately key in shaping the nature and degree of women's political participation in the post-communist context, and directly responsible for women's political involvement characterised by (1) an aversion to political mobilisation, (2) hostility towards a Western feminist agenda, and (3) negative attitudes towards affirmative action for women. The immediate result of this outlook was the abolition of gender quotas for state legislatures and a sharp drop in the numbers of female MPs.

Coupled with the decrease in the DRW in post-communist Bulgaria was a low level, or even an absence, of substantive representation. The transition context proved particularly harmful, as women's issues were submerged in the 'larger' issues of democracy and economic restructuring (Graham and Regulska 1997: 6). Accordingly, women's interests were bundled together with those of the unemployed or the pensioners, preventing once again the emergence of a distinct women's agenda. Hostility towards women's equality as a state project – which recalled memories from the communist past, as well as rejection of the Western feminist discourse seen as irrelevant to the East European context – further hindered substantive representation and the emergence of a genuine discussion and understanding of women's issues and interests.

Given such legacies, another characteristic of post-communist political life is the absence of strong women's parties.[8] In Bulgaria, the PBW has been one of the parties with the lowest registered performance, scoring a meagre 0.38 per cent in the 1997 election. The unique position that the party had in the 2001 election, when it became a partner of NDSV, allowed it to negotiate the nomination of many more female candidates (Kostadinova 2003: 311), resulting in NDSV having the highest percentage of women's representation in post-communist Bulgarian politics (*see* Table 5.1). But after failing to gather the necessary 7,000 signatures to register for the 2011 local elections, the PBW virtually disappeared.[9] Not characterising itself as feminist, and neither promoting nor drawing support from feminist groups (Kostadinova 2003: 310), the PBW is a clear example of the effect of the legacy of womanism. Its brief history further demonstrates that the increased number of women in politics does not necessarily lead to the articulation of women's interests and improved substantive representation.

Yet the numbers of women participating in politics should not be neglected, especially if we consider the status of those female leaders. Although women's parties have remained weak and underdeveloped, the number of women occupying executive positions in Eastern Europe, and in Bulgaria in particular, has risen dramatically in recent years. Forest (2011: 5) reports that there were 11 women of

---

8.   Women's parties were found in a few post-communist states, mostly within the Post-Soviet Republics (Krook and Rashkova 2006). Only three of these parties – the Shamiram Women's Party of Armenia, the Lithuanian Women's Party, and the Women of Russia – managed to enter national parliaments in the early and mid-1990s.

9.   'Партията на жените е аут от изборите' ('The Women's Party is out of the elections'), *Trud*, 11 August 2011.

ministerial rank and 27 women with the ranks of state secretary and deputy minister in the period 1989–99, while these numbers for the 1999–2009 period were 14 and 53, respectively. Female executives have further enjoyed greater access to 'big' ministries such as Economy, Finance and Defence, as well as to other high ranking political positions. Although efforts to feminise the executive have had populist undertones at times, particularly in Bulgaria's last government,[10] the increased prominence of female executives is undeniable. While the effect of such presence on women's substantive representation is yet to be seen, we argue that women occupying key executive positions constitute what we refer to as 'substantive presence': influential female politicians occupying key positions, which may contribute to an improved SRW in the future. Women's political presence is a necessary step towards the achievement of actual, and more voiced, representation of women, for example by providing for political discussions of women's issues (such as the attempt to start a women parliamentary lobby group).

Interviews with two influential female politicians, Anastasia Moser, a former leader of the Centre-right Agrarian Party, and Ekaterian Mihailova, formerly a co-chair and chair of the parliamentary group of the most right-wing political formation in Bulgaria – DSB – enable us to explore further questions of substantive representation. Our interviewees were chosen based on their political popularity and significant role in post-communist politics, their rightist political views, and of course their sex. While the accounts of the two women sometimes exhibit significant differences, both respondents suggest that the SRW in Bulgaria is still lacking. And unlike more developed countries, where feminist scholars would claim this turf for the Left, in Bulgaria, and perhaps in most former communist states, the parties on the Left are no more substantively representative of women than are parties on the Right. In fact, all female prime ministers and heads of state elected or designated in post-communist Eastern Europe have been recruited to the centre-right (Forest 2011: 19).

Our interviews indicate the presence of gender inequalities and discrimination both in politics and at a broader social level, as well as disagreement on the issue. While Moser argues that gender equality in Bulgaria exists only on paper and much remains to be done, Mihailova states that the question of gender equality is not salient in Bulgarian politics. 'To a large extent Bulgaria is blessed in this respect', she argues, continuing: 'this is one of the good things we inherited from socialism' (Mihailova 2012, interview). Yet, Mihailova notes that women are always expected to deliver more – give a bit more effort, have a bit more knowledge, be a bit more confident – in order to be given access to this traditionally male domain. She further acknowledges serious problems at a broader social level, such as pronounced discrimination in hiring practices and wages for women. Such practices, Mihailova argues, have led to the feminisation of some professions. Judges, for example, are primarily women because of the low pay.

---

10. In Bulgaria, feminisation has been used as an electoral strategy both by NDSV and GERB, in trying to overcome widespread corruption and meet European values (Forest 2011: 6).

These diverging opinions indicate a lack of shared awareness or consensus around gender inequalities. While some Bulgarian women notice discriminatory behaviour, others do not always identify it as such. Mihailova, for example, does not perceive of a different role for male and female politicians, but admits that women are subject to higher standards, and are also expected to be more moderate and tolerant. She is also a strong opponent of quotas, subscribing to the common negative view towards affirmative action for women. 'I believe that one should occupy a position not because of their gender but based on qualities'; 'I would be rather insulted to know that I've been elected to parliament only because I am a woman' (Mihailova 2012, interview). Ilonszki and Kostova find this view to be prevalent among Bulgarian female politicians (Ilonszki and Kostova 2003: 670), something that might illustrate the effect of past legacies.

A lack of awareness of gender inequality obviously makes it hard for women to organise and act to eradicate inequalities. Moser participated in one such initiative in the mid-1990s – an attempt to start a female lobby group within parliament. The initiative died at the outset, evidencing the low substantive representation. While women in post-communist politics have been much more influential than their communist predecessors, they rarely champion initiatives that promote women's interests. Hence, we can argue that substantive representation remains rather limited. Increasing awareness, therefore, is key and this is where Moser views her most significant contribution as a female politician. 'In Bulgarian society', she argues, 'such awareness is, at best, still very modest' (Moser 2012, interview).

Equality and awareness call for a broader change in mentality. Bulgaria possesses a very patriarchal culture, where 'women are still running around men, slaving, instead of establishing an equal partnership in marriage and in the family' (Moser 2012, interview), a trend also seen in the political sphere. One of the recurring factors that would lead to more gender equality is, in the view of Moser, a change in attitudes. While she recognises the importance of the law, she argues that respecting the law and having a consciousness sensitive to gender issues are more important in achieving equality. In contrast, Mihailova does not discuss the necessity of changing attitudes and perceptions, but views legal action and institutions as the driving force for addressing women's issues. Legislative and institutional instruments are, in her view, the important first step to addressing gender equality.

Recognising the legacies of passivity and womanism as the major obstacles to both descriptive and substantive representation, Moser repeatedly argues that women need to take action on their own. Mihailova's disapproval of gender quotas, in turn, recalls the negative attitudes towards affirmative action. Resonating with womanist essentialism, Mihailova ascribes inequalities in the political sphere to differences in gender behaviour. 'The feminist discourse', she further states, 'is very far from us' (Mihailova 2012, interview).

While Moser is hopeful that feminist organisations can overcome historical legacies, Mihailova does not expect the emergence of strong feminist organisations. This is in part because of the existence of women's organisations at party level. While DSB does not have a women's organisation (but offers training for female politicians), Mihailova views such organisations positively as they create an opportunity for cooperation with women's organisations in other European parties, and thus provide an extra channel for cooperation. Overall, she sees gender relations evolving in a positive direction.

On the question of how the role of women differs at each end of the political spectrum, we can say that there is no striking difference between the numbers of women on the Left and women on the Right (with the Right having slightly higher numbers in the last decade). Yet the latter have had a much more marked political path, and this is largely because they occupy much more influential posts. After leading the Agrarian Party for over a decade, Moser has now been succeeded by another woman, who defeated the male contender for leadership in the internal party election gaining 80 per cent of the vote. Many other political parties, especially other Centre and Right parties, have also included a number of female politicians in key posts. By comparison, no Left party has had a female leader to date (Moser 2012 interview). Women from the Right are also more likely to occupy more powerful positions while in parliament – they become members of the Foreign Affairs Committee or the Constitutional Changes Committee. Importantly, according to Mihailova, there is symbolic value across the board in promoting women to high posts, over and above the question of their numbers. On the parliamentary committees in which Mihailova takes part, women constitute at least one-third of the members. And she contends that in her party women have serious presence at both local and national levels. Similarly, Moser argues that the percentage of women in politics, and in high-level positions in general, shows how democratic and advanced a country is. While this share has increased in Bulgaria, it is still quite low.

Conclusion

This chapter has examined the representation of women in a post-communist society, offering unique insights about the well-established, but recently increasingly challenged, link between Left political parties and the fight for gender equality. As the introductory chapter to this volume argues, it is time that gender and politics scholars start examining how women act for women across the political spectrum. In this context, Eastern European countries, and in our particular case Bulgaria, offer an untapped opportunity for extending gender and politics research on DRW and SRW and the relationship between the two. As a post-communist country where 'conservatism' and 'gender equality' are still terms in the making, Bulgaria exhibits a trend – perhaps one unexpected by Western scholars – in which the number of conservative women is on a par, if not greater, than that of socialist women. Furthermore, our study shows that these women have made and are making a greater mark on the country's daily politics than many women of the Left under communism, where the higher level of descriptive representation was ultimately 'symbolic' or tokenistic. We also see that parties on the Right include more women in their governing bodies and place women on more electable positions on their party lists than do their counterparts on the Left.

These characteristics of women's representation in Bulgaria prompt our claim that the link between stronger and perhaps better women's representation and the parties of the Left is not sustainable, at least in the post-communist cases. Not only is the term *equality* taken to mean something negative and linked to the past, due to the legacies of communism, but women of the Left, as our study shows, have carried on to a great extent the role they had in the past, which was more often than not associated with taking on lower positions, positions with less authority and prestige than those of their male counterparts. Women on the Right have, on the contrary, been involved with influential politics. And while we find that most of these women's political actions have not favoured women *per se*, thus emphasising the lack of fulsome SRW in Bulgaria at the moment, we argue that what we are currently observing is *substantive presence* of women, a necessary condition, in our opinion, for changing social attitudes, acceptance, and awareness of (in)equality.

Acknowledgements

We would like to gratefully acknowledge the support of the European Research Council (ERC starting grant 205660) in the preparation of this chapter, and the help of Desislava Pavlova with data gathering.

List of interviews

Mihailova, Ekaterina (2012) Sofia.
Moser, Anastasia (2012), Washington, D.C. (conducted over Skype).

References

Anderson, L. S. (2006) 'European Union gender regulations in the East: the Czech and Polish accession process', *East European Politics and Societies*, 20 (1): 101–25.

Delinesheva, M. and Kmetova, T. (2005) *The Corridors of Power: Women and Men in Governance*, Gender Equality Monitoring Agency Series, Sofia: Center of Women's Studies and Policies.

Enyedi, Z. (2006) 'Party politics in post-communist transition', in Katz, R. and Crotty, W. (eds), *Handbook of Party Politics*, London: Sage Publications, pp. 228–38.

Fodor, E. (2004) 'The state socialist emancipation project: gender inequality in workplace authority in Hungary and Austria', *Journal of Women in Culture and Society*, 29 (3): 783–813.

Forest, M. (2011) 'From state-socialism to EU accession: contrasting the gendering of (executive) political power in Central Europe', paper presented at the Second ECPR Conference, Budapest, 12–15 January.

Graham, A. and Regulska, J. (1997) 'Where political meets women: creating local political space', *Anthropology of East Europe Review*, 15 (1): 4–12.

Harvey, J. (2002) 'Re-theorizing emancipation: remembering 'gender equality' in Eastern European womanist thought', *Anthropology of East Europe Review*, 20 (1): 27–39.

Ilonszki, G. and Kostova, D. (2003) 'Warum weniger fraunspolitisch mehr sein kann. Parlamentarische Representation von Frauen in Bulgarien un Ungarn', *Osteuropa*, 2003/5, 661–74.

Jones, M. (1998) 'Gender quotas, electoral laws, and the election of women: lessons from the Argentine provinces', *Comparative Political Studies*, 31 (1): 3–21.

Kostadinova, T. (2003) 'Women's legislative representation in post-communist Bulgaria' in Matland, R. E. and Montgomery, K. A. (eds), *Women's Access to Political Power in Post-Communist Europe*, New York: Oxford University Press, pp. 304–20.

Kostova, D. (1998) 'Women in Bulgaria: changes in employment and political involvement', in Jaquette, J. S. and Wolchik, S. L. (eds), *Women and Democracy: Latin America and Central and Eastern Europe*, Baltimore: Johns Hopkins University Press, pp. 203–21.

Krook, M. L. and Rashkova, E. (2006) 'The emergence and impact of women's parties: a comparative analysis of Western and Eastern Europe', unpublished manuscript.

Linkova, M. (2007) 'Moving target: gender equality in science in enlarged Europe', *Kontext: časopis pro gender a vědění*, 1: 2–11.

NSEGE (2009) National Strategy for the Encouragement of Gender Equality for the Period 2009–2015, Sofia: Ministry of Labour and Social Policy, available at: www.mlsp.government.bg/equal/normativ.asp (in Bulgarian; last accessed 19 March 2012).

Phillips, A. (1995) *The Politics of Presence*, Oxford: Clarendon Press.

Popa, R. M. (2003) 'The socialist project for gender (in)equality: a critical discussion', *Journal for the Study of Religions and Ideologies*, 6 (Winter): 49–72.

Walker, A. (1983) *In Search of Our Mother's Garden: Womanist Prose*, San Diego, CA: Harcourt.

Chapter Six

Motherhood, Representation and Politics: Conservative Women's Groups Negotiate Ideology and Strategy

Ronnee Schreiber

Introduction

In August 2008, John McCain surprised the United States by nominating Alaska Governor, Sarah Palin to be his running mate in the presidential elections. The press, along with interest groups, activists and the general public were quick to comment. Opponents of Palin considered her to be too inexperienced, right wing and unpredictable for the nation's second highest office. Supporters praised her 'maverick' sensibilities, forthrightness and outside-the-Beltway mentality. Shaping many of these conversations was one important fact – that Palin is the mother of five children. From August until Election Day in November, references to her gender and maternal status influenced the campaign and generated public discussions about whether or not mothers of young children should seek elective office (Gibson and Heyse 2010). Discussions of mothers in politics made their reappearance in 2010, when Palin herself invoked her maternal identity to promote other conservative women running for office. She warned that 'Mama Grizzlies', i.e. mothers active in politics, were 'banding together, rising up, saying, "No – this isn't right for our kids and for our grand-kids. And we're gonna do something about this"'.[1] Fast forward to 5 June 2011, when another conservative mother of five, Congresswoman Michele Bachmann (R-MN), announced her intention to run for President of the United States. As with Palin, Bachmann's bid for office generated debate about gender roles and the place of mothers in politics. Given that both women were running in high-profile races, these cases provide excellent lenses through which public deliberations about gender roles, motherhood, conservatism and representation can be examined.[2]

---

1. Palin's ad can be viewed at http://www.youtube.com/watch?v=fsUVL6ciK-c (accessed 5 May 2014).

2. The introduction and sections of the data analysis published here also appear in 'Gender roles, motherhood and electoral politics: conservative women's organisations frame Palin and Bachmann', forthcoming in *Journal of Women, Politics and Policy*.

During the 2008 elections, some criticised McCain and the Republican Party for advancing a candidate who seemed to contradict the central tenets of social conservatism. Social conservatives represent an important base of support for the Republican Party (Green *et al.* 2004). Premised on theological beliefs about the need for male leadership in (heterosexual) families and gendered values about the primacy of women as caretakers, social conservatives generally believe that women should prioritise their roles as mothers when their children are young (*see* e.g. Schlessinger 2008; LaHaye and Crouse 2001; Lewis and Yoest 1996). Republicans are also less likely than Democrats to support a woman, especially the mother of young children, running for office (Stalsburg 2010; Sanbonmatsu and Dolan 2009; Pew Research Center 2008). Relatedly, scholars have found an inverse correlation between the numbers of social conservatives in a state and the number of women who serve in their respective state offices (Merolla *et al.* 2007). Republican voters also shy away from Republican women candidates because they perceive them as being too liberal (Falk and Kenski 2006; King and Matland 2003). Even economic conservatives, who do not tend to espouse traditional views about gender roles, have argued that due to gender differences, women are better suited than men to be primary caretakers and have advocated for policies that reflect this sentiment (Schreiber 2012a).

Despite these prevailing gender role norms, women have a long history of political participation in conservative movement politics. Conservative women's activism has included organising national opposition to constitutional amendments (e.g. the Equal Rights Amendment and the Women's Suffrage Amendment) and challenging laws in favour of legal abortion, same-sex marriage and government-funded family leave (Schreiber 2012a; Rymph 2006; Hardisty 1999; Marshall 1997; Klatch 1987; Mansbridge 1986). They also founded political action committees and organisations that raise money and train women to run for office.[3] Throughout many of these efforts, conservative women have argued that their status, or potential status, as mothers means that women can offer different, but valuable, insights in the political realm as compared to their male counterparts. When presented with a choice, for example, Republican voters prefer candidates who are mothers to childless women (Stalsburg 2010).

Historically, then, conservatives have grappled with a conflict between ideology and political realities when it comes to women's roles in the public sphere, including the realm of professional politics. This is becoming increasingly the case. Wilcox notes that even male-led socially conservative groups have shifted their rhetoric about traditional gender roles due to social and economic changes (Wilcox 2004). Women, including those with young children, are entering the workforce in record numbers.[4] And, more importantly for this study, Republican women are running in growing numbers for elective office and thus need support

---

3.   For example, the Susan B. Anthony List supports pro-life women candidates.

4.   *See* 'Labor force participation rate of mothers 1975–2007' (2011) US Bureau of Labor Statistics, available at http://data.bls.gov (accessed 5 May 2014).

from conservative voters and party leaders.[5] Republicans are also well aware that a gender gap in favour of Democrats means that they must target women voters and encourage women's political activism. George W. Bush's 'W. Stands for Women' campaign in 2004 featured Republican women leaders touring the country in an effort to mobilise women to vote for him,[6] and more recently, conservative women's organisations have organised against the Left's 'War on Women' campaign.[7] Indeed, one conservative woman leader assessed the candidacies of Palin and Bachmann through the lens of Republican motherhood, and articulated a reconceptualisation of mothers' political roles:

> Traditional republican motherhood – in which women served on the sidelines as political and moral compasses for men – is clearly obsolete. Today, instead, we see a new kind of republican motherhood emerging. And in the year of the big-R Republican woman, Michele Bachmann just might be its matriarch … The goals of modern republican mothers are broadly similar to those of the original ones: to foster a relationship between citizen and state in which the citizen is sovereign over government. But whereas the republican mother of our Founding era participated in politics only indirectly, the new republican mother plays a decidedly active role in our public life. Gender has been not overcome, but integrated (Schaeffer 2011).

Given the conflict between conservative views about gender roles and motherhood with economic and political shifts and realities, this chapter analyses how national organisations that claim to represent conservative women, framed Palin's and Bachmann's bids for office. Specifically, I show how they make gendered claims about women's interests to negotiate their ideological beliefs about traditional familial roles with their interest in promoting women in politics. In addition, I explore how well these claims fit with conservative ideology and what these cases can tell us about gender, representation and conservative politics more broadly.

How these representatives of conservative women talk about Palin and Bachmann coincides with Type II claims as defined by Celis and Childs in this book's Introduction. That is, their claims are gendered, but not feminist. For example, although feminists argue that gender roles are socially constructed, conservatives consider them to be naturally derived. Feminists have also argued that public and private spheres are mutually constitutive, meaning, for example, that public policies and values affect who we expect to care for children within the family (Okin 1998). Conservatives generally urge political leaders to think of the family in private terms and allow members within it to make decisions without government 'interference', as long as the couple leading the family is married and

---

5. *See* http://www.cawp.rutgers.edu (accessed 5 May 2014) for complete data on women running for office.

6. *See* http://www.gwu.edu/~action/2004/bush/bushorgwomen.html for more information (accessed 5 May 2014).

7. *See* for example, http://www.cblpi.org/resources/article.cfm?id=221 (accessed 5 May 2014).

heterosexual.[8] To this end, conservative women activists seek to mobilise women to support policies like tax cuts for businesses that offer flexi-time (Schreiber 2012a). How the organisations under study frame Palin's and Bachmann's bids for office corresponds well with conservative views about motherhood, suggesting a quality of fit between the organisations under study and the women they claim to represent.

However, because there are social and political shifts that conservatives must address, and because interest groups seek to attract and mobilise new members or adherents, the correlation between claims and quality of fit must also be understood in this context. That is, in evaluating how well the conservative women's groups under study represent conservative women, we need to take into account the myriad goals of representational actors. In this case, conservative women's groups frame issues in ways that reflect the conservatism of their base, thus suggesting congruency. But since they also aim to negotiate among the tensions within conservatism articulated earlier, as well as appeal to women who may not explicitly identify as conservative, their interest articulation also can be regarded as pushing ideological boundaries. This 'stretching' of meanings about motherhood and politics enables political actors to mobilise potential adherents and expand their scope of influence (Lombardo *et al.* 2009).

Data, methods and definitions

Inductive qualitative data analysis (Thomas 2006) is employed to evaluate how conservative women's organisations framed Palin's and Bachmann's roles as women and mothers running for office. Groups under study are Concerned Women for America (CWA), Independent Women's Forum (IWF), Eagle Forum (EF), Network of enlightened Women (NeW), Clare Booth Luce Policy Institute (CBLPI) and Smart Girl Politics (SGP) (*see* Appendix for more information about these groups). These organisations all claim to represent women, are national in scope, and are central to the burgeoning conservative women's movement taking hold in the United States (Schreiber 2010a). Since these advocates see it as their mission to speak as and for conservative women, they can be considered representatives of women's interests, thus demonstrating that representational politics is not a process limited to the interaction between elected officials and their constituencies. In addition, the media take them seriously as representatives of women, meaning that how they frame mothers' interests becomes part of the public dialogue (Schreiber 2010b; Spindel 2003; Flanders 1996).

Data for this study come from statements made about Palin and Bachmann by these conservative women's organisations. The time span for these data is between

8. I do not mean to diminish the consequences of conservative anti-gay activism, and I recognise that conservative rhetoric about the relationship between the public and private is inconsistent with some conservative movement policy goals. This study, however, is concerned with mothers' roles *vis-à-vis* other members of their families and within the workplace, and when talking about these mothers, conservative women's organisations assume they are heterosexual.

August 2008 and January 2011 for Palin (these dates reflect the time between the announcement of Palin's candidacy to three months after the 2010 elections where she engaged in high-profile campaigning for other candidates) and June 2011 to January 2012 for Bachmann (these dates reflect the time period for which she was a candidate in the Republican primaries for US President). On the organisations' websites, separate searches for 'Palin', 'Bachmann', 'mother' and 'motherhood' (many of the documents contain two of these terms) were undertaken. In addition, within the time frames noted, major newspapers and magazines were searched via Lexis/Nexis by entering each organisation's name coupled with the phrase 'Palin' or 'Bachmann' to gather any articles or editorials in which organisational leaders were quoted on the topic. Finally, two organisations – IWF and CBLPI – send me regular newsletters and fundraising appeals and these documents were also analysed.[9] Overall, 142 documents were analysed – 79 from the organisations' websites and 63 from news sources (articles and/or editorials in newspapers or online news sites and magazines). Since Palin was on the national agenda longer than Bachmann, and her general election run for vice president was the first by a Republican woman, there are more stories and analyses of her by conservative women's organisations (eighty-eight for Palin versus fifty-four for Bachmann, some of which also contained discussions about Palin). To determine the frames most often invoked by these organisations, the 142 documents were read and the overall themes used to talk about these political actors were recorded. From this list of general themes, those employed when the organisations talk about Palin, Bachmann, gender roles and motherhood were re-analysed and a major frame – 'supermom' – was found. Comprising this major frame are two sub-frames: 'conservatism' and 'femininity'. Both the major frame and sub-frames conform tightly with Type II claims.

For the purposes of this study, 'Republican' and 'conservative' are conflated because the Republican Party platform promotes both traditional gender roles and the call for women to engage politically. The word 'conservative' is used in both its social and economic contexts. Social conservatives in the US are usually Protestant evangelicals who lobby for policies that prohibit abortion, same-sex marriage and pornography, but promote prayer in public schools and a strong and well-funded US military. Economic conservatives favour free-market capitalism, less regulation on businesses and low taxes. Their tendency toward libertarianism means that they generally shy away from supporting laws that ban abortion or same-sex marriage. The term 'traditional' is used to refer to the belief that families should consist of heterosexual married couples where men are the primary wage-earners and women are the primary caretakers of their children and household functions. Finally, the use of the term 'feminism' reflects how conservative women activists conceptualise it. Generally, when these leaders talk about the feminist movement they are mostly referring to nationally organised interests, like the

---

9. CBLPI sends its members the *Luce Ladder* – a biannual glossy newsletter that averages twelve pages per issue.

National Organization for Women (NOW) and/or well-known individual feminist leaders and scholars. Generally, these organisations and actors support women's equal rights under the law and/or believe that women's oppression relative to men is the result of discrimination. In addition, they argue that women's status is predominantly shaped by processes of institutional and structural inequality, not individual actions or circumstances. Like their conservative counterparts under study here, these groups are 'mainstream', in that they work directly with government institutions and political actors.

Organisational framing strategies

Frames are organisational resources that provide diagnoses of problems in need of alteration and help elicit rationales to encourage people to engage in corrective actions; they are shaped by the political goals and intentions of the actors (Lombardo *et al.* 2009; Stone 2002; Tarrow 1992; Snow *et al.* 1986). As such, frames are specific constructions that 'give meaning to reality' and shape how it is understood (Verloo 2005: 20). Frames can act as resources for organisations and leaders, and enable them to both make direct representational claims and appeal to a wider, and perhaps untapped, group of adherents. This discourse has practical implications in terms of policy outcomes as well, since some version of these debates will be translated into public policy and social practice (Verloo *et al.* 2009; Ferree and Mueller 2004; Stone 2002).

Organisational frames are rarely static, since activists need to adapt to changing political, social and economic contexts. Indeed, many concepts, like motherhood, are contested, and are in part constructed to account strategically for shifting conditions (Lombardo *et al.* 2009). To align with, and account for, changes, activists may engage in 'stretching' the meaning of a concept to extend its relevance to potentially new adherents or a different audience. Building on theories of 'frame extension' (Snow *et al.* 1986), Lombardo *et al.* show how ideas about gender both factor into, and are shaped by, frame stretching (2009). In the cases under study here, women unaffiliated with conservative groups may not be compelled by traditional conservative conceptualisations of maternal obligations and gender roles, but might be interested in other gendered claims that are not explicitly feminist. Thus, conservative women's organisations might benefit from stretching and thus aligning their motherhood frames to reflect a wider range of opinions about gender roles and motherhood. This adaptation is essential for conservatives if they want to recognise social and economic changes, appeal to more women, and increase the number of Republican women in elected office. In so doing, they also influence how policymakers and the public understand motherhood and politics.

Framing is strategic, but advocates' discourse is not necessarily devoid of the central ideas and values they hold dear (Lombardo *et al.* 2009). Such a shallow strategy could backfire, as the organisations would be failing to promote their goals and/or be accused of selling out. They might also lose members if, as representatives, they do not articulate ideas that fit with members' beliefs (Snow *et al.* 1986). The challenge for the women's organisations under study is deciding how to frame motherhood in ways that attend to cultural and political factors that contradict some central tenets of conservatism (especially social conservatism), but do not alienate their adherents. These groups must continue to appeal to, and represent, their bases, and also demonstrate that they have ideological commitments worthy of the attention of potential members. Thus, the frames that are likely to be successful are those that can both resonate with adherents, and also speak to new groups of people. This process has its limits – the frames put forth by these organisations can be constraining and offer a version of conservative motherhood that still gives a nod to traditional understandings of femininity and gender roles. As conservative women's organisations make representational claims about women's interests and participate in public debates about gender and politics, their messages shape cultural norms about what it means to be a mother and influence women's roles in politics more broadly. Organisational rhetoric also produces a new set of conservative views about motherhood that suggest conservative movement actors are adjusting their strategies to adapt to the changing expectations of conservative women in politics as well as influencing public debates about mothers in politics. Thus, they challenge feminist conceptualisations of women's interests and exemplify the importance of having conservative women participate in politics in articulating Type II claims.

Conservative women frame Sarah Palin and Michele Bachmann

The major frame articulated by these conservative women's organisations is 'supermom'. Grouped under the 'supermom' frame are two sub-frames that ultimately qualify which mothers would make suitable national leaders according to these organisations: 'conservativism' and 'femininity' (*see* Verloo 2005 for a discussion of major frames and sub-frames). Thus, not only are Palin and Bachmann 'supermoms', but they also are decidedly conservative and feminine, hence rendering them *conservative* supermoms. As already noted, in the past, conservative women have chastised feminists for allegedly promoting the notion that women 'can have it all'. That is, they have challenged the notion that women can and should seamlessly balance raising children, holding a job in the paid workforce, and enjoying intimate relationships with their partners. In other words, they criticised the idea of the supermom. Nonetheless, in talking about Palin and Bachmann, conservative women applaud them for finding ways to fit it all in, indicating a shift from their previous rhetoric. Palin, for example, is praised for providing 'a model for how some women can manage motherhood and a professional career' (Easton 2008b) and for appealing 'to women who want to "have it all" – including staying happily married to the love of their youth … and bearing his children' (Crouse 2009). And, she is revered because '[s]he's a woman who believes that it's possible for a woman – and a mother of five children at that – to hold down a full-time CEO job overseeing a multi-billion-dollar budget' (Allen 2008). Extending this beyond Palin, Crouse also praises Bachmann and 'numerous other outstanding female leaders' for having found ways to 'do it all' (Crouse 2011).

These 'supermom' accolades do come with the need to meet important conditions. Palin and Bachmann are heralded as such because they abide by personal and political beliefs that are central to social and economic conservativism, thus casting them as '*conservative* supermoms'. First, they allegedly yield to their families, especially their husbands. Many social conservatives promote a traditional version of family life in which heterosexual families are led by men. This does not mean that women have no say, or that couples do not negotiate with one another. However, scholars have shown that conservative evangelicals, who are so important to the Republican Party, still claim adherence to the idea of male spiritual authority within the family unit (Gallagher and Smith 1999). Palin purportedly follows these values and 'has a family willing to work together' (Crouse 2008). In addition, according to conservative women, Palin's strength comes from her recognising that she 'doesn't need feminist approval for her lifestyle; the only person whose OK she needs for her double career as mother and politician is her husband's; and he seems very happy with Sarah' (Schlafly 2008).

For Bachmann's part, her public admission that she adheres to 'Biblical submission' helps solidify her social conservative credentials. The meaning of submission in this context is not necessarily clear-cut, even among the women who observe it (Snyder-Hall 2008; Griffith 1997). Generally, it stems from abiding by a biblical passage that says: 'Wives, submit yourselves unto your own husbands, as unto the Lord' (Ephesians 5:22).[10] Bachmann's acknowledgement that she believes in submission generated public debate and scrutiny. It also forced conservative women to offer an explanation that would satisfy concerns that Bachmann could be independent and lead a nation. Responding in the *Washington Post* to criticism that Bachmann's decision making would be unduly influenced by her husband, CWA's Crouse argued:

> Michele Bachmann, who has served notably as a United States congresswoman and is currently a presidential candidate, is now under scrutiny regarding how she could, as a Christian president, balance submission and leadership. In the context of women in leadership, it is important to note that biblical submission is about harmony and well-being within the home and the relationship between a husband and a wife; it has nothing to do with leadership responsibilities, except that no one – even the president of the United States – should treat others with disrespect, expect a subservient spirit from anyone or demand total surrender of another person's will. Thus, a woman who willingly submits to her husband – and enjoys his equal submission, nurturing and cherishing – does not have a similar relationship with the men at work. Some women in the workplace are the boss, the leader, the one in charge; other women are in

---

10. Ephesians 5:25 also says, 'Husbands, love your wives, even as Christ also loved the church, and gave himself for it'.

subordinate positions, working under the direction of someone else. In any work situation, a Christian woman (or man) should be considerate of others and not treat others in a disparaging or demeaning manner. A Christian woman or man in leadership must lead and fulfill the responsibilities for which they are accountable both to God and to those whom they are serving in a leadership capacity (Crouse 2011).

And although IWF members do not tend to be social conservatives, one of its leaders suggested that challenges to Bachmann's religious beliefs were essentially sexist:

I don't know the extent to which similar counsel is given to men in the Bible, but I know that modern Christian thinkers would encourage men to also sacrifice their personal desires for the good of the family, and to consider the needs of their wives. The language may be different, but the core understanding is that a functioning marriage and family requires putting the unit before individual desires. Obviously, there is more tension in how these power relationships are discussed when it's the woman, rather than the man, who is the politically powerful figure (Lukas 2011).

In addition to exemplifying socially conservative values about gender roles, Palin and Bachmann are also pro-life. Opposition to abortion is central to the agenda of some conservatives and many of them believed that McCain was not aggressive enough in promoting anti-abortion policies. Given that some Republican voters think Republican women are more liberal, especially with regard to abortion policies (Sanbonmatsu and Dolan 2009), highlighting Palin's and Bachmann's outspoken pro-life views help quell that concern. Palin's decision to bear a child with Down's syndrome meant that she received the blessing of social conservatives. Her son Trig symbolises her commitment to motherhood and to her working to oppose the legality of abortion, as noted by CWA:

The Palins' decision to have Trig, their 5th child and a Down Syndrome baby, is indicative of the pro-life and pro-family values that make the Palin family so distinctive and rile the left to such hatred (Crouse 2009).

Bachmann received similar accolades when Schlafly endorsed her for President:

Most important, Michele has the courage to be a leader among her peers … [s]he is a real champion in speaking up for values we care about. Michele is a woman of faith and the mother of a beautiful family. She has a 100 per cent pro-life record and is a strong supporter of traditional marriage (Quoted in Shear 2011).

In addition to praising them for their abortion positions, conservative women's organisations extolled Palin and Bachmann for bolstering the conservative economic policies of the Republican Party:

After decades of being tarred as sexists, conservatives and the GOP [Grand Old Party] base are understandably proud to have women making their case in support of limited government and free markets. These women obviously do appeal to an audience – particularly fellow women – that has often tuned out similar messages when voiced by the standard white male conservatives (Lukas 2011).

Further qualifying the supermom is the sub-frame of 'femininity'. Palin is deemed to be full of 'grace' and someone who exudes 'femininity'. Michelle Easton, President of CBLPI, tells us that Palin 'holds her baby onstage because she wants to publicly embrace being a woman in all its facets' (Easton 2008a). Palin's nod to motherhood, coupled with her endorsing conservative policy goals, 'proves', according to IWF, 'that you don't have to hold the political viewpoints and cultural prejudices of the Left to succeed as a woman. And [Palin] does it all with grace and charm' (IWF fundraising letter dated 4 December 2008; emphasis in original). In an interview with the *Washington Post*, IWF President Michelle Bernard summed it up this way: '[s]he is feminine and she is fashionable and that is okay now' (Romano 2008). In these ways, 'femininity' references both how Palin looks (she wears make-up and skirts), and her personal convictions (she emphasises the centrality of her husband and children in her life), and thus factors into what type of supermom is legitimate. Bachmann generated similar reactions from conservative women. In an interview discussing the potential effects of Bachmann's 'feminine' dress and appearance, CBLPI's Cordova told a CNN reporter that: 'I actually think it's really great. I think that you can embrace your femininity in the way that you look and still be a smart, intelligent woman' (CNN 2011).

In addition to their styles and personae, Palin and Bachmann are also consistently praised for seeking office for the right reasons: that is, not to gain power or authority, but to help people. Here conservative women offer a 'feminised' account of their quest for national office, and one that is more consistent with how we understand traditional notions of mothering and gender roles, thus reinforcing the Type II nature of their claims. To this end, Karen Agness, founder of NeW, a conservative organisation for college women, praised Palin's life choices and goals:

Palin chose to marry her high school sweetheart, stating proudly during her acceptance speech, 'We met in high school, and two decades and five children later he's still my guy'. She chose to have children. And she chose to focus her time on raising her children, pursuing public office not to climb the political ladder, but to make her community better for her children. During her acceptance speech she said, 'I was just your average hockey mom, and signed up for the PTA [Parent–Teacher Association] because I wanted to make my kids' public education better. When I ran for city council, I didn't need focus groups and voter profiles because I knew those voters, and knew their families, too' (Agness 2008).

Bachmann was also touted as a role model due to her 'feminine' leadership goals. CBLPI's Cordova told a reporter that Bachmann '[s]tands up for her beliefs. It's not about power or title. People call her crazy for speaking up, but younger conservative women really look up to her' (quoted in Rosenblum 2009).

In framing Palin and Bachmann as feminine leaders, conservative women offer a new ideal for young women and a way for conservatives to both fit with their conservative base, and also reach out and mobilise a fresh group of potential adherents. Another statement by NeW's Agness affirmed the relative value of such a strategy:

> NeW's success is a product of college women rebelling against the feminist message that dominates campus and trying proactively to find ways to increase their level of happiness. Young women are seeking a new message – one that embraces femininity, acknowledges that there are sex differences and values the role of women as mothers and in the workplace (Agness 2008).

Emphasising femininity while encouraging women's desires for professional satisfaction helps to stretch the meaning of conservative gender roles and enables these advocates to speak to young women entering the workforce and to those eager to run for elective office. Given that in 2010, the majority of 20–24-year-olds with college degrees in the paid labour force were women, this is particularly salient.[11]

Complementing the femininity sub-frame is discourse that celebrates women's toughness. On Palin, CWA's Crouse argued that '[s]he is not the kind of person who gives in to bullies, but she is the kind of mother who protects her children– something that those who hate her don't seem to understand' (2009). CBLPI's Camille Hart commented that '[e]ven in the face of vicious personal attacks, Palin responds with a cheerful toughness and refuses to play the victim' (Hart 2009). Teri Christoph, of SGP, said of Bachmann and her conservative counterparts: 'You have to have a very strong backbone in being a conservative woman running for office' (quoted in McVeigh 2012). Bachmann is also described by one CWA supporter as having 'the strength and tenacity to do what's necessary to lead this nation' (Targeted News Service 2011). Coupling femininity with traditional conceptualisations of masculinity suggests that Palin and Bachmann can be 'ladies', but also be counted on to run a country. Such complex descriptions are necessary for most women who run for higher office, regardless of their partisan affiliations. People expect, and prefer, women to be communal, warm and kind, while they expect men to be agentic, aggressive and self-directed. The latter set of characteristics also coincides with traits the public expects national leaders to exhibit (Eagly 2007). This places women at a disadvantage and causes them to experience a double bind (Carroll 2009; Eagly 2007; Jamieson 1995). Descriptions

---

11. *See* 'Gender and college recruiting', April 2011. The full report can be found at http://www.naceweb.org/gender/ (accessed 5 May 2014).

of Palin and Bachmann as being both feminine and tough help to navigate between these cultural demands as well as keep them in line with conservative views about gender roles and differences. Palin's 'Mama Grizzly' image precisely captures this tension and attempts to reconcile it. In her advertising, Palin offers this sentiment: 'You thought pit bulls were tough. Well, you don't want to mess with the mama grizzlies'.

The 'femininity' sub-frame not only makes these candidates more appealing to conservative men and women because they allegedly conform to gender role norms, it is also used to distinguish Palin and Bachmann from feminists on ideological grounds. Given that Republican voters shy away from supporting Republican women because they assume they are more liberal (King and Matland 2003), positioning them in opposition to feminists could help counteract that effect. For example, CBLPI's Easton praised Palin because she 'exudes a "can do" optimism without the usual feminist "it's tough to be a woman leader" bitterness' (Easton 2008a). CWA's Crouse employed strong anti-feminist language to celebrate Palin's femininity:

> Palin illustrates that a woman can be feminine while being a strong, smart leader. Sarah Palin's feminine appearance, charm, and rhetoric transformed the dowdy image of female leadership à la Betty Friedan, Bella Abzug, Madeline Albright, or Janet Reno. With her casual and humorous approach to public speaking and her down-home expressions, she made harsh feminist diatribes seem empty, meaningless, out-of-touch and out-of-date. Her savvy, confident demeanor reflects her sense of self as a wife, mother and accomplished career woman. Like Margaret Thatcher, Palin's soft exterior is a stark contrast to her tough inner strength. Unlike Nancy Pelosi's surgically induced gash of a smile, which is hard to endure, Palin simply lights up the room when she enters it (Crouse 2009).

Conservative women argue that Palin's nomination and Bachmann's bid for President represent what feminists have long worked for – women's entrance into higher levels of public office. But they also contend that feminists' disapproval of Palin and Bachmann reveals flaws in feminist ideology and the movement itself. That is, feminists should have endorsed Palin and Bachmann if they really cared about moving more women into positions of institutional power. That they chose not to support them reveals, according to these advocates, that feminists are self-serving and hypocritical (Schreiber 2012b). Since conservative women activists vie with feminists over the right to represent women and interpret women's interests, these debates also further conservative women's goal of denouncing their political opponents and laying claim to their right to speak on behalf of women. For example, NeW's Agness chastised the feminist National Organization for Women (NOW) for not supporting Palin:

NOW is not a broad-based movement representing all women. While NOW argues in abstract terms of choice, there is only one correct choice for NOW. They promote empowerment, but only if that power is used to push their agenda. NOW may disagree with Palin on some of the issues. Vigorous debate is valuable in American society. Yet, it is improper, unnecessary and discrediting for NOW to completely disown Palin. She is, after all, a living example of what second wave feminists claimed to be about: empowering women to make choices and giving them the opportunity to do so. NOW, women and all Americans should celebrate Palin for the woman she is and the possibilities she symbolises for women. She is truly a liberated woman (Agness 2008).

Here, the 'truly liberated woman' is re-imagined in the form of Sarah Palin. Invoking 'femininity' to describe her and Bachmann captures the desire of conservative women's organisations to re-inscribe traditional gender roles, while supporting the 'liberated' women who disrupt them as supermoms.

Conclusions

This chapter has provided new insights into how conservative women's organisations that claim to represent women navigate among views about gender roles, motherhood, ideology and politics. Through it, we have gained a more nuanced and richer understanding of representation, conservative movement politics and women's political participation. Palin's and Bachmann's willingness to challenge conservative gender role norms is framed as acceptable because these norms correspond with a concept of motherhood that is otherwise consistent with conservative values. In these cases, working mothers are embraced if they fit within particular, and what some might consider constrained, notions of femininity, and promote conservative policies. Here conceptualisations of gender roles are stretched to allow them to appeal to more people, but are not so broad as to be identical to those endorsed by most feminist political actors. Those who believe that we need more women in public office, but who are anxious about, if not critical of, feminist ideology, will likely find this comforting and may be drawn to these conservative women's organisations and their claims to represent them. This framing strategy also yields a new maternal image – one that has the power to transform our beliefs about women and politics, with an alternative gendered conceptualisation of political leadership. Conservative women's groups offer, then, a complicated understanding of motherhood that affirms women's professional decisions, but also limits how they may go about achieving them. Power for its own sake is considered unfeminine, but seeking elected office is not, at least under certain circumstances. Running for office when you are the mother of five is acceptable, but it is best accomplished with your husband's blessing and sharing of domestic obligations.

Public support for Palin and Bachmann from conservative women leaders makes it more difficult for other conservatives to denounce women working outside of the home. It will moreover be likely to encourage the Republican Party to step up its efforts in supporting women's bid for higher office, regardless of their age or their maternal status. From the point of view of gender equality, having more mothers in elective office sends an important symbolic message about the need for attention to women's rights and the recognition of women's wide-ranging abilities. That these conservative women's organisations so heartily promoted a women's bid for vice president, for example, validates that women belong in the 'public sphere'.

In 2010, a record number of Republican women ran for, and won seats in, the US Congress. During upcoming elections, we can expect to see subtle but necessary shifts in conservative rhetoric about motherhood, gender roles and politics. In some ways this is good news for feminists who have argued that women's maternal status should not impede their professional progress. Of course, the articulation of transforming rhetoric about gender roles, or the increase in the number of conservative mothers in office, does not mean that feminist public policies will be forthcoming. As discussed at the beginning of this chapter, conservative women's groups are making Type II claims that are explicitly not feminist. Palin's and Bachmann's professional choices are met in part with approval because they appear to have addressed work-family tensions privately. Privatised solutions are more consistent with conservative values. Thus, there is no consideration of how government policies might make it easier for women with children to make strides in the paid workforce – something US feminists have sought in their advocacy struggles. And, that Palin and Bachmann are framed as abiding conservatives who are attentive to the wills of their families also confirms something feminists have lamented for some time – that women who work outside the home 'must be presented as being as exemplary mother[s] to justify [their] employment' (Johnston and Swanson 2003: 3).

Thus, while we should recognise that conservative women's groups rightfully can and do represent women's interests, we must also specify clearly that their participation may not result in feminist outcomes. Hence, delineating between 'feminist' and 'gendered' interests (or Type I and Type II claims) is critical to comprehending the intersection of gender and political representation, as well as understanding the enduring contest between feminists and conservatives over motherhood and politics (Schreiber 2012a).

Appendix

Table 6.A.1: Appendix: Conservative women's organisations

Organisation	Year founded	Issue priorities
Concerned Women for America (CWA)	1979	Religious liberty; national sovereignty (e.g. opposes UN); anti-abortion; opposition to gay rights; opposition to pornography; education
Clare Booth Luce Policy Institute (CBLPI)	1993	Providing leadership training and mentoring to conservative university women; promoting conservative curriculum on college campuses; school choice
Eagle Forum (EF)	1972	National sovereignty; anti-abortion; opposition to gay rights; immigration; English only language; opposition to feminism
Independent Women's Forum (IWF)	1992	Women in Iraq; women and work; courts/judges; national security; health/science; education; international women's rights; violence against women
Network of enlightened Women (NeW)	2004	Foster education and leadership skills of conservative university women; education
Smart Girl Politics (SGP)	2008	Energy independence, school choice in education, health care

References

Agness, K (2008) 'Sarah Palin: a liberated woman', 7 September, available at http://townhall.com/columnists/karinagness/2008/09/07/sarah_palin_a_liberated_woman/page/full (accessed 5 May 2014).

— (2009) 'A NeW direction for female happiness', 29 September, available at http://townhall.com/columnists/karinagness/2009/09/28/a_new_direction_for_female_happiness/page/full (accessed 5 May 2014).

Allen, C. (2008) 'When lipsticked pigs fly', *Independent Women's Voice*, 29 October available at http://iwvoices.com/detail.php?c=1404764&t=When-Lipsticked-Pigs-Fly (accessed 23 May 2014).

Carroll, S. J. (2009) 'Reflections on gender and Hillary Clinton's presidential campaign: the good, the bad, and the misogynic', *Politics and Gender*, 5 (1): 1–20.

CNN (2011) *American Morning*, aired 31 August.

Crouse, J. S. (2008) 'Bless her heart: poor Sarah Palin', *Concerned Women for America*, 1 October, available at http://www.cwfa.org/bless-her-heart-poor-sarah-palin/ (accessed 5 May 2014).

— (2009) 'Thank you, Sarah Palin', *Concerned Women for America*, 23 July, available at http://www.cwfa.org/thank-you-sarah-palin/ (accessed 23 May 2014).

— (2011) 'Michele Bachmann: Biblical submission and servant leadership', *Washington Post*, 29 July.

Eagly, A. (2007) 'Female leadership advantage and disadvantage: resolving the contradictions', *Psychology of Women Quarterly*, 31 (1): 1–12.

Easton, M. (2008a) 'Sarah shows the way', *National Review Online*, 23 October, available at http://www.nationalreview.com/articles/226076/sarah-shows-way/michelle-easton (accessed 5 May 2014).

— (2008b) 'Sarah Palin, multitasker', *Washington Times*, 28 October, available at http://www.washingtontimes.com/news/2008/oct/28/a-multitasker/?page=all (accessed 5 May 2014).

Falk, E. and Kenski, K. (2006) 'Issue saliency and gender stereotypes: support for women as presidents in times of war and terrorism', *Social Science Quarterly*, 87 (1): 1–18.

Ferree, M. M. and Mueller, C. M. (2004) 'Feminism and the women's movement: a global perspective', in Snow, D., Soule, S. and Hanspeter, K. (eds), *The Blackwell Companion to Social Movements*, Malden, MA: Blackwell Publishing, pp. 576–607.

Flanders, L. (1996) 'Conservative women are right for media mainstream', *Extra!* 1–3 (March–April).

Gallagher, S. and Smith, C. (1999) 'Symbolic traditionalism and pragmatic egalitarianism', *Gender and Society*, 13 (2): 211–33.

Gibson, K. L. and Heyse, A. L. (2010) '"The difference between a hockey mom and a pit bull": Sarah Palin's faux maternal persona and performance of hegemonic masculinity at the 2008 Republican National Convention', *Communication Quarterly*, 58 (3): 235–56.

Green, J., Rozell, M. and Wilcox, C. (2004) *The Values Campaign?: The Christian Right and the 2004 Elections*, Washington, D.C.: Georgetown University Press.

Griffith, R. M. (1997) *God's Daughters: Evangelical Women and the Power of Submission*, Berkeley, CA: University of California Press.

Hardisty, J. (1999) *Mobilizing Resentment*, Boston, MA: Beacon Press.

Hart, C. (2009) 'Sarah Palin: a conservative, a lady, a leader', Clare Boothe Luce Policy Institute, 15 June, available at http://cblpi.org/resources/article.cfm?ID=201 (accessed 5 May 2014).

Jamieson, K. H. (1995) *Beyond the Double Bind: Women and Leadership*, New York, NY: Oxford University Press.

Johnston, D. D. and Swanson, D. H. (2003) 'Undermining mothers: a content analysis of the representation of mothers in magazines', *Mass Communication and Society*, 6 (3): 243–65.

King, D. C. and Matland, R. E. (2003) 'Sex and the grand old party: an experimental investigation of the effect of candidate sex on support for a Republican candidate', *American Politics Research*, 31 (6): 595–612.

Klatch, R. (1987) *Women of the New Right*, Philadelphia PA: Temple University Press.

LaHaye, B. and Crouse, J. S. (2001) *A Different Kind of Strength*, Eugene OR: Harvest House Publishers.

Lewis, D. S. and Yoest, C. C. (1996) *Mother in the Middle*, Grand Rapids MI: Zondervan Publishing House.

Lombardo, E., Meier, P. and Verloo, M. (2009) 'Stretching and bending gender equality: a discursive politics approach', in Lombardo, E., Meier, P. and M. Verloo (eds), *The Discursive Politics of Gender Equality: Stretching, Bending and Policy-Making*, London: Routledge.

Lukas, C. (2011) 'A woman can take her marriage (and husband) seriously and still be an independent politician', *Independent Women's Forum*, 20 July, available at http://www.iwf.org/blog/2432310/A-Woman-Can-Take-Her-Marriage-(and-Husband)-Seriously-And-Still-Be-An-Independent-Politician (accessed 5 May 2014).

McVeigh, K. (2012) 'Does the GOP have a problem with women?' *The Guardian*, 10 January, available at http://www.guardian.co.uk/world/2012/jan/10/gop-women-problem (accessed 5 May 2014).

Mansbridge, J. (1986). *Why We Lost the ERA*, Chicago IL: University of Chicago Press.

Marshall, S. E. (1997) *Splintered Sisterhood*, Madison, WI: University of Wisconsin Press.

Merolla, J., Schroedel, J. R. and Holman, M. R. (2007) 'The paradox of Protestantism and women in elected office in the United States', *Journal of Women, Politics and Policy*, 29 (1): 77–100.

Okin, S. M. (1998) 'Gender, the public and the private', in Phillips, A. (ed.), *Feminism and Politics*, Oxford: Oxford University Press, pp.115–41.

Pew Research Center (2008) 'Revisiting the Mommy Wars after Palin: politics, gender and parenthood', Pew Research Center, 15 September, available at http://www.pewsocialtrends.org/2008/09/15/revisiting-the-mommy-wars/ (accessed 5 May 2014).

Romano, L. (2008) 'Ideology aside, this has been the year of the woman', *Washington Post*, 24 October, available at http://www.washingtonpost.com/wp-dyn/content/article/2008/10/23/AR2008102303827.html (accessed 5 May 2014).

Rosenblum, G. (2009). 'Conservative calendar is for young women, not old debates', *StarTribune*, 30 September, available at http://www.startribune.com/featuredColumns/63000262.html (accessed 5 May 2014).

Rymph, C. (2006) *Republican Women: Feminism and Conservatism from Suffrage through the Rise of the New Right*, Chapel Hill, NC: University of North Carolina Press.

Sanbonmatsu, K. and Dolan, K. (2009) 'Do gender stereotypes transcend party?', *Political Research Quarterly*, 62, 485–94.

Schaeffer, S. L. (2011) 'A good candidate is hard to find', *The Hill*, 13 September.

Schlafly, P. (2008) 'Feminists against Palin – shame on you', *SFGate*, 21 September, available at http://www.sfgate.com/default/article/Feminists-against-Palin-shame-on-you-3194173.php (accessed 5 May 2014).

Schlessinger, L. (2008) 'Sarah Palin and motherhood', *Dr Laura Blog*, 2 September, available at http://www.drlaurablog.com/2008/09/02/sarah-palin-and-motherhood/ (accessed 5 May 2014).

Schreiber, R. (2010a) 'Conservative women as leaders of organizations', in O'Connor, K. (ed.), *Gender and Women's Leadership: A Reference Handbook*, New York NY: Sage Press, pp. 237–24.

— (2010b) 'Who speaks for women? Print media portrayals of feminist and conservative women's advocacy', *Political Communication*, 27 (4): 432–52.

— (2012a) *Righting Feminism: Conservative Women and American Politics with New Epilogue*, New York, NY: Oxford University Press.

— (2012b) 'Dilemmas of representation: conservative and feminist women's organizations react to Sarah Palin', in Blee, K. M. and Deutsch, S. M. (eds), *Women of the Right: Comparisons and Interplay Across Borders*, State College, PA: Penn State University Press, pp. 273–90.

Shear, M. D. (2011) 'Bachmann and Perry make final appeal to social conservatives', *New York Times*, 27 December, available at http://thecaucus.blogs.nytimes.com/2011/12/27/bachmann-and-perry-make-final-appeal-to-social-conservatives/?_php=true&_type=blogs&_r=0 (accessed 5 May 2014).

Snow, D., Rochford, E. B. Jr, Worden, S. K. and Benford, R. D. (1986) 'Frame alignment processes, micromobilization, and movement participation', *American Sociological Review*, 51 (4): 464–81.

Snyder-Hall, R. C. (2008) 'The ideology of wifely submission: a challenge for feminism?', *Politics & Gender*, 4: 563–86.

Spindel, B. (2003) 'Conservatism as the "sensible middle": the independent women's forum, politics and the media', *Social Text*, 21 (4): 99–125.

Stalsburg, B. L. (2010) 'Voting for mom: the political consequences of being a parent for male and female candidates', *Politics & Gender*, 6 (3): 373–404.

Stone, D. (2002) *Policy Paradox: The Art of Political Decision Making*, New York, NY: Norton.

Targeted News Service (2011) 'Bachmann campaign adds Conservative leader Tamara Scott as Iowa co-chair', *Targeted News Service*, 18 November, available at http://targetednews.com/pr_disp.php?pr_id=3686323 (accessed 5 May 2014).

Tarrow, S. (1992) 'Mentalities, political cultures and collective action frames', in Aldon, M. and Mueller, C. M. (eds), *Frontiers in Social Movement Theory*, New Haven, CT: Yale University Press.

Thomas, D. R. (2006) 'A general inductive approach for analysis of qualitative evaluation data', *American Journal of Evaluation*, 27 (2): 237–46.

Verloo, M. (2005) 'Mainstreaming gender equality in Europe: a critical frame analysis approach', *Greek Review of Social Research*, 117: 11–34.

Wilcox, B. (2004) *Soft Patriarchs, New Men*, Chicago, IL: University of Chicago Press.

Chapter Seven

Conservative Women and Executive Office in Australia and New Zealand

Jennifer Curtin

Introduction

In June 2013, after a long and intensely personal campaign to undermine her leadership, Julia Gillard, Australia's first woman prime minister was ousted by former Labor leader Kevin Rudd.[1] Labor went on to lose the national election in September that year, and a new Liberal–National coalition government took office led by Tony Abbott. Abbott had been named and shamed by Gillard as a misogynist in her now-famous 'sexism' speech in parliament, and women voters were not convinced of his likeability during his time as opposition leader. Then, on becoming prime minister, Abbott caused a media frenzy and re-ignited charges of sexism when he selected only one woman to his Cabinet.

This limited presence of conservative women in Australia's federal Cabinet contrasts with the case of New Zealand, which has an increasingly strong record of selecting women for political leadership on both the left and the right. Between 1997 and 2008 New Zealand had two successive women prime ministers, Jenny Shipley (1997–9), leader of the National Party followed by Labour's Helen Clark (1999–2008). Clark's Cabinet comprised 30 per cent women and the centre-right National leader John Key has continued this trend since winning government in 2008 and 2011.

Thus, while research indicates that parties of the left have tended to be more 'female- friendly' in terms of both the descriptive and substantive representation of women (Htun and Power 2006; Sawer *et al.*, 2006; Curtin 2008), less is known about how conservative parties understand and practice 'female' friendliness. As such, this chapter takes up the call by Celis and Childs (2012) to go beyond a focus on explicitly 'feminist' actors and policies (most often represented by parties of the left) by reviewing both the descriptive and substantive representation of, and by, women from the major parties of the right in Australia's Liberal Party and New Zealand's National Party.

---

1. The spelling of 'Labour' differs in the two countries (the Australian Labor Party dropped the 'u' while the New Zealand Labour Party retained it). Where the parties are referred to collectively, the original spelling is used.

More specifically this chapter examines the presence, the speeches and the acts of 'conservative' women Cabinet ministers in Australia and New Zealand, in an attempt to identify and explain any evident trends. In doing so, it is necessary to reflect on what both 'conservatism' and 'feminism' has meant in these two Westminster settler societies, where egalitarianism overrode privilege and establishment as a core colonial value (Brett 2003; Belich 2001; Simms 1979). Indeed, in both Australia and New Zealand, the major party on the right, in its modern form, has viewed itself as a 'broad church', encompassing both conservative and liberal (gendered) traditions. Theoretically then, there has been room for women in these parties to speak and act for women in a variety of ways, including as feminists.

In practice however, party discipline remains a core convention that constrains opportunities for women on both sides of the political divide to act across party lines or independently for women (for exceptions *see* Sawer 2012; McLeay 2009). With this in mind, the chapter reviews the first speeches of liberal/conservative women who have gone on to become Cabinet ministers and assesses the extent to which they use these speeches to identify themselves as women (A), to name particular women or women's issues as the subject of their speech (B) and to advocate for women's rights and/or gender equality (C; *see* Tables 7.1 and 7.2). While parliamentary speeches and debates are regularly used as source material to investigate the substantive representation of women, MPs' maiden speeches provide them with the opportunity to outline their individual (rather than just their party's) values at the start of their political career.

Revealing the extent to which women speak within Cabinet is more difficult; the Westminster tradition of collective responsibility ensures policy debate within the executive remains invisible to researchers. However, although the prime minister selects portfolios for ministers, there are opportunities to indicate preferences through party forum, committee work and parliamentary debates. What women say on entering parliament and what they ultimately do as ministers is 'not determined exclusively by their own preferences' (Horn *et al.* 1983: 265) and as such, may be analytically tenuous. Nevertheless, the objective here is to begin to unravel how the substantive representation of women is expressed by liberal/ conservative women in New Zealand and Australia, by 'exploring interventions at various points in political processes' to identify claims, acts and outcomes for women (Celis and Childs 2012: 215).

What becomes apparent is that at different times, conservative/liberal women have sought to advance women's interests as mothers and as workers. While these claims and acts may not be articulated in terms that reflect transformative feminist ideas (Squires 1999), they may be defined as liberal feminist (a version of Type I claims as noted by Celis and Childs in the introduction). In recent years, the picture has become more complex. Some conservative/liberal women ministers' claims on behalf of women have become more muted or absent, at least by comparison to their maiden speeches, while others have embraced neoliberal discourse leading to an alternative, anti-feminist, Type I claim. The small sample of women included in this analysis makes it impossible to generalise but reveals that there is considerable diversity of representation of women by women inside conservative/liberal parties.

Table 7.1: Conservative women ministers' first speeches, New Zealand, 1930–2011

	Date elected	Framing 'women' in maiden speech				Cabinet term/s	Portfolios
		Identify as a woman (A)	Name women as subject (B)	Advocate for women (C)	Women's issues identified		
Hilda Ross	1945	Y	Y	Y	Well being of women and children; quality of domestic work, anti-factory work for women	1949–57	Without portfolio, Social Security (in 1957)
Ruth Richardson	1981	Y	Y	Y	Women's full participation in public life	1990–93	Finance
Jenny Shipley	1987	Y	Y	Y	Equal economic opportunity; domestic violence	1990–99	Social Security, Health, State Services, Women's Affairs, Prime Minister
Georgina te HeuHeu	1996	Y	Y	N	Māori women; self-determination, Treaty of Waitangi settlements	1998–99; 2008–11	Women's Affairs, Courts, Pacific Island Affairs
Pansy Wong	1996	N	N	N	No explicit mention; recognises she is first Asian MP	2008–10	Women's Affairs, Ethnic Affairs
Anne Tolley	1999	Y	Y	Y	More women in parliament; equal opportunity	2008+	Education, Police
Judith Collins	2002	Y	Y	N	Portrayal of women as over-represented as solo mother beneficiaries	2008+	Police, Justice
Paula Bennett	2005	Y	Y	N	Choice for women to stay at home; welfare for those in need; anti-welfare dependence	2008+	Social Security
Kate Wilkinson	2005	N	N	N	No mention – identifies as a monarchist and pro-deregulation	2008+	Labour, Conservation
Hekia Parata	2008	Y	Y	Y	Welfare dependency; women and children as victims of violence; Māori community development	2011+	Education
Amy Adams	2008	Y	N	N	Child of a solo mother but 'self starter'; no women's issues mentioned	2011+	Internal Affairs, IT and Communications, Environment

Table 7.2: Conservative women ministers' first speeches, Australia, 1930–2011

		Framing 'women' in maiden speech					
	Date elected	Identify as a woman (A)	Name women as subject (B)	Advocate for women (C)	Women's issues identified	Cabinet term/s	Portfolio
Enid Lyons	HR 1941	Y	Y	Y	Social security, declining birth rate, child endowment, housing, family well being	1949–51	Vice President Executive Council (no portfolio)
Margaret Guilfoyle	Senate 1971	Y	Y	Y	Being the 'voice for women of Australia' across issues; economy	1975–83	Education, Social Security, Finance
Amanda Vanstone	Senate 1984	N	Y	N	General discussion of equality; Aboriginal and youth issues	1996–2007	Employment/Education, Justice, Family/ Community Services, Women, Immigration
Jocelyn Newman	Senate 1986	N	Y	N	Women who follow their husband into politics	1996–2001	Social Security, Women, Family/Community Services
Kay Patterson	Senate 1987	Y	Y	Y	Number of women in parliament; volunteer work and girl guides; living standards	2001–07	Health, Family/ Community Services, Women
Helen Coonan	Senate 1996	Y	Y	Y	'Relentless' need for women to juggle work family; flexible work	2001–07	Revenue, Communications
Julie Bishop	HR 1998	N	N	N	Generic mention of equal opportunity	2003–07;	Ageing, Education, Women, Foreign Affairs

Conservatism and feminism in Australia and New Zealand

Australia and New Zealand have long been considered a perfect pair for comparative research because of their numerous similarities (Castles 1985; Chappell and Curtin 2013). They are settler societies that are geographically and culturally close, and both were early adopters of the female franchise.[2] Both inherited the Westminster parliamentary system, albeit with different adaptations made over time: Australia is federal, bicameral and majoritarian at the national level while New Zealand is unitary, unicameral and has featured a proportional representation electoral system since 1996. The latter has produced an increase in the number of parties represented in the New Zealand parliament, but despite this, government formation in both countries continues to be dominated by the two major parties. New Zealand's National Party and the Liberal Party in Australia are the dominant 'conservative' parties, although at the federal level in Australia the Liberals govern in coalition with the rural-based Nationals.

The establishment of conservative or centre-right parties in these settler societies came later than that of Labour. In response to a long period of industrial unrest in the late 1800s, the Labour movements in Australia and New Zealand created their parties (in 1901 federally in Australia and in 1916 in NZ) as a means to advance further the rights and interests of workers (Aimer 2010; Crisp 1955). By contrast, non-Labour politicians formed several parties on the right, although the stability of these was undermined by rural/urban and protectionist/free trade divisions (Jaensch 1994; Miller 2005). It was not until 1936 in New Zealand, and 1945 in Australia, that a single unified party on the right was born, embedding a two-party dominance that is a feature of both countries' House of Representatives.

Scholars have been wary of invoking a traditional British notion of 'conservative' when seeking to understand the political tradition of the non-Labour parties in the Antipodean context (Brett 2003; Gustafson 1986; Shorter 1974; Simms 1982). Judith Brett argues that the question of whether the Australian Liberal Party is conservative or liberal is fraught and in part dependent on the party leadership. For example, she notes that former Liberal Prime Minister John Howard believed the Party was the trustee of both the classical liberal and conservative traditions, combining a liberal economic policy and a conservative social policy. Under his leadership this translated into support for market based or neoliberal economic policies, combined with support for families and a disinterest in (if not open hostility to) gender equality policies (Brett 2003; Maddison and Partridge 2007). It would be tempting to believe that this position exemplifies the major centre-right party in Australia, but its origins suggest otherwise. For example, in 1949, Liberal Prime Minister Menzies was keen to stress the Party's commitment to a forward-looking liberalism and to 'scotch suspicions that it was a reactionary party focused mainly on the status quo' (Brett 2003: 1). And Liberal Prime Minister Deakin (1903) would never have countenanced the description

---

2. Although in Australia, extension of the vote did not include all indigenous women until 1962.

'conservative', regarding it as the name for those who defended unwarranted and entrenched privilege (Brett 2003). Early Liberal leaders in New Zealand exhibited similar perspectives (Gustafson 1986). It was under Liberal premiers that women won the right to vote (1893), that workers' rights to negotiate collectively were legalised (1894) and old age pensions introduced (1898).

This is not to say that there have not been conservative tendencies within these parties of the centre-right. Australia's interwar prime ministers, Lyons and Bruce, facing what they saw as urgent threats to Australia's 'fundamental institutions and values' were, according to Brett, comfortable with the term 'conservative' (Brett 2003: 2). In New Zealand, the rural divisions of the party were often nervous of the liberalism evident amongst the urban sections of the party (Gustafson 1986). However, in neither country was the name 'Conservative Party' ever chosen. And leaders and members of the National Party in New Zealand and the Australian Liberal Party consistently saw their respective organisations as having the potential to encompass both liberal and conservative ideas and voters (Brett 2003; Shorter 1974).

This lack of clarity around defining 'conservative' politics in Australia and New Zealand has also been a subject of debate in feminist politics. For example, to counter claims that providing women with political rights as citizens would undermine the established moral order, Australian suffragists argued that the traditional roles of women were not being displaced, but complemented: 'There is no reason why women's sphere should be circumscribed. Her duty begins in the home but it does not end there ... No woman could be so much interested in a budget speech or an electoral Bill [as] to forget to put the chops on' (cited in Sawer and Simms 1993: 30; *see also* Lovell-Smith 1992, on New Zealand).

Moreover, Marilyn Lake (1993) claims that early arguments for maternal rights made by women in Australia were radical in that their aim was to provide an element of economic independence for women located in the domestic sphere. By contrast Anne Summers (1994) argues that while the women who stood up for these claims might have been radical politically, their conservative, maternalist approach to women's rights undermined the potential of this radicalism. Yet as other feminist scholars have argued there has long been recognition that state interference in the family was essential to protect the rights of children and women in Australia and New Zealand (Sawer 2003; Nolan 2000). Feminist activists in the 1970s and 1980s in both countries drew heavily on this reformist tradition of state intervention in their claims for public policy initiatives to address intra-family income distribution, sexual and domestic violence, to regulate prostitution and pornography and to support issues relating to women's health and economic well-being (Sullivan 1997; Nolan 2000; Curtin and Sawer 1996; Curtin and Teghtsoonian 2010; Gustafson 1986).

Parties on the right of the political spectrum recognised early on that accessing the women's vote was important for electoral success. In Australia, separate political organisations became a key strategy for mobilising women with the best known Liberal women's organisation being the Australian Women's National League (AWNL), established in 1903. The League, declaring that its members wanted to do more than provide tea and scones for their male counterparts, focused instead on candidate selection, participating in election campaigns and ensuring women's social and political rights were addressed by Liberal Party policy (Fitzherbert 2004). When Robert Menzies formed the modern Liberal Party in 1944, the AWNL negotiated itself permanent representation on the Federal Executive of the party, guaranteed positions on state executives and state councils, and the creation of women's sections in the party (Fitzherbert 2004; Sawer and Simms 1993).

In her exploration of conservatism and feminism in Australia, Marian Simms (1979) argues that the categorisation of feminism as radical or militant has belied its plurality and as such, has tended to exclude women's groups that pursued women's rights albeit within the confines of conservative social, political and sexual mores. Simms argues that 'conservative' women's activism has been incorrectly dismissed as a defender of the hierarchical status quo, whereby political, social and economic (and gender) inequalities are tolerated as part of the natural order. Her empirical findings reveal that self-professed conservative women's organisations associated with Australian parties of the right have a long history of demanding legal and political equality for women, and working for women's right to economic independence, thereby challenging their own party's perspectives on the role of women in society (Simms 1979). As such, these conservative women's claims for gender equality could be viewed as feminist in a liberal–reformist sense, as were the suffragists' claims before them.

The in-depth qualitative work of Heather Devere on women's political attitudes in New Zealand reveals a disjuncture between the conceptualisation of the traditional left-right spectrum, feminism, and where to put women's responses to women's issues (Devere 1993; *see also* Devere and Curtin 1993). Although Devere found that National-identifying women were less likely to label themselves feminist, they believed in equal pay and equal opportunity, a role for the state in assisting women in need and the right to political equality. This resonates with what is known about women in the National Party historically. Women's auxiliaries and branches were a feature of the both Labour and non-Labour parties in the early twentieth century (Devere and Curtin 2009; Gustafson 1986). With the establishment of the National Party in 1936, the auxiliaries morphed into women's sections and grew in number and membership. While focused primarily on fund-raising and recruiting women into the party as members (rather than as candidates), these sections lobbied the party on women's issues and some argued for dedicated women's representation within the party hierarchy. There was some progress in this regard – women's sections were granted delegates to conference, and in 1974, 'Woman Vice President' became a formal position on the party executive (Gustafson 1986).

The institutionalised involvement of women in the Australian Liberal Party from the 1940s also ensured it became an attractive party to women in terms of party membership (Brennan 2002). This AWNL legacy ultimately led to the development in 1981 of the Liberal Feminist Network, established to support women who wanted to enter politics. While the Network itself did not last beyond the 1980s, Liberal women continued to promote the need to increase women's parliamentary representation with the creation of the Liberal Women's Forum (Whip 2003). Unlike its predecessor, the programme was not labelled explicitly as feminist, and nor did it deal with issues of policy. Rather, its goal was to identify and encourage individual women to stand for election and assist them in their campaign to do so (Brennan 2002). However, over the past twenty years there has been a number of Liberal Party women elected whose self-portrayal has been avowedly feminist, and who have worked to protect women's economic and social rights through their committee work in parliament, suggesting that conservative/liberal party women may identify as feminists and take up feminist claims (Curtin 2013).

It is perhaps unsurprising to find that for many decades women voters in Australia and New Zealand were more likely to support the liberal/conservative parties in preference to Labour. Without going into the respective Labour Party histories, in summary it would be fair to say that until the women's movement's demands of the 1970s infiltrated Labour thinking, the Party saw itself primarily as representative of the working man and protector of the family wage. Women's demands for equal pay and equal opportunity were often seen as undermining the broader 'class' struggle, and until women entered the party and the union movement *en masse*, were largely ignored. So while some scholars have argued that women were more likely than men to be conservative voters because of their lower levels of higher education and labour force participation, others have also argued that Labour was for many years an unattractive prospect for women voters (Campbell 2006; Curtin 2003, 2014b; Hill 2006).

Finally, it is important to recognise that in both Australia and New Zealand the Liberal and National parties have, over time, become the 'natural' party of government. Between 1949 and 1999, Labour in New Zealand held office only three times – in 1957–60, 1972–5 and 1984–90. In Australia a similar trend is evident, with Labor forming government from 1972–5 and 1983–96. Although longevity in office may now have become a thing of the past, such trends highlight the importance of studying women in liberal/conservative government.

The descriptive representation of conservative women in Australia and New Zealand

New Zealand women won the right to stand for parliament (1919), seventeen years later than their Australian sisters. Although women in both countries then stood as candidates, the numbers elected were low. In New Zealand, between 1919 and 1951, 35 women stood as candidates 55 times in 11 elections and 8 by-elections. Eight of the 35 during this period were from the conservative side of politics and two were successful (Bootham 1989).[3] In Australia prior to the 1950s less is known about the number of women candidates who stood for election, although

---

3. In this early period it was not uncommon for women to replace their husbands or fathers after they died in office.

there was a period prior to World War II when a significant number of women eschewed political parties and stood for election as independents (Costar and Curtin 2004; Curtin 2003). Yet in these early years liberal/conservative women in Australia fared better than their New Zealand sisters in terms of their appointment to Cabinet. The first Australian women to gain ministerial office at both the state and federal levels were all from the conservative side of politics although there were only eight of them in the whole period from 1947–79.

Although large-N comparative studies indicate that the total number of women elected to parliament is a key determinant of their appointment to Cabinet (Davis 1997; Siaroff 2000), growing the number of conservative women MPs to increase the pool of ministerial eligibles also matters. In Australia and New Zealand Cabinets include about twenty ministers and, in the case of the conservative parties, the selection process is led by the party leader who appoints all ministers and allocates portfolios. Table 7.3 indicates that over time, the number of liberal/conservative women candidates and parliamentarians has increased in both countries, although progress has been slow and the Liberal/National parties are laggards compared to parties on the left.

However, the patterns are different across the two countries. In terms of the overall numbers and proportion of women elected to parliament since the 1930s, New Zealand women have fared better than women in Australia. Progress was incremental until the late 1970s but in 1981 the number of New Zealand women elected doubled, and this growth continued until 2008. Although the initial spike in the early 1980s was a result of Labour standing women in safe seats, greater numbers of liberal/conservative women followed several elections later, with women constituting 27.1 per cent of the National Party MPs in 2013.

The numbers of women elected in Australia also began to increase in the 1980s, but in proportional terms their presence did not reach double figures until 1996. The significant increase in women elected in 1996 appears to be a direct result of Australian Labor's 1994 gender quota rule, with evidence of a gender contagion effect on Liberal Party candidate selection (Curtin and Sexton 2004). More women were selected to safe and marginally Liberal seats than in previous years, and the swing to the Party in 1996 ensured they were elected. However since 2007, the representation rate of Liberal women has been in decline. In the 2013 election the Liberal–National coalition won back over 20 seats, taking their total from 59 to 91. This included an increase of four women, but the overall proportion of women in the new government has dropped from 23.7 to 19 per cent.

Selection to Cabinet depends on a range of factors including personal and political resources and experience. But first and foremost is the need to secure a safe seat or list position, to ensure incumbency over time thereby enabling women to build a strong constituency base and support within the party. After her election in 1945, Hilda Ross, who went on to become New Zealand's first female conservative Cabinet minister, commented that 'if a woman did become a candidate it would be for an "iffy" seat, not a safe one' (cited in Gustafson 1986: 284). Although the advent of a mixed member proportional system has increased women's chances of being elected to the New Zealand parliament, thereby increasing the pool

Table 7.3: Conservative women parliamentarians and ministers, Australia/New Zealand, 1930–2011

	New Zealand			Australia				
	All women MPs	Conservative women MPs	Conservative women in cabinet	Conservative women in cabinet	Conservative women MPs	All women senators	Conservative women Senators	Conservative women in cabinet
	n (%)	n (%)	n	n (%)	n (%)	n (%)	n (%)	n
1930s*	1–3 (2.5)	0	0	0	0	0	0	0
1940s	2 (2.9)	2 (5.2)	1**	2 (2.7)	1 (2.3)	2 (5.6)	1 (50)***	1†
1950s	4 (5)	1 (2.2)	1	0	0	5 (8.3)	4 (13.3)	1†
1960s	4–6 (5.6)	2 (4.4)	0	1 (0.8)	1 (1.9)	4 (6.7)	3 (10.7)	1#
1970s	4 (4.5)	2 (4.3)	0	1 (0.8)	0	6 (9)	3 (8.6)	1
1980/1	8 (8.7)	2 (4.2)	0	3 (2.4)	0	10 (15.6)	5 (17.9)	1
1984##	12 (11.6)	2 (5.4)	n/a	8 (5.4)	1 (1.5)	14 (18.4)	6 (18.2)	n/a
1987	14 (14.4)	3 (7.5)	n/a	9 (6.1)	1 (1.6)	17 (22.4)	8 (23.5)	n/a
1990	16 (16.5)	8 (11.9)	2	10 (6.8)	3 (4.3)	18 (23.7)	8 (23.5)	n/a
1993	21 (21.2)	5 (10)	1	13 (8.8)	4 (6.2)	16 (21.1)	7 (19.4)	n/a
1996	35 (28.3)	8 (18.2)	2	23 (15.5)	18 (19.1)	23 (30.3)	8 (21.6)	1
1998/9	37 (29.2)	8 (20.5)	n/a	33 (22.3)	17 (21.2)	22 (28.9)	9 (25.7)	1
2001/2	35 (28.3)	6 (22.2)	n/a	38 (25.3)	18 (21.9)	23 (30.3)	8 (22.8)	2
2004/5	40 (33.1)	12 (25)	n/a	37 (24.7)	17 (19.1)	27 (35.5)	9 (23.1)	4
2007/8	41 (33.6)	16 (27.6)	6	40 (26.7)	13 (20)	27 (35.5)	10 (27.8)	n/a
2010/11	39 (32.2)	16 (27.1)	6	37 (24.7)	14 (23.7)	30 (39.5)	10 (29.4)	n/a

Sources: New Zealand Electoral Commission, available at http://www.elections.org.nz/research-statistics; Australian Parliamentary Handbook, available at http://www.aph.gov.au/About_Parliament/Parliamentary_Departments/Parliamentary_Library/Parliamentary_Handbook (both accessed 23 June 2014).

Notes: *Averages have been used in the decades because the numbers are so small; ** Hilda Ross entered cabinet in 1949 and continued until 1957; ***Annabelle Rankin was the first woman to be granted a portfolio (Housing) but she remained a Minister outside Cabinet; † Enid Lyons' term was 1949–51; # The Senate included only 36 people in the 1940s – this increased to 60 in the 1950s; ## The election of 1983 is missing from this table; the 1983 government lasted less than two years; n/a = Labor was in government during these periods.

of ministerial eligibles, electoral volatility means that predicting winnable list positions is difficult. By contrast most single member district seats are relatively safe; such seats are increasingly necessary for a political career, but theoretically less accessible to women candidates (Curtin 2012). In 2011, four of the six female members of the National Cabinet held safe seats. The remaining two held marginal urban seats, but because of the dual candidature rules they were assured a safe list position if they continued to perform in Cabinet.

In Australia, it is the Senate – the country's Upper House – that functions under a proportional representation electoral system, and this is the chamber where women have been able to establish their political careers. The electoral cycle is six years, parties have control over list ordering, and over time the Liberal–National coalition has begun to put more women in the top three positions at half-Senate elections. Indeed, to date, only two Liberal women MPs have been selected to Cabinet – the first being Dame Enid Lyons in 1949 and the second being Julie Bishop in 2013.[4] Thus the Senate has become a critical pathway for conservative/ liberal women into the executive.

In 1966, Australian Liberal Senator Annabelle Rankin became the first woman to be minister responsible for a government department (Housing), although this was not a Cabinet position. It was not until late 1975, when Liberal Senator Margaret Guilfoyle entered Cabinet as Minister for Education, that a woman held a portfolio inside Cabinet. In 1976, Guilfoyle became Minister for Social Security and she remained in Cabinet for more than seven years as the only woman. She still holds the record as Australia's longest-serving woman Cabinet minister. With the arrival of the Howard Coalition government in 1996, the number of women in Cabinet increased to two and by 2005 it stood at three.

Despite the contrasts in electoral systems and state architecture it is evident that over the past twenty years, the liberal/conservative parties in Australia and New Zealand became increasingly open to the election of women MPs, thereby growing the pool of ministerial eligibles. In both countries women now constitute at least one-quarter of the centre-right caucus. Yet only in New Zealand do we see women from the centre-right being selected to Cabinet in proportion to their party's parliamentary representation. Since 2008, liberal/conservative women have constituted 30 per cent of the National Cabinet, with three Māori women and the first Asian woman selected by Prime Minister John Key. By contrast, and despite having two sources of qualified potential ministers and a long history of representing Liberal women, the Australian Liberal Party leaders have continued to select few women. This suggests that while the Party might see itself as a 'broad church' and its women may be 'liberal' in orientation, the Party retains a strong conservative element whereby a gendered hierarchical status quo is tolerated as part of the natural order.

---

4.   However, Senators cannot go on to become Prime Minister.

Conservative women's claims and executive office

Although the focus on the descriptive representation reveals the extent to which executive power is shared between conservative women and men, it is widely accepted that numbers alone may not be the 'true' test of women's influence within political elites. What also matters when trying to ascertain influence, according to Baer, is the extent to which these women leaders are able to 'capitalize on their leadership posts' (2003: 135–6). While Baer's point is linked to increasing women's political influence through leadership, her broader argument might also be applied to conservative women ministers. They may have been few in number but this in itself does not prevent them from performing 'critical acts' on behalf of, or in the name of, women (Childs and Krook 2006).

To date, most of the published work on the substantive representation by women ministers has focused on the work of Labour women (Curtin 2008; Curtin and Sawer 2011). Certainly, the small number of conservative women selected to Cabinet in Australia and New Zealand over time limits the potential for generalisation. Nevertheless a qualitative exploration of how these women have 'spoken' and 'acted' for women is a useful first step towards understanding the factors that might facilitate or constrain the substantive representation of women by liberal/conservative women.

In Westminster systems the Cabinet is the 'black box' of politics in that collective responsibility prevents scholars from reviewing the debates that occur behind closed doors. This limits our capacity to 'know' how women ministers represent women's claims in the process of debating policy decisions. As such this analysis draws from two sources to shed some light on how conservative women represent women. The first is through an analysis of first or 'maiden' speeches of the conservative women who later became Cabinet ministers and the second is through a cursory review of the extent to which the legislative and policy decisions taken by these women as ministers reflect their initial representation of claims for women.

We should not necessarily expect to find explicit references to women's interests in the process of policy decision making; ministerial career progression may depend on women being 'silent' or 'masking' a feminist representative claim (*see* Carroll 1984a; Curtin 2008). Moreover, choosing to speak for selective groups in making public policy might actually further the backlash politics already identified around women's issues. Finally, over time centre-right parties in Australia and New Zealand have become increasingly neoliberal in their economic orientation, and this is reported to have had a detrimental impact on the lives of women (McClelland and St John 2006; Curtin and Devere 2006).

Nevertheless, 'maiden' or first speeches are a useful source of identifying how MPs first represent themselves. These speeches are a traditional rite of passage and enable the new MP to speak uninterrupted, sometimes for up to thirty minutes. The speeches are a verbal and symbolic record of new parliamentarians' aspirations, motivations, issue concerns and philosophical orientations at the outset of their parliamentary careers. The audience includes the general public, their particular constituents, their party colleagues and leaders. Research by Horn *et al.* (1983: 232) indicates that in the New Zealand context, maiden speeches are seen by women MPs as an opportunity to speak to the electorate, tell them 'who you are' and what 'action you want to see taken' on a range of issues.

As noted in Table 7.3, of all conservative women that have entered national parliament in Australia and New Zealand since 1930, only eighteen have gone on to hold Cabinet positions (seven in Australia and eleven in New Zealand). Tables 7.1 and 7.2 offer a more complete picture of these women and provide several points worthy of note. It is clear that during the post-war period prior to the economic crises associated with stagflation and the collapse of Keynesianism in the late 1970s, liberal/conservative women parliamentarians in both countries saw a role for the state to assist women in need, to protect women and children from economic deprivation, and to enhance the quality of women's lives.

Australia's Enid Lyons was a Catholic mother of twelve children and in her maiden speech she saw herself as an advocate for women's role as mothers and for the health and well-being of children. Over the six years that followed, Lyons spoke in the House on many subjects of relevance to women: housing, clothing, child endowment, the domestic economy, maternity services, discrimination against married women in the workforce, service women's pay, widows' pensions and the nationality of married women. When she was appointed to Cabinet in 1949 it was as Vice President of the Executive Council, and although it was a significant honour she was disappointed not to have been granted a portfolio. She labelled her role 'toothless', commenting that she thought it unlikely that Menzies wanted her in Cabinet at all, and that she was there 'to pour the tea' (Lyons 1972).

As Minister of Welfare of Women and Children and then Minister of Social Security, New Zealand's first conservative woman minister Hilda Ross also took a close interest in the problems facing welfare recipients and women as mothers. But she also supported the campaign for equal pay launched by female public servants and advocated compulsory domestic education courses for all girls and women, no matter what their career choice. Her work as a minister reflected the issues she raised in her maiden speech, and her belief in the role of the state in assisting women led to her being labelled the 'Mother of New Zealand' (Dalley 2012).

From 1975 until the mid-1980s both countries were governed by centre-right governments, and both countries had vocal women's movements making demands for policy change. Carroll (1984b) argues that noisy external constituencies can create an impetus for the selection of women to Cabinet, but New Zealand Conservative Prime Minister Robert Muldoon resisted such symbolic appeasement, selecting no women to his three consecutive cabinets between 1975 and 1981. By contrast, Australian Prime Minister Malcolm Fraser selected Margaret Guilfoyle, first as the low-ranked Minister of Education, then later as Minister of Social Security, and then Minister of Finance. Guilfoyle championed the importance of women in politics in her maiden speech and throughout her ministerial career, as well as in her post-parliamentary life. In 1994, she noted that, unless women were positioned in the Cabinet, then the effect of more women in parliament would not be felt in the arena where the decisions are taken and the policy directions are set (Guilfoyle 1995).

During the 1980s, radical economic policy changes were undertaken by the Lange/Douglas Labour government in New Zealand and to a lesser extent by the Hawke–Keating Labor government in Australia (Castles *et al.* 1996). Deregulation of the financial and labour markets resulted, and increased means testing was applied to social welfare. The significance of this period for women should not be underestimated. Labour governments established the foundations of a neoliberal turn in policy making, embraced and enhanced by incoming liberal/conservative governments in the 1990s. Although Labour women ministers during this period worked to ensure women's social rights were protected from economic and labour market reforms, the overarching direction of government policy was fixed.

It is evident from the first speeches of many of the women entering parliament for the liberal/conservative parties in Australia and New Zealand during the 1980s and 1990s that expecting the welfare state to protect women from the vagaries of the market, and interventions around equal pay for work of equal value and to support other social services, were no longer countenanced. Where women were mentioned at all, the language of self-reliance, individual responsibility and irresponsible solo mothers becomes more apparent. It is perhaps unsurprising then, that upon entering Cabinet these women are charged with roles that involve removing state services from women's lives. While it is not uncommon to see women receive social portfolios, the women charged with these portfolios during a time of economic austerity became key advocates for their governments, and were reviled by many for their role in targeting women's economic well-being (Curtin and Teghtsoonian 2010).

New Zealand's two most high-profile National women ministers of the 1990s, (Ruth Richardson, Minister of Finance, and Jenny Shipley, Minister of Social Welfare and later Prime Minister), oversaw a massive overhaul of the welfare state and labour market in New Zealand. Family payments were cut, targeting was introduced and individual work contracts became the norm, decimating trade unions and stalling any progression on the minimum wage – all of which had a negative impact on women and children (McClelland and St John 2006). Continuing in this vein, since 2008, National's Paula Bennett, Minister of Social Development has also targeted solo mothers, linking benefit payments with workforce participation and offering contraceptive incentives to young women considered at risk. Her approach to this issue has led a number of commentators to accuse her of 'beneficiary bashing' (Curtin 2014b).

Welfare dependence featured in most of the first speeches given by women entering the New Zealand parliament since the 1990s, although only Bennett and Judith Collins single out women as the primary beneficiaries and invoke negative images of these women. By contrast, the first speeches of recent Australian women ministers do not feature women's welfare dependence to the same extent. While equality of opportunity is mentioned by several, and the juggling of work and family by one, women's issues are largely absent from the speeches of these women. But as with the case of New Zealand, women ministers were allocated the portfolios responsible for reforming and cutting welfare to women (Whip 2003).

In New Zealand, Women's Affairs is a standalone portfolio, and it is interesting to note that the last liberal/conservative senior woman minister to hold this portfolio was Jenny Shipley. Elsewhere, analyses of Jenny Shipley's work as Minister of Women's Affairs suggest that she attempted to advance other policies for women, including legal reforms to combat domestic and family violence (which is reflected in her first speech), but was constrained by the overarching strategic direction of the National Government (Curtin and Teghtsoonian 2010; Chappell and Curtin 2013). Since the election of the liberal/conservative National government in 2008, Women's Affairs has rarely been represented in Cabinet, and the gender mainstreaming work previously undertaken by the ministry has virtually disappeared (Curtin 2014a).

In Australia, women's affairs has been organised differently, with the prime minister nominated as spokesperson for women, with a Minister Assisting. Under consecutive Liberal governments, the Office for the Status of Women has been downgraded regularly and, apart from Kay Patterson, the women selected to be the Minister Assisting, had not demonstrated a strong commitment to women's issues in their first speeches. Indeed, as Ministers Assisting, these women presided over a period of significant dismantling of legislation protecting the legal rights of women, including the abolition of the Affirmative Action Act in 1994, (the Act was established in 1986 and abolished in 1994) and the watering down of the Sex Discrimination Act (Whip 2003; Maddison and Partridge 2007). There were a number of Liberal Party women who broke ranks with their leadership to fight against these reforms but in doing so they undermined their chances of future Cabinet selection.

Those women who have gone on to become liberal/conservative ministers in recent years have been subdued in both their claims and acts for women, in contrast with the claims and acts of liberal/conservative women prior to the 1990s. While these early women ministers may have presented a more conservative view of women's role, and the state's role in 'protecting' women and children, they also advocated for women's rights to be free from discrimination in paid work and in politics. This reflects Simms' findings that conservative women can make feminist claims and undertake feminist acts, if feminism is defined as reformist in orientation (Simms 1979). However, more recently liberal/conservative women ministers in both Australia and New Zealand appear to have chosen to remain silent on issues relating to women's equality. The increasingly hegemonic status of economic neoliberalism and anti-welfarism appears to have limited conservative/liberal women representative acts, while the anti-benefit claims being made by some women ministers do little 'to forge responsive connections with women and women's groups' (Dodson cited in Reingold 2008: 137).

Conclusions

Although Australia and New Zealand were pioneers of women's political rights, in both countries it took many decades before women's absence from parliament and public decision making became a political issue. And while conservatives led the way in Australia in terms of women's ministerial representation this did not become a trend. By contrast, in New Zealand the presence of women prime ministers and the selection of women as ministers from both sides of politics over the past decade appears to have resulted in a 'normalisation' of women's access to executive politics. Yet compared to earlier generations of women ministers, few have spoken as advocates for women on entering parliament. A different trend is evident in Australia. While there has been a consistent core of Liberal Party feminists elected to parliament in Australia over the past fifteen years, few of these women are selected for Cabinet, and when they are, their public voice for women is muted, if not silenced by collective responsibility and possibly the threat of demotion. In 2011, Curtin and Sawer wrote that conservative governments now have difficulty resisting expectations of female presence in the ministry. However in 2013 Australian Prime Minister Tony Abbott proved them wrong. This suggests that the representation of women by women in parties of the right remains contingent on the conservative or liberal leanings of the party leadership and the discursive space available in a neoliberal environment.

References

Aimer, P. (2010) 'Labour', in R. Miller (ed.), *New Zealand Government and Politics* (5th edn), Melbourne: Oxford University Press, pp. 474–85.

Baer, D. (2003) 'Women, women's organisations and political parties', in Carroll, S. (ed.), *Women and American Politics: New Questions, New Directions*, Oxford, Oxford University Press, pp. 111–45.

Belich, J. (2001) *Paradise Reforged: A History of the New Zealanders from the 1880s to the year 2000*, Auckland NZ: Allen Lane (Penguin Press).

Bootham, V. (1989), 'Women political candidates in New Zealand general election 1919–1951', unpublished history essay, Victoria University of Wellington.

Brennan, D. (2002) 'Women and political representation', in Summers, J., Woodward, D. and Parkin, A. (eds), *Government, Politics, Power and Policy in Australia* (7th edn), Sydney: Pearson, pp. 269–88.

Brett, J. (2003) *Australian Liberals and the Moral Middle Class: From Alfred Deakin to John Howard*, New York: Cambridge University Press.

Campbell, R. (2006) *Gender and the Vote in Britain: Beyond the Gender Gap?* Colchester: ECPR Press.

Carroll, S. (1984a) 'Women candidates and support for feminist concerns: the closet feminist syndrome', *Western Political Quarterly*, 37 (2): 307–23.

— (1984b) 'The recruitment of women for cabinet-level posts in state government: a social control perspective', *Social Science Journal*, 21 (1): 91–107.

Castles, F. (1985) *Working Class and Welfare: Reflections on the Political Development of the Welfare State in Australia and New Zealand, 1890–1980*, Wellington: Allen and Unwin (Port Nicholson Press).

Castles, F., Gerritsen, R. and Vowles, J. (eds) (1996) *The Great Experiment: Labour Parties and Public Policy Transformation in Australia and New Zealand*, Auckland: Auckland University Press.

Celis, K. and Childs, S. (2012) 'The substantive representation of women: what to do with Conservative claims?', *Political Studies*, 60 (1): 213–25.

Chappell, L. and Curtin, J. (2013) 'Does federalism matter? Evaluating state architecture and family and domestic violence policy in Australia and New Zealand', *Publius: The Journal of Federalism*, 43 (1): 24–43.

Childs, S. and Krook, M. L. (2006) 'Should feminists give up on critical mass? A contingent yes', *Politics and Gender*, 2 (4): 522–30.

Costar, B. and Curtin, J. (2004) *Rebels with a Cause: Independents in Australian Politics*, Sydney: University of New South Wales Press.

Crisp, L. F. (1955) *The Australian Federal Labour Party, 1901–1951*, London: Longmans Green.

Curtin, J. (2003) 'White women and the federal vote, 1902–1949: challenging the idea of women's conservatism', in J. Chesterman and D. Philips (eds), *Selective Democracy: Race, Gender and the Australian Vote*, Melbourne: Circa, pp. 112–126.

—   (2008) 'Women, political leadership and substantive representation of women in New Zealand', *Parliamentary Affairs*, 61 (3): 490–504.

—   (2012) 'Gendering parliamentary representation in New Zealand: a mixed system producing mixed results', in Tremblay, M. (ed.), *Women and Legislative Representation*, New York: Palgrave Macmillan, pp. 191–202.

—   (2013) 'Gender, politics and the representation of women', in Fenna, A., Robbins, J. and Summers, J. (eds), *Government, Politics and Power in Australia* (10th edn), Frenchs Forest NSW: Longman/Pearson, pp. 311–28.

—   (2014a) 'The evolution of gender equality policy making in New Zealand', in Hill, M. (ed.), *Studying Public Policy: An International Approach*, Bristol: Policy Press, pp. 115–126.

—   (2014b) 'From presence to absence? Where were women in the 2011 election?' in Vowles, J. (ed.), *The New Electoral Politics in New Zealand*, Wellington: Institute for Governance and Policy Studies, Victoria University of Wellington, pp. 125–140.

Curtin, J. and Devere, H. (2006) 'Global Rankings and Domestic Realities: Women, Work and Policy in Australia and New Zealand', *Australian Journal of Political Science*, 41 (2): 193–208.

Curtin, J. and Sawer, M. (1996) 'Gender equity in the shrinking state: women and the great experiment', in Castles, F., Gerritsen, R. and Vowles, J. (eds), *The Great Experiment: Labour Parties and Public Policy Transformation in Australia and New Zealand*, Auckland: Auckland University Press, 149–69.

—   (2011) 'Oceania', in Bauer, G. and Tremblay, M. (eds), *Women in Executive Power: A Global Overview*, London/New York: Routledge, pp. 45–64.

Curtin, J. and Sexton, K. (2004) 'Selecting and electing women to the House of Representatives: progress at last?', paper presented to the Australasian Political Studies Association, Adelaide, Australia, 29 September–1 October.

Curtin, J. and Teghtsoonian, K. (2010) 'Analysing institutional persistence: the case of the Ministry of Women's Affairs in Aotearoa/New Zealand', *Politics & Gender*, 6 (4): 545–72.

Dalley, B. (2012) 'Ross, Grace Hilda Cuthberta', in *Dictionary of New Zealand Biography: Te Ara – The Encyclopedia of New Zealand*, available at http://www.TeAra.govt.nz/en/biographies/5r25/ross-grace-hilda-cuthberta, accessed 10 March 2013.

Davis, R. H. (1997) *Women and Power in Parliamentary Democracies*, Lincoln, NE: University of Nebraska Press.

Devere, H. (1993) *Political Labels and Women's Attitudes*, unpublished PhD Thesis, Auckland: University of Auckland.

Devere, H. and Curtin, J. (1993) 'A plurality of feminisms', *Political Science*, 45 (1): 6–26.

— (2009) 'Rethinking political connections: women, friendship, and politics in New Zealand', in McMillan, K., Leslie, J. and McLeay, E. (eds), *Rethinking Women and Politics: New Zealand and Comparative Perspectives*, Wellington: Victoria University Press, pp. 87–111.

Fitzherbert, M. (2004) *Liberal Women: Federation to 1949*, Sydney: Federation Press.

Gustafson, B. (1986) *The First Fifty Years: A History of the New Zealand National Party*, Auckland: Reed Methuen Publishers.

Guilfoyle, M. (1995) 'Women, parliament and cabinet', *Canberra Bulletin of Public Administration*, 78, 21–4.

Hill, L. (2006) 'Women's interests and political orientations: the gender voting gap in three industrialized settings', in Chappell, L. and Hill, L. (eds), *The Politics of Women's Interests: New Comparative Perspectives*, London/ New York: Routledge, pp. 66–92.

Horn, P., Leniston, M. and Lewis, L. (1983) 'The maiden speeches of New Zealand Women MPs', *Political Science*, 35 (2): 229–66.

Htun, M. and Power, T. (2006) 'Gender, parties, and support for equal rights in the Brazilian Congress', *Latin American Politics and Society*, 48 (4): 83–104.

Jaensch, D. (1994) *Power Politics: Australia's Party System*, Sydney: Allen and Unwin.

Lake, M. (1993) 'A revolution in the family: the challenge and contradiction of maternal citizenship', in Koven, S. and Michel, S. (eds), *Mothers of a New World: Maternalistic Politics and the Origins of Welfare States*, London: Routledge, pp. 378–95.

Lovell-Smith, M. (1992) *The Woman Question: Writings by Women Who Won the Vote*, Auckland NZ: New Women's Press.

Lyons, E. (1972) *Among the Carrion Crows*, Adelaide: Rigby.

Maddison, S. and Partridge, E. (2007) 'How well is Australian democracy serving women?' Focused Audit Report no. 8, *Democratic Audit of Australia*, Canberra: Australian National University.

McLeay, E. (2009), 'Spare the rod? The story of how Sue Bradford, Green Party MP 1999–2009, fought for the rights of New Zealand children and changed the law', paper presented to the Public Leadership Workshop, Canberra: Australian National University, 26–7 November.

McClelland, A. and St John, S. (2006) 'Social policy responses to globalisation in Australia and New Zealand, 1980–2005', *Australian Journal of Political Science*, 41 (2): pp. 177–191.

Miller, R. (2005) *Party Politics in New Zealand*, Melbourne: Oxford University Press.

Nolan, M. (2000) *Breadwinning: New Zealand Women and the State*, Christchurch: Canterbury University Press.

Reingold, B. (2008) *Legislative Women: Getting Elected, Getting Ahead*, Boulder CO: Lynne Rienner.

Sawer, M. (2003) *The Ethical State? Social Liberalism in Australia*, Melbourne: Melbourne University Press.

— (2012) 'Gender divisions: crossing the floor for women', *International Political Science Review*, 33 (3): 320–35.

Sawer, M. and Simms, M. (1993) *A Woman's Place: Women and Politics in Australia*, Sydney: Allen and Unwin.

Sawer, M., Tremblay, M. and Trimble, L. (2006) *Representing Women in Parliament: A Comparative Study*, London: Routledge.

Shorter, C. (1974) 'Political thoughts in New Zealand: the ideologies, the values, and beliefs of the New Zealand National and Labour parliamentary parties', unpublished Masters thesis, Auckland: University of Auckland.

Siaroff, A. (2000) 'Women's representation in legislatures and cabinets in industrial democracies', *International Political Science Review*, 21, (2): pp. 197–215.

Simms, M. (1979) 'Conservative feminism in Australia: a case study of feminist ideology', *Women's Studies International Quarterly*, 2 (3): 305–18.

— (1982) *A Liberal Nation: The Liberal Party and Australian Politics*, Sydney: Hale and Iremonger.

Squires, J. (1999) *Gender in Political Theory*, Cambridge: Polity Press.

Sullivan, B. (1997) *The Politics of Sex: Prostitution and Pornography in Australia since 1945*, Cambridge: Cambridge University Press.

Summers, A. (1994) *Damned Whores and God's Police*, Ringwood: Penguin.

Whip, R. (2003) 'The 1996 Australian Federal Election and its aftermath: a case for equal gender representation', *Australian Feminist Studies*, 18 (40): 73–97.

Chapter Eight

(Re)Presenting Women: Gender and the Politics of Sex in Contemporary Italy

Roberta Guerrina

Introduction

Berlusconi's ascendancy to power in 1994 was a critical juncture in the politics of gender in Italy. His leadership was marred by numerous scandals and has been widely criticised for the sexualisation of women's political participation (Hooper 2011; McRobbie 2011). It is perhaps too soon to assess the long-term impact of the Berlusconi years on Italian social norms, though Newell (2009) and Benini (2012) have already identified and expressed concern about the exploitation of women's bodies in the media. From a gender perspective, Berlusconi's version of centre-right politics does not construct a new gender ideology so much as exploit already established – i.e. dominant – norms that juxtapose women's sexuality, mothering and religiousness to create a multifaceted form of dominant femininity. This chapter outlines how this process determines, and arguably limits, the ability of women in government to represent the interests of women as a constituency.

The history of women's participation and representation in Italian politics is complex and has been defined by the dominance of Catholic values in both society and politics. Berlusconi's rise to power resulted from the disintegration of the old Christian Democratic Party (DC) that dominated Italian politics in the post-war period. His leadership was predicated on a mixture of liberal economic policies and conservative social policy. Following the general election defeat in 2006, Berlusconi sought an alliance of convenience with other parties of the centre-right. These included, amongst others, National Alliance (AN) and the Union of Christian and Centre Democrats (UDC). This new umbrella party – *Popolo della Libertà*/People of Freedom (PdL) – provided a platform for the renewal of a conservative political agenda that aspired to economic reform whilst supporting Italian conservative/Catholic values (Edwards 2011; Pasquino 2008).

The Berlusconi IV government (2008–12) brought together three conservative visions – AN, *Forza Italia* and Christian Democracy. This chapter examines this government in order to highlight the impact of gender ideologies on women's position as citizens and political actors. Seeking to map gender politics in a particular phase of contemporary Italian history, the main aim is to expose the impact of the *Popolo della Libertà*'s competing discourses on gender and the ways in which women in the government have positioned themselves in relation to the party's political ideology, the politics of gender, and women's representation more broadly. In particular, it looks at the interface of social conservatism and populism in the politics of the centre-right and how it defines/curtails the political agency of women in the government.

The joining of three key conservative forces in the country under the banner of the *Popolo della Libertà* provides a useful starting point for analysing the politics of gender in the Italian right. The populist nature of Berlusconi's politics also allows for a wider commentary about emerging gender ideologies in the country. Analysing the tension between symbolic and substantive representation, the framing of gender ideologies and the public performance of dominant norms, provide a platform for a more detailed examination of the state of gender politics in Italy. The chapter evaluates the quality of women's political representation along the following lines: (1) political leadership and performance –as both members of a party and independent actors; (2) representation of women's interests; (3) media coverage and depiction *vis-à-vis* the relationship with the party leadership.

Methodological considerations

In understanding the role of women of the centre-right in representing women's interest in Italy, Butler's discussion of performativity is instructive:

> As a public action and performative act, gender is not a radical choice or project that reflects a merely individual choice, but neither is it imposed or inscribed upon the individual, as some post-structuralist displacements of the subject would contend. The body is not passively scripted with cultural codes, as if it were a lifeless recipient of wholly pre-pen cultural relations. But neither do embodied selves pre-exist the cultural conventions which essentially signify bodies. (Butler 1988: 526)

The peculiarities of political relations in the country, as defined by the events that characterised Italian politics during the Second Republic, require the adoption of a discursive methodology to unpack the role of values – and biases – in shaping women's access to power and the performance of gender norms in the theatre of politics.

Specifically, the chapter focuses on the political performance of Mara Carfagna in her position as Equal Opportunities Minister in the Berlusconi IV cabinet, although it is also illustrative of a wider debate about Italian conservatism. Her position as Equal Opportunities Minister makes her a prime candidate for analysing the politics of women's representation. The role is supposed to provide a platform for the substantive representation of women's interests in the private sphere, the economy, and politics. Public critiques of Carfagna's political trajectory (*see* for instance, Ventura 2009) highlight tensions within the centre-right about the role and position of women within Italian society, Berlusconi's (personal) gender politics, and the ability of the *Popolo della Libertà* (PdL) to represent women's interests.

Adopting a discursive approach to the analysis of the socio-political context within which Carfagna operated and the media coverage of her work as junior minister, I unpack popular perceptions of her role as a public/political figure. Drawing on Butler's (1990, 1988) work on performativity, this highlights how the performance of gender norms as a public act legitimises the hegemonic gender order.

The way politics and gender interface in the new conservative agenda promoted by the PdL should not, however, be seen as the establishment of a new gender ideology. There is a continuous line running between the gender paradigm of the Fascist regime to the family-centred values of the post-war Christian Democrats and through to Berlusconi's gender ideology. Understanding the values, tensions and idiosyncrasies of contemporary Italian conservatism requires a brief historical overview of the politics of gender since the Fascist regime. The chapter then goes on to look at the impact of the 1992 reforms triggered by large-scale investigations into political corruption (known as *Mani Pulite*) and Berlusconi's rise to power, which is inextricably linked to the history of the 'Second Republic'. The transition from a complex gender identity based on Catholicism, mothering and sexuality to one that is based predominantly on the commodification of sexuality is then examined. Women ministers in Berlusconi IV are found to be invested symbolically with this new gender identity through their performance of hegemonic gender norms, in a political setting that is increasingly reminiscent of popular TV. This chapter thus concludes by posing the question of whether a normalisation of Berlusconi's gender ideology will be the enduring legacy of the Second Republic. Women's sexuality thus becomes once again a site of contestation.

Women and politics in historical context

Women's relationship with the Italian state is embedded in a history of struggle and contestation, which has been the focus of a number of studies. Most of these make reference to the influence of fascism, Catholicism and the post-war settlement in shaping gender discourse in Italy. One of the defining features of post-war politics is the interface between political and religious conservatism. Despite a strong leftist tradition, gender politics and consequently women's participation in the public sphere has been shaped largely by socially conservative values centred on the traditional family (for details *see* Durham 2001; Guerrina 2005; Longo and Sangiuliano 2007).

The fascist legacy is still evident in the scope and nature of the socio-economic cleavages that continue to define political relations in the country. Moreover, the Italian state has a long tradition of controlling women's bodies – expressed particularly in the politics of motherhood, reproductive rights, and sexuality – in order to shape social policies (Calloni 2001; Danna 2004; Guerrina 2005). For instance, the continued elevation of maternalism to the position of a national institution reflects the state's preference for the traditional (extended) family to fulfil key welfare roles. This triangular relationship based on the interface of gender power hierarchies, exploitation of women's sexuality, and the politics of mothering has become part of the very fabric of the post-war Italian state. It also highlights the centrality of conservative norms in the evolution of social policies and politics.[1]

Contemporary feminist claims for increased recognition of women's rights and representation have to be understood within this broader context that defines public perceptions of gender and the performance of dominant norms in political institutions. These have shaped the nature of the Italian gender order in the post-war transition and the First Republic, and help understand the values that shaped acts of public performance of the hegemonic gender order (Butler 1988) during the Berlusconi years.

What is particularly important to highlight in relation to the gendered nature of Italian politics is the way in which women's bodies – political representation, reproductive rights, mothering, especially – have been the discursive playground for a number of 'higher' political and ideological battles that have defined the history of post-war Italy. Women's position and role in society have therefore become central to the emerging identity of the nation. Women's political invisibility is thus substituted by a normative power struggle between different political forces (Calloni 2009). It is in this context that we have to understand the influence of the Church within the institutions.

After the nineteenth-century unification of Italy, and before the advent of fascism, it is possible to witness the birth of various organisations fighting for improved working conditions in industries employing primarily women (Kaplan 1992). By the end of the second decade of the twentieth century, a different kind of women's movement started to develop around the advent of 'feminine fascism'. This marks the beginning of the regime's efforts to manipulate – and control – women's position in society and the family. Fascism exploited existing cultural norms about women and mothering to support a pro-natalist agenda that ultimately established femininity and mothering as public institutions in the hands of the state. The fascist regime therefore consolidated a social framework built upon representations of women as carers and cared for (De Grazia 1992; De Grand 1976; Guerrina 2005; Durham 2001).

The regime openly sought to construct and dominate women's bodies, identity and sexuality. As De Grazia (1992) highlights, it was a relationship in which the regime was the ruler and Italian women were ruled over. There was something very paternalistic about this relationship that the post-war Italian state has retained in the way social policy is formulated and discharged. Despite the early rhetoric, the regime forced mothers back into the home thus excluding women from the public sphere, and consequently, politics. Indeed, the politicisation of the private sought to reinforce the traditional gender division of labour. Various slogans, aiming at exalting women's social role in the reproductive process, reinforced these assumptions about gender roles. With the support of the Catholic Church, the

---

1. This assessment is in keeping with Sainsbury's (1999) typology of welfare states based on the interaction between the state, the market and the family.

fascist regime tried to push its authority even further by pursuing new institutional policies aimed at establishing a new type of social involvement that would 'recast older notions of maternity and fatherhood, femaleness and masculinity' (De Grazia 1992: 2). In this context, women therefore became the guardians of traditional family values (Durham 2001). Importantly, this pathway to political recognition plays into the hands of the dominant gender order, which has become reified through its relationship with formal state institutions.

Women's contribution to the resistance during World War II was the catalyst for a new debate about women's political participation and representation. The introduction of universal suffrage in 1945 is an important milestone for the feminist movement, which sees its efforts tied to the politics of the left (Cutrufelli *et al.* 2001: 138–40; Ergas 1982). However, the historic compromise between the left and the Catholics that led to the establishment of a post-war government was to shape the way in which the *questione femminile* (women's position and role in politics and society) would be framed in the new republican constitution. And, in this way, conservative gender norms and ideologies became not only institutionalised but also part of the very fabric of the Italian state.

The 1948 Constitution includes a (generic) right to equality between men and women (Art. 3), as a recognition of women's position as citizens. However, it also includes a normative agenda about women's roles in society. Article 29 sets out the position of the family, stating:

> [T]he Republic recognises the rights of the family as a natural society *based upon marriage*. Marriage is based upon moral and legal equality of the partners, within the limits established by the law to safeguard the unity of the family. [emphasis added]

Article 37 takes this further, outlining the key principles of the maternalist ideology that underpins the post-war Italian state:

> The working woman has the same right and, for equal work, the same remuneration due to a man. *Working conditions should permit the fulfilment of her essential family function and ensure adequate protection to the mother and the child.* [emphasis added]

Framing women's public and private position in terms of the role of the mother in the family is a clear indication of the influence of conservative Catholic values in Italian republican tradition.

Reflecting on the opportunities and constraints of Italian politics for the feminist movement in the early 1980s, Ergas (1982: 258) claimed that 'the complex system of alliances constructed by the Christian Democrats (DC) effectively worked against the realisation of equality for women'. As the dominant social and political force of the First Republic, the Christian Democrats defined the position of gender power structure and ideologies of the Italian state. The achievements of the 1970s, e.g. the 1971 maternity protection law, the 1977 equal opportunity law and the

1978 abortion law, should be seen as a challenge to the dominant discourse and were largely the result of an active women's movement associated with the left (Ergas 1982; Cutrufelli *et al.* 2001).

Women's enduring support for socially conservative values promoted by the DC in the post-war era was key to maintaining the party's position of power. Mattei Dogan's survey of voting behaviour in the 1950s and 1960s points to the crucial role of women voters. This ideology was constantly negotiated through women's role as mothers rather than as sexual objects. It is in this context that women would appear to feel greater affinity with the values of the centre-right, which was seen as less exploitative and more family-focused (Corbetta and Cavazza 2008: 273–4).

The dominant gender frame that became normalised in the First Republic was therefore one that speaks to women's role and position in the family. Much of the feminist writing at this time sought to provide a detailed critique of the tensions attached to women's position in Italian society, particularly the double burden and imposition of a femininity defined by either self-sacrifice or the objectification of sexuality.

The political landscape: The Second Republic and the rise of Berlusconi

The rise of Berlusconi, the advent of new communication technologies and the shift towards some form of what Bodrunova (2013) termed 'mediacracy' provide the foundation towards a new gender contract based on the commodification of women's sexuality. This new form of political practice and debate provided an ideal platform for Berlusconi's populist politics. His popularity was built upon the exploitation of accepted social norms that derived their basis from the social conservatism of the post-war era. Exploiting the dominant gender paradigm was part of Berlusconi's approach to generating broad-based appeal. Gandini's interrogation of Italian 'videocracy' (Madsen 2012) provides an equally useful frame of analysis to understand the cooptation of national public institutions as vehicles for the transmission of particular values, as presented in Walby's (1990) model of 'public sexism'. In this context, the gender models advanced by media outlets first, and then political institutions, should not be seen as a point of departure, but as the exhortation of one particular dimension of femininity.

The investigation into high-level political corruption (*Mani Pulite*) that led to the collapse of the First Republic marked a period of transition for Italian politics. The post-1992 era was supposed to change radically the way in which the Italian political system operated. One area of change that was largely overlooked by all political actors was women's political representation. Women thus continue to be largely absent from mainstream political institutions (Longo and Sangiuliano 2007: 5–6). The longed-for change in the political order thus appears to be more superficial than initially claimed, or had been hoped for (Donovan 2003).

In terms of women's representation, the disbanding of traditional political parties in favour of wider coalitions that eventually brought to power Berlusconi's *Forza Italia* and Fini's *Alleanza Nazionale should* be providing an opening for women to enter formal politics in larger numbers. Ergas theorised that when political systems are in flux or transition women have an opportunity to increase their representation within formal institutions. Transition, for Ergas, implies a significant change in the norms that underpin the political system in question, thus providing an opening for traditionally marginal groups, in this case women. (Ergas 1982: 254). Yet, the transition that took place in post-1992 Italy did not achieve a radical reformulation of political institutions or a step-change in women's political participation. Although women's representation has nearly doubled since 1996, Berlusconi's leadership has also transposed a particularly sexualised gender ideology, already widely present in his media outlets, to the political sphere. This process, I contend, has served to crystallise power hierarchies and women's public role as frames for hegemonic masculinities.

The disappearance of a political gender gap relating to men and women's voting preferences is an interesting starting point for the analysis of political representation post-1992. Corbetta and Cavazza (2008: 277, 281) theorise this shift was the result of women's greater participation in the labour market and the declining influence of Catholicism in politics.

With Berlusconi's ascent to power the influence of the Church is replaced by the power of mass media, particularly as the main force/sources for political socialisation (Corbetta and Cavazza 2008). The centrality of media had important repercussions for the Italian political landscape. First, it reinforced Berlusconi's personal position and popular appeal through his control of media outlets. In this way, personality and presentation have become more important and replaced ideology as drivers for political participation (Campus 2010). Second, his control of media outlets has enabled him to influence popular beliefs about men and women, thus shaping gender norms throughout the country (Paladino *et al.* 2013). According to Campus (2010), the mediatisation – i.e. framing political events in keeping with media requirements – of Italian politics has ultimately had the impact of limiting opportunities to contest gender norms. Paladino *et al*'s (2013: 12) study of psychological drivers leading to public protest against Berlusconi in 2009 found that 'support for these beliefs [hostile sexism] lowered women's negative emotional reactions of anger to Berlusconi's behaviour and, in turn, their participation in protest'. This suggests that the historical socialisation of women along Catholic lines and the legacy of 'feminine fascism' have provided a platform for the mediatic processes currently at work. It also shows that women remain marginal within political discourse and are still defined by the performance of hegemonic gender norms, e.g. mothering and sexuality (Paladino *et al.* 2013).

Accepting the assumption that mass communication and media have played a significant role in shaping Italian political identity over the last thirty years, it is also important to look at the role of Berlusconi's controlled media outlets in consolidating dominant values around (1) women's role in society and (2) women's sexuality. Talking about Berlusconi in an interview with Gutiérrez and Boselli in 2009, Chiara Volpato's critique of his blatant objectification of women is unforgiving:

[Berlusconi] has imposed a model of a superficial woman. A woman whose main function is decorative. An object. A woman who doesn't exist for herself but through the eyes of men. […] This model exists in other countries, but here it is the only model offered by mass media. (Volpato in Gutiérrez and Boselli 2009)

This analysis essentially points to the commodification of sexuality as a form of capital that has occurred in Italian society as a result of the liberalisation of mass communication. Again, this process is not new, but builds upon gender power hierarchies at the core of the socially conservative model that has characterised Italian socio-political structures and relations for the best part of a century.

Calloni (2009) links this shift in social imagination to the evolution of market-driven, neo-liberal values in the country. Commodification of sex and sexuality thus plays into a well-established gender ideology. As she further points out, the populist style of Berlusconi's politics serves only to normalise the explicit objectification of women's bodies in order to enhance and frame a particular form of hegemonic masculinity. Berlusconi's entry into the political domain has simply provided an additional stage where the dominant gender ideology can be performed. The ideological framework becomes legitimised through state institutions. For Calloni (2009) this is further evidence of the kind of social and political stagnation affecting the country that is ultimately undermining achievements in the area of women's rights obtained in the 1970s. In the XV Legislature, which covers the tenure of the fourth Berlusconi government, only 157 seats (out of a total of 985) in the Italian Parliament (upper and lower chambers) were held by women. This is a mere 17.23 per cent in the lower chamber (Camera dei Deputati) and 13.43 per cent in the upper chamber (Senato) (Table 8.1). Moreover, no woman has yet been the leader of a major political party. The party structures remain male dominated with only a few high-profile women promoting a feminist agenda in Parliament (Gutiérrez and Boselli 2009).

The quality of women's political representation, symbolic and substantive, remains poor, particularly when compared to other EU member states. Guadagnini and Donà's (2007: 162) data on Italy show that on 'most indicators of gender equality Italy is still one of the most backward countries in Europe'. Despite the criticisms of the Berlusconi governments in the 1990s and 2000s, the long-term impact of the gender ideology espoused by the Italian political leadership will be felt for generations to come. The absence of public endorsement for comprehensive critiques of Berlusconi's gender ideology and the absence of a coherent equality programme, as outlined by the Shadow Report (2005; see also Guadagnini and Donà 2007), is indicative of the pervasiveness of these values in Italian society and political leadership. For Calloni (2009) the current situation reflects a shift from a paternalistic vision of women's emancipation – i.e. one focused on mothering – to a commodification of women's sexuality in support of a neo-liberal agenda. Far from subverting established norms and hierarchies, it uses women's bodies as a battleground for the consolidation of a particular economic, political and ideological model. In this context, women's position in the public

Table 8.1: Women's political representation in Italy during the Second Republic

Year		Lower chamber (%)	Upper chamber (%)
1992	XI Legislature	8.12	9.12
1994	XII Legislature	15.34	8.71
1996	XIII Legislature	11.35	7.69
2001	XIV Legislature	11.47	7.69
2006	XV Legislature	17.23	13.43
2008	XVI Legislature	20.50	17.92
2013	XVII Legislature	32.00	28.75

Sources: Italian Senate data; Camera dei Deputati data; Calloni and Cedroni (2011)

Table 8.2: Representation of women in the Italian executive during the Second Republic

Year	No. of women	Total no. (cabinet)	Women's representation (%)	President of the Executive (PM)
2013	7	21	33.0	Letta
2011	3	26	11.5	Monti
2008	6	26	23.0	Berlusconi IV
2006	6	26	23.0	Prodi II
2005	2	24	8.3	Berlusconi III
2001	2	24	8.3	Berlusconi II
2000	5	25	20.0	Amato II
1999	6	26	23.0	D'Alema II
1998	6	30	20.0	D'Alema
1996	3	24	12.5	Prodi
1995	1	21	4.7	Dini
1994	1	28	3.5	Berlusconi

Source: Presidenza del Consiglio dei Ministri http://www.governo.it/Governo/Governi/governi. html (accessed 14 May 2014).

sphere – as media and political figures – is supposed to support women's role in the domestic sphere – as mothers and sex objects. A direct line can be drawn between much of the discourse currently being articulated today and the regime's construction of the ideal woman (Guerrina 2005; Durham 2001; Kaplan 1992; De Grazia 1992).

By the time Berlusconi resigned as prime minister in November 2011, there were five women in his cabinet (*see* Table 8.2). Largely holding what are considered to be marginal portfolios – equal opportunities, European affairs, youth, tourism, environment and education – and with an average age of thirty-four on taking up their positions in the executive, these cabinet women have been criticised for simply helping to augment Berlusconi's masculinity. Media focus on the largely ephemeral characteristics of the new ministers helped to crystallise the showbiz image of the 2008 executive (e.g. Babington 2008; Moore 2008; Kington 2010). It is interesting to note, however, that despite the media attention received by the women in the Berlusconi cabinet, this group remains largely under-studied as a political phenomenon in academia.

Representation in the media: Matrons, show girls and hegemonic masculinities in contemporary Italian politics

The rise of women in the Berlusconi government poses important questions about the impact of dominant gender norms within state institutions on women's public roles (Butler 1988, 1990). Confrontation and exchange with mass media further crystallises the centrality of such models. Lack of a counter discourse about women's representation and leadership – and more generally women's presence in the public sphere – ultimately consolidates established narratives about women's position and contribution in society: that women should be in the private sphere. The appointment of Mara Carfagna as Equal Opportunities Minister in the Berlusconi IV government provides an excellent case for the analysis presented here. Mara Carfagna's quick rise through the ranks of *Forza Italia* was the source of much speculation in the press. Her career ultimately served to consolidate Berlusconi's position, and a narrowly conceived populist form of femininity in the public sphere. It is through such processes that political institutions have become a theatre for this public performance of hegemonic gender norms, and hierarchies of power already at work within wider society have been legitimised. The nature and quality of public debates surrounding Carfagna's appointment highlight furthermore how hegemonic discourses and counternarratives share a common vision of femininity that centres around women's position in the family and sexuality (as discussed previously).

Sofia Ventura's (2009) wholesale critique of the portayal of women in *Forza Italia* for the Fondazione Futuro – a right-wing think tank associated with Gianfranco Fini – was intended to challenge the public exploitation of women's femininity and sexuality within Italian politics and specifically the centre-right. Ventura's analysis highlights how women's bodies are used in both politics and the media to frame leading (male) personalities, in this case Berlusconi. She calls for a shift in the way women are presented and present themselves in the political theatre and, in so doing, she provides a critique of Italian political and social structures. Unfortunately, the focus of her article and the associated debate on Berlusconi's *velinismo* (i.e. using attractive women to enhance the masculinity of the 'lead male' in public settings) only serve to marginalise further the role these women have played in Italian politics (Tonelli 2009). Moreover, even though it is now increasingly clear that this particular gender paradigm is not supported by all parties at both ends of the political spectrum or by a large section of the Italian population, what remains missing is a clear alternative vision of femininity that does not fall back on women's mothering as a source of emancipation (Paladino *et al.* 2013).

Ventura's (2009) article is a response to the candidature of many young women associated with the world of entertainment in the European elections of 2009. This choice of candidates, she argues, not only undermines women's position in the political sphere, it also undermines the legitimacy of key political institutions more generally. She openly criticises Berlusconi for his overtly exploitative behaviour and the crystallisation of a well-established trend of using young and attractive women to frame public figures in the media. Ventura's analysis focuses mainly on the use of women's bodies and youth to present an image of renewal and change within Berlusconi's PdL (Anon 2009). In this a mono-dimensional image of women centred on sexuality is promoted, thus consolidating the position of the hegemonic male as dominant and in control. What is interesting to note is that this image is not entirely dissimilar from that advocated by the fascist regime in the 1940s (Tonelli 2009).

There is much to be said for this critique. Yet an alternative reading shows that this particular narrative about 'Berlusconi's women' is as exploitative as the discourse it is trying to criticise. Looking at media representations of Carfagna's political career highlights a tendency towards voyeurism that undermines a serious appraisal of the gender ideology that her image represents (*see* for instance, Pisa's (2008) report for the *Daily Mail*). As Calloni points out, women's position and bodies are portrayed through the eyes of others. Individual ministers thus become an example of Butler's (1993) interpretation of 'the body as situation', meaning, as Chambers and Carver (2008: 66–7) explain: 'the body serves both to constrain and to enable our capacity for action'. From this perspective, the agency of women ministers working with and for Berlusconi is thus limited by the strategic use of the 'bodies' in the public sphere. Their agency – their ability to substantively represent women's interests – thus becomes curtailed by political structures and (gendered) social norms.

Media representations: Exploiting the paradigm

Berlusconi's populist politics are evident in the choice of candidate selection. Since taking on the leadership of *Forza Italia*, many of his candidates had very visible/media-centred pathways to public office. The visibility of this 'new' political leadership exposes the individuals concerned to considerable public/

media scrutiny. This trend has had specific repercussions for women, particularly if drawn from the Berlusconi media, which tends to use women in supportive and framing roles for male personalities (Cotta and Verzichelli 2002).

In this context, there is little doubt that Carfagna's position is highly performative. Her candidature and her appointment as Equal Opportunities Minister institutionalised a highly sexualised gender paradigm that is embedded in the image presented during her media career. A nuanced assessment of the impact of her performance has to take into consideration how she has discharged her role and the values she should endorse and promote. It is also interesting to note that much of the coverage of Berlusconi's women portrays them as largely voiceless. The exploitation of their bodies and image has thus been carried out by both supporters and critics.

Given the high level of media attention Carfagna received throughout her tenure in the Berlusconi cabinet, it is useful to look at the nature and quality of the coverage and reporting. This provides, first, useful insights into public perceptions of an individual's role in government; second, it illustrates dominant assumptions about gender and how an individual performs gender norms. An initial assessment of different forms of coverage shows that television reports and interviews are more likely to focus on personality, sexuality, and femininity than articles and interviews printed in the press. This can be explained by the nature of the medium and the visual focus of television, which allows for acts of public performance both from the interviewer and the interviewee.

Cotta and Verzichelli (2002: 148) observed that under Berlusconi's leadership ministers came from a wide range and varied backgrounds:

> The profiles of individual ministers range from the technocrat, selected because of his functional abilities, through the 'personal loyalist' directly recruited by the Prime Minister to assist with the implementation of the political agenda, to the more traditional figure of the 'party watch-dog', who has to represent his party's official position within the governing coalition.

Taking this position as the starting point for analysis of Carfagna's representation in the media, it is interesting to note that she is often portrayed as a clear party loyalist. This is in keeping with Ventura's analysis of the use of women as *veline* (i.e. sirens) for the party leadership. In particular, the representation of Carfagna as a 'loyalist' links her political profile and image to that of Berlusconi. It also means that she is unlikely to be perceived as an independent political figure.

Ventura (2009) produced the most extensive critique of women in the Berlusconi IV cabinet from a conservative standpoint. It is therefore useful to unpack her critique. Three dimensions are identified as underpinning the performance of women in the cabinet: (1) her individual traits; (2) her substantive performance as a political figure; (3) her relationship with Berlusconi. Each of these dimensions includes a number of nodes or frames. Individual traits include considerations about Carfagna's femininity, sexuality and appearance. Substantive performance includes consideration of her ability as an Equal Opportunities Minister and the range of issues/topics that defined her political agenda. Finally, her relationship with Berlusconi considers issues relating to her performance as 'party loyalist', as well as issues relating to various scandals reported during his tenure as prime minister. The main problem with the way this critique is formulated and presented is that it fails to produce a counter narrative or an alternative gender model. Such an approach would require a more detailed and nuanced critique of core values and power structures – e.g. the family and gender hierarchies – upon which Italian society and politics are built. Costamagna's televised interview with Carfagna in 2012 (discussed in full later) is a good example of this process. Whereas Carfagna herself sought to engage in a discussion about women's position in Italian society, the interviewer kept referring back to her personal life and circumstances.

There are two interlinked dimensions to this discussion: first, Carfagna's complex relationship with the party defining/limiting her role in the executive as secondary and supportive; second, it positions her as a frame, much like a *velina*, for 'Berlusconi's gender order'. The juxtaposition of institutional power structures with the performative nature of her role, in other words, defines her position in the public sphere both as a representative of Italian conservatism – as defined by the PdL – and as a politician seeking to represent women's interests in government. Accordingly, it curtails her ability to represent women's interests in government effectively.

Printed press

This subsection presents the findings of the analysis of 328 newspaper articles from both ends of the political spectrum. The articles were selected on the basis that they identified Mara Carfagna specifically as Equal Opportunities Minister. This identification positions her as a member of the executive and as a representative of women's interests. The articles were all published between 2008 and 2012 to cover her tenure in government.

Table 8.3 shows the seven frames that dominated the coverage; most of the coverage – notably – focused on her political performance (64 per cent of the total coverage), looking at her interaction with issues such as employment rights, gender stereotyping, harmful traditional practices, representation in decision making and violence against women. There is little in the way of an open critique of her performance in this data, and much of what there is, makes frequent reference to political scandal and her personal links to the party's leadership. Some 15 per cent of the coverage explicitly mentions the former prime minister. Moreover, a total aggregate of 11 per cent of the coverage is either critical or concerned with scandal of some kind.

The analysis of media representations of Carfagna's performance uncovers two additional trends: (1) media interest and focus on scandals diminish the longer she is in office; (2) coverage of Carfagna's work in the area of equal opportunities increases towards the end of her tenure. It would appear that the largely exploitative coverage that characterised reports and stories soon after her appointment as Equal Opportunities Minister give way to a more substantive engagement presenting

Table 8.3: Printed press – frequency and content analysis of articles discussing Carfagna's performance

Discursive nodes	No. of times reported
Berlusconi	78
Critique	37
Femininity	20
Political performance	341
Private life	8
Scandal	30
Values	14
Total number	528

Carfagna as a political figure and member of the executive. Ventura's (2009) analysis of women's position in the Berlusconi IV government clearly fits into the wider critique of Carfagna's work at the beginning of her tenure as minister, when her position in the executive is portrayed very much as secondary and supportive of Berlusconi's masculinity – i.e. what Ventura calls *velinismo*. What the analysis of press coverage highlights is that the closer she is perceived to be to Berlusconi, the less effective she is regarded as a public figure. This ultimately limits her ability to represent women's wider interest, because media interest is diverted from substantive topics to issues of a personal and ephemeral nature (Figure 8.1). Such analysis points to Carfagna's ability to acquire and assert agency as a political figure, something that is reconsidered in respect of TV coverage.

In terms of Carfagna's political performance, the analysis presented here focuses on her effectiveness at representing women's interests. Figure 8.2 provides a detailed breakdown of issues and topics that define her work as Equal Opportunities Minister. It is interesting to note a fairly critical coverage of her position of lesbian, gay, bisexual and transgender (LGBT)[2] issues in the first couple of years as minister. Her public views expressed in 2008/9 about sexuality are in keeping with the public performance of the kind of heteronormative values at the heart of Berlusconi's gender order. The settlement with the Arcigay group in 2009 constitutes a notable shift in position but should not be seen as a detailed critique of these same values. The focus of Carfagna's political agenda in relation to promoting women's rights focused in particular on the issues of violence against women, representation in decision making (*quote rosa*, i.e. quotas), equal opportunities and employment rights. If the frequency of coverage represents her work and media interest in a particular issue, the low incidence of gender stereotyping as a topic of discussion indicates a vacuum in the development of a counter narrative to public representations of women in Italy, something that

---

2.   LGBT stands for lesbian, gay, bisexual and transgender.

Figure 8.1: Focus of media coverage

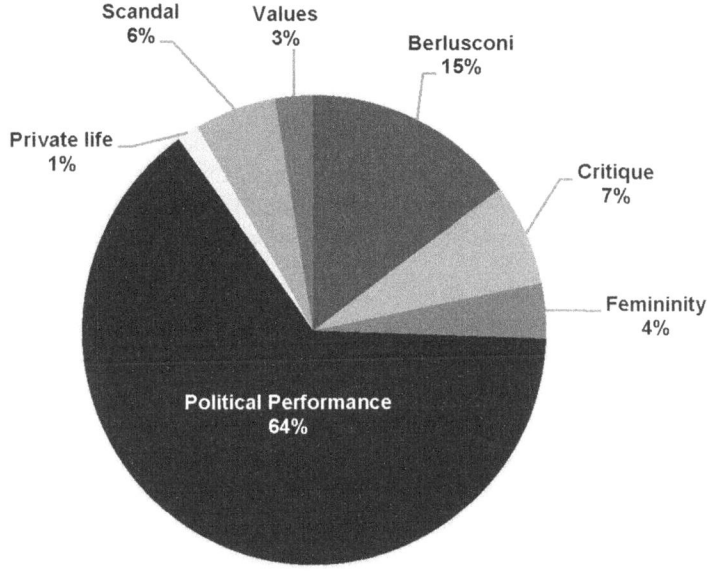

Figure 8.2: Frequency and issues covered relating to substantive representation

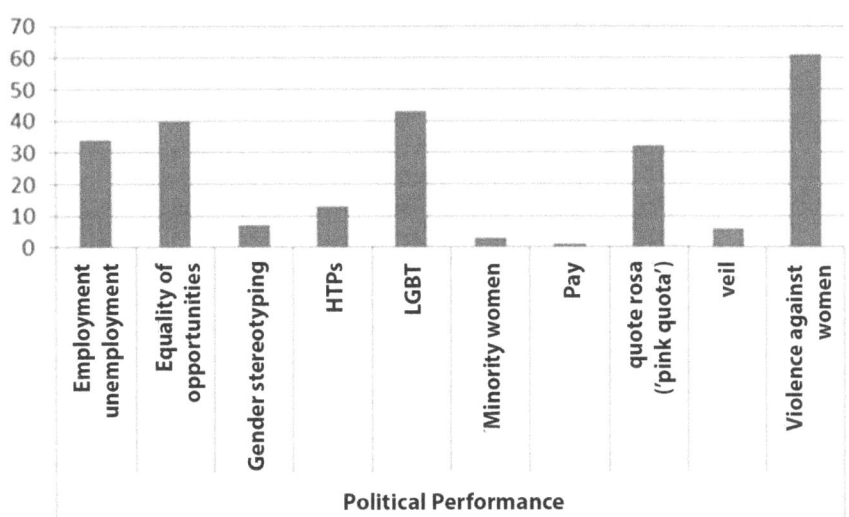

Campus (2010) identified as one of the most significant problems in relation to women's position in Italian society.

Newspaper coverage of Carfagna's tenure in government presents a mixed picture of her political performance. It also suggests that she was better able to represent women's interests as a minister once she gained confidence in her position in the executive, thus indicating a much greater degree of agency than originally presented in the media. This analysis thus points to Carfagna's pathway to politics and membership of the government as ultimately limiting her ability for manoeuvre in the executive. The appointment of Carfagna, a fairly junior and inexperienced individual with close links with the leadership of the party, helps to marginalise further the role of what has traditionally been seen as a secondary portfolio.

Television coverage

Much of the critique of Carfagna's work as Equal Opportunities Minister comes from various TV interviews where the discussion has centred on her private life, physical attributes, and her relationship with the prime minister. My analysis focuses on a particular interview held on 8 March 2012, carried out by Luisella Costamagna on the TV Programme Robinson (RAI3), after the dismissal of the Berlusconi IV government. This particular programme is interesting both for the way the debate was presented and structured and for the actual content of the interview.

The staging and format of the interview seems to set in opposition two women, both performing (and thus reinforcing) a dominant form of femininity. Questions focus predominantly on Carfagna's personal experience of working in politics, her pathway to a position in the cabinet and her career in the media prior to entering politics. The issue of sponsorship is implicit throughout the discussion, as is the public performance of gender norms. Issues such as physical attributes and the value of a sexualised femininity are both implicit and explicitly addressed. The interview lasted just over thirty-three minutes. The nature of the questions posed to Carfagna during the first seventeen minutes focused almost entirely on her personal past, media career, sponsorship and her trajectory from media personality to government minister. This discussion was followed by two minutes' in-depth questioning about Berlusconi's position and control of media outlets. This was an introduction to a wider discussion about Berlusconi and sexual scandal. Berlusconi's personal interest in her career was also the subject of detailed scrutiny. The first substantive questions about the representation of women's rights and Carfagna's performance as an equal opportunities minister came twenty-two minutes into the interview. This line of questioning however lasted just over two minutes, when Costamagna (the interviewer) returned to Carfagna's views about the Berlusconi candidature for the 2013 elections. The interview finally ends with a brief (forty-five second) discussion of women's representation in politics and decision making. This (belated) discussion, however, is rather superficial. Figure

Figure 8.3: Breakdown of issues covered in 2012 interview

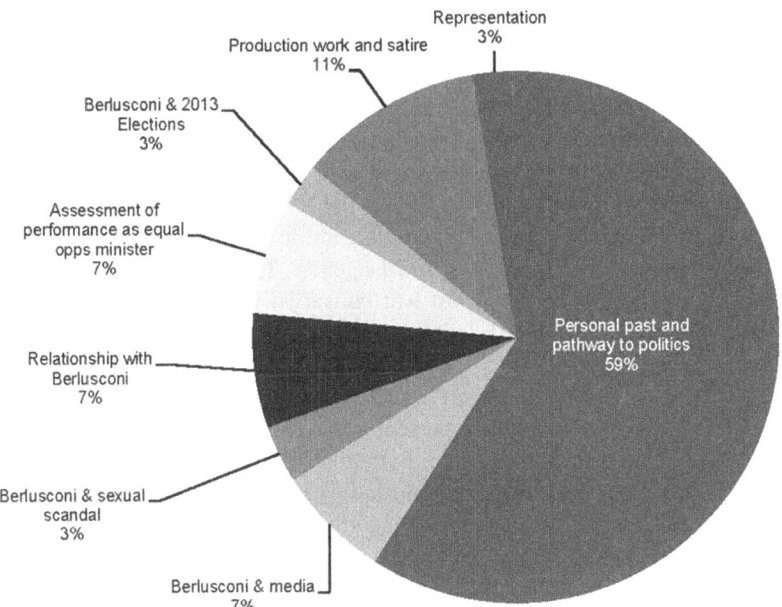

8.3 provides a detailed breakdown of issue coverage in the interview. Discussion of Carfagna's career trajectory and Berlusconi accounts for 79 per cent of the total interview. Only 10 per cent of the discussion focused on substantive issues relating to women's interests.

Two frames are especially dominant in the interview: (1) sexuality, and (2) image. The focus on the interviewee's personal traits was at the expense of a meaningful discussion of key issues relating to equality, representations of women and gender stereotyping in Italy. Clearly, this represents a missed opportunity to raise awareness and engage in a meaningful discussion about women's position and role in contemporary Italian society, politics and economics. Far from establishing such a meaningful discussion and counter discourse about women's position in Italian society, the interview reinforces the dominant gender order. This focus on individual and personal traits exploits Carfagna in an assertion of power that is designed to discipline women's voices in public spaces.

These observations ultimately lead to the conclusion that individual women's agency to represent women's interests in politics is framed by the nature and scope of sponsorship associated with an individual's career. The failure of the Italian political system to challenge the clientelist nature of party structures in the transition between the First and Second Republic ultimately undermines the ability of individual women to act for and on behalf of women in a way that is transformative.

Conclusions: Enduring tensions between symbolic positioning and substantive representation

This chapter has mapped how Carfagna's position in Berlusconi's government performed a specific function in supporting a dominant gender ideology – and one that was particularly conservative, in that it defined women's public position in relation to mothering and sexuality. As outlined earlier the performance of both of these gender norms is key to the conservative paradigm as performed in Italy. The analysis of media coverage has uncovered how Carfagna has become emblematic of a dominant form of femininity.

This raises important questions about the ability of Italian conservative parties to promote an openly feminist political agenda. The historical baggage of the right in Italy is something that post-war conservative parties constantly have to contend with, particularly in relation to the enduring gender models associated with the Christian Democrats. The focus on mothering, gender difference, and women's role in the private sphere poses an additional challenge for women in conservative parties seeking to represent women's interests in government. The case of Carfagna is illustrative of this trend. Her ability to represent women's interests in her position of Equal Opportunities Minister is framed – and limited – by public perceptions of her career as depending upon sponsorship from the leader of the party. What is particularly worthy of notice is that in trying to challenge and hold her – and Berlusconi – to account, the media crystallised the dominant gender ideology. The exploitation of Carfagna as a political figure in this way highlights the extent to which the media buys into the dominant gender order. This is particularly evident in the absence of an alternative model of femininity in public discourse and debate.

References

Anon (2005) Shadow Report: 'Sulla Situazione Italian a 10 anni dalla conferenza ONU sulle donne, Pechino, 1995', available at http://www.noidonne.org/articolo.php?ID=00001 (accessed 30 June 2014) (n.p.).

——— (2009) 'Veline come Eurocandidate del Pdl? Fare Future dice no', available at http://news.panorama.it/politica/Veline-come-Eurocandidate-del-Pdl-FareFuturo-dice-stop (accessed 30 June 2014).

Babington, D. (2008) 'Ex-showgirl starts in Berlusconi's female cast', Reuters, US Edition, 8 May, available at: http://www.reuters.com/article/2008/05/08/us-italy-government-women-idUSL0880971820080508 (accessed 1 June 2013).

Benini, S. (2012) 'Televised bodies: Berlusconi and the body of Italian women', *Journal of Italian Cinema & Media Studies*, 1 (1): 87–102.

Bodrunova, S. (2013) 'Fragmentation and polarization of the public sphere in the 2000s: evidence from Italy and Russia', *Global Media Journal*, 3 (1): 1–35.

Butler, J. (1988) 'Performative acts and gender constitutions: an essay in phenomenology and feminist theory', *Theatre Journal*, 40 (4): 519–31.

——— (1990) *Gender Trouble: Feminist and the Subversion of Identity*, London: Routledge.

——— (1993) *Bodies that Matter: On the Discursive Limits of Sex*, London: Routledge.

Calloni, M. (2001) 'Debates and controversies on abortion in Italy', in McBride Stetson. D. (ed.) *Abortion Politics, Women's Movements and the Democratic State: A Comparative Study of State Feminism*, Oxford: University Press.

——— (2009) 'In Italia, tra donne e TV fine di un' alleanza'. Available at: http://http://www.resetdoc.org/story/00000001454 (accessed 5 May 2014).

Calloni, M. and Cedroni, L. (2011) 'Le donne nelle istituzioni rappresnetativie dell' Italian Republicana: una ricognizione storica e critica'. Available at http://www.unimib.it/upload/gestioneFiles/__corso2009/dispensecorso2012/callonicedronidonnealparlamento.pdf (accessed 30 June 2014).

Campus, D. (2010) 'Political discussion, views of political expertise and women's representation in Italy', *European Journal of Women's Studies*, 17, 249–68.

Chambers, S. and Carver, T. (2008) *Judith Butler and Political Theory: Troubling Politics*, London: Routledge.

Corbetta, P. and Cavazza, N. (2008) 'From the parish to the polling booth: evolution and interpretation of the political gender gap in Italy, 1968–2006', *Electoral Studies*, 27, 272–84.

Cotta, M and Verzichelli, L. (2002) 'Ministers in Italy: notables, party men, technocrats and media men', *South European Society and Politics*, 7 (2): 117–52.

Cutrufelli, M. R., Doni, E., Gaglianone, P. *et al.* (2001) *Il Novecento delle Italiane: Una Storia Ancora da Raccontare*, Rome: Editori Riuniti.

Danna, D. (2004) 'Italy: the never-ending debate' in Outshoorn, J. (ed.) *The Politics of Prostitution: Women's Movements, Democratic States and the Globalisation of Sex Commerce*, Cambridge: Cambridge University Press.

De Grand, A. (1976) 'Women under Italian Fascism', *Historical Journal*, 19 (4): 947–68.

De Grazia, V. (1992) *How Fascism ruled Women: Italy 1922–1945*, Berkeley, CA: University of California Press.

Donovan, M. (2003) 'A second republic for Italy?' *Political Studies Review*, 1, 18–33.

Durham, M. (2001) *Women and Fascism*, London: Routledge.

Edwards, P. (2011) 'The Berlusconi anomaly: populism and patrimony in Italy's long tradition', *South European Society and Politics*, 10 (2): 225–43.

Ergas, Y. (1982) 'Feminism and the Italian party system: women's politics in a decade of turmoil, *Comparative Politics*, 14 (3): 253–79.

Guadagnini, M. and Donà, A. (2007) 'Women's policy machinery in Italy between European pressures and domestic constraints', in Outshoorn, J. and Kantola, J. (eds) *Changing State Feminism*, Basingstoke: Palgrave Macmillan, pp. 164–81.

Guerrina, R. (2005) *Mothering the Union: The Politics of Gender, Equality and Maternity Rights in the EU*, Manchester: University Press.

Gutiérrez, M. and Boselli, O. (2009) 'Where are the women? Part 1', *Inter Press Service*, available at: http://www.ipsnews.net/2009/09/politics-italy-where-are-the-women-part-1/ (accessed 5 May 2014).

Hooper, J. (2011) 'Berlusconi's scandals – timeline', *The Guardian*, 14 October, available at: http://www.guardian.co.uk/world/2011/oct/14/berlusconi-scandals-timeline (last accessed 1 June 2013).

Kaplan, G. (1992) *Contemporary Western European Feminism*, London: Routledge.

Kington, T. (2010) 'A weathergirl, a Miss Italy Contestant and a showgirl: Berlusconi unrepentant over election choices', *The Guardian*, 28 February, available at: http://www.guardian.co.uk/world/2010/feb/28/silvio-berlusconi-single-man-showgirls (accessed 5 May 2014).

Longo, V. and Sangiuliano, M. (2007) *Issue Histories Italy: Series of Timelines of Policy Debates*, Vienna: QUING Project, available at: http://www.quing.eu/files/results/ih_italy.pdf (accessed 5 May 2014).

Madsen, O. J. (2012) 'Baudriallard and videocracy: the virtual absence of the political', *International Journal of Baudriallard Studies*, 9 (3) (n.p.), available at: http://www.ubishops.ca/baudrillardstudies/vol-9_3/v9-3-madsen.html (accessed 5 May 2014).

McRobbie, A. (2011) 'Beyond post-feminism', *Public Policy Research*, 18 (3): 179–84.

Moore, M. (2008) 'Berlusconi apoints [sic] former showgirl to cabinet', *The Telegraph*, 7 May, available at: http://www.telegraph.co.uk/news/worldnews/europe/italy/1936102/Silvio-Berlusconi-apoints-former-showgirl-to-cabinet.html (accessed 5 May 2014).

Newell, J. (2009) 'Italy during the Berlusconi years: the economy and society', in Albertazzi, D., Brook, C., Ross, C. and Rothenberg, N. (eds) *Resisting the Tide – Cultures of Opposition in the Berlusconi Years*, London: Continuum.

Paladino, M.P., Zaniboni, S., Fasoli, F., Vaes, J. and Volpato, C. (2013) 'Why did Italians protest against Berlusconi's sexist behaviour? The role of sexist beliefs and emotional reactions in explaining women and men's pathways to protest', *British Journal of Social Psychology*, available at: http://onlinelibrary.wiley.com/doi/10.1111/bjso.12023/full (accessed 5 May 2014).

Pasquino, G. (2008) 'The 2008 Italian national Elections: Berlusconi's third victory', *South European Society and Politics*, 13 (3): 345–62.

Pisa, N. (2008) 'Former topless model joins Berlusconi's cabinet as Italy's equalities minister', *Mail Online*, 9 May, available at: http://www.dailymail.co.uk/news/article-564760/Former-topless-model-joins-Berlusconis-cabinet-Italys-equalities-minister.html#ixzz1rLPKby9b (accessed 5 May 2014).

Sainsbury, D. (ed.) (1999) *Gender and Welfare Regimes*, Oxford: University Press.

Tonelli, M. (2009) 'Basta Veline in Politica. L'alto la della fondazione fini', *La Republica*, April available at: http://www.repubblica.it/2009/04/sezioni/politica/elezioni-2009–1/futuro-veline/futuro-veline.html (accessed 5 May 2014).

Ventura, S. (2009) 'Donne in Politica: il "velinismo" non serve', Fondazione Roberto Franceschi, 28 April, available at: http://www.fondfranceschi.it/cogito-ergo-sum/donne-in-politica-il-velinismo-non-serve (accessed 15 August 2013).

Walby, S. (1990) *Theorizing Patriarchy*, Oxford: Blackwell.

Chapter Nine

Conservative Women MPs' Constructions of Gender Equality in Finland

Johanna Kantola and Milja Saari

Introduction

> For the wellbeing of Finns and for the success of Finland, it is crucial that resources of the nation are being utilised full out, [and] that men and women are equal in working life and also that the resources of the nation's parenthood, fathers and mothers, are utilised full out (Sari Sarkomaa, woman MP; National Coalition Party, speech 58a).

This quotation is from a political process that took place in 2010 around Finland's first ever Government Report on Gender Equality (Gender Equality Report 2011). The comments are made by a woman MP from the conservative National Coalition Party and are, in many ways, representative of the debate. First, conservative women MPs were particularly active in the debate and hence both emerged and confirmed their position as shapers of the national gender equality discourse. Second, their way of framing and legitimising gender equality issues strengthened the focus on resources, the economy and the nation. As a result, the traditional Finnish way of defining gender equality in the leftist context of the Nordic welfare state was further moved in the direction of neoliberal governance (*see* Kantola *et al.* 2012; Nousiainen *et al.* 2013).

In this chapter, we are interested in exploring further these initial observations. Our empirical case study consists of a quantitative and qualitative analysis of the parliamentary debates that took place in the Gender Equality Report. We focus on the feminist and gendered claims made by the women MPs regarding three issues: (1) reconciliation of work and family, (2) equal pay, and (3) gender violence – to study the shifts in the hegemonic discourse on gender equality. Traditionally, the left-wing approach has focused on economic equality, the economic independence of women, equality for working mothers (and nowadays also fathers), and the state's role in providing the necessary services that enable women to work in the labour market. The right-wing/conservative discourse has traditionally highlighted family as distinct from the public sphere and held that families/mothers have the right to choose to stay at home if they so desire. We are interested in these constructions against the political backdrop of neoliberal governance that foregrounds the language of individuals, choices, markets and opportunities and that, among other things, renders gender equality a technical question of numbers and the 'right' policies and tools (Kantola and Squires 2012). The shifts in gender equality discourse documented here seem paradoxically to bring together the traditionally leftist talk about social structures and inequality, and right-conservative talk about individuals and their choices. Hence, it is difficult to trace traditional and socially conservative constructions of gender roles from the debates. At the same time, we suggest, the neoliberal focus on the individual woman and her rights effectively masks the more conservative gender constructions that actually underpin this traditional woman's conservative constructions.

The Gender Equality Report is an illuminating case, as it both looks into the objectives and measures of the government gender equality policy that have been pursued over the past ten years, and sketches the outlines for future gender equality policy. Its foci range from decision making, education and research, to working life, men and gender violence. The report was prepared by the government's Gender Equality Unit, in a process that was seen at first as bureaucratic and apolitical – it involved mainly civil servants and researchers and excluded political parties, civil society and labour market organisations. The governing parties, however, rejected the first draft of the report and accepted only a significantly shortened version with many findings merely annexed to the report. The report was debated twice, in the Finnish parliament and in the parliamentary Committee of Working Life and Equality, giving MPs a chance to express their views on gender equality issues. As MPs can choose whether to participate in parliamentary and committee debates, the level of participation is taken as an expression of interest in the issue. The parliamentary debates are not only recorded but also televised, highlighting the performative aspects of debates and the individual MPs' speeches. Ultimately, the Speaker of the Parliament decides to whom to give the speaking turns and, in so doing, shapes the debate.

The relationship between gender and conservative parties has most often been studied through questions of representation, both descriptive and substantive: do conservative women get elected and why; what is their position in the party hierarchy; do they make claims to represent women or act for women; and do they act for women's issues in terms of sponsoring bills or acting across party lines (Childs and Webb 2012; Reingold 2008; Swers 2002)? In our research also, we compare the claims made by the different political actors. However, we ask a slightly different set of questions, namely: How do conservative women MPs construct gender equality in the parliamentary debates? Can these constructions be distinguished from 'leftist' gender equality claims? Do the women MPs focus on structuralist explanations of remaining gender inequalities (leftist), or do they highlight individuals, families and their right to choose (right-wing/conservative)? What consequences do these constructions have for the overall gender equality discourse in the country?

Contextualising gender and conservatism in Finland

Whilst conservatism comes in many forms, characteristically it emphasises individual rights and opportunities, the pursuit of self-interest in a free market economy, the rejection of state intervention in the private sphere, and natural inequality between individuals' abilities (Bryson and Heppell 2010, p. 33–4). In terms of gender relations, conservatism has traditionally emphasised complementary gender roles and the importance of women's nurturing and reproductive roles, as well as the family and its central role in reproducing social cohesion. Traditionally, left-wing parties, with their understanding of structural inequalities and more progressive gender roles, have been thought to provide better avenues for advancing feminist claims for gender equality.

A number of scholars have, however, started to explore the self-proclaimed 'feminisation' of conservative parties (on the UK, *see* Bryson and Heppell 2010; Childs and Webb 2012). For instance, the valorisation of the values and practices of women's traditional gender roles in the family and in relation to mothering, and a commitment to equal opportunities in the market, can unite conservative claims with those seeking to advance gender equality (Bryson and Heppell 2010: 39; Childs and Webb 2012).

The Finnish party system does not show clearly where to start studying right-wing or conservative parties in Finland. The country has a multi-party political system with eight parties sitting in the current parliament. Figure 9.1 illustrates a generalisation of how the parliamentary parties are usually divided along left-right and liberal–conservative axes in Finland, according to the nodal points that are highlighted in their gender equality discourse.

Traditionally, the three biggest parties, namely the Centre Party, the National Coalition Party and the Social Democrats (SDP), have fought to be the biggest prime ministerial party to form the government. This has, in part, resulted in a lack of polarised ideological differences and a search for a common centre ground (Paloheimo and Raunio 2008: 21). During the 2007–11 parliamentary term – the focus of this study[1] – the Centre Party, the National Coalition Party, the Green Party and the Swedish People's Party formed the right–green government. The representation of women in the parliament was 42 per cent, and in the government 60 per cent (12 women and 8 men) (2007). Parties and their seats in the parliament (2007–11) and the share of women MPs are presented in Table 9.1.

Of these political parties the National Coalition Party, The Finns, the Centre Party, the Swedish People's Party and the Christian Democrats are seen to be on the (centre) right, and the Social Democrats, the Left Alliance and the Green Party on the left although the Green Party is clearly more individualistic than the other left parties (Paloheimo 2008: 38–9, 54–5). Although the division between the left and the right is not as stark in Finland as in some other European countries, the parties on the right share some core values that differentiate them from those

---

1. Our data date back to 2010 therefore uses statistics from the results of the 2011 elections.

Figure 9.1: Generalisation of the Finnish parliamentary parties and the axes of liberal–conservative and left-right in the context of gender equality discourses

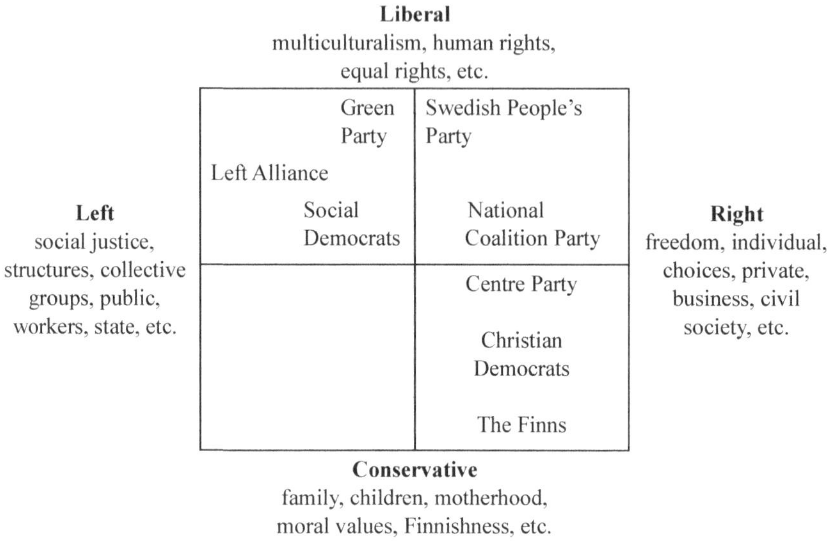

Liberal
multiculturalism, human rights,
equal rights, etc.

	Green Party	Swedish People's Party	
Left Alliance			
Left social justice, structures, collective groups, public, workers, state, etc.	Social Democrats	National Coalition Party	**Right** freedom, individual, choices, private, business, civil society, etc.
		Centre Party	
		Christian Democrats	
		The Finns	

Conservative
family, children, motherhood,
moral values, Finnishness, etc.

on the left. The former emphasise the importance of family for social cohesion, freedom rather than equality (with the exception of The Finns who emphasise the rights of the poor and the old), and the free market rather than regulation or state intervention (Paloheimo 2008: 30). There are also some significant differences between the right-wing parties, with the Swedish People's Party being a liberal party in terms of its pro-immigration and multiculturalism stance, and The Finns, being socially very conservative and nationalist. The National Coalition Party and the Swedish People's Party are very much on the right in terms of economic values, and The Finns more on the left. There are also differences within parties, with the National Coalition Party having both conservative and liberal factions.

As in other western democracies, feminist research has established that Finnish left-wing parties' representation of women's concerns has traditionally been more in line with feminist and women's movement demands (Holli 2006). Women's descriptive representation has also been higher in left-wing parties, although right-wing parties have recently caught up (Kuusipalo 2011). In terms of institutional structures, Finnish political parties have women's organisations, and a fixed percentage of party funding (which has varied between 8 and 12 per cent) goes to 'women-specific' activities. Such regulation has encouraged for example the right-wing populist party, The Finns, to establish a women's organisation in order

Table 9.1: Parties and their seats in the Parliament (2007–11) and the share of women MPs (per cent)

	Left Alliance	Social Democrats	Green Party	Centre Party	National Coalition Party	Swedish People's Party	Christian Democrats	The Finns
Seats, 2007–11	17	45	15	51	50	9	7	5
Women MPs (%)	18	56	67	27	40	56	57	20

for them not to lose party funding (Luhtakallio and Ylä-Anttila, forthcoming). Increasingly, women MPs in the conservative parties play a crucial role as shapers of gender equality discourse and policy. In recent years, women's parliamentary representation in the conservative National Coalition Party has come to parallel that of left-wing parties, and, furthermore, Finland's two female prime ministers (Anneli Jäätteenmäki, 17 April–24 June 2003, and Mari Kiviniemi, 22 June 2010–22 June 2011) have come from the conservative Centre Party.

Finnish women's party organisations have a long history of cross-party cooperation in parliament and civil society. This has ensured a certain degree of consensus surrounding what is constructed as women's interests – a hegemonic discourse about gender equality – and a learning process for those coming into the context from 'outside'.[2] Cooperation takes place in the Coalition of Finnish Women's Associations (NYTKIS, established in 1988), which includes the women's organisations of all political parties, and in the parliament's women's MPs network, established in 1991. The achievements of these networks include, for example, the reform of the Childcare Act in the 1990s, which extended the right of statutory public childcare to all children under the school age of seven, as well as building broader consensus about the policies needed to achieve gender equality. This consensus covers such issues as women's political representation, the gender pay gap, women's participation in the labour market, reconciling work and the family, and violence against women. Nevertheless, analyses of the causes of inequalities and political and the policy solutions required to overcome these vary greatly between the parties – suggesting competing conceptions of what is in women's interests (Celis *et al.* forthcoming).

---

2. By 'outside', we mean new parties like The Finns and their MPs, who had to find a means to discuss gender equality in a way that is both compatible with the party's overall political rhetoric and with the present hegemonic gender equality discourse in the country.

Research design and material

Our research material consists of the Government Report on Gender Equality (21 October 2010), the preliminary debate in plenary session (18 November 2010), the committee report of the Employment and Equality Committee (25 February 2011), and the second reading in plenary session (2 March 2011).[3] Three gender policy areas, namely (1) reconciliation of work and family, (2) equal pay and (3) gender violence are chosen because of their centrality to gender equality, as Katja Taimela, woman MP, Social Democrats, makes clear (speech 18b):

> Issues concerning gender equality can also vary a lot in their size. There is a lot to be done in relation to special groups. However, the biggest gender equality issues resonate with society at large. They are issues related to pay, parenthood and violence.

The three debates moreover relate to different dimensions of gender equality, with equal pay being a labour market issue (often conceptualised as an economic right), the reconciliation of work and family both a labour market and a family issue (often framed as a social right) and the issue of violence is traditionally framed as a private issue that feminists have fought to move to the public sphere (bodily right). The focus on three key issues enables us therefore to analyse their differences and similarities. In terms of our research questions, a focus on these three debates is particularly useful for at least two other reasons. First, they represent both old and new gender equality issues in the country, with work and family, and equal pay having a long history in the country's gender equality policy, whereas violence has entered the political agenda more recently. We hypothesise that the different historical trajectories may have relevance to the ways in which left- and right-wing women MPs construct the issues and for the similarities and differences between these constructions. Second, the differences between left- and right-wing parties have traditionally been stark in relation to these three issues. In work and family, the differences centre on the notion of family and the role of women therein, as well as the public–private division and the role of the state in upholding this distinction. In respect of equal pay, the most evident difference between left and right is that the former promotes legal duties that target the employer, whilst the latter usually resists them. In relation to gender violence, the difference has traditionally been that the left has framed the issue in terms of a feminist 'violence against women' discourse and emphasised the need to change societal power relations to eradicate violence, whereas the right has framed the issue in terms of 'family violence' that results from interpersonal problems (Siukola 2004; Kantola 2006). Yet, despite such differences left- and right-wing parties have, in practice, negotiated an 'uneasy balance' in terms of state policy surrounding reconciliation of work and family. This uneasy balance consists of a

---

3. The minutes for the plenary sessions and the report can be downloaded in Finnish from the Parliament's webpage http://www.eduskunta.fi.

mixed system which combines parental leave that is partly funded by the state, day care services that are mainly provided by the public sector (to reflect the left-wing demand for state responsibility), and a system of home care allowance in which the state and municipalities pay for a parent to take care of a child at home (to reflect the right-wing demand for choice for parents).[4] In this chapter, we are interested in analysing the shifts in these traditional constructions.

Parliamentary group speeches open up the debate

To characterise the overall constructions of gender equality in Finland we begin by analysing the opening speeches of the parliamentary debate on the Equality Report (18 November 2010). These consist of the Minster of Equality's speech, which introduces the issue, and the parliamentary group speeches that follow before the floor is opened to individual MPs. In this opening of the debate, it is noteworthy that three out of the eight parliamentary group speeches were given by men MPs (Centre Party, National Coalition Party, Left Alliance), all known for their active role in establishing the Parliamentary Men MPs' Network as a counter actor to the traditional cross-party Parliamentary Women MPs' Network. The tone of the parliamentary group speeches, however, was more moderate than the overall debate, as they represented the stances taken by the political parties on the issue of gender equality. For example, in this case, the women's organisations of some of the parties had been consulted about the contents of the speeches as they came so close to their specific area of expertise and interest.

Some key characteristics of the Finnish debate on gender equality can be discerned from these opening speeches. First, a number of speeches – including that of the Minister for Equality Stefan Wallin (man, Swedish People's Party) – suggest that Finland is a model country for gender equality. In making this claim, speakers appeal to global gender equality indices and the fact that Finnish women gained the right to vote in 1906. In this debate, such arguments were also used to say that as a pioneer Finland had a particular duty to push its gender equality policies forward, although feminist research considers such rhetorical strategies as a key way to downplay continuing and existing gender equality problems in the country (Julkunen 2010; Holli 2002).

One particular area where gender equality is often said to have been achieved is that of political representation, a claim that was articulated in a number of

---

4.   While we were finalising this chapter in August 2013, the Government presented a new home care allowance model as part of the discussions for the next year's budget. The new model would divide the home care allowance period (approximately two years per child) evenly between the father and the mother. If one of the parents did not use his/her 50 per cent of the allowance period, the family would lose that time from their state supported parental leave. The model is justified by promoting gender equality in working life and in the family. This model came as a surprise to Finnish people, and also to us researchers. The new model is an example of the decisions made in our 'rainbow' government, where both the left and right are represented. Future research will have a new interesting case to study in this renewed model, in which gender equality policies and families' choices clash in discussions about parental leave.

MPs' speeches. This was contrasted with a new theme of women's low/under-representation in economic decision making and a demand to increase the number of women on company boards (e.g. the Minister, the National Coalition Party, the Green Party). Of these the Green Party openly supported corporate board quotas and the conservative National Coalition Party spoke positively about quota effects in relation to political decision making, indicating the acceptability of this controversial issue even for parties on the right.

Nearly all parties addressed the reconciliation of work and family, the gender pay gap and gender violence as key issues where gender inequalities still persist. Of these, the reconciliation of work and family was most hegemonic, in the sense that it was mentioned by all eight of the political parties represented in the parliament, and by the Minister. This of course reflects the constructions of gender equality that centre on the importance of women and men's equal opportunities to participate in the labour market. All parties also used arguments that fathers' care roles make men healthier and happier, and emphasised how women bring new resources to the economy. The gender pay gap was mentioned as a key remaining gender inequality problem by the Minister and five political parties both on the left and right (the Centre Party, the SDP, the Left Alliance, the Christian Democrats, The Finns). Gender violence was also mentioned by five political parties, on both the political left and right (the National Coalition Party, the SDP, the Left Alliance, the Swedish People's Party, the Christian Democrats, The Finns). However, rather than framing it as violence against women or gender violence, MPs spoke most about 'violence in intimate relationships' that concerned children, women and men, as discussed in more detail below.

In addition to the three gender equality policy themes there was a fourth hegemonic theme that was discussed by the Minister and five political parties: men's equality concerns (the Centre Party, the National Coalition Party, the SDP, the Left Alliance, the Green Party). The specific themes included men's health, custody rights, and the risk of men being marginalised in society. The emphasis placed on this topic reflects not only the active stance taken on the issue by the Finnish men's movements and organisations, but also the more traditional character of gender equality discourse in Finland, namely its harmony, symmetry and gender balance between women and men. The parliamentary group speeches emphasised how, for example: 'The Finns need to be told that equality benefits everyone' and that 'Advancing gender equality is our shared concern' (Risto Autio, man, Centre Party, cf. Jari Larikka, man, National Coalition Party), and that 'Good gender equality work supports the goals of both genders' (Kari Uotila, man, Left Alliance).

Differences in foregrounding certain topics among the parties included the emphasis that the SDP, the Left Alliance and Christian Democrats placed on gendered poverty and the importance of welfare state services to gender equality. In line with their general emphasis on openness and tolerance, the Green Party promoted the marriage rights of same sex couples and the Swedish People's Party spoke of the rights of immigrants.

Analysing the speeches: Who speaks in the plenary sessions?

Here we analyse who speaks in the plenary sessions and takes most of the speech turns: are they women/men, and are they right-wing/conservative women MPs or left-wing/Green women MPs? The data consist of the two plenary sessions. The reason why we focus only on women in this phase of our research[5] is that we wish to tease out the differences and similarities between women MPs in these two different political groups in respect of how active they are in discussing gender equality at the highest political arena – the parliament – and to analyse the congruencies and differentiations that are evident in discussion of work and family, equal pay and gender violence.

There were 77 MPs in the group of left-wing/Green parties in the Finnish parliament, of which 38 were women (49 per cent) (*see* Table 9.2). Women from the left-wing/Green parties comprised 45 per cent of all women MPs and 19 per cent of all MPs in the parliament. The group of right-wing conservatives included 123 MPs of whom 46 were women MPs (37 per cent). The conservative women formed 55 per cent of all women MPs and 23 per cent of all MPs. To round the percentages: half of the MPs in the group of left-wing/Green parties were women whereas little more than one in three right-wing conservative MPs was a woman.

The right-wing National Coalition Party had the most speaking turns (30) (*see* Table 9.3). Of these, 16 were held by women MPs and 14 by men. The Social Democrats came second with 22 speaking turns (16 by women, 6 by men). Third was the Centre Party with 20 speaking turns (11 by women, 9 by men). Speaking turns are more evenly shared between women and men in the Coalition Party and in the Centre Party than in the Social Democrats, where women spoke more often than men. The Christian Democrats and The Finns had three speaking turns respectively. None of these speeches was given by a man. In the first plenary session none of the women MPs in the Left Alliance ($N = 3$) gave a speech and only one in the second. In the second plenary session, none of the Green Party's women MPs spoke ($N = 10$).

Notable in Table 9.4 is that right-wing/conservative MPs had more speaking turns (67 per cent) than left-wing/Green MPs (33 per cent). In both categories women MPs had more speaking turns (58 per cent, respectively) than men. Women MPs in the group of left-wing/Green parties took 19 speaking turns in the plenary sessions, whereas the women MPs in the group of right-wing-conservatives took 39 speaking turns: almost double the amount. In the group of right-wing conservative MPs there were 46 women, and in left-wing/Green parties, there were 38. The greater number of right-wing conservative women MPs explains some of the difference but nevertheless, right-wing conservative women were much more active than left-wing/Green women MPs in these debates, especially when compared to their share of right-wing conservative party seats. This begs the

---

5. The differences and similarities between women and men MPs in both right-wing/conservative and left-wing/Green parties will be analysed in the next phase of our research.

Table 9.2: Women in the parliament and in the plenary sessions

	Left Alliance	Social Democrats	Green Party	Centre Party	National Coalition Party	Swedish People's Party	Christian Democrats	True Finns	Åland Islands MP	Total
Women in plenary sessions	1	10	1	4	6	2	2	1	1	28
Men in plenary sessions	3	3	1	5	4	1	0	0	0	17
Seats in the Parliament 2007	17	45	15	51	50	9	7	5	1	200
Women in parliamentary group 2007	3	25	10	15	20	5	4	1	1	84
Parliamentary group: women (%)	18	56	67	29	40	56	57	20	100	42
Speeches by women MPs (total) in the parliamentary group (%)	33	40	10	27	30	40	50	100	100	

Table 9.3: Speeches in the plenary sessions (parties, men and women)

	Left Alliance	Social Democrats	Green Party	Centre Party	National Coalition Party	Swedish People's Party	Christian Democrats	The Finns
Plenary session 1								
Women	0	9	2	6	9	4	3	2
Men	4	3	2	9	8	2	0	0
Subtotal	4	12	4	15	17	6	3	2
Plenary session 2								
Women	1	7	0	5	7	2	0	1
Men	2	3	0	0	6	3	0	0
Subtotal	3	10	0	5	13	5	0	1
Total	7	22	4	20	30	11	3	3

Table 9.4: Speeches in the plenary sessions (left-wing/Green Party and right-wing conservative, men and women)

	Speeches by women	Speeches by men	Speeches total	Speeches by left wing/Green parties total	Speeches by right-wing conservative parties total	Speeches by left-wing/Green Party women	Speeches by left-wing/Green Party men	Speeches by right-wing conservative party women	Speeches by right-wing conservative party men
Plenary session 1	35	28	63	20	43	11	9	24	19
Plenary session 2	23	14	37	13	24	8	5	15	9
Total	**58**	**42**	**100**	**33**	**67**	**19**	**14**	**39**	**28**
%	58	42	100	33	67	58	42	58	42

Table 9.5: Themes under the topic of work and family in women MPs' speeches

Theme	Left Alliance	Social Democrats	Green Party	**Left-wing/ Green total**	Centre Party	National Coalition Party	Swedish People's Party	Christian Democrats	The Finns	**Right-wing conservative total**	**Total**
Work and family (in general)	1	16	2	**19**	11	16	5	3	3	**38**	**57**
Sharing the costs of parental leave in a more just way between state and employers in different sectors	1	3	1	**5**	8	8	1	2	1	**20**	**25**
6+6+6 parental leave model	0	3	2	**5**	0	1	3	0	2	**6**	**11**
Fathers' role and position in families	0	0	0	**0**	2	3	3	0	1	**9**	**9**
Single parents	0	5	0	**5**	1	1	0	0	1	**3**	**8**
Women in executive positions in corporations and public administration	0	2	1	**3**	0	5	0	0	0	**5**	**8**
Women entrepreneurs	1	0	0	**1**	2	4	0	0	0	**6**	**7**
Poverty (women, families with children)	0	5	0	**5**	0	0	0	1	0	**1**	**6**
Rights of fathers in divorce	0	1	0	**1**	0	4	0	0	0	**4**	**5**
Day care	0	1	0	**1**	0	1	1	0	1	**3**	**4**
Home care allowance	0	0	0	**0**	1	1	0	0	0	**2**	**2**

following question: could it be that gender equality issues seem more relevant to right-wing parties than to leftist and green parties?

In the plenary sessions, 12 individual women MPs from the left-wing/Green Party group (32 per cent) spoke, and 16 individual women MPs from the right-wing-conservatives (35 per cent). In respect of both groups, this means that two-thirds of women MPs in the Finnish parliament did not speak. The mean number of speeches allowed to each individual woman MPs in both groups was about three. There was no significant difference in the activity between the groups of women MPs in a numerical sense. However, because of the sheer majority of women MPs in the right-wing conservative group, in practice, they dominate the discussion. Qualitatively, they also seem to have delivered the most passionate speeches on gender equality, women, and their situation both in Finland and globally:

> Instead of stepping aside and being content in admiring the [gender equality] results that we have gained [in Finland], we as the pioneers of gender equality [of the world], are obligated to set even more ambitious goals. (Anna-Maja Henriksson, Swedish People's Party, woman,[6] speech 7a)

Left-wing/Green Party women MPs appeared not to be able to stand out in the debate. There were simply not enough of them present at the debates; too few of them spoke; and their speeches did not stand out from other contributions. Whether MPs choose to speak in the plenary, or not, signals the priority that they place on the issue at hand: only one of the three women MPs in the Left Alliance, ten of the 25 Social Democrat women MPs, and only one of the ten Green Party women MPs chose to do so. In the right-wing/conservative women MPs' group the equivalent numbers were: National Coalition Party, 16 speeches, Centre Party 11, Swedish People's Party 6, Christian Democrats 3 and The Finns 3 speeches by women MPs. On this basis we conclude that gender equality can no longer be called a leftist political issue in Finnish parliamentary politics. Groups from left/ Green parties and right-wing/conservative parties have all promoted their political agendas in respect of gender equality in the debate.

Analysing the debates: What themes are addressed in the plenary sessions?

In addition to analysing the division of speech turns in the plenary debates, we also examined what topics were discussed under the themes of work and family, equal pay and gendered violence, and by whom. As illustrated above, the traditional role of women in the leftist parties as the articulators of gender equality discourse is changing. In this section, we focus on women's speeches to analyse what this means for the overall contents and discourses of gender equality.

---

6. All the citations from here on will be from speeches made by a woman MP.

Work and family

Women MPs gave 58 speeches: 57 of these discussed the theme of work and family and how to reconcile them, which reflects the centrality of the issue in the Finnish gender equality discourse (*see* Table 9.5). There were some differences between left- and right-wing women MPs on the issues emphasised. Right-wing/conservative women MPs discussed to a greater extent sharing the costs of parental leave between the state and employers in different sectors, and the father's role and position in families – especially in a situation when parents have divorced. Left-wing/Green women MPs more frequently took up the themes of single parents, and poverty among women and families with children. The Finnish women's organisations, including NYTKIS, have called for a new model called '6+6+6' (months) as a new way of dividing parental leave between parents. This has gathered some support among both left- and right-wing women MPs.

Equal pay

Surprisingly, equal pay was the least discussed topic among the three analysed here. Equal pay is often considered as the main topic in gender equality discourse in Finland, and one would have expected it to have a more prominent place in the plenary debates. However, fewer than half of all speeches given by women MPs, only 28 of the 58, discussed equal pay (*see* Table 9.6).

Eight of the 20 speeches given by right-wing/conservative women MPs mentioned girls' and women's educational and career choices when they discussed equal pay. Only one of the left-wing/Green women MPs (Päivi Lipponen, woman, Social Democrats, speech 2b) talked about girls' and women's career choices: 'they should be encouraged to apply to jobs that pay better and have traditionally been male dominated'. This kind of argumentation, which emphasises individuals and their choices rather than gendered structures in society and working life, is usually more common in right-wing/conservative gender equality discourses than the leftist ones.

Right-wing/conservative women MPs also talked about temporary and atypical work as a gender equality problem and as one cause of the gender pay gap. They also repeatedly posed the issue of low wages in female-dominated jobs in the public sector, whilst left-wing/Green women MPs did not mention this subject. It is notable too how these gender equality topics were combined with right-wing/ conservative political agenda, which usually promotes public expenditure cuts and flexibility in the workforce.

In the speeches of women MPs, the topic of equal pay frequently overlaps– and is interwoven – with the topic of reconciliation of work and family life:

> It is a fact that women's salaries are still lower than men's [and] each child will reduce a woman's salary, and finally this all can be seen in the pensions (Päivi Lipponen, Social Democrats, speech 2b).

Table 9.6: Themes under the topic of equal pay in women MPs' speeches

Theme	Left Alliance	Social Democrats	Green Party	Left-wing/ Green Total	Centre Party	National Coalition Party	Swedish People's Party	Christian Democrats	The Finns	Right-wing conservative Total	Total
Equal pay in general	0	7	1	8	7	9	1	2	1	20	28
Girls' and women's educational and career choices	0	1	0	1	4	4	0	0	0	8	9
Parental leave system and its costs	0	0	0	0	1	6	0	0	0	7	7
Temporary and atypical work more common for women	0	2	0	2	3	2	0	2	0	7	9
Tripartite: The Equal Pay Programme	0	3	1	4	2	1	1	0	1	5	9
Low wages in female-dominated jobs in public sector	0	0	0	0	2	1	1	0	0	4	4
Women's family responsibilities	0	1	0	1	0	3	0	1	0	4	5
Role of tripartite labour system and social partners	0	1	0	1	1	1	0	2	0	4	5
DUO: Women's pay and men's health	0	1	0	1	3	0	1	0	0	4	5
Role of children's upbringing and primary education	0	1	0	1	1	1	0	0	0	2	3
Segregation in labour market	0	2	1	3	1	0	0	0	1	2	5
Attitudes and gender stereotypes	0	1	1	2	1	0	0	1	0	2	4
Women's lack of briskness in asking for more pay or the inability to mark the price of their work	0	0	0	0	1	1	0	0	0	2	2
Role of state and government	0	1	0	1	1	1	0	0	0	2	3

Tabke 9.6 cont'd

Theme	Left Alliance	Social Democrats	Green Party	Left-wing/ Green Total	Centre Party	National Coalition Party	Swedish People's Party	Christian Democrats	The Finns	Right-wing conservative Total	Total
Need to develop gender equality legislation and tools to promote equal pay at the workplace level	0	1	0	1	1	0	0	1	0	2	3
Need to develop job evaluation schemes	0	2	0	2	1	0	0	0	0	1	3
Gendered structures in society and economy	0	2	0	2	0	0	0	1	0	1	3
Gendered income and feminisation of poverty	0	2	1	3	0	1	0	1	0	1	4
Wage discrimination based on sex	0	0	0	0	0	0	0	0	0	1	1

Table 9.7: Themes under the topic of gender violence in women MPs' speeches

Theme	Left Alliance	Social Democrats	Green Party	Left wing/Green total	Centre Party	National Coalition Party	Swedish People's Party	Christian Democrats	The Finns	Right wing-conservative total	Total
Gender violence (in general)	1	10	1	12	6	11	6	3	1	27	39
Framed as intimate partnership violence	0	4	0	4	1	1	1	3	1	7	11
Framed as violence against women	0	1	1	2	0	2	0	3	0	5	7
Framed as family violence	0	0	0	0	1	2	0	0	0	3	3
Resources for shelters	0	2	0	2	1	2	0	2	0	5	7
Importance of CEDAW for Finland	0	1	0	1	0	0	3	2	0	5	6
Funding for the programme	0	0	0	0	1	0	3	1	0	5	5
No reconciliation (sovittelu)	0	0	0	0	1	0	0	2	0	3	3
Women as victims	0	3	0	3	0	0	1	1	1	3	6
Men as victims	0	1	0	1	1	0	2	0	0	3	4
Issues that concern immigrants	0	3	0	3	0	0	1	1	0	2	5
Violence as crime	0	0	0	0	0	0	0	1	1	2	2
Economic efficiency	0	0	1	1	1	0	1	0	0	2	3
State responsibility	0	0	0	0	1	0	1	0	0	2	2
Police resources	0	1	0	1	0	0	0	0	1	1	2
Women as perpetrators	0	1	0	1	1	0	0	0	0	1	2
Individual responsibility	0	0	0	0	1	0	0	0	0	1	1
Men as perpetrators	0	0	0	0	0	0	0	0	0	0	0

The most common way in which right-wing/conservative women MPs talked about equal pay was in the context of criticising the Finnish parental leave system and the uneven distribution of its costs:

> It is a serious fact that as long as there are more costs to the employer for employing a female employee than a male one, the discrimination against women will continue in the labour market. It can be seen in a severe way in women's salaries, in temporary jobs and as hindrances in women's careers (Sari Sarkomaa, National Coalition Party, speech 58a).

Both of the quotations above employ the concept of a fact. However, facts based on statistics are not solid truths, and are constantly politically contested. There is an ongoing and never-ending debate in Finland about how big the gender pay gap is. And in the plenary debates, there is much 'statistics speech' concerning the gender pay gap, and some speeches focus on reiterating statistics when discussing equal pay. However, there are very few concrete actions and proposals aimed at narrowing the gender pay gap, even though everyone seems to be of the mind that equal pay is important and must be promoted. Table 9.4 presents the themes that women MPs have discussed in relation to the topic of equal pay, which makes for an extensive list of policy-making tools. It runs the gamut from bringing up boys and girls in a more gender-equal way, to developing more accurate job evaluation schemes. Notably, in the context of promoting equal pay, the responsibility of the state as a major employer in the public sector, alongside the government's budgetary power, is mentioned in only three speeches. Interestingly enough, two of them were given by a right-wing conservative woman MP, even though it has traditionally been the left that has advocated state responsibilities in gender equality matters.

Gender violence

Although the overall number of references to violence is lower than those to work and family, Table 9.7 shows that gender violence is now established as a key gender equality issue in official Finnish discourse. It is brought up in debate by both left- and right-wing women MPs (in 39 out of the 58 speeches). This is remarkable in the Finnish context in the sense that gender violence was, for a long time, not considered a relevant problem. Such violence was framed as 'family violence' caused by alcoholism and solved by the social policy sector of the welfare state, and, importantly, both women and men were seen as perpetrators (*see* Kantola 2006). Table 9.7 shows, however, that reports and statements about gender violence issued by international actors, such as the UN committee for CEDAW (the Convention on Elimination of All Forms of Discrimination Against Women), substantiate the importance of this issue.

Despite the new prominence of the topic, Table 9.7 also illustrates the long shadow of family violence discourse. The new and gender-neutral concept, 'intimate partnership violence' is used more often than 'violence against women' by women MPs from both left- and right-wing parties. Other characteristics of this framing involve seeing both women and men as victims of 'intimate partnership violence'. Notably, no women MP directly addressed men as perpetrators of violence but women were explicitly brought up as perpetrators of violence in two instances by both left and right. This reflects, at least according to feminist analysis (Nousiainen *et al.* 2013) a certain lack of understanding of questions of gendered power in the debate.

Another prominent question illustrated by Table 9.8 is that of resources. Both left- and right-wing women MPs have called for more resources for shelters, funding for the new programme on violence against women, and adequate police resources. In sum, Table 9.8 shows that there is surprisingly little difference between the left- and right-wing women MPs in the ways in which they address gender violence in this debate. This may partly be due to the above-mentioned fact that left-wing/Green women MPs did not attend the plenary sessions in the report as much as right-wing women MPs did. Additionally, men's equality activists have been successful in framing the issue in gender-neutral terms.

Conservative shifts in gender equality discourses

In the above quantitative and qualitative analysis, we have traced both the new hegemonies of the Finnish gender equality discourse, and the displacement of earlier discourse, in relation to work and family, equal pay and gender violence. Below we map out three trends: (1) gender equality as a numerical phenomenon, (2) gender equality defined in terms of productivity and efficiency, and (3) the costs of parental leave constituted as the bottleneck point of gender equality.

Gender equality as a numerical phenomenon

> European Council recommends that Finland should have one family place in a shelter for every 10,000 citizens which means 500 shelter places altogether in Finland. We only have 123 shelter places and 21 shelters. (Merikukka Forsius, National Coalition Party, speech 20a)

In the plenary sessions and in the government's report, one can find several examples of the numerical terms in which Finnish MPs talk about gender equality. As men's poorer health and shorter lifespan have become a topic on the gender equality agenda, an old slogan 'Woman's euro is 82 cents' has received an insertion: 'Man's year is 11 months'. The need for renewing the Finnish parental leave system is condensed into a new model: '6+6+6' (also strongly advocated by women's organisations), where the mother has six months' leave, the father has six months' leave and parents could decide how to spend the additional six months' leave. There is also discussion about the gender quota system (a 40:60 per cent quota) for public boards and municipal committees being extended to include stock exchange listed companies.

When gender equality demands are put into numbers they are, arguably, easier to grasp and a brisk tone can be adopted in equality debates. For example, it is far easier to demand 377 shelter places than to talk about the gendered nature of violence in Finland and about gendered power structures that reproduce violence against women. Numerical needs and demands moreover, represent problems in gender equality as solvable and as a matter of scarce financial resources. However, representing the problem in this way focuses only on symptoms, not the root causes of the problem, which lies – at least according to feminist analysis – in the gendered and social power structures, institutions and practices. Condensing the issue into technical numbers in this way also reflects the shift in the discourse towards more 'right-wing' ways of framing gender equality, as one of efficiency and appropriate management (Kantola 2010; Kantola and Squires 2012).

Productivity, efficiency and gender equality

Also from the point of view of the national economy, it is an unbearable situation that young families have to write off their dreams for children because of the demands of working life and for economic reasons. This is an important equality question for women and for men as well (Elsi Katainen, Centre Party, speech 45a).

A reduction in family violence also reduces sick leave and diminishes the costs of public health care and thereby makes the society function and develop better (Ulla Karvo, National Coalition Party, 44a).

Demands for the state to promote gender equality are often justified in terms of an economic rationale. An example of this kind of reasoning can be seen in the words of MP Sari Sarkomaa's, which opens the chapter, and also in the quotation from MP Elsi Katainen above. In these, gender equality is framed not as an issue of human rights but as an economic concern: taking care of equality has instrumental value rather than being of value in itself. Gender equality problems are therefore constructed as bad household management in 'our home', the Finnish nation:

The Finns espouse developing the parental leave system in a way that would be based on the '6+6+6' model. This model would support sharing the costs of parental leave in a balanced way and it would further motivate fathers to stay home to care for their children … However, The Finns do not wish to see matters only as gender issues but in a more comprehensive manner. For example, fixed-term contracts are a big problem for individuals – whether this individual is a man or a woman (Pirkko Ruohonen-Lerner, The Finns, speech 9a).

This quotation from MP Pirkko Ruohonen-Lerner, the only woman MP in the parliamentary group of populist party The Finns in 2007, is an example of the uneasy relationship between gender equality demands and populist conservatism.

She was one of the very few women MPs in plenary sessions to show explicit support for the '6+6+6' model and The Finns is one of the few parties that have expressed their commitment to the model. However, in the same speech MP Ruohonen-Lerner manages to distance herself and her party from any feminist inclination to criticise women's position in the labour market. However, this kind of problem representation (Bacchi 2009), focuses only on attending to symptoms, not the root causes of the problem, which lies – at least according to feminist analysis – in gendered and social power structures, institutions and practices. Hence, the feminist argument that it is not enough to focus only on the individual level (the individual suffering from a fixed-term contract is far more often a woman than a man) is neatly and conveniently dismissed. This illustrates the relative lack of interest in the right-wing parties for pushing for a structural gender analysis of society.

Costs and funding as bottlenecks of gender equality

> As long as these costs [from parental leave] burden only sectors dominated by women [gender] equality cannot be achieved [...] I think that it is more important to leave the practical decisions about child care to families themselves than [impose] parental leave quotas for fathers (Leena Rauhala, Christian Democrats, speech 51a).

> Violence against women is estimated to cost society over 90 million Euros per year and the actions put forward in the Programme against violence against women would cost about 15 million Euros (Heli Järvinen, Green Party, speech 15a).

In the parliamentary debate, one particular issue has become identified as a problem that is key to gender inequalities in relation to work and family: the costs that (especially women's) maternity and parental leave (especially of women) impose on employers. These costs are considered as a bottleneck, which if removed, would resolve gender inequality in the field of employment. A similar bottleneck in relation to violence is constructed around the funding of the shelters and of the programme addressing violence against women. Again such depictions represent a simplification of the complex problems of gender segregation in the labour market and gender violence. The framing masks other problems too, such as unequal power relations and the lack of political will, and makes it easier not to talk about and deal with them. Solutions tend to be technical, and involve different calculative measures that divide money between the state and different employers or organisations.

Finnish Conservative claims: Not feminist or gendered but gender-neutral claims

Karen Celis and Sarah Childs (in this volume) introduce a new pair of concepts in analysing women's substantive representation and representational claims: feminist claims (Type I claims) and gendered claims (Type II claims). This distinction emphasises that conservative representatives make both kinds of claims, feminist and gendered claims, and that there is a difference between them. Type II (gendered) claims differ from the Type I (feminist) claims because they presuppose commitment to women's traditional roles and experiences as mothers, care givers, and victims of violence. They might also be underpinned by more explicit anti-feminism. In both types, the claims may be framed in terms of improving women's lives. However, to count as women's substantive representation (Celis *et al.* forthcoming), acts and claims for women in both kinds of claim should be: (1) directly constructed as being of importance to women; (2) presented as affecting only women; (3) discussed in terms of gender difference; (4) spoken of in terms of gendered effects; and/or (5) framed in terms of equality between women and men.

In our analysis, all the above-mentioned criteria can be met implicitly in the conservative women MPs' speeches, but the most prominent and explicit of them is the fifth one: claims framed in terms of equality between women and men. This reflects the character of the gender equality discourse in Finland, namely its strive for harmony, symmetry and gender balance between women and men. 'Women's interests' are seldom discussed explicitly, and hardly ever without the parallel perspective of men and their interests and needs in gender equality policies. Therefore, 'women's interests' in Finnish political rhetoric are usually embedded in gender neutrality and therefore not articulated explicitly. Gender and gendered roles are ever present but masked in gender neutrality and harmony. Therefore, gender roles and stereotypes concerning women exist in the parliamentary debates but they are harder to catch, analyse and criticise because of their implicit form. Men's interests in gender equality are articulated in the debates too: men's health and earlier mortality, fathers' custody rights and the right to claim an equal share of parenthood in the family. In sum: in Finnish gender equality debate, the male gender is visible whilst female is not.

However, in the Finnish case, there is a notable party difference in the way conservative women MPs put forward Type 1 claims (feminist) and Type II claims (gendered). Right-wing women from the National Coalition Party and the Swedish People's Party are more inclined to use traditional liberal feminist vocabulary: rights, individual women, choices, opportunities, education, career and merit. Gendered claims (Type II) that arise from women's traditional roles and experiences as mothers and care givers (mother, family, children, care, love, nurture, home care allowance), are strongly present in the Finnish conservative discourse, but they are not discussed in such terms in the parliament, not even by the more gender-conservative women MPs from the Christian Democrats, the Centre Party and The Finns. The hegemonic neoliberal way of framing gender equality as a matter of gender-neutral individual/family choices and opportunities provides a shield behind which conservatives in Finland are seemingly safe from accusations of old gender stereotypes and maintaining the status quo of the existing gender power order.

Another reason why it is hard to find explicitly gendered claims in the conservative women MPs' speeches can be found in the technical way in which gender equality is discussed in the parliamentary debates. Instead of discussing gender per se, gender differences, gendered interests or gendered power orders, MPs condense gender equality to gender equality policy measures: for example, the best way to renew the parental leave system; in what ways should or could the Gender Equality Act be tightened up; and how to encourage employers to conduct gender equality plans in workplaces. It seems that in the current political climate, gender equality can be discussed only in such technical terms.

Conclusion

When gender is masked in gender neutrality and women's interests are not explicitly and separately articulated, are the claims of Finnish conservative MPs for women's substantive representation? In our view, even if the claims are not explicitly feminist or gendered, in Finnish gender-neutral (if not gender-blind) political culture they can still put forward politics that are 'for women'. However, there are many kinds of women, and it is important to ask for whom and to what kinds of women the conservative women MPs are talking and acting. In fact, these imaginary women and their supposed gender equality policy interests are precisely where the axes of left-right and liberal-conservative are reproduced all over again in political debates.

In spite of the current hegemonic gender equality discourse in Finland that is embedded in the neoliberal capitalist political culture and focuses on technical, numeric and individual policy responses to gender equality problems, the left can still be distinguished by the way it puts forward poverty as a gender equality problem (single mothers and women as low-income wage earners in cooking, cleaning and caring, for example). The right highlights women who are small entrepreneurs and women as top executives (highly educated women's career paths, reconciling family and business, getting through the glass ceiling, etc.). Liberals bring in the discourse of human rights, multiculturalism, minority rights (including sexual and gender minorities), and international treaties, and Finland's obligation to comply with them. Conservatives build their gender equality discourses on the heterosexual nuclear family and stress the importance of care and moral values, and in the case of the conservative party The Finns, also the Finnish nation.

Ideological differences between what kinds of women are being represented and what kinds of gender equality themes are put forward by the left and right, or Liberals and Conservatives, seem to exist especially in issues that are linked to the period of growth and expansion of the Finnish social-democratic wage earners' welfare state (after the Second World War till the 1990s) and its 'women friendly' public sector and services, and the role and responsibilities of the state in providing them. When matters such as equal pay, the reconciliation of work and family, equal career paths and social justice are discussed, different ideological discourses can be traced even among the current hegemonic neoliberal and individually oriented gender equality discourses.

However, gender violence seems to differ from this pattern of ideological differences in gender equality discourse. In Finland, violence against women and gendered violence emerged as a gender equality policy issue in the 1990s at the same time as Finland joined the Council of Europe (1989), the Soviet Union fell apart (1991) and the severe economic recession legitimised the retrenchment of the welfare state. In 1995 Finland joined the European Union and so the fundamental rights in Finland were renewed. Violence against women and gender violence started to be framed in a new way, as a matter of human rights and anti-discrimination. In this new frame, women's party organisations and networks (NYTKIS, etc.) were able to find a common language and join their forces against gender violence across the ideological and party lines. International human and women's rights treaties joined women's political forces, but at the same time the treaties were imports that did not resonate well with existing Finnish ideological political culture, which was very much class-based. The policy problem of gender violence was formed at a time when individuals, their rights and right-wing ideologies were gaining a strong footing in the Finnish post-Cold War political landscape. It is no wonder that the left remains silent in the parliamentary debates in our data: at the moment, gender equality can plausibly be discussed politically either in a right–liberal or a right-wing conservative way. The right–liberal way focuses on individual women, men and their families and choices, whereas right-wing conservatives base their agenda on morals and on heterosexual families. In Figure 9.1, the box that would combine leftist values with structures, morals, culture and safety, remains empty. Being leftist and conservative just does not attract voters: political talk about structures and (gender) power orders is 'so last season'. Accordingly, the new left is stuck with the discourse of individuals and choices if it wishes to separate itself from conservative communist ideals and ideologies. Structural themes such as the gendered division of labour flash up a few times in the women MPs' arguments but are quickly followed by neoliberal individualism:

> If the division of labour between the sexes in which a woman nurtures and a man is a bread-winner is not broken up [gender] equality cannot be attained. Care must be re-evaluated in society and divided between men and women. However, we [the Christian Democrats] do not support separate parental leave quotas for fathers but instead we wish to leave the practical decisions concerning child care to families themselves. (Tarja Tallqvist, Christian Democrats, speech 8a)

This quotation is a good example of the uneasy balance between feminist and left-wing discourse on structures and divisions and right-wing conservative politics, which draws a sharp line between private and public spheres of life. The two arguments in the citation are put forward as linked together in a balanced way and yet they represent two competing and different political discourses. Can these two coexist or must the one yield to the other? In the case of the woman MP in question, Tarja Tallqvist, these two ways of promoting gender equality could not coexist: she defected from Christian Democrats to Social Democrats during the last parliamentary term and did not get re-elected in the parliamentary elections of 2011.

By analysing the interconnections between left- and right-wing/conservative discourses that reconcile work and family, equal pay, and gender violence, we do not want to reproduce old stereotypes that leftist parties would somehow be more inclined to promote feminist demands in Finland and that right-wing parties would not. It seems that there are tendencies to promote women's issues (in a broad sense of the concept) in all parties but their basic assumptions on the problem of the representation of gender equality problems differ between left and right; in other words they conceptualise differently what is in the interests of women (Celis *et al.* forthcoming). The crucial question for future research is therefore: in what ways can neoliberal capitalism and its unwillingness to talk in a language of structures, state responsibilities and public services coexist in a balance – no matter how uneasy that would be – with feminist views of gender equality in politics?

References

Bacchi, C. L. (2009) *Analysing Policy: What's the Problem Represented to Be?* Melbourne: Pearson Education Australia.

Bryson, V. and Heppell, T. (2010) 'Conservatism and feminism: the case of the British Conservative Party', *Journal of Political Ideologies*, 15 (1): 31–50.

Celis, K., Childs, S., Kantola, J. and Krook, M. L. (2014) 'Constituting women's interests through representative claims', *Politics & Gender*, 10(2): 149–174.

Childs, S. and Webb, P. (2012) *Sex, Gender and the Conservative Party: From Iron Lady to Kitten Heels*, Basingstoke: Palgrave Macmillan.

Government Report on Gender Equality (2011) Ministry of Social Affairs and Health 2011:4, available online http://www.stm.fi/c/document_library/ get_file?folderId=2765155&name=DLFE-15811.pdf (accessed 5 May 2014).

Holli, A. M. (2002) 'Suomalaisen tasa-arvopolitiikan haasteet', in Holli, A. M., Saarikoski, T. and Sana, E. (eds) *Tasa-arvopolitiikan haasteet*, Helsinki: WSOY and TANE), pp. 12–30.

— (2006) 'Strong together? A comparative study of the impact of the women's movement on policy-making in Finland', in Hellsten, S. K., Holli, A. M. and Daskalova, K. (eds) *Women's Citizenship and Political Rights*, Basingstoke and New York: Palgrave Macmillan, pp. 127–53.

Julkunen, R. (2010) *Sukupuolen järjestykset ja tasa-arvon paradoksit*, Tampere: Vastapaino.

Kantola, J. (2006) *Feminists Theorize the State*, Basingstoke: Palgrave Macmillan.

— (2010) *Gender and the European Union*, Basingstoke: Palgrave Macmillan.

Kantola, J. and Squires, J. (2012) 'From state feminism to market feminism?', *International Political Science Review*, 30 (4): 382–400.

Kantola, J., Nousiainen, K. and Saari, M. (eds) (2012) *Tasa-arvo toisin nähtynä. Oikeuden ja politiikan näkökulmia tasa-arvoon ja yhdenvertaisuuteen*, Helsinki: Gaudeamus.

Kuusipalo, J. (2011) *Sukupuolittunut poliittinen edustus Suomessa. Acta Universitatis Tamperensis; 1614*, Tampere: Tampere University Press.

Luhtakallio, E. and Ylä-Anttila, T. (forthcoming) 'Gender in numbers and contents: The Finns party effect'.

Nousiainen, K., Holli, A. M., Kantola, J., Saari, M. and Hart, L. (2013) 'Theorizing gender equality: perspectives on power and legitimacy', *Social Politics*, 20 (1): 41–64.

Paloheimo, H. (2008) 'Ideologiat ja ristiriitaulottuvuudet', in Paloheimo, H. and Raunio, T. (eds) *Suomen puolueet ja puoluejärjestelmä*, Helsinki: WSOY, 27–58.

Paloheimo, H. and Raunio, T. (2008) 'Puolueiden rooli ja tehtävät demokratiassa', in Paloheimo, H. and Raunio, T. (eds) *Suomen puolueet ja puoluejärjestelmä*, Helsinki: WSOY, pp. 11–24.

Reingold, B. (2008) 'Women as officeholders, linking descriptive and substantive representation', in Wolbrecht, C., Beckwith, K. and Baldez, L. (eds) *Political Women and American Democracy*, Cambridge: Cambridge University Press, pp. 128–47.

Siukola, R. (2004) 'Poliittinen puolue ja naisen paikka? Naispoliitikon toiminnan mahdollisuudet ja rajat kansallisessa kokoomuksessa', in *Naistutkimus-Kvinnoforskning*, 17 (4): 22–33.

Statistics Finland (2009) 'Fixed-term employment relationships decreased in 2009', Helsinki: Statistics Finland, available at http://www.stat.fi/til/tyti/2009/15/tyti_2009_15_2010-06-01_kat_001_en.html (accessed 5 May 2014).

Swers, M. L. (2002) *The Difference Women Make: The Policy Impact of Women in Congress*, Chicago: University of Chicago Press.

Chapter Ten

Feminist Proposals and Conservative Voices: The Substantive Representation of Women in Argentina

Jennifer M. Piscopo

Introduction

In Latin America, statutory gender quotas have combined with closed-list proportional representation systems to raise women's legislative representation throughout the region. In Argentina, Mexico, Costa Rica, Ecuador, and Bolivia, for instance, women comprise 25 to 40 per cent of the lower or unicameral chamber of Congress. Consequently, researchers have signalled the importance of women's descriptive representation for advancing women's substantive representation, highlighting feminist policy outcomes such as strengthened domestic violence and sexual harassment laws, liberalised access to reproductive health services, and generalised legal protections for women (Franceschet and Piscopo 2008; Miguel 2012; Schwindt-Bayer 2010; Waylen 2008).

Yet questions remain regarding how uniformly female and male legislators support substantive feminist representation, and whether substantive representation could in fact undermine feminist policy goals. The generalised understanding that many Latin American women hold feminine, maternal identities rather than feminist, radical identities yields conflicting approaches to gender equality (Craske 1999; Franceschet *et al.* 2012). Since quotas ensure that parties of all ideological positions elect relatively equivalent proportions of women, female legislators in Latin America are most likely not uniformly feminist. Yet scholarship on other powerful actors, such as the Catholic Church (Blofield 2006; Htun 2003), indicates that *male*-dominated institutions are frequently the most ardent defenders of traditional social arrangements. These observations signal the need for more in-depth analyses of sex differences and ideological differences in legislative representation.

This chapter draws on the theoretical framework of representation as claims-making to compare Type I (feminist) substantive representation to Type II (gendered) substantive representation in the case of Argentina. Following Celis and Childs (Introduction, this volume), distinctions are made first between women's issues and women's interests, and second between liberally feminist and traditionally gendered representative claims. 'Women's issues' captures the broad policy areas that particularly affect female citizens: for instance, policies addressing marriage and divorce, reproductive health, and sex trafficking target women because longstanding beliefs associate women with domesticity and sexual submission. To address a women's issue does not imply a particular view of women: issue representation becomes interest representation as legislators make proposals – make claims – about specific policy approaches. For example, feminists may see women's interests as best advanced by promoting contraception, whereas traditionalists may see contraception as inimical to women's interests because of its ability to undermine motherhood. The latter claim insists on women's traditional gender roles, while the former promotes feminist policy goals.

The substantive representation of women (SRW) in the Chamber of Deputies, the lower house of the Argentine Congress, is explored using bill introduction data from 2005–11. Deputies are elected for four-year terms, with half of the 257-member chamber renewing every two years. In 2005, Argentina's 30 per cent electoral quota law, passed in 1991, became maximally effective due to electoral code revisions that strengthened the placement mandate: women comprised 35.8 per cent of the lower chamber for the 2005–7 term, 36 per cent for the 2007–9 term, and 38.5 per cent for the 2009–11 term. Women's presence is proportionally distributed across all the political parties. Consequently, if leftist parties are more amenable to feminist policy goals, and if rightist parties are more dedicated to traditional gender roles, then feminist substantive representation and gendered substantive representation should both occur in Argentina.

The data demonstrate, however, that traditionalists have presence (absolute numbers) but not strength (relative numbers) when proposing policies in Argentina. Feminist proposals dominate the legislative agenda. These findings are supported through a three-part analysis: first, the overall introduction of SRW bills (issues) is examined; second, SRW bills are analysed for content, meaning whether they conceive of women as individual rights-bearers (feminist interests) or embedded family members (gendered interests); and third, these different visions of women are qualitatively compared, focusing on representative claims made in policy proposals on pregnancy and families.

Bills are classified as gendered when they view women as embodied subjects and tie women to their maternal roles, and bills are classified as feminist when they view women as autonomous citizens and liberate women from traditional roles. The categorisations also distinguish legislative activity focused on women from legislative activity focused on children. On the one hand, the longstanding identification of Latin American women with motherhood makes the well-being of women inseparable from the well-being of children. On the other hand, many policy areas involving child development do not directly (or even indirectly) invoke women as mothers. Once these child welfare bills ('children's bills') are separated from feminist bills and gendered bills, it becomes apparent that, in the Argentine Congress, very few legislators support a wholesale return to traditional values. Instead, many legislators – especially male legislators – spend significant time focusing on children. The gendered Type II proposals, while an absolute minority, target women as mothers and position women's interests as subservient to the interests of children and the nation.

Left and right in Latin America

Political scientists typically group leftist ideologies as those political beliefs that favour an expanded welfare state, wherein social programmes are supported by redistributing tax resources from the wealthy to the disadvantaged. Conversely, rightist ideologies support curtailing redistribution in order to advance capitalism: individuals compete freely in unrestrained markets, receiving rewards according to ability and skill, and policies that 'correct' for the unequal distribution of opportunities, privileges, and rights are not needed. Conservatism typically refers to this variant of economic liberalism, while liberalism typically signifies the leftist belief that structural forces, rather than individual capabilities, drive inequality. Women's substantive representation in Latin America – especially feminist representation – has consequently benefited from the election of leftists, as leftists of both sexes support distributive and rights-oriented policies more than rightists of both sexes (Htun and Power 2006).

Nonetheless, left and right ideologies in Latin America are complicated determinants of parties' positions on gender equality. Latin American nations have not experienced uninterrupted periods of democracy; they have endured populist regimes that bypassed representative institutions and military dictatorships that actively suppressed political and civil rights. Many also experienced devastating civil wars between Marxist-inspired insurgents and authoritarian leaders. More recently, economic neoliberalism has expanded free trade and curtailed the welfare state, integrating Latin America into global markets while accelerating the gap between the rich and the poor. This chapter cannot provide a complete account of all these political transformations, but some broad notes on their implications for feminism are important.

Expansions of women's political and economic rights typically occurred first in the region's populist regimes, in power from the late nineteenth century to the early-to-mid twentieth century. Charismatic leaders such as Juan Perón in Argentina granted suffrage, created educational and employment opportunities, and encouraged community organising. This incorporation of women into the state hinged, however, on their domestic roles: for instance, women received public assistance to form and work in day care crèches, food kitchens, and poverty relief programmes (Kampwirth 2010; Lavrín 1995). Hence, early Latin American feminists leveraged women's familial roles to justify their expanded legal protections and social involvement: women's care taking was framed as essential to the health, stability, and growth of the nation. These beliefs persist, undergirding the region's contemporary welfare system: for instance, conditional cash transfers provide family aid only when female household heads engage in specific childrearing tasks (Molyneux 2009). In Latin America, the liberal expansion of citizenship rights and the redistribution of economic wealth often coexists with, and depends upon, a traditional reification of women's roles as wives and mothers. Populist parties still exist and still enjoy electoral success. Consequently, a Latin American leftist can support redistributive policies while nonetheless holding traditionally gendered views about women and families.

Latin America's experiences with dictatorship and democratisation also have profoundly shaped views of women's rights and roles. Under the authoritarian regimes in the second half of the twentieth century, military generals and civilian leaders restricted political liberties and disappeared suspected Marxists or communists.[1] On the one hand, women's mothering roles were exalted by autocratic leaders: women were essential to the production and reproduction of the national family, one based on spiritual (Catholic) virtue and economic (capitalist) discipline. On the other hand, motherhood granted women unique public power to *resist* authoritarianism: throughout South America, women mobilised to shame authoritarian leaders for disappearing their children and thus destroying the very families the regimes claimed to protect. Today, Latin American activists use motherhood to justify their activism on behalf of working-class families (Eltantawy 2008) and victims of criminal and domestic violence (Bejarano 2002). However, other female activists and politicians use motherhood to resist the social and political changes brought by democratisation and, more recently, globalisation. In this conservative view, modernity has corrupted the moral order by destroying family life (Kampwirth 2005).

While motherhood was mobilised by authoritarian and democratic forces, socialist rebel groups throughout Latin America incorporated women as soldiers and leaders. These groups adopted a more classically Marxist platform that promoted women's full economic, social, and sexual equality. With democratisation, most guerrilla groups demobilised and reconstituted as political parties. The socialist project thus remains strong in the region, organising activists and politicians under the contemporary goals of resisting globalisation on behalf of the poor, attaining freedom for historically repressed groups (women, indigenous peoples, and LGBT individuals), and redistributing wealth and political power.

These ideological legacies are all present in Argentina, which democratised following the collapse of the 1976–83 dictatorship. Since then, Argentina has typically been classified as a two-party system, in which the *Partido Justicialista* (PJ), the party of populist Juan Perón, competes for power with the *Unión Cívica Radical* (UCR). Yet Peronism has fractured during the presidencies of Néstor Kirchner (2003–7) and Cristina Fernández de Kirchner (2007–2015). The PJ and the UCR remain the two largest parties, but the country's closed-list proportional representation (PR) system has allowed numerous third parties and PJ splinter parties to increase in size and strength. Multipartism in the Argentine Congress has increased dramatically, with between thirty-five and forty parties occupying seats in the Chamber of Deputies since the mid-2000s.

Further, the popular view that most Argentine parties are ideologically fluid groupings of electorally opportunistic individuals (Torre 2005) obscures critical variations. Some upstart parties are indeed provincially based vehicles for personalistic power that lack ideological coherence; others, however, such

---

1.   The term refers to how Latin American dictatorships abducted and imprisoned suspected dissidents; without bodies, the victims of state violence were 'disappeared' rather than murdered.

as *Propuesta Republicana* (PRO) and the *Coalición Cívica* (Civic Coalition) are institutionalised, programmatic, and increasingly powerful across multiple provinces. Nonetheless, a left-right typology can be developed using the region's and the country's political history as well as legislators' ideal points from 1999 to 2007 (Alemán *et al.* 2009), bill introduction and roll call votes from 1999 to 2011, and field interviews from 2005, 2007, and 2009 (*see* Piscopo 2011 for an extended discussion).

The left side consists of parties representing populism and socialism. Parties expressing populist ideologies include the Kirchners' *Frente para la Victoria* (Victory Front) and the numerous PJ splinter parties. These 'PJ dissident' parties have formed in opposition to the Kirchners, but remain committed to populist-style policies that fund social welfare programmes, support labour unions, and generally guarantee employment, healthcare, education, and other assistance to the working classes. Still, viewpoints in all Peronist parties are incredibly heterogeneous (Levitsky 2005), and, though these parties belong on the 'populist left', legislators' beliefs may in practice span the ideological spectrum. The 'socialist left' parties, by contrast, are more ideologically coherent. These consist of the longstanding *Partido Socialista* (the Socialist Party) and the contemporary leftist parties formed around the Civic Coalition. These liberal parties advocate equal rights and critique the structural inequalities of globalisation; they have a younger, more feminised membership and leadership structure than the populist parties.

Legislators on the populist left are hypothesised to be as likely to make Type I (feminist) claims as Type II (gendered) claims. Populism in Latin America has historically viewed women as national mothers, but Peronism in Argentina has become increasingly ideologically eclectic; the 'populist left' label in Argentina may not convey any particular view of women. Legislators on the socialist left, by contrast, have consistent commitments to equal rights, and these leftists are hypothesised to make exclusively Type I claims.

The right side of the ideological spectrum consists of parties representing economic neoliberalism and social conservatism. 'Neoliberal right' refers to parties that are principally concerned with economic issues and advocate for curbing the welfare state, advancing free trade, and opening markets. The UCR, while not historically a neoliberal right party, has become associated with such policies by virtue of opposing the Kirchners' Peronism since 2003.[2] The 'conservative right' characterises a small but influential number of parties (such as *Acción República*) that endorse the neoliberal agenda but also advocate a return to traditional moral, social, and spiritual values. Both sets of parties are hypothesised to make exclusively Type II claims. Since neoliberalism in Latin America has meant deregulating economic activity while maintaining control over women and the family (Craske 1998), politicians on the neoliberal right might implicitly, if not explicitly, take traditional positions on matters relating to women's place in the private sphere.

---

2. Roll call voting in Argentina unfolds according to a government–opposition dynamic, regardless of parties' ideological commitments (Jones *et al.* 2009).

Women's issues, sex, and party ideology in Argentina

Together, the hypotheses suggest that all parties will substantively represent women, but that only socialist left parties will exclusively undertake feminist substantive representation. Yet the representation of women's interests requires that a women's issue policy be introduced, which raises a more immediate question: how frequently does SRW – of any type – occur in the Argentine Congress? To answer this question, bills introduced in the Argentine Congress between 2005 and 2011 are examined. No bills are omnibus bills: each proposal deals with a discrete policy.[3] In total, 11,899 bills were introduced by 574 legislators, 364 (63.4 per cent) of whom are male and 210 (36.6 per cent) of whom are female. Male legislators introduced 60.1 per cent of the bills and female legislators introduced 39.9 per cent of the bills, proportions roughly equal to their total numbers in Congress.

Women's issues bills are identified using the bills' titles and *fundamentos* [fundamentals]. In Argentina, titles are highly descriptive and often suffice for identifying the policy area: for example, a typical title reads, 'The right of all women to interrupt their pregnancy within the first 12 weeks of gestation in any medical centre in the country'.[4] Further, each legislator attaches a letter, known as a *fundamento*, which explains her rationale in authoring the bill. To qualify as a 'women's issue bill' – hereafter referred to as an SRW bill – the title or *fundamento* has to (1) identify the policy area as wholly or mostly affecting women or (2) invoke women as the targets or beneficiaries. This approach provides an advantage on previous SRW studies because it does not presume, *ex ante*, that only certain policy areas affect women. For example, rather than predetermining that all finance bills are 'men's issues' and that all health bills are 'women's issues' (Schwindt-Bayer 2006), any bill that identifies women as the policy object gets considered an SRW bill. Further, the classification is content neutral: whether the bill takes a feminist or traditional perspective on women's rights does not matter. For instance, policies to expand and restrict abortion access were coded as SRW bills (where 1 = SRW bill and 0 = all others). The measurement captures simply whether the bill draws legislative attention to women, irrespective of the claim.

Yet the study does distinguish between proposals that target women and proposals that target children. Previous SRW studies from Latin America have drawn from historical and cultural realities to treat children and families as women's issues (Schwindt-Bayer 2006). Yet such decisions imply that *all* policies that benefit children also benefit women, by virtue of the presumed inextricable psychosocial connection between women and children – a categorisation that obscures important variations within proposals on children and the family.

Consider two proposals. One would further penalise non-custodial parents who shirk childcare payments. This proposal might assist mothers – in that female

---

3. Only symbolic bills were eliminated from the dataset, as follows: property transfers between the federal and provincial governments; declaring days, places, or buildings in commemoration of persons or events; declaring historic sites; and issuing commemorative money.

4. Bill 2700-D-2008.

household heads gain more leverage over 'deadbeat' fathers – but the *fundamento* reveals that the legislator's primary concern is for children. Further, the proposal uses gender-neutral language that discusses parents' (not mothers') legal duties. The other proposal would equalise men's and women's custodial rights in divorce cases: here, the *fundamento* reveals the legislator's desire to eliminate legal distinctions that disadvantage women in family law. The first proposal primarily intends to help children; the second primarily intends to help women. Consequently, bills that may disproportionately affect women in practice (i.e. child support) qualify as women's issues bills only if the title or *fundamento* explicitly indicates a concern for women's welfare. Bills that target children, however, are retained and categorised as 'children's bills', in order to explore further how conceptualising and coding children as a women's issue affects conclusions about SRW.

Three measures of SRW bills are thus constructed and presented. The first measure follows traditional research practices by grouping together all SRW bills targeting children with all SRW bills targeting women. Just over 12 per cent of all bills (1,442 of 11,899) introduced in the Argentine Congress between 2005 and 2011 addressed women and children. The second and third measures use the criteria outlined in the previous paragraph, dividing the SRW bills into those that focus on women, versus those that focus on children. This disaggregation yields a 'women only' measure (789 bills) and a 'children only' measure (653 bills).

Table 10.1 compares male and female legislators' bill introduction rates across all three SRW measures. In all cases, female legislators write the majority of SRW bills. Men's SRW activity is nonetheless quite high. Male legislators write 41.5 per cent of all SRW bills, revealing a relatively small gap between men's seat share in the chamber (3/5) and their authorship share of SRW bills (2/5). An important difference emerges, however, when SRW bills are disaggregated: female legislators write 64.4 per cent of the 'women only' bills, but only 51.3 per cent of the 'children only' bills. Conversely, male legislators write 35.6 per cent of the SRW bills that target women, but 48.7 per cent of the SRW bills that target children. Male legislators are relatively more active on children's issues than on women's issues, and female legislators are relatively more active on women's issues than on children's issues. These proportions suggest that conflating women's issues and children's issues may *over-estimate* male legislators' substantive representation of women.

A probit regression goes further, examining the marginal effects of legislators' sex and party membership on SRW. Bills are the unit of analysis, and the model predicts the likelihood of an SRW bill being introduced relative to a non-SRW bill during the 2005–7 and 2007–9 congressional terms.[5] The independent variables are constructed in relation to the bills' authors, and include legislators' sex, party membership, party rank, incumbency status, expertise, and constituency. Sex and party membership are dummy variables. For sex, 1 = female and 0 = male; for party, the categories are socialist left, populist left, neoliberal right, and

---

5.   The regression models omit the 2009–11 term due to changes in availability of data for the control variables.

Table 10.1: Bills on women and children introduced to the Argentine Chamber of Deputies, 2005–11

	Women and children	Women only	Children only
Male legislators	41.5% (599)	35.6% (281)	48.7% (318)
Female legislators	58.5% (843)	64.4% (508)	51.3% (335)
Total	100.0% (1,442)	100.0% (789)	100.0% (653)

conservative right, where 1 = member and 0 = non-member and socialist left is the omitted category. Legislators' incumbency (1 = incumbent; 0 = no) and party rank (operationalised as list position and logged to reduce the scale) control for the low prominence afforded to women's issues: lower-ranked legislators may eschew women's issues in order to accumulate prestige, whereas higher-ranked legislators may have the freedom to pursue women's issues. Legislators' expertise and constituency may also drive bill introduction. Expertise is operationalised as whether or not the legislator sits on the committee that evaluated the bill (yes = 1 and no = 0) and constituency effects are captured by the province's Gender Development Index.[6]

As Table 10.2 shows, legislators' sex, rather than party membership, is the strongest predictor that an introduced bill will be an SRW bill. A women's issue proposal is more likely to be introduced by a female legislator, and the effect of legislators' sex is statistically significant across all three SRW measures. However, the magnitude of the effect of sex does change. In model (2), which examines women only bills, the effect of sex is strongest and, in model (3), which examines children only bills, the effect of sex is weakest. These findings are consistent with the descriptive statistics presented in Table 10.1: female legislators are absolutely more likely than male legislators to introduce policy proposals on women's issues and children's issues, but male legislators are relatively more likely to focus on children's issues than women's issues.

Aside from year-specific effects, none of the control variables attained significance. Party membership only predicted the likelihood of writing an SRW bill on women: in model (2), women's issues proposals are less likely to be introduced by members of neoliberal right parties relative to socialist left parties. This outcome supports the observation that neoliberal right parties are organised principally around economic goals. Conservative right parties, by contrast, adopt platforms that reaffirm the traditional role of mothers and families. Though not significant, the regression coefficients in models (1) and (2) indicate that conservative right parties, relative to socialist left parties, are more likely to introduce SRW bills on women. Recall, however, that the coding of women's issues is content neutral: rightist legislators may be more active than leftist legislators on women's issues, but they may not make feminist claims about women's roles.

6. Data on legislators is from the *Directorio Legislativo*, a yearbook published for each term of the Argentine Congress. Data on provincial GDI is from the United Nations.

Table 10.2: The likelihood of introducing an SRW bill relative to a non-SRW bill in Argentina, 2005–9 (probit regression coefficients)

	(1) Women and Children	(2) Women Only	(3) Children Only
female	.4351 (6.22)***	.5142 (7.03)***	.2002 (2.79)***
populist left	-.0648 (0.50)	-.1269 (0.92)	.0436 (0.04)
conservative right	.2179 (0.87)	.3688 (1.18)	-.1201 (0.57)
neoliberal right	-.1842 (1.43)	-.2561 (1.71)*	-.0386 (0.32)
list position	-.0024 (0.07)	.0252 (0.61)	-.0319 (0.83)
incumbency	-.1216 (1.28)	-.0979 (0.84)	-.0991 (1.48)
expertise	-.0668 (0.94)	.0206 (0.28)	-.0989 (1.47)
provincial GDI	1.048 (0.00)	.8996 (0.47)	.8471 (0.61)
2006	.0107 (0.15)	.0044 (0.05)	.0103 (0.13)
2007	-.1688 (2.12)**	-.1384 (1.57)	-.1409 (1.73)*
2008	-.1142 (1.40)	-.0261 (0.28)	-.1796 (2.37)**
2009	-.1651 (1.76)*	-.1919 (1.81)*	-.0732 (0.87)
constant	-2.004 (1.60)	2.307 (1.46)	-2.214 (1.96)**
n	8008	8008	8008
Pseudo R^2	0.0298	0.0469	0.0105
Wald Chi^2	64.87	75.46	26.28

Notes: *** $p < .001$; ** $p < .05$; * $p < .10$, t-statistics in parentheses.

Women's issues: The predominance of feminist claims

A more precise exploration of SRW thus disaggregates women's issues into women's interests, separating SRW bills that adopt a feminist perspective (Type I) from SRW bills that adopt a traditional perspective (Type II). When classifying claims, Celis and Childs argue for establishing specific metrics by which to judge feminist claims, which might include commitments to gender justice or the provision of equal opportunities in the public sphere (2012: 218). Conversely, gendered claims might emphasise commitments to women's roles and experiences as mothers and caregivers (Celis and Childs, Introduction, this volume), and/or rejections of justice-oriented or equality-oriented proposals when they erase or elide 'natural' sex differences. Using these criteria, the women-only SRW bills can be divided into Type I and Type II proposals and compared to the children's bills. This analysis shows the absolute and relative strength of Type I claims when compared to Type II claims. Female legislators raise women's and children's issues more frequently than male legislators, but both predominantly support the feminist project.

Feminist, or Type I bills, advance gender justice by granting women rights and benefits not through their social position (e.g. as wives and mothers) but as autonomous citizens exercising dominion over mind and body. These bills make claims about women's *individual status* in seven policy areas: (1) civil code or family law modifications equalising women's legal standing (e.g. inheritance); (2) 'pro-choice' bills guaranteeing access to abortion, contraception, family planning, infertility services, and sexual health education; (3) health bills acknowledging needs beyond pregnancy (e.g. mammograms and treatment for anorexia); (4) employment bills protecting women's right to work (e.g. job protection during maternity leave); (5) non-discrimination bills promoting general equality goals (e.g. international women's rights treaties); (6) social assistance bills equalising and extending entitlements (e.g. setting women's retirement benefits equal to men's); and (7) proposals to combat sex trafficking, violence against women, and domestic violence. With the exception of area (2), all legislative proposals initially identified as belonging to these policy areas moved in a feminist direction: that is, no proposals sought to remove employment benefits or protections from domestic violence.

Gendered, or Type II, bills treat women not as individual right-bearers, but as relational subjects who gain status through traditional, nuclear families. These measures centre on the primacy of women's mothering and care taking roles; the claims range from seemingly benign celebrations of maternalism to deliberately polemical statements against feminism (the latter interpreted as denying sex differences and thus destroying families). These claims about women's *family status* fall into three policy areas: (1) supporting women as anchors of the family and fortifying the traditional family; (2) curtailing access to sexual education, family planning, contraception, and abortion ('anti-choice'); and (3) extending healthcare and other social programmes to pregnant women, unborn children, and new infants. While the latter group does expand the welfare state, these 'pro-natal' measures deny women's autonomous decision-making capacity. For example, a 2009 proposal to fund a national breastfeeding campaign stated that 'the majority [of new mothers] need help, encouragement, assistance, and training immediately following birth, in order to *enjoy* the feeding and care of their children'.[7] Another 2009 proposal required that women impregnated via sexual assault – who are legally entitled to abortions – receive economic subsidies to assist with child rearing.[8] These measures are consonant with an Argentine tradition of pro-natal social conservatism that opposes family planning and supports welfare for mothers and infants (Barrancos 2006; Lopreite 2008). In enhancing mothers' dependence on state tutelage and largesse, these Type II bills benefit women insofar as they fulfil traditional gender roles.

Finally, children's bills are those legislative proposals identified previously as falling into the SRW category of 'children only'. Previous research, by referring to

---

7.   Bill 0671-D-2009. Emphasis added.
8.   Bill 0853-D-2009.

'children/family bills' (Schwindt-Bayer 2006), has potentially conflated women's interests in mothering specifically with women's interests in child development generally. It seems necessary, however, to distinguish between gendered proposals related to motherhood and families (Type II claims) and child-centred proposals related to young people's well-being. For example, a bill that creates a national youth volunteer programme encourages civic-mindedness; this measure neither fortifies the traditional family nor trains women in mothering. Here, *child welfare* bills propose to (1) penalise predatory sex crimes (e.g. prevention of paedophilia), (2) provide social assistance to children (e.g. child support from absentee parents and subsidies for handicapped youth), or (3) improve general well-being (e.g. school credit for volunteer work).

Table 10.3 shows the total numbers of feminist, gendered, and children's bills introduced in the Argentine Congress between 2005 and 2011. Feminist bills are the most frequent: of the 1,442 SRW proposals introduced in the Argentine Congress, 48.8 per cent made Type I claims, 45.3 per cent focused on children, and 5.9 per cent made Type II claims. Traditional perspectives are represented, but weakly: legislators wrote 704 feminist bills compared to eighty-five gendered bills. Within these trends are some notable differences between male and female representatives. Both male and female legislators make few Type II claims, but vary in focusing on feminist claims or children's well-being. Of those SRW bills written by female deputies, the majority (54.8 per cent) made Type I claims, whereas of those SRW bills written by male deputies, the majority (53.1 per cent) focused on children. The data indicate the importance of avoiding a wholesale conflation of child welfare with women's interests: if women's interests and children's interests are intertwined, the dedication of male legislators to the substantive representation of *women* – especially from a feminist perspective – could be over-estimated.

Yet male legislators are not entirely silent on advancing women's interest from a feminist perspective, as Type I bills account for 40.2 per cent of their total SRW activity. Nonetheless, relative to female legislators, male legislators introduce fewer feminist proposals overall and fewer feminist proposals in all policy areas save employment rights. In the areas of family law and violence against women, female legislators' bill authorship is double male legislators' bill authorship; in combating discrimination and recognising health needs other than pregnancy, female legislators' bill authorship is *quadruple* male legislators' bill authorship. The outlying category of employment rights might be due to the many proposals that expand maternity leave benefits, particularly in cases of ill or handicapped children. While these proposals remain feminist, in that the *fundamentos* discuss the importance of women's participation in the paid labour force, an alternative conceptualisation views these proposals as facilitating women's caregiving responsibilities. If expanded maternity leave means improved childcare, then male legislators' greater relative attention to employment rights might be an additional, though implicit, manifestation of their concern for children.

Dividing the data by party further reveals the greater importance of sex in predicting SRW concentrations. Throughout the period of study, the Argentine Chamber of Deputies was dominated by the populist left, namely the Kirchners'

Table 10.3: Feminist, gendered, and children's bills introduced in the Argentine Congress, 2005–11

Feminist/Type I	Female legislators	Male legislators	Total
Civil code and family law modifications	14.7% (124)	9.2% (55)	12.4% (179)
Pro-choice	8.5% (72)	6.8% (41)	7.8% (113)
General women's health	3.3% (28)	1.0% (6)	2.4% (34)
Employment rights	8.1% (68)	12.0% (72)	9.7% (140)
Non-discrimination and gender equality	8.1% (68)	2.3% (14)	5.7% (82)
Social assistance	0.5% (4)	0.4% (2)	0.4% (6)
Violence against women and sex trafficking	11.7% (99)	8.5% (51)	10.4% (150)
Subtotal	54.8% (463)	40.2% (241)	**48.8% (704)**
Gendered/Type II			
Nuclear family fortification	0.9% (8)	1.7% (10)	1.2% (18)
Anti-choice	1.2% (10)	1.7% (10)	1.4% (20)
Pronatalism	3.3% (27)	3.3% (20)	3.3% (47)
Subtotal	5.5% (45)	6.7% (40)	**5.9% (85)**
Children			
General child well being	29.5% (249)	37.4% (224)	32.8% (473)
Sex crimes against children	4.5% (38)	7.7% (46)	5.8% (84)
Social assistance to children	5.7% (48)	8.0% (48)	6.7% (96)
Subtotal	39.7% (335)	53.1% (318)	**45.3% (653)**
Total	100% (843)	100% (599)	100% (1,442)

Frente para la Victoria and the Peronist splinter parties. In the 2009–11 congressional term, for example, the *Frente para la Victoria* held eighty-seven seats in the Chamber of Deputies, and the smaller Peronist parties held seventy seats, yielding a combined total of 158 of 257 seats.[9] Thus, due to absolute numbers, populist left legislators introduced the vast majority of SRW initiatives when compared to legislators from other parties (populists introduced 53.2 per cent of the feminist bills, 73.3 per cent of the gendered bills, and 61.6 per cent of the children's bills). These aggregate data suggest a slight preference among the populist left for Type II claims, but a more thorough analysis controls for parties' uneven weight by examining SRW trends within each party category.

---

9. Author's counts based on IPU election data, which can be accessed from IPU for the 2009–11 election period: *see* http://.ipu.org/parline-e/reports/arc/2011_09.htm (accessed 14 May 2014).

Table 10.4: Feminist, gendered, and children's bills by party, 2005–11

	Socialist left		
	Female legislators	Male legislators	Total
Type I/feminist	71.5% (188)	44.4% (44)	64.1% (232)
Type II/gendered	0.4% (1)	0% (0)	0.3% (1)
Children	28.1% (74)	55.6% (55)	35.6% (129)
Total	100% (263)	100% (99)	100% (362)
	Populist left		
	Female legislators	Male legislators	Total
Type I/Feminist	45.5% (204)	43.4% (170)	44.6% (374)
Type II/Gendered	6.5% (29)	8.7% (34)	7.5% (63)
Children	48.0% (215)	47.8% (187)	47.9% (402)
Total	100% (448)	100% (391)	100% (839)
	Neoliberal right		
	Female legislators	Male legislators	Total
Type I/Feminist	57.8% (63)	25.7% (26)	42.4% (89)
Type II/Gendered	4.6% (5)	2.0% (2)	3.3% (7)
Children	37.6% (41)	72.3% (73)	54.3% (114)
Total	100% (109)	100% (101)	100% (210)
	Conservative right		
	Female legislators	Male legislators	Total
Type I/Feminist	34.8% (8)	14.3% (1)	30.0% (9)
Type II/Gendered	43.5% (10)	57.1% (4)	46.7% (14)
Children	21.7% (5)	28.6% (2)	23.3% (7)
Total	100% (23)	100% (7)	100% (30)

Table 10.4 presents this analysis. For the socialist left, the hypothesis is confirmed: the vast majority of bills (64.1 per cent) introduced by socialist legislators make feminist claims about women's individual status. Moreover, women within the socialist left parties made more feminist claims relative to their male colleagues: Type I bills account for 71.5 per cent of the SRW bills authored by female leftists, compared to only 44.4 per cent of the SRW bills authored by male leftists (the differences between the sexes are statistically significant at the 1 per cent level). Only one bill introduced by a socialist left deputy made a gendered claim: this proposal sought to protect family homes from debt collectors, but is coded as Type II because the *fundamento* focuses not on women's property rights,

but on the nuclear family's need for stability.[10] As predicted, deputies belonging to socialist left parties exclusively make Type I claims when representing women; female leftists also appear more active on questions of women's individual status when compared to male leftists, who appear more active on children's well-being.

For the populist left, the hypothesis that legislators are as equally likely to make Type I or Type II claims receives partial support. More proposals authored by members of Peronist parties make feminist claims (374 bills) when compared to gendered claims (63 bills), suggesting an overall trend within the populist left to support the feminist project. However, populist legislators make more gendered claims relative to socialist legislators: Type II bills account for less than 1 per cent of socialist legislators' bill authorship, but 7.5 per cent of populist legislators' bill authorship. Traditional views of women's roles will find more sympathies in populism than socialism. Populist legislators also make more claims about children's welfare, as children's bills account for 47.9 per cent of SRW activity on the populist left, compared to 35.6 per cent of activity on the socialist left. There are no statistically significant differences between men and women in the populist left parties, with most bills authored by female deputies and male deputies focusing on children.

The data also show support for both Type I and Type II claims within the neoliberal right parties, disconfirming the hypothesis that legislators favouring economic liberalism would also support traditional gender roles. Legislators on the neoliberal right in fact author a large number of feminist bills (89) compared to gendered bills (7), a trend consistent with the socialist and populist parties. This difference is statistically significant and markedly pronounced in comparing women to men: on the neoliberal right, 57.8 per cent of women-authored bills are feminist, compared to only 25.7 per cent of male-authored bills. Conversely, 72.3 per cent of male-authored proposals focus on children, compared to only 37.6 per cent of female-authored proposals.

Only conservative rightists dedicate most of their SRW activity to Type II claims, as anticipated. Framing women's interests in relation to their family roles accounts for 46.7 per cent of conservative legislators' SRW activity, with no statistically significant differences between male and female co-partisans. Moreover, legislators on the conservative right do not make these claims *exclusively*: 30 per cent of their SRW activity also goes to proposals that frame women in feminist terms. Like the populist left, both conservative and neoliberal right parties appear to host legislators with heterogeneous views on women's interests.

Together, the data offer important insights on extant conceptualisations of SRW. First, researchers should separate legislative proposals aimed at women – whether in relation to women as individuals or women as mothers – from legislative proposals aimed at children. In Table 10.4, if children's issues were removed from the analysis, the data would show the following divisions between feminist

---

10. Bill 0375-D-2010.

proposals and gendered proposals, respectively: socialist parties, 99.5 per cent to 0.5 per cent; populist parties, 85.6 per cent to 14.2 per cent; neoliberal parties, 91.7 per cent to 8.3 per cent; and conservative parties, 39.1 per cent to 60.9 per cent. These numbers reveal that all parties, save the socially conservative parties, support the expansion of women's individual rights, and that even the socially conservative parties do not wholly reject the feminist project. Overall, Type II proposals are fewer relative to Type I proposals, which should assuage feminists' fears about conservatives' ability to roll back gains for women, at least in the Argentine case. Further, conflating women's interests with children's interests can lead researchers to improperly estimate the extent to which legislators of diverse ideologies support feminism.

Second, separating out children from women reveals important comparative trends in male legislators' approaches to social issues. Children's association with the home means that child welfare constitutes a gendered issue, but many proposals target children's interests not in the private sphere, but in the public sphere (i.e. bills that focus on children as students). When legislative proposals making claims about children's well-being are treated as analytically distinct from proposals making claims about women's rights and familial roles, male legislators are found to be consistently more concerned about children relative to female legislators. Female legislators absolutely introduce more bills on children when compared to men (Table 10.1), but male legislators relatively introduce a greater proportion of children's bills than women's bills, both as a whole and within their parties (Table 10.4). This trend raises the possibility that children may be a 'men's interest'. As legislative chambers become more feminised, do male legislators feel more comfortable dedicating their voices to children rather than women?

Helping women, protecting children: An anatomy of claims

Gendered claims account for a small proportion of overall proposals introduced in the Argentine Congress, but constituents who support traditional values will nonetheless find their viewpoints represented. This representation becomes apparent by comparing the Type I and Type II claims made in the *fundamentos* of bills addressing two high-valence women's issues: carrying pregnancies to term and fortifying nuclear families. As shown in Table 10.5, these bills correspond to the gendered policy areas of nuclear family fortification and pronatalism, and the feminist policy areas of abortion liberalisation (a subset of the 'pro-choice' bills identified previously). Legislators from the populist left introduced the bulk of the proposals in all three policy areas, but were particularly active on pronatalism, which resonates with Latin American populism's tradition of treating mothers as national treasures. Indeed, claims made by legislators introducing pro-natal bills or family bills demonstrate how gendered proposals – though an absolute minority – continue to frame women as clients who gain rights and benefits *through* their maternal roles.

Consider the contestation over carrying pregnancies to term. Under the Argentine penal code, abortions are legally available to women with life- or health-

Table 10.5: Introduction of bills in three SRW areas by party, 2005–11

	Socialist left	Populist left	Neoliberal right	Conservative right	Total
Abortion liberalisation (feminist)	34.5% (10)	48.3% (14)	17.2% (5)	0% (0)	100% (29)
Pronatalism (gendered)	0% (0)	80.9% (38)	8.5% (4)	10.6% (5)	100% (47)
Nuclear family formation (gendered)	5.6% (1)	66.7% (12)	5.6% (1)	22.2% (4)	100% (18)

threatening pregnancies, or women impregnated by rape or incest. Qualifying women must obtain a judicial authorisation, however, and such permission is typically withheld in practice. Ongoing civil society mobilisation to liberalise abortion has resulted in two competing women's interests: relaxing abortion procedures in order to guarantee women's access, or discouraging abortions through the provision of state assistance to pregnant women (the latter initiatives are coded as 'pro-natal' rather than anti-choice since they do not prohibit abortion outright).

Proponents in both camps claim to protect women and children. For instance, a proposal to waive the judicial authorisation required for abortions in the cases of anencephaly (a terminal foetal disorder), introduced by a female legislator of the socialist left, argues that administrative permission 'harms the mother's right to physical and psychological health as well as the well-being of her family (spouse and [existing] children)'.[11] A similarly aimed bill noted that women should decide 'freely and with dignity what to do with a [bad] pregnancy' and that free choice in the case of rape or foetal birth defects is consonant with protecting the human rights of women.[12] Moreover, this proposal and another – both introduced by female legislators of the populist left – argued that forcing women to continue pregnancies when faced with foetal disorders could provoke a 'psychological catastrophe', because the women would essentially be birthing infants doomed to die.[13] In these *fundamentos*, feminist legislators claimed that the maternal–infant bond is harmed, not enhanced, when women must bear unhealthy or unwanted children.

Yet many legislators from the populist left, as well as some from the neoliberal and conservative right, make gendered claims: state aid – not abortions – should assist women with high-risk or rape-induced pregnancies. For example, a bill to promote the 'integrated assistance of women pregnant as a result of a violation against their sexual integrity', stated its object to 'protect women, boys, and girls'. Here, protection does not mean making legally permissible abortions easier to

---

11. Bill 1627-D-2005.

12. Bill 5223-D-2008.

13. Bills 5223-D-2008 and 0725-D-2006.

attain; it means that the 'state take charge of the victims'. The proposal requires that the state provide 'medical, psychological, and social assistance, with the goal of restoring the [woman's] life and that of her son or daughter'. As such, this bill, introduced by a populist male legislator, requires that women forcefully impregnated receive an economic subsidy and join the national adoption registry.[14]

Similarly, a proposal introduced by a female legislator on the neoliberal right also exhorts subsidies for rape-induced pregnancies, to 'prioritise the well-being of the mother and her child'.[15] However, women should receive these subsidies only if they reject abortion, because 'a woman who has experienced this hardship but commits herself to saving a life should be elevated to the status of heroine'. For this reason, the woman should receive the subsidies whether she chooses adoption or parenthood, because 'she fulfilled her duty of giving birth to the child despite her terrible state, and for this [act] she deserves compensation'. Another proposal, one authored by a female legislator of the populist left, guarantees psychological counselling for women during their pregnancies, in order to 'prevent post-partum depression and to ensure that women truly enjoy their motherhood, which will benefit the woman as well as the boy or girl to be born'. The proposal asserted that the nation's health centres must 'prioritise motherhood', because mothers-to-be 'are deserving of all the necessary attention in order to bring their children into the world with security, contentment, and support'.[16]

A common claim made by legislators authoring pro-natal bills is thus that pregnant women – especially those deemed 'at risk' – have diminished decision-making capacities that can be restored via state interference. Legislators with traditional values help women by directing them on the proper path of motherhood. These claims also appear in pro-natal bills to create breastfeeding campaigns and national breast milk banks; here, motherhood is portrayed as the best option for women *and* the nation. For example, a female populist legislator noted that breastfeeding 'strengthens the mother–child relationship, and becomes especially important when women who work must be separated from their children for most of the day'. Additionally, breastfeeding saves families 'time and money that would have been spent on formula', and ultimately 'ensures the health of the boys and girls of the nation'.[17] Likewise, a similar proposal authored by a female legislator from a neoliberal right party stated, 'Mothers who breastfeed contribute to the country by ensuring healthy, intelligent and self-confident children'.[18] Breastfeeding instructions, like psychological counselling, guide women in fulfilling their exalted role as mothers.

These pro-natal bills are inherently paradoxical. On the one hand, they target women as constituents and beneficiaries, and count as SRW proposals on women,

14. Bill 0853-D-2009.
15. Bill 3247-D-2007.
16. Bill 3150-D-2010.
17. Bill 2454-D-2007.
18. Bill 0671-D-2009.

not children. On the other hand, they portray women's interests as *in service to* the interests of children. Most of the pro-natal bills that focus on pregnancy and breastfeeding assistance, and as such elevate motherhood to a national public good, are authored by female legislators. Male legislators, by contrast, mostly author pro-natal initiatives focused on the detection and treatment of foetal illnesses caused by negligent mothers, such as foetal alcohol syndrome or HIV. Even within this policy area of Type II claims, the foci of male and female legislators vary, with male legislators more likely to chastise women.

These sex differences in tone also appear in the Type II claims related to nuclear family fortification. Here, male legislators justified state assistance by focusing on failed mothers: for instance, in proposing a conditional cash transfer programme, a populist male deputy wrote that families needed 'mothers' (not 'women') to 'improve their education to obtain more profitable employment' and 'enhance their commitment to the stable nurturing of their children'.[19] Female legislators, by contrast, proposed social programmes in more empowering, but still gendered and traditional, terms. In wishing to distribute copies of the Argentine civil code to all households, a female populist deputy described family law as the 'vehicle through which the Argentine woman can defend her children, her home, and her rights as a consumer because, in the twenty-first century, no one can dispute that it is women who must fortify the family as an institution'.[20] Focusing on mothers as failed, rather than in need, may be one way that male legislators speak for children – albeit indirectly – even when making Type II claims.

Conclusion

Gendered claims in the Argentine Congress, while present, are in the minority. Across all parties save the conservative right, male and female legislators introduce significantly more feminist claims when compared to gendered claims. Support for women's traditional roles does exist, but state resources are not often appropriated for the cause: few Type II proposals exit committees, while more Type I proposals not only exit committees, but advance to plenary debate and vote (Piscopo 2011). From a feminist perspective, then, the Argentine case is reassuring: despite the ideological attachment of many legislators to traditional views of women's roles, policy projects ultimately treat women as individual right-bearers, not nationalist mothers. The predominance of feminist proposals, however, does not mean that Type II claims lack legitimacy. Future research could explore whether these Type II claims are responsive to constituents, as Celis and Childs (this volume) suggest: are conservative constituents aware that their interests, while not sufficiently popular to alter laws, at least appear on the agenda?

Further, research should extend the party and content analysis to other Latin American cases. The absence of effects for party ideology on the representation of

---

19. Bill 2375-D-2009.

20. Bill 4635-D-2007.

feminist and gendered claims may well be particular to the Argentine case, where parties are internally heterogeneous and opportunistic rather than programmatic. Further, the distinction between women's interests and children's interests, while improved upon in this analysis, remains conceptually fraught. A detailed look at pro-natal bills and nuclear family fortification bills does suggest that Type II claims, while they target women as policy beneficiaries, may also implicitly target children. Future work should explore whether, for conservative legislators, women's interests are ever truly separable from children's interests. For male legislators in particular, severance may be difficult. This possibility suggests that feminist legislators will face ongoing challenges in introducing and passing any policy, such as those liberalising reproductive choice, that sever women from their maternal roles.

References

Alemán, E., Calvo, E., Jones, M. P. and Kaplan, N. (2009) 'Comparing co-sponsorship and roll-call ideal points', *Legislative Studies Quarterly*, 34 (1): 87–116.

Barrancos, D. (2006) 'Gender, sexuality, and reproduction in 20th century Argentina', *Journal of Women's History*, 18 (6): 123–50.

Bejarano, C. L. (2002) 'Las Super Madres de Latino América: transforming motherhood by challenging violence in Mexico, Argentina, and El Salvador', *Frontiers*, 23 (1): 126–50.

Blofield, M. (2006) *The Politics of Moral Sin*, New York: Routledge.

Celis, K. and Childs, S. (2012) 'The substantive representation of women: what to do with conservative claims?', *Political Studies*, 60 (1): 213–25.

Craske, N. (1998) 'Remasculinisation and the neoliberal state in Latin America', in Randall, V. and Waylen, G. (eds), *Gender, Politics and the State*, New York: Taylor & Francis, pp. 100–20.

—— (1999) *Women and Politics in Latin America*, London: Routledge.

Eltantawy, N. (2008) 'Pots, pans, and protests: women's strategies for resisting globalization in Argentina', *Communication and Critical/Cultural Studies*, 5 (1): 46–63.

Franceschet, S. and Piscopo, J. M. (2008) 'Quotas and women's substantive representation: lessons from Argentina', *Politics & Gender*, 4 (3): 393–425.

Franceschet, S., Piscopo, J. M. and Thomas, G. (2012) 'Motherhood and politics in Latin America: continuity and change', paper presented at 'Mothers and Others' Workshop, Banff, Canada, 8–9 November.

Htun, M. (2003) *Sex and the State*, Cambridge: Cambridge University Press.

Htun, M. and Power, T. J. (2006) 'Gender, parties, and support for equal rights in the Brazilian Congress', *Latin American Politics and Society*, 48 (4): 83–104.

Jones, M. P., Hwang, W. and Micozzi, J. P. (2009) 'Government and opposition in the Argentine Congress, 1989–2007: understanding inter-party dynamics through roll call vote analysis', *Journal of Politics in Latin America*, 1 (1): 67–96.

Kampwirth, K. (2005) 'Resisting the feminist threat: antifeminist politics in post-Sandinista Nicaragua', *Feminist Formations*, 18 (2): 73–100.

—— (ed.) (2010) *Gender and Populism in Latin America: Passionate Politics*, University Park: Pennsylvania State University Press.

Lavrín, A. (1995) *Women, Feminism and Social Change in Argentina, Chile, and Uruguay, 1890–1940*, Lincoln, NE: University of Nebraska Press.

Levitsky, S. (2005) 'Crisis and renovation: institutional weakness and the transformation of Argentine Peronism, 1983–2003', in Levitsky, S. and Murrillo, M. V. (eds), *Argentine Democracy: The Politics of Institutional Weakness*, University Park, PA: Pennsylvania State University Press, pp. 181–206.

Lopreite, D. (2008) 'Challenging the Argentine gender regime?', paper presented at the APSA Annual Conference, Boston, MA, 28–31 August.

Miguel, L. F. (2012) 'Policy priorities and women's double bind in Brazil', in Franceschet, S., Krook, M. L. and Piscopo, J. M. (eds), *The Impact of Gender Quotas*, New York, Cambridge University Press, pp. 103–18.

Molyneux, M. (2009) 'Conditional cash-transfers: a "pathway to women's empowerment"', Pathways of Women's Empowerment Project, available at http://www.pathwaysofempowerment.org/archive_resources/conditional-cash-transfers-a-pathway-to-women-s-empowerment-pathways-brief-5 (accessed 14 May 2014).

Piscopo, J. M. (2011) 'Do women represent women? Gender and policy in Argentina and Mexico', PhD dissertation, University of California, San Diego.

Schwindt-Bayer, L. A. (2006) 'Still supermadres? Gender and policy priorities of Latin American legislators', *American Journal of Political Science*, 50 (3): 570–85.

—— (2010) *Political Power and Women's Representation in Latin America*, New York: Oxford University Press.

Torre, J. C. (2005) 'Citizens versus political class: the crisis of partisan representation', in Levitsky, S. and Murrillo, M. V. (eds), *Argentine Democracy: The Politics of Institutional Weakness*, University Park, PA: Pennsylvania State University Press, pp. 165–80.

Waylen, G. (2008) 'Enhancing the substantive representation of women: lessons from transitions to democracy', *Parliamentary Affairs*, 61 (3): 518–34.

Chapter Eleven

Mapping 'Feminist' Demands Across the French Political Spectrum

Rainbow Murray and Réjane Sénac

Introduction

Two assumptions frequently recur in literature on the substantive representation of women (SRW). The first is that, all other things being equal, women are more likely than men to seek to represent women's interests, and to do so more effectively than men (*see* for example, Campbell *et al.* 2010; Lovenduski 2005; Phillips 1995; Sapiro 1981). The second is that left-wing parties are more feminist in their ideology and practice, resulting in policies more likely to be acknowledged as SRW by feminist researchers (Kittilson 2006). It therefore follows that left-wing women might be the group most likely to represent women, with right-wing men being the least likely to initiate SRW. This argument creates a certain tension for right-wing women politicians whereby their sex predicts that they should be concerned with women's issues, while their ideology indicates that this concern might not be feminist in direction. In turn, this raises questions of whether the fact of representing a group in the descriptive sense of 'standing for' is sufficient to guarantee the representation of 'its' interests in the substantive sense of 'acting for', as Hanna Pitkin (1972) herself suggested of descriptive representation per se.

Recent gender and politics literature underlines to a much greater extent the need to question relationships between the descriptive and substantive representation of women (Celis and Childs 2008, 2012; Dahlerup 1988; Krook and Childs 2010; Mansbridge 1999; Phillips 1998; Rymph 2006; Sénac 2012; Wängnerud 2000). Childs and Krook's notion of the critical actor (2006; 2008) provides for a more nuanced account that recognises that gendered and/or feminist motivations can in principle transcend the sex of the actor, even as they admit that most critical actors are likely to be women. Added to this is research that questions the association between women's substantive representation and leftist feminists (Childs and Webb 2012a, 2012b; with Marthaler 2009, 2010; Celis and Childs 2012). Valuable research certainly exists to demonstrate that left-wing parties, collectively, have a better track record than right-wing parties regarding SRW, which is defined as policies that are broadly in tune with feminist goals (Caul 1999, 2001; Kittilson 2006). However, this overall trend does not preclude the possibility of SRW by individual critical actors within right-wing parties.

Indeed, with a growing presence of women politicians in right-wing parties in a number of western democracies, it is important to reevaluate the relationship between gender, party and SRW, as Celis and Childs (2012) suggest. In order to investigate the possibility that SRW is not limited to a particular ideology or group of actors, gender and politics scholars must reconsider how SRW is defined (Celis *et al.* 2008, 2009), with differences linked to ideological interpretations of which problems matter (what are women's issues) and which solutions are acceptable (what is considered to be in women's interests). Hence, the possibility of SRW by conservatives challenges the assumption that leftist women representatives have a monopoly on acting on women's interests, as they define them.

In this chapter we take France as a case study in order to examine the possibility of conservative SRW and to map 'feminist' approaches across the French political spectrum. We do so first by testing the claims of conservative representatives and, secondly, by considering 'conservative representative claims and actions as part of an economy of gendered representative claims' (Celis and Childs 2012: 218). In so doing, and following Celis and Childs, we too eschew attempts to place conservative representatives on a continuum with 'non-substantive representation of women/anti-feminist/conservative' on the one hand, and the 'substantive representation of women/feminist/leftist' on the other.

The principle of gender equality has been enshrined in the French constitution since 1946,[1] and key debates over this principle have included contraception rights in 1965, abortion rights in 1974, and claims for gender parity in the 1990s, with presidential elections acting as a focal point (Bereni 2007; Dahlerup 2008; Murray 2008; Sineau 2011a). In the 2012 French presidential election, there was intense media coverage of gender equality, not least in respect of equal pay, violence against women, and gender parity. An analysis of the different manifestos in the 2012 presidential election campaign (Sénac and Parodi 2013), together with a survey conducted among members of the French National Assembly, illustrates how attitudes to representation differ by sex and party. Fifty-two interviews were undertaken during the period January-June 2011. The sample includes 29 women and 23 men, drawn from parties on the right (21) and left (31).[2] Quantitative analysis of policy priorities, using data from private members' bills (*propositions de loi*), written questions, and oral questions to the government, are also analysed.

---

1. Cf. The preamble of the 1946 Constitution, included in the preamble of the 1958 Constitution, specifying that 'the law guarantees to women, in every aspect, equal rights to men'.

2. All members of parliament were sent an interview request, and our initial sample comprised those deputies who responded positively to this request. Using a snowballing sampling technique, we used recommendations from our initial interviewees to help us procure further interviews. It is therefore likely that our sample is biased, as it is skewed towards those who were willing to partake in a study of gendered representation. To limit the effects of this bias, we encouraged our interviewees to recommend colleagues of all viewpoints, including those who were hostile to parity. While those sympathetic to women's representation are almost certainly over-sampled, we did obtain respondents from across the political spectrum, and this is reflected in the views expressed. To protect the anonymity of our interviewees, we identify them only by their gender and ideological affiliation. We list deputies as being left-wing or right-wing, rather than identifying their party affiliation. This protects the identity of members of smaller parties on the left or right.

Comparisons are undertaken on a number of dimensions, including how deputies view their role as representatives, and their experiences of being in parliament; equality between men and women in the 2012 presidential election campaign; attitudes towards the law on parity; and how different actors have embraced, rejected, or accepted gender parity. In so doing, it is possible to identify critical actors 'for women', and consider the importance that deputies attach to gender.

Gender equality and substantive representation in the 2012 French presidential election

The 2012 presidential election came at a time when feminism was undergoing a revival and gender equality was gaining media coverage. Contributing to this phenomenon were the world economic crisis, Dominique Strauss-Kahn's indictment for sexual assault, and the tradition of using presidential elections as an opportunity to force gender onto the agenda.

The period between the two rounds of the election was characterised by a re-politicisation of gender, including a feminist campaign arguing that 'the rights of women come from the left'.[3] This was followed by the publication of an opinion piece on 25 April 2012 in the daily newspaper *Liberation* signed by 150 feminist personalities stemming from civil society, declaring their support as feminists for the left-wing candidate, François Hollande. Hollande's subsequent nomination of France's first parity government was in keeping with his electoral campaign, in particular his forty commitments 'to guarantee women's rights and transform society towards more equality'.[4] One of these pledges was fulfilled through the nomination of Najat Vallauf-Belkacem as a fully-fledged Minister of Women's Rights, similar to the Ministry of Women's Rights entrusted to Yvette Roudy (1981–6) by François Mitterrand (Dauphin 2010; Stetson and Mazur 2010).

The main French political parties addressed the issue of gender equality through a series of events prior to the election, including the UMP's conference on 'The place of women in society' on 21 June 2011; 'Where are the women?' organised by the *Nouveau Centre* (New Centre) on 7 March 2011; and the debate 'How to disrupt the sexual order' by the Greens (EELV) on 31 March 2011. The Socialist Party chose to include the theme of gender equality in its 'Conference on real equality' (*Convention pour l'égalité réelle*[5]), the text of which was adopted by the National Council on 9 November 2010. A subsection of the document is entitled 'Providing the means to achieve male/female equality', contained within the section on 'The same rights for all citizens'.

---

3.   *See* http://www.lesdroitsdesfemmespassentparlagauche.wordpress.com/pourquoi-cette-campagne/ (accessed 5 May 2014).

4.   *See* http://www.laboratoiredelegalite.org/spip.php?action=acceder_document&arg=197&cl e=6b1d13fe1c666a5180e954ec01fc60e0101e7ccd&file=pdf%2F40_Engagements_pour_l_ egalite_F-H_Francois_Hollande.pdf (accessed 22 May 2015).

5.   *See* http://www.parti-socialiste.fr/static/9243/convention-nationale-egalite-reelle-le-texte-en-debat.pdf (accessed 5 May 2014).

Candidates' manifesto pledges for gender equality

An analysis of candidates' programmes in terms of family policy sheds light on ideological and partisan differences between the parties. Focusing first on left-wing parties, the Left Front (*Front de gauche*) is clear in its objective 'to eliminate patriarchy', as are the Greens, who seek 'to place gender equality at the heart of the transformation of society'. The Left Front issued an appeal for gender equality in March 2012, arguing that 'feminist demands should no longer be a pretext but [should] be the centre of political debate in 2012'.[6] Note however that these parties' programmes do not reveal whether they aim more towards the model of the universal worker – denounced by Nancy Fraser as androcentric – or towards the model of the universal supplier of care (Fraser 2012; Fraser and Honneth 2003), where 'the State intervenes to favour the lack of differentiation between the roles of men and women' (Dauphin 2011: 321).

Turning to the right-wing parties, the UMP and the *Mouvement Démocratique* (MoDem) both recognise the need to establish a 'gender agreement' (Letablier 2009) to help women balance their personal and professional lives – a perspective that corresponds to Fraser's (1994, 2005) caregiver parity model. In other words, the purpose is not to make women's lives the same as men's, but rather 'to eliminate the cost of the difference' (Fraser 2005: 177–8). Accordingly, public policies aim to provide opportunities for women to combine care work and employment, by creating generous benefit programmes and facilitating part-time work. This model is linked to the defence of the complementarity between the sexes and heteronormativity as the foundation for the social contract (Pateman 1988; Sénac-Slawinski 2007, 2009). This link was embodied by a proposal to create a public inquiry into the introduction and dissemination of gender theory ('*théorie du gender*') in France by a group of UMP Members of Parliament on 7 December 2012.[7]

Focusing on the National Front (*Front National*, or FN), Marine Le Pen's presidential campaign offered a symbolic representation: she was 'a woman of her time [...] free, [...] modern, [...] divorced, the mother of three children'.[8] Through her personal story, Marine Le Pen emerged as a representative of women, apparently sharing the same difficulties with them: 'women know nothing about the 35-hour week [...]. Women are submitted to a "double burden": an often fascinating job and a family life to be led'. FN policies supported the principle of 'national priority' and a pro-birth policy. There would be: a lowering in the retirement age for mothers having brought up at least three children or having brought up a disabled child; the creation of a parental salary (rather than just a maternal salary) amounting to 80 per cent of the SMIC (guaranteed minimum wage) from the second child; and the up-rating and indexation on the cost of living of family allowances.

---

6.   *See* http://www.placeaupeuple2012.fr/feminisme/ (accessed 5 May 2014).

7.   *See* http://www.assemblee-nationale.fr/14/propositions/pion0482.asp (accessed 5 May 2014).

8.   *See* http://www.marinelepen2012.fr, following the link headed 'Marine' (accessed 1 May 2012).

The National Front programme is further characterised by the defence of the national priority principle for employment, accommodation and social benefits. Thus, allowances would be reserved for families in which at least one parent is French. In the same vein, the party's defence of free choice 'not to have an abortion' through the development of prevention, antenatal adoption, or improvement in family benefits should be interpreted as a means of not alienating the established FN electorate. More generally, the FN understands the family to be an 'irreplaceable institution', a 'basic unit of society' which 'has to establish itself exclusively through the union of a man and a woman to procreate from a father and mother'. This is why the FN opposes 'any demand for the establishment of same-sex marriage and/or adoption by homosexual couples'. Such sentiments correspond to the expectations of loyal FN voters, the majority of whom are male, pensioners, with few or no qualifications. At the same time, Le Pen's more liberal declarations constitute an opening towards younger, 'disengaged' voters from the moderate right, and 'remobilised' voters (Perrineau 2011, 2012a), whose profile is 'more female, young (25–34 years old), middle class (mid-level employees and clerical employees), who have obtained their high school diploma and completed some kind of post-high school education and whose income is low and/or insufficient' (Perrineau 2012b: 3). In particular, the policy transition from a maternal to a parental salary (thus envisaging stay-at-home fathers) was designed to reflect the renewal of the FN electorate, which was younger and more used to modern family models.

Parity and SRW

Parity laws: Strategic alliances

If parties' pronouncements at the time of elections are one indicator of their position on the SRW, it is also necessary to examine the implementation of these policies once they are in power (Childs 2008; Franceschet and Piscopo 2008), in order to capture the distinction between claims making and acting for women.[9] For ten years (2002–12), France was governed by a right-wing majority led by the UMP party. This time frame coincides with the implementation of France's 'parity' law (Bereni and Lépinard 2004; Bereni and Revillard 2007; Mossuz-Lavau 1998; Scott 2005; Sénac-Slawinski 2008a, 2009), which obliges political parties to put forward equal numbers of male and female candidates for most elections. Although the law has been limited in its effectiveness in the National Assembly[10] (Dahlerup 2007; Murray 2010a, 2010b; Ross 2002), it has helped raise the proportion of women in parliament from 12 per cent (2002) to 18 per cent (2007) and 27 per cent

---

9. We carried out interviews with more than fifty deputies of the 13th legislature.

10. The two main causes for this ineffectiveness are as follows. First, the law focuses on the number of candidates rather than on seats; thus, parties tend to field women in unwinnable seats. Second, the sanction for disregarding the law is quite weak.

(2012). As noted elsewhere (Murray 2004), some parties on the right, including the UMP, have chosen to sacrifice a portion of their state finance (the penalty for failing to respect parity for legislative elections) rather than select 50 per cent female candidates. At the same time, and while still wary of so-called 'positive discrimination', the UMP has softened its attitude towards parity, with some of its original detractors now starting to recognise its worth. France has a small, but growing, contingent of right-wing women deputies who belong to the governing party and have had the opportunity to act for women, even if this opportunity might be constrained by these women's ideology and marginalization within their party.

France's 'parity' law has been one of the most divisive issues of direct relevance to women. It has traditionally received more support on the left than on the right and the only deputy to vote against the original law was Christine Boutin, a female deputy on the right. However, attitudes towards parity have crossed gender and partisan lines. Recent research (Sénac-Slawinski 2008b) indicates that attitudes towards parity are starting to shift among women on the right, as they move from resistance to acceptance of the law. Two sources of tension emerged for right-wing women when our interviewees were asked about parity. The first was an internal tension: a desire for fair representation had to be reconciled with an ideological hostility towards equality guarantees (Lovenduski 2005). The second was an external tension, whereby feminist views and/or sympathy towards gender parity might place them in conflict with their own party and in an uneasy alliance with deputies on the left.

These tensions were very present in the arguments presented by right-wing women. The majority of this group of interviewees denied that parity had helped them secure their own position in politics, whereas women on the left were much more open in acknowledging the role that parity had played in helping them to enter politics. One right-wing woman, for example, claimed that she had arrived in politics 'without parity',[11] while another stated that 'parity did not have an effect because I was elected in my own name, without support from my party. It's not parity but my wish to stand. […] You mustn't hide behind parity. […] In my case, the parity law did nothing for me'.[12]

A third said that her election was 'not because I was a woman'.[13] Two others recognised that they were chosen because they were women, but did not see this as an advantage because they had been selected to run for a seat believed to be unwinnable.[14] This scenario was echoed by another woman on the right, who said:

---

11. Interview 1, right-wing woman, interviewed in Paris, 18 January 2011.

12. Interview 14, right-wing woman, interviewed in Paris, 17 February 2011.

13. Interview 24, right-wing woman, interviewed in Paris, 17 February 2011.

14. Interview 25, right-wing woman, interviewed in Paris, 4 May 2011; interview 52, right-wing woman, interviewed in Paris, 25 May 2011.

the parity law contributed […] that's clear. That's true. Because, as if by magic, there were four female candidates. But it's also true that they were difficult constituencies to win, so, hmm, it did nothing to shake things up for men [laughs], and I also saw other female colleagues who were placed in similar seats to me. When she was asked to clarify whether it was effectively a reserved seat for women she replied, laughing, 'no, rather a hopeless seat!'[15]

Parity was therefore seen by several right-wing women as irrelevant, or even unhelpful. One claimed 'parity undermines women's interests because we come to hear that we are here because we are women and not out of merit. It has to be handled carefully to ensure it doesn't turn against women'.[16] This viewpoint echoes longstanding unease with the concept of parity among right-wing politicians. Parity sits uncomfortably alongside right-wing ideology, which favours individual over group identity. Parties on the French right prefer traditional roles for women, and argue that women should not be forced into politics if they are not ready and willing to enter (Opello 2006). The tendency to blame a shortage of women on supply-side factors is, then, used here to justify women's ongoing under-representation since the introduction of parity. But the testimony of women politicians suggested that the problem was more one of demand. One argued that 'this is a law made by men, for men. There are as many women as men on party lists but in the positions of responsibility […] women aren't there. Parity is just a sleight of hand, it's just for show'.[17] Another stated:

we are very often placed in constituencies that aren't very winnable. […] This shocked me. You have to prove that you have far more qualities just to get an equal role, and be recognised as being far superior to what is expected for a man. And this bothers me because I am from a generation that imagined that by the year 2000 we would have won all the battles. But [the battle] is far from won.[18]

Another woman from her party concurred, stating that 'women are outnumbered and are not taken seriously. You have to do more to get recognition when you're a woman'.[19]

---

15. Interview 34, right-wing woman, interviewed in Paris, 18 January 2011.

16. Interview 9, right-wing woman, interviewed in Paris, 1 February 2011.

17. Interview 14, right-wing woman, interviewed in Paris, 17 February 2011.

18. Interview 20, right-wing woman, interviewed in Paris, 8 March 2011.

19. Interview 6, right-wing woman, interviewed in Paris, 26 January 2011.

Power-sharing as a cross-party claim

Despite this disenchantment with the reality of parity, there was also growing acceptance of the principle of this mechanism for increasing women's presence in politics. One right-wing woman conceded that 'at first I was against it because it was a Socialist law and I'm from the UMP, but now I recognise with hindsight that it is well founded'.[20] Another admitted that 'women must be represented and representatives in equal measure, and it's for this reason that parity was necessary'.[21] Some women on the right are even enthusiastic about parity. One interviewee sought to introduce a quota law in 1996, proposed together with a male colleague, but the law never got off the ground because they were 'lynched' by their party colleagues. 'Everyone said, "let things happen naturally", but I said "if things were happening naturally there wouldn't be 50 women in parliaments, there would be 250 or 200", so what is natural about this situation?'[22] She went on to declare that 'going from a minority, when we are actually a majority in the real world, to parity, is not only a question of social justice and democracy, but also, quite simply, a question of modernity'.[23] These comments were echoed by a right-wing colleague, who said of gender equality: 'Do we need laws? I completely agree – yes. Because there is a glass ceiling, and we need to break it. Therefore, of course the law is indispensable, and I am one of those who are convinced that without a law we will not make progress'.[24]

Where women do support parity, this has created an external tension, because their views place them closer to their left-wing counterparts than to men within their own party. One right-wing woman acknowledged this explicitly, claiming that the left 'are a bit ahead of us on that issue, yes. Yes, they are further ahead'.[25] She recounted a time when she drew attention to the insufficient application of the parity law during a parliamentary debate, 'and the left applauded me, and the right was furious that I said this'.[26] Another recognised that 'it's true that in parliament there is solidarity between women that crosses party lines. It's very strong'.[27] At the same time, right-wing ideology has offered different solutions to problems, which allow women to distinguish themselves from their left-wing counterparts while still supporting a feminist point of view. One woman gave the example of women's subordination within society, where her position had shifted from one of protection to one of the empowerment of women.

---

20. Interview 20, right-wing woman, interviewed in Paris, 8 March 2011.

21. Interview 25, right-wing woman, interviewed in Paris, 4 May 2011.

22. Interview 53, right-wing woman, interviewed in Paris, 22 June 2011.

23. Ibid.

24. Interview 46, right-wing woman, interviewed in Paris, 22 March 2011.

25. Ibid.

26. Ibid.

27. Interview 52, right-wing woman, interviewed in Paris, 25 May 2011.

I have often said, including to my Socialist colleagues, who often approached the problem from a position of protection, that we have been advocating protection for 15 years now, and I completely supported it, but from now on we will have no new progress unless it comes from women themselves.[28]

This is one of numerous examples of what might be termed right-wing feminism. The feminism declared by a number of our interviewees was sincere, passionate and ideologically coherent. Irrespective of their other political views, there was no denying that these women cared about women's rights and were willing to defend them. One interviewee, who was a former Women's Minister in a right-wing government, said:

I had a grandmother [...] who was very feminist, she was one of the suffragettes... I asked myself a lot of questions about women's lives... because I realised that we were in a world where responsibility and power was held by men... I had a very strong feminist consciousness because I felt that it was through feminism that we could really change the lives of women and of society. I had this perception when I was young and I decided to build my life around this feminist political path [...] I said to myself 'I am going to succeed and I am going to show that women can succeed'.[29]

This deputy modelled her life upon her feminist ideals, refusing to marry, defending the right for women to challenge accepted gender roles and redefine social norms. For example, 'when I arrived at parliament, in a navy blue trouser suit, I went up to the dispatch box and an usher said, "you are in trousers, ma'am", and I said, "you'd better get used to it because you will change before I do"'.[30] Another described how she mobilised within her party to ensure the nomination of a woman as vice-president of the National Assembly, and how she and her feminist colleagues rallied against the male domination within her party and within parliament more broadly. Even when referring to her own decision to stand down as mayor in a large city, she ensured that her successor was also a woman, saying, 'I couldn't pass it on to anyone other than a woman!'[31]

Feminism within the UMP is not universal, demonstrating the importance of critical actors. For the most part, these actors are women, including notable right-wing feminists such as Roselyne Bachelot-Narquin, founder of the Parity Observatory; Nicole Ameline, former Women's Minister; and Françoise de Panafieu, a staunch supporter of parity who successfully stood as a dissident candidate in the parliamentary constituency where she was also mayor after her party refused to make her the official nominee. We could also add to the list Marie-

---

28. Interview 53, right-wing woman, interviewed in Paris, 22 June 2011.
29. Ibid.
30. Ibid.
31. Interview 46, right-wing woman, interviewed in Paris, 22 March 2011.

Jo Zimmerman, former president of the Parity Observatory and former president of the parliamentary Delegation for Women's Rights, and Chantal Brunel, former Justice Minister and former president of the Parity Observatory, even though neither of these women self-identifies as feminist. In addition, Rachida Dati, former Justice Minister, followed in Panafieu's footsteps by standing in the constituency where she was mayor against the outgoing UMP prime minister, and vocally critiquing the UMP for its lack of commitment to parity. Following her defeat in June 2012, she created a UMP women's group that united right-wing women in the fight for greater presence and influence within the party. While the group's mission is clearly feminist in its goal of getting more women into power, it frames this goal in terms of making the UMP more modern and reflective of French society.[32]

The above list of right-wing feminists is certainly not exhaustive; Dati's group counts more than 100 UMP politicians who have signed up to support women's inclusion within the party. Not all the critical actors are women, even if feminist men are a rare find within the UMP. One right-wing man spoke at length about his support for women's representation, declaring that 'if you do not have the intelligence to understand that you need to offer a fair and equal place to women then you have understood nothing of how society works'.[33] He added that when there are elections within the UMP for internal party roles, 'I automatically tick all the women candidates to ensure that their representation is at least proportionate to their presence within the party parliamentary group'.[34] While he may be the exception that proves the rule, the point remains that feminism is the exclusive preserve neither of women, nor of the left.

Deputies' behaviour and the SRW

An empirical study of policy preferences tested whether these impressions of gender differences among representatives were borne out in reality. Data were gathered from private members' bills, written questions and questions to the government, in order to identify whether men and women prioritised different issues. For each of these types of parliamentary activity, the data was gathered from the website of the National Assembly (http://www.assemblee-nationale.fr), and coded into thirty-eight different policy areas. For private members' bills, the mean number of bills proposed within each policy area was calculated in order to determine the top six priority areas for different groups of deputies. A similar approach was taken for parliamentary questions, except that percentages for each policy area were calculated before taking the mean scores, in order to compensate for large disparities in the numbers of questions asked by different deputies.

---

32. *See* http://www.adroitetoutes.fr/ (accessed 25 September, 2013).

33. Interview 19, right-wing man, interviewed in Paris, 3 March 2011.

34. Ibid.

The resulting tables illustrate where men and women from different parties had different issue priorities.

Although most policy is initiated by the government in France, individual deputies can also initiate bills (*propositions de loi*). These tend not to be passed, especially when introduced by a member of an opposition party, although bills on valence issues can sometimes succeed. Nevertheless, deputy-initiated bills are used as a way of drawing attention to particular issues and signalling that action has been taken on a policy of importance to an individual deputy. Table 11.1 reveals that during the 13th legislature the most commonly addressed issue area for almost all groups of deputies was administrative matters – constitutional affairs, local politics, the civil service, civil registers and some public services. The only group not to focus most on this area was left-wing women. Health is also a bigger priority for women than for men, while commerce is of less importance to women. Women's equality issues are a top priority for left-wing women and are also a high priority for right-wing women, whereas they were a very low priority for men of both party groups. These findings suggest that French women deputies are more likely than men to be substantively representing women, with a much higher level of interest in initiating legislation pertaining directly to women's issues. This sex gap is far more striking than any partisan difference.

Written questions are asked by deputies as a means of learning more about an issue or bringing an issue to a minister's attention; they are also an indicator of the SRW. While questions often pertain to issues of importance at constituency level, Table 11.2 reveals that there was partisan convergence between men and women on most issues but that women prioritised welfare more highly than men, and were less interested than men in administrative issues.

Questions to the government are the most high profile of all parliamentary activities, as they are televised and watched by a large audience. The coveted question slot tends to focus on an issue of contemporary relevance; deputies may propose questions in advance, but these may be replaced at short notice with a topical question that needs to be addressed quickly.[35] The high-profile nature of these questions means that they are carefully managed by parties. Our analysis demonstrates that gender stereotypes emerge more frequently in questions to the government (which are chosen by parties) than in other types of question (chosen by deputies). This pattern emerges less clearly when focusing only on the most common policy areas, but some sex differences can still be seen in Table 11.3. For right-wing women, questions on the family are the fourth most frequent policy area, followed by welfare – both issues that are not frequently addressed by men. Left-wing women ask more questions on education and again show less interest in administrative issues.

---

35. Questions to the government are asked in an hour-long session twice a week, with deputies allowed a maximum of two minutes to ask their question, followed by a two-minute response by the minister. These very strict time limits mean that these questions are of limited effectiveness as a way of holding the executive to account.

Table 11.1: Policy priorities measured by Private Members' Bills

Policy priority	Men			Women		
	Right-wing	Left-wing	All	Right-wing	Left-wing	All
1	Admin	Admin	**Admin**	Admin; health	Women; health; transport	**Health**
2	Law and order	Commerce	**Law and order**	Law and order		**Admin**
3	Commerce	Law and order	**Commerce**	Foreign policy		**Law and order**
4	Health	Welfare; politics; environment	**Welfare**		Agriculture; welfare; foreign policy; law and order	**Women; foreign policy**
5	Welfare		**Health**	Welfare; commerce; housing; women		
6	Tax		**Tax**			**Welfare**

Source: http://www.assemblee-nationale.fr/13/documents/index-proposition.asp (accessed 19 June 2014).

Table 11.2: Policy priorities measured by written questions

Policy priority	Men		Women	
	Right-wing	Left-wing	Right-wing	Left-wing
1	Health	Administration	Health	Welfare
2	Administration	Education	Welfare	Education
3	Welfare	Health	Tax	Health
4	Tax	Welfare	Commerce	Administration
5	Education	Law and order	Administration	Law and order
6	Transport	Pensions	Agriculture	Pensions

Source: www2.assemblee-nationale.fr/recherche/questions (accessed 19 June 2014).

Table 11.3: Policy priorities measured by questions to the government

Policy priority	Men			Women		
	Right-wing	Left-wing	All	Right-wing	Left-wing	All
1	Foreign policy	Administration	**Foreign policy**	Foreign policy	Law and order	**Law and order**
2	Agriculture	Finance	**Administration**	Law and order	Commerce	**Commerce**
3	Law and order	Foreign policy	**Agriculture**	Agriculture	Education	**Education**
4	Transport	Pensions	**Law and order**	Family	Pensions	**Foreign policy**
5	Commerce	Tax	**Commerce**	Welfare	Agriculture	**Welfare**
6	Administration	Commerce	**Transport**	Transport	Administration	**Agriculture**

Source: http://www2.assemblee-nationale.fr/recherche/questions (accessed 19 June 2014).

Overall, our data on questions indicate that differences between men and women are quite small in most areas, albeit with some important caveats. Men and women of both parties have fairly similar preferences on most issues, but policy areas of particular relevance to women are prioritised only by women and not by men. In addition to policies pertaining directly to women's rights, women are also more likely to focus on related areas such as healthcare, welfare, and education. In some cases, the gap between the sexes is greater than the gap between parties, indicating that sex/gender identity can sometimes be a greater predictor of legislator behaviour than ideology. This finding reinforces Phillips' claims (1995) for a politics of presence rather than focusing exclusively on a politics of ideas.

The gender of parliamentary activity as seen by deputies

When our interviewees considered whether some issues were gendered, a number were identified as being of particular relevance to women, especially by interviewees on the left. These issues included violence, parity, youth, maternity, children, infants, elderly people, disabled people, women's rights, reproduction, bioethics, health, education and sexuality. One left-wing man explained that 'women notice the problems that men do not know about because they have not experienced them'.[36] However, a different left-wing man argued that gender differences were exaggerated, not least by women: 'they wish, they claim that these differences exist, but I don't see them. If it were anonymised you would not know whether it was a man or a woman talking, you can't tell the difference'.[37] In contrast to the tendency of most left-wing interviewees to emphasize sex differences, several right-wing women sought to downplay them, and expressed frustration at the use of stereotyping. One argued that 'you mustn't limit women to social policy. Take security for example – when a woman talks about it, she has as much experience as a man, even if people find that surprising. But women in the UMP are pigeonholed into social policy, for example dependents, nurses, family, education, healthcare, parenthood, elderly people, etc'.[38]

Another right-wing woman regretted that there were not more women involved with budgetary issues. She was also one of several women to complain that when certain 'female' policies were debated, men did not get involved. She gave the examples of incest and addiction, stating that only women attended the debate on the former and were much more likely to contribute to the committee discussion on the latter.[39] A reluctance of right-wing women to be typecast was also shared by some women on the left. One claimed that 'there are some women that really don't

---

36. Interview 3, left-wing man, interviewed in Paris, 20 January 2011; a sentiment closely echoed by a right-wing woman, who claimed that 'women will deal with subjects and issues that men don't think of because they haven't faced these problems' (interview 9, Paris, 1 February 2011).

37. Interview 11, left-wing man, interviewed in Paris, 9 February 2011.

38. Interview 6, right-wing woman, interviewed in Paris, 26 January 2011.

39. Interview 14, right-wing woman, interviewed in Paris, 17 February 2011.

want to be "feminists" because that provokes an aggressive response'.[40] Another stated:

> I refuse to say that there are some jobs for men and others for women. [...] Hardly any women work on transport, which is a shame as the majority of users of public transport are women and no one attaches any importance to this. But transport is gendered; according to surveys, women have different expectations, they want a regular, reliable service that is certain to get them to the school or nursery on time, far more than they want sophisticated technology.[41]

This woman argued that women were needed across the policy spectrum to get unexpected insights such as this, adding: 'I haven't seen men asking these sorts of questions'. She advised:

> it is a fundamental error for women to focus on "women's" policy areas, they need to go elsewhere. It's often the expectations of male politicians (and even women sometimes), who give them responsibility for these issues. On the contrary, you need to go and work on those issues that you wouldn't ordinarily think to focus on'.[42]

These attitudes indicate that, while right-wing women seemed to be the most uncomfortable with the restraints placed on them by gender stereotypes, left-wing women can also feel the need to challenge gendered expectations. Men from both parties were more likely to accept the notion of gendered differences, and less likely to view them as limiting or as a problem for women.

Conclusion

This chapter has analysed the representative claims made during the 2012 French presidential campaign, and the parliamentary acts by representatives in the preceding parliament. In respect of the former, there was a consensus on the principle of gender equality. At the same time, the 2012 presidential election provided an opportunity for public debate on the political implementation of gender equality. Voters perceived that, on this subject, the positions of the French political parties were different and competing (Sénac and Parodi 2013). The manifestos of left-wing parties called for reform of gender hierarchies, while those of the right-wing parties favoured the notion of the complementarity of the sexes and the need for equal treatment. Left-wing party policies, and in particular those of the Greens (*Europe Ecologie les Verts*) and the Left Front (*Front de gauche*), propose a model of 'transformation' (Fraser 2005: 107–44) that seeks to identify 'the systems and the structures at the origin of indirect discrimination' and 'remedy' them (Rees 1995: 46–8). The translation of these electoral differences into voting preferences

---

40. Interview 33, left-wing woman, interviewed in Paris, 18 January 2011.

41. Interview 17, left-wing woman, interviewed in Paris, 2 March 2011.

42. Ibid.

presents a generational more than a gender divide (Sineau 2011b). Younger voters, who tend to have more progressive attitudes towards gender relations, are more likely to vote to the left, while older voters, where women form a majority due to greater longevity, continue to prefer parties of the right.

Our French case study reveals, then, that the interaction between sex, gender and party is highly complex. On the whole, women demonstrate higher levels of gender consciousness than men, with more awareness and experience of sex discrimination. They are more willing to acknowledge certain gender differences, while studiously avoiding certain gender stereotypes. They are also more likely to act for women, with issues of concern to women (such as women's rights, welfare and education) receiving higher priority by women MPs than by men. Differences also emerge between parties on the left and on the right. Right-wing men are more likely than men on the left to be dismissive of the existence of gender discrimination, and more willing to ascribe traditional gendered traits and portfolios to women. Right-wing women are less comfortable acknowledging the role of parity in their political advancement, and are more likely to use universalist rhetoric rather than embracing difference feminism. However, these general trends meet with frequent exceptions. There were large differences between individuals, such that it was often difficult to categorise responses by gender or by party.

Nevertheless, what is clear from our analysis is that left-wing women do not have a monopoly on the SRW. Right-wing women faced internal conflicts when gender equality measures contradicted other aspects of their ideology, and external conflicts when their advocacy of women's interests placed them at odds with their male-dominated party. Yet many of the right-wing women interviewed demonstrated a clear commitment to increasing the descriptive and substantive representation of women. In numerous instances, they advocated positions that were feminist, and sometimes overtly so. At times, these positions led them to form alliances with women on the left, while on other occasions they offered policy positions that were ideologically distinct but still clearly feminist in their orientation. They have also managed to forge a number of successful alliances with sympathetic men within their own party. This may help to explain why the French right has achieved some policy successes on women's rights, despite a large amount of indifference, if not hostility and resistance, to women's interests by many right-wing men. Critical actors on the French right have fought hard to keep women-friendly policies on the agenda. While it remains the case that the left has a better track record for gender equality, with both men and women on the left more likely to espouse feminist positions, French women on the right have proven that conservatism and feminism can indeed go hand in hand.

Acknowledgements

The research presented here was funded by the Leverhulme Trust through a Leverhulme Research Fellowship, and by the City of Paris through a Research in Paris grant. The authors wish to thank Sarah Childs and Karen Celis for their judicious and patient editing. We also thank all our interviewees for their time and candour.

References

Bereni, L. (2007) 'Feminism and the Republic', *French Politics*, 5 (3): 187–228.
Bereni, L. and Lépinard, E. (2004) 'Les stratégies de légitimation de la parité en France', *Revue Française de Science Politique*, 54 (1): 71–98.
Bereni, L. and Revillard, A. (2007) 'Des quotas à la parité: "féminisme d'Etat" et représentation politique (1974–2007)', *Genèses*, 67: 5–23.
Campbell, R., Lovenduski, J. and Childs, S. (2010) 'Do women need women MPs? A comparison of mass and elite attitudes', *British Journal of Political Science*, 40 (10): 179–194.
Caul, M. (1999) 'Women's representation in parliament: the role of political parties', *Party Politics*, 5 (1): 79–98.
— (2001) 'Political parties and the adoption of candidate quotas: a cross-national analysis', *Journal of Politics*, 63 (4): 1214–29.
Celis, K. and Childs, S. (2008) 'Introduction: the descriptive and substantive representation of women: new directions', *Parliamentary Affairs*, 61 (3): 419–25.
— (2012) 'The substantive representation of women: what to do with conservative claims?', *Political Studies*, 60 (1): 213–25.
Celis, K., Childs, S., Kantola, J. and Krook, M. L. (2008) 'Rethinking women's substantive representation', *Representation*, 44 (2): 99–110.
— (2009) 'Constituting women's interests through representative claims', paper presented at the APSA Annual Conference, Toronto, Canada, 3–6 September.
Childs, S. (2008) *Women and British Party Politics*, London: Routledge.
Childs, S. and Krook, M. L. (2006) 'Should feminists give up on critical mass? A contingent yes', *Politics & Gender*, 2 (4): 522–30.
— (2008) 'Critical mass theory and women's political representation', *Political Studies*, 56 (3): 725–36.
Childs, S. and Webb, P. (2012a) *Sex, Gender and the Conservative Party: From Iron Lady to Kitten Heels*, Basingstoke: Palgrave Macmillan.
— (2012b) 'Gender politics and conservatism: the view from the British Conservative Party grassroots', *Government and Opposition*, 47 (1): 21–48.
Childs, S., Webb, P. and Marthaler, S. (2009) 'The feminization of the Conservative Parliamentary Party: party members' attitudes', *Political Quarterly*, 80 (2): 204–13.

—   (2010) 'Constituting and substantively representing women: applying new approaches to a UK case study', *Politics & Gender*, 6 (2): 199–223.

Dahlerup, D. (1988) 'From a small to a large minority: women in Scandinavian politics', *Scandinavian Political Studies*, 11 (4): 275–298.

—   (2007) 'Electoral gender quotas: between equality of opportunity and equality of result', *Representation*, 43 (2): 73–92.

—   (2008) 'Gender quotas – controversial but trendy: on expanding the research agenda', *International Feminist Journal of Politics*, 10 (3): 322–8.

Dauphin, S. (2010) *L'État et les droits des femmes: Des Institutions au Service de l'Égalité?* Rennes: Presses Universitaires de Rennes.

—   (2011) 'Action Publique et Rapport de Genre', in Milewski, F. and Périvier, H. (eds), *Les Discriminations entre les Femmes et les Hommes*, Paris: Presses de Sciences Po, pp. 313–41.

Franceschet, S. and Piscopo, J. M. (2008) 'Gender quotas and women's substantive representation: lessons from Argentina', *Politics & Gender*, 4 (3): 393–425.

Fraser, N. (1994) 'After the family wage: equity and the welfare state', *Political Theory*, 22 (4): 591–618.

—   (2005) *Qu'est-ce que la Justice Sociale? Reconnaissance et Redistribution*, Paris: La Découverte.

—   (2012) *Le Féminisme en Mouvements. Des années 1960 à l'Ere Néo-libérale*, Paris: La Découverte.

Fraser, N. and Honneth, A. (2003) *Redistribution or Recognition? A Political–Philosophical Exchange*, London: Verso.

Kittilson, M. C. (2006) *Challenging Parties, Changing Parliaments: Women and Elected Office in Contemporary Western Europe*, Columbus, OH: Ohio State University Press.

Krook, M. L. and Childs, S. (eds) (2010) *Women, Gender and Politics*, Oxford: Oxford University Press.

Letablier, M.-T. (2009) 'Régimes d'État-Providence et Conventions de Genre en Europe', *Informations Sociales*, 151: 102–9.

Lovenduski, J. (2005) *Feminizing Politics*, Cambridge: Polity.

Mansbridge, J. (1999) 'Should blacks represent blacks and women represent women? A contingent "yes"', *Journal of Politics*, 61 (3): 628–57.

Mossuz-Lavau, J. (1998) *Femmes/Hommes: Pour la Parité*, Paris: Presses de Sciences Po.

Murray, R. (2004) 'Why didn't parity work? A closer examination of the 2002 election results', *French Politics*, 2 (3): 347–62.

—   (2008) 'Fifty years of feminizing France's Fifth Republic', *Modern & Contemporary France*, 16 (4): 469–482.

—   (2010a) *Parties, Gender Quotas and Candidate Selection in France*, Basingstoke: Palgrave Macmillan.

—   (2010b) 'Linear trajectories or vicious circles? The causes and consequences of gendered career paths in the National Assembly', *Modern & Contemporary France*, 18 (4): 445–59.

Opello, K. (2006) *Gender Quotas, Parity Reform and Political Parties in France*, Oxford: Lexington Books.

Pateman, C. (1988) *The Sexual Contract*, Stanford: Stanford University Press.

Perrineau, P. (2011) 'Marine Le Pen: Voter pour une Nouvelle Extrême Droite?' in Perrineau, P. and Rouban, L. (eds), *La Solitude de l'Isoloir: les Vrais Enjeux de 2012*, Paris: Autrement, Frontières, pp. 25–38.

—   (2012a) 'Marine Le Pen: un Héritage qui Fructifie?', in Duhamel, O. and Lecerf, É. (eds), *L'État de l'Opinion 2012*, Paris: TNS/SOFRES/Seuil: 55–70.

—   (2012b) 'La renaissance electorale de l'électorat frontiste', CEVIPOF research note, 5, April, available at http://www.cevipof.com/fr/les-publications/notes-de-recherche/bdd/publication/966 (accessed 22 May 2014).

Phillips, A. (1995) *The Politics of Presence*, Oxford: Clarendon Press.

—   (1998) 'Democracy and representation: or, why should it matter who our representatives are?' in Phillips, A. (ed.), *Feminism and Politics*, New York: Oxford University Press: 224–40.

Pitkin, H. F. (1972) *The Concept of Representation*, Berkeley, Los Angeles: University of California Press.

Rees, T. (1995) *Women and the EC Training Programmes: Tinkering, Tailoring and Transforming*, University of Bristol, School of Advanced Urban Studies: Policy Press.

Ross, K. (2002) 'Women's place in "male" space: gender and effect in parliamentary contexts', *Parliamentary Affairs*, 55: 189–201.

Rymph, C. E. (2006) *Republican Women: Feminism and Conservatism from Suffrage through the Rise of the New Right*, New York: University of North Carolina Press.

Sapiro, V. (1981) 'When are interests interesting? The problem of political representation of women', *American Political Science Review*, 75 (3): 701–16.

Scott, J. W. (2005) *Parité! L'Universel et la Différence des Sexes*, Paris: Albin Michel.

Sénac-Slawinski, R. (2007) *L'Ordre Sexué: La Perception des Inégalités Femmes–Hommes*, Paris: Presses Universitaires de France.

—   (2008a) *La Parité*, Paris: Presses Universitaires de France.

—   (2008b) 'Justifying parity in France after the passage of the so-called parity laws and the electoral application of them: the 'ideological tinkering' of political party officials (UMP and PS) and women's NGOs', *French Politics*, 6 (3): 234–56.

—   (2009) 'Parity and the sexual order', in Mousli, B. and Roustang-Stoller, E. A. (eds), *Women, Feminism, and Femininity in the 21st Century – American and French Perspectives*, New York and London: Palgrave

Macmillan, pp. 133–54.

Sénac, R. (2012) *L'invention de la diversité*, Paris: Presses de Sciences Po.

Sénac, R. and Parodi, M. (2013) 'Tracking change in the french-style gender gap: through the 2012 Presidential Election', *Revue française de science politique* (English), French Election 2012 (1), 63 (2): 19–42.

Sineau, M. (2011a) 'L'égalité femmes/hommes: question-clé pour 2012?', note Enjeux, CEVIPOF élections 2012, 4, available at http://www.cevipof.com/rtefiles/File/AtlasEl3/noteSINEAU.pdf (accessed 5 May 2014).

—— (2011b) *La Force du Nombre: Femmes et Démocratie Présidentielle*, 2nd edn, Paris: Éditions de l'Aube.

Stetson, D. M. and Mazur, A. (2010) *The Politics of State Feminism: Innovation in Comparative Research*, Philadelphia, PA: Temple University Press.

Wängnerud, L. (2000) 'Testing the politics of presence: women's representation in the Swedish Riksdag', *Scandinavian Political Studies*, 23 (1): 67–91.

Chapter Twelve

Representing Women's Interests and the UK Conservative Party: 'To the Left, To the Right', Party Members, Voters and Representatives

Rosie Campbell and Sarah Childs

Introduction

The study of the 'gender gap' in attitudes and party of vote has developed in response to the high profile gender gap in US elections; a greater proportion of women than men have voted for every Democratic presidential candidate since 1980 (Andersen 1999; Box-Steffensmeir *et al.* 1997; Burden 2008; Burns 2001; Carroll 1988, 1999; Chaney *et al.* 1998; Conover 1988; Duke Whitaker 2008; Edlund and Pande 2002; Mueller 1988; Norris 2001). Interest in the subject has spawned an international literature that assesses the extent to which the US gender gap can be found elsewhere (Wängnerud 2000; Norris 1999; Inglehart and Norris 2000; Gidengil and Harell 2007; Campbell 2006). The research has become ever more nuanced and sophisticated with complex theoretical models employed to explain why men and women might prefer different political parties (Alvarez and McCaffery 1999; Burden 2008; Greenberg 2001; Dolan 2010).

To some extent the British case remains an outlier in this literature. There is little in the way of a 'gender gap' in political attitudes or behaviour in Britain (Campbell 2006, 2012) and British research that has tested Norris and Inglehart's claim that women across the developed world are moving to the left has produced mixed results (Norris 1999; Steel 2003; Hayes 1997; Inglehart and Norris 2000; Campbell 2006, 2012). It is apparent that women in Britain have not simply shifted their allegiances from the Conservatives to the Labour Party, and although the Labour Party had some advantage among younger women in 1997 and 2001, there is little evidence to show that this was sustained in 2005 and 2010 (Campbell 2012). The British case therefore provides an interesting example for furthering the study of gender and political attitudes and behaviour.

The absence of an aggregate sex gap among voters does not mean that sex and gender differences do not play out in UK electoral politics. Recent research has shown that the aggregate-level similarity between men and women's political attitudes may mask intra-party differences; a recent study of Conservative party members established that women party members are significantly to the left of men on a range of economic issues (Childs and Webb 2009, 2012; Webb and Childs 2012). This sex gap in Conservative attitudes is interesting in and of itself, but it is also potentially increasingly politically salient in the current economic climate and in a context of massive planned public expenditure cuts. Should Childs and Webb's findings be replicated beyond the membership to the party's support base, the implications are likely to be more significant not only for future intra-party discipline (the focus of Childs and Webb's interest), but also for the possible reemergence of a 'modern' gender gap in vote choice at the next British general election. Using the British Election Study 2010[1] we therefore assess, in this chapter, the extent to which Childs and Webb's observed Conservative sex gap among party members is also evident among Conservative party supporters and identifiers, in other words, among the Conservatives' core voters.

Context

The 2010 United Kingdom general election ushered in a Conservative-led Coalition government. Having been out of power for more than a decade, the Conservative party had engaged in a process of modernization and repositioning so as to be more electorally competitive (Bale 2010). One part of this 'detoxification' process involved a conscious decision to feminise the party (Childs and Webb 2012). The new leader, and now Prime Minister, David Cameron was explicit about his desire to both rectify the 'scandalous' under-representation of women in his parliamentary party and to win back women voters.[2] He was especially focused on attracting the votes of younger women and working mothers, with a series of what can be categorised as liberally feminist policies, not least in respect of equal pay, flexible working, and maternity and paternity leave and pay (Campbell and Childs 2010).[3] Since the election, however, the Conservatives, as the leading party in the current Coalition, have been on the receiving end of repeated gendered criticism, not least, for failing to see how the government's deficit reduction plans disproportionately and negatively affect women. Theresa May, then Minister for Women and Equality, as well as Home Secretary, first warned the Treasury that it must undertake a gender audit of its emergency budget back in 2010. Labour's Yvette Cooper (Shadow Minister for Women),[4] the Fawcett Society and the Women's Budget Group[5] have all produced figures since to show that Coalition

---

1. The British Election Study was conducted by Harold Clarke, David Sanders, Marianne Stewart and Paul Whiteley and funded by the ESRC (*see* http://bes2009-10.org/, accessed 5 May 2014).

2. It has been argued that without women voters there would have been continuous Labour governments in the post-1945 period (Harmen and Mattinson 2000).

3. Even if his commitment to recognise marriage in the tax system smacked more of social conservatism.

4. *See* http://www.guardian.co.uk/politics/2010/oct/22/cuts-women-spending-review (accessed 5 May 2014).

5. *See* http://www.wbg.org.uk (accessed 30 June 2014).

cuts to public services, benefits, and public sector jobs have been overwhelmingly negative for women. Women make up 65 per cent of public sector employees in Britain, and the Office for Budget Responsibility has forecast that the public payroll will be reduced by 710,000 by 2015 (Office for Budget Responsibility, Autumn 2011).[6] The March 2012 budget similarly came under attack for targeting women, inter alia, with cuts to child tax credits, child benefit, and pension income tax benefits.[7]

Defenders of the government refute charges that the Coalition is ideologically 'anti-women'. Rather, the differential impacts are said to simply reflect the fact that women are the greater users, receivers, and employees of the state – 'collateral damage' perhaps, but with little to do with gender politics per se. In contrast, Coalition critics have raised the question of how the government – both Conservative and Liberal Democrat – appears not to have noticed that its policies would impact more heavily on one sex. Was this a failure of descriptive and substantive representation, of Coalition women representatives being too few, and of failing to 'act for' women?[8] The all important 'quad' of leading Conservative and Liberal Democrat Cabinet Ministers are all male; women numbered only five in the Coalition's first Cabinet, four in its second, and are all Conservative women MPs; and on the government benches women make up only 16 per cent of the parliamentary Conservative party and a mere 12 per cent of the Liberal Democrats' MPs are women, compared with more than 30 per cent in the parliamentary Labour Party.

Adding to feminist academic analysis and Westminster village talk, there has also been extensive media copy suggesting that women voters are turning away from the Conservative party.[9] Although the evidence from the polls is variable, it is clear that within the Conservatives there is much concern, and indeed reaction, over this possibility: a 'women's policy advisor' was appointed (February 2012) to coordinate the 'fight back'– although this was only part of her brief; MPs, mostly but not exclusively women, have established a Conservative party Women's Forum (2011); and a series of mini policy announcements, for example on forced marriage, have been pushed out, seemingly to 'fill' in the gap in the government

---

6. Economic and Social Data Service, Quarterly Labour Force Survey Household Dataset, April–June 2010.

7. *See* http://fawcettsociety.org.uk/index.asp?PageID = 1268; http://www.guardian.co.uk/lifeand-style/2012/mar/30/women-paying-price-osborne-austerity (accessed 5 May 2014).

8. Of course, such a claim remains underpinned by an uncritical assumption that Conservative and Liberal Democrat women Ministers and Members of Parliament are ideologically predisposed to want to act for women in this direction (Celis and Childs, 2011).

9. *See* http://blogs.spectator.co.uk/coffeehouse/2012/03/camerons-pitch-to-women-voters/ (accessed 19 June 2014); http://www.guardian.co.uk/commentisfree/2011/oct/02/david-cameron-women-voters?utm_source = feedburner&utm_medium = feed&utm_campaign = Feed%3A +theguardian%2Fcommentisfree%2Frss+%28Comment+is+free%29 (accessed 5 May 2014); http://www.guardian.co.uk/politics/interactive/2011/sep/13/leaked-memo-women-coalition-government (accessed 5 May 2014). Consideration of the Liberal Democrats and women's representation lies beyond the remit of this paper: *see* Evans (2011).

programme. Even so, there remains a nagging question in the academic and public realm as to whether Cameron's Conservative party has effectively walked away from its commitment to gender equality, in the face of an economic context that demands, in the view of the party and Coalition leadership, a very particular set of responses: read, austerity economics.[10] We do not attempt to answer the normative question as to whether the Conservative party are failing to recognise women's different political priorities, but we do investigate whether there is a gender dimension to public attitudes on economic issues, particularly cuts in public expenditure, among Conservative supporters and identifiers. In so doing, we speak to wider concerns of gender politics scholars and political scientists in the UK and beyond.

This chapter extends analysis that sought to capture the feminisation efforts of the Conservative party between 2005 and 2010 (Childs and Webb 2012). One part of this earlier study investigated the political attitudes of party members and elites prior to the 2010 general election.[11] Informed by existing research that points to intra-party sex differences across all the main parties on the 'women's terrain', Childs and Webb established that Conservative women party members are visibly to the left of men on economic issues – issues that are rarely considered to be directly or explicitly gendered – in addition to their more widely known, more feminist positioning, on explicitly gendered issues (Childs and Webb 2012). Childs and Webb found that on a seven-point self-placement left-right measure, women placed themselves slightly to the left of men, closer to the neutral category; the mean score for women was 5.22 and for men it was 5.38 (Childs and Webb 2012, 124). They also found that women were slightly to the left of men on Heath *et al'*.s socialist/*laissez-faire* scale (Heath *et al.* 1993) and slightly more authoritarian on the liberal–authoritarian scale (Childs and Webb 2012: 125). The most sizeable sex differences were in response to two items, censorship and attitudes to 'big business'. In total 18 per cent more women than men agreed with the statement 'censorship of films and magazines is necessary to uphold moral standards', and 5 per cent more women than men agreed with the statement 'Big business benefits owners at the expense of workers'.

Childs and Webb ran an ordinary least squares (OLS) regression with the tax/spend item as the dependent variable and found a sex effect even after age, social grade, terminal education age and ideological grouping were controlled for (Childs and Webb 2012, Table 7.9). Our analysis, jumping off from Childs and Webb's, centres on the extent to which the left/right sex gap on economic issues among Conservative members is also evident among Conservative supporters and identifiers. As such, this chapter adds to our knowledge about the variation

10. The failure of the party to publish its candidate selection data, as per the 2010 Speaker's Conference Recommendations, means that we cannot determine whether they have walked away from the first dimension of feminisation either: that is, the descriptive representation of women.

11. Chapter Eight also looks at voters for all parties at the 2010 GE; in this chapter we look just at conservative identifiers and supporters.

between elite and mass attitudes, an established area of political science (Jennings 1992; Fleishman 1988; Nie and Andersen 1974; Converse 1964) that has been concerned mostly with ideological consistency and issue constraint. Most studies of elite/mass attitudes focus on whether political elites have more coherent, internally consistent sets of attitudes and beliefs than ordinary members of the public. Here, instead, we are assessing whether the sex differences found among a political elite (Conservative party members) by Childs and Webb are also evident at a mass level (among Conservative supporters and identifiers). Conceptually we move away from a two-tier elite/mass comparison and instead conceive of a more complex hierarchy of political commitment combined with power; we imagine political commitment and power as a pyramid. The least committed – those people for whom the height of political activity is to vote occasionally – form the base (the party voter), and sitting at the apex are those whose whole lives are consumed by political activity (the elected members). The hierarchy is also delineated by political power; ordinary voters have the least power, and elected politicians have the most. In between these two groups – voters and MPs – are party supporters, party members and parliamentary candidates. Party supporters retain a loyalty to the party between elections but have little direct power over party decision-making; party members sign up and pay their dues and have a vote in the selection of their local parliamentary candidate; parliamentary candidates devote time and money to their selection and election campaigns and are most likely plugged into party networks. Rather than considering voters as a whole, as many elite/mass studies do, we compare two layers from this pyramidal account: party members and supporters/identifiers. Future research will collect data on MPs and parliamentary candidates (in a study of the 2015 British General Election). As such this research is the first step towards understanding more fully how gender interacts with political attitudes across all of the layers in the hierarchy of the British Conservative party.

Sex differences and possible explanations

There is a popular currency to deride Conservative women's politics as the politics of the falsely conscious: to talk of 'Stepford Wives'. Indeed, the title of Beatrix Campbell's analysis of women Conservatives in the 1980s asked the simple question 'Why do women vote Tory?' Although she took the opinions of the Conservative women she interviewed seriously, it is not unfair to suggest that Conservative women's politics are often regarded by feminists, and those on the left, as suspect. What they need – and we parody somewhat here – is some good old-fashioned consciousness-raising. A similar approach has been taken by scholars of the gender generation gender gap, who regard right-wing women's 'traditional' values as a remnant from times past when women were largely confined to the private sphere, with restricted access to higher education and paid employment (Inglehart and Norris 2000; Norris 1999; Campbell 2006). From this perspective Conservative women voters might still be understood to be suffering from a false consciousness that will, over time, slowly die out. The decline of the traditional gender gap in the UK and the emergence of a gender generation gap, which broadly, but not completely, maps onto the period in office of New Labour (1997–2010), appeared to provide some evidence of this; mirroring the emergence of the gender gap found in the US. However, analysis of the 2010 British general election suggests that the UK Conservatives had been rather effective at restoring their traditional advantage among women voters (Childs and Webb 2012; Campbell and Childs 2010; Campbell 2012). Explaining away Conservative support among women as a historic legacy now looks rather premature.

Before proceeding to the analysis it might therefore be helpful to think about why we might expect to see such a sex difference and to develop testable hypotheses. First, there is an argument that can be made from the international literature. In a number of Western industrialised countries women's political attitudes have moved to the left of men's (Inglehart and Norris 2000). British women also tend to have more egalitarian attitudes to gender relations, homosexuality and racial discrimination (Ford 2008; Campbell 2011; Campbell *et al.* 2010), and some studies have shown that younger women tend to have more left-leaning attitudes than younger men, although these differences are not persistent over time and across surveys (Campbell 2006). Nevertheless, the sex difference among the attitudes of Conservatives found in this article *in respect of the economy* might possibly be accounted for by a more general trend evident within the whole population.

> H1: The sex gap in left-right economic attitudes among Conservative supporters and identifiers can be explained by more left-leaning attitudes held by women than by men in the general population.

There are several reasons why we might expect women to be to the left of men on economic issues. Women are the majority of primary carers of young children and it can be argued that this might shift them to the left politically; perhaps because the psychological impact of mothering may make women more altruistic (Ruddick 1989; Lehman *et al.* 1995), or because they tend to prioritise state services such as health and education for their children rather than reductions in taxation.

> H2: The sex gap in left/right economic attitudes among Conservative supporters and identifiers can be explained by the impact of parental status on women's attitudes.

In addition, women tend to be financially less well off after divorce than men and tend to be over-represented in lower income households, and these conditions may account for any left-leaning tendency among women.

> H3: The sex gap in left/right economic attitudes among Conservative supporters and identifiers can be explained by women's average lower household income.

An alternative approach emphasises women's authoritarian attitudes relative to men on some issues; particularly on censorship, which women are still considerably more likely to support than men (Campbell 2006). We might argue, in light of this, that perhaps Conservative women who are economically to the left are at the same time, more authoritarian on social issues. This hypothesis reflects accounts that identify women's greater religiosity and moral conservatism as one of the causes of the 'traditional gender gap' (Norris 1999) – the Conservative's historic advantage among women voters, which was at its peak in the post war years but declined to negligible levels in the late 1970s. From this perspective women might be drawn to the Conservative party because of its association with traditional moral values rather than *laissez-faire* economics. Accordingly, it may be that the sub-groups of women who vote for, support, or are members of the Conservative party are more likely to be drawn from the moral right. If this is the case their views of economic issues might be less important to their identification as Conservatives than their liberal/authoritarian position. If this is the case, the implications for the Conservative party electorally may be lessened, as women may continue to feel at home in, and supportive of, a Conservative party that articulates their interests on the social/authoritarian axis even as it diverges from them on the economic axis.

> H4: The sex gap in left/right attitudes towards economic issues among Conservative supporters and identifiers results from women having more authoritarian values than men.

A third potential explanation for the sex difference in Conservatives' political attitudes on the economy might stem from the sex segregation of employment sectors that characterises the UK. Given that we know women are significantly more likely than men to be employed in the public sector, if women associated with the Conservative party are also employed more often in the public sector than men, then they might well be more likely to support public spending rather than reduced taxation. In other words, we might be able to explain away the sex difference over tax and spend among Conservatives by reference to another causal factor: public sector employment. Sex, in this case, is not the driver of attitudinal dispositions.

> H5: The sex gap in left/right attitudes towards economic issues among Conservative supporters/identifiers is an indirect effect of the larger proportion of women employed in the public sector than men and the tendency for public sector workers to be to the left on economic issues *vis-à-vis* private sector workers.

Finally, any sex difference we find might be an artefact of men's generally greater interest in politics than women. It is well established that women report less interest in politics than men and tend to do less well in political knowledge quizzes (Burns 2001; Campbell and Winters 2008; Andersen 1975; Frazer and

MacDonald 2003; Mondak and Anderson 2004). Consequently, it is important to identify whether any sex gaps we find in political attitudes are generated by women placing themselves disproportionately in the 'neutral' categories because they have less interest in the survey questions.

H6: The sex gap in left/right attitudes towards economic issues among Conservative supporters/identifiers results from more women than men placing themselves in the middle or neutral category.

Analysis

Conservative supporters

Turning to Conservative supporters, we first examine supporters' self-placement on the tax/spend question in the face-to-face post-election 2010 British Election Study (BES) (*see* Figure 12.1). Respondents to the survey were asked to place themselves on a zero-to-ten scale. Zero indicated that 'government should cut taxes and spend much less on health and social services'; ten that 'government should raise taxes a lot and spend much more on health and social services'. The reference to health in the item is most likely to produce sex differences, as women tend to report greater interest in health policy issues than men (Campbell and Winters 2008; Campbell 2006; Wängnerud 2000). There is a small, but statistically significant difference between men and women Conservative supporters' responses: the mean responses were 5.09 for men and 5.83 for women.[12]

Examination of Figure 12.2 shows a peak in the responses for both men and women at the middle of the scale and the differences between the sexes are not enormous. However, it is clear that women more often than men favoured increasing services, and men more often than women favoured cutting taxes.[13] Furthermore, this sex difference cannot be accounted for by the fact that women in the whole population generally respond to this question to the left of men: among the whole sample women were on average just 0.37 points further towards spending more than men (half the Conservative sex gap). Thus, comparing Conservative supporters against the whole distribution, and with other parties, reinforces the claim that Conservative women supporters are to the left of men on the tax/spend

---

12. The mean difference is significant at the 0.001-level ANOVA (analysis of variance). The data are weighted by the post-election face-to-face weight 'postwtgt'.

13. On first glance this sex difference seems pretty marginal. Yet, when we compare the mean responses of Labour and Conservative supporters (6.14 and 5.48) respectively, we can see that the 0.7 points in sex difference is actually slightly larger than the 0.65 points in ideological difference between supporters of the Labour and Conservative parties. In other words, whilst the sex difference *within* the Conservative party is not large, it is bigger than the gap *between* Labour and Conservative supporters, when we might have expected the latter gap to be the larger as the ideological gap between the parties is usually much greater than the gap between the sexes (Campbell *et al.* 2010: 40).

Figure 12.1: Responses to the tax/spend item in the Conservative members' survey

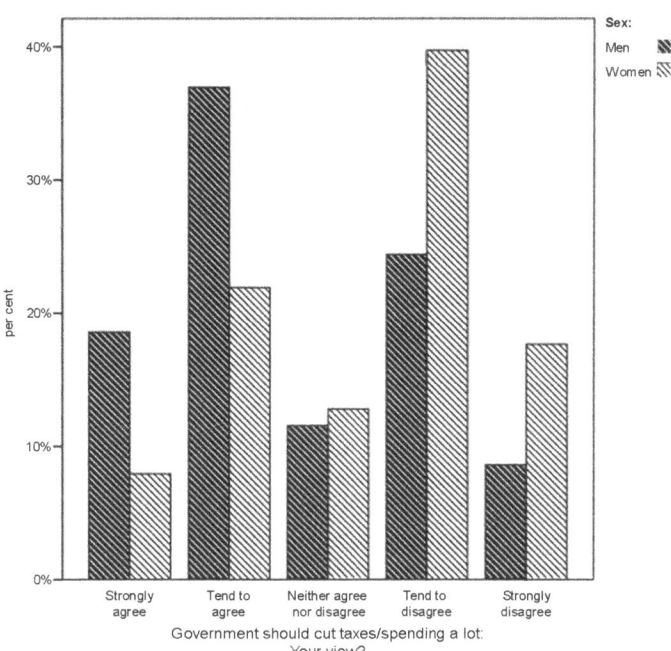

Notes: N = 1690; differences significant at the 0.001 level chi-squared test.

issue and refutes hypothesis one, namely, that the sex gap among Conservative supporters is an artefact of an overall sex gap in the population.

Respondents to the 2010 BES mail-back survey were also asked to place themselves on a left/right scale.[14] There was no statistically significant mean difference between Conservative-supporting men and women, although women placed themselves marginally to the left of men (*see* Figure 12.3). This finding suggests that when asked directly about whether they think of themselves as to the left or to the right, Conservative women do not appear to 'think' of themselves as being as leftist as their answers to the tax/spend questions suggest they are. Why this is the case is unclear: perhaps women 'mislabel' themselves, denying just how to the left they are. Alternatively, they might be basing their self-placement on issues other than, or in addition to, tax and spend. For example, if you are to the right on issues on the liberal/authoritarian axis, your preference regarding tax and spend might be less relevant to your own understanding of your overall political position. To put it another way, in thinking about being 'left' or 'right', voters might well imagine a 'two by two' left/right, social authoritarian/libertarian model, and not just a single left/right economic dimension.

---

14. The self-placement left/right scale was coded from 1 = left to 10 = right.

Figure 12.2: Conservative supporters' responses to tax/spend question by sex, 2010 (post-election face-to-face BES)

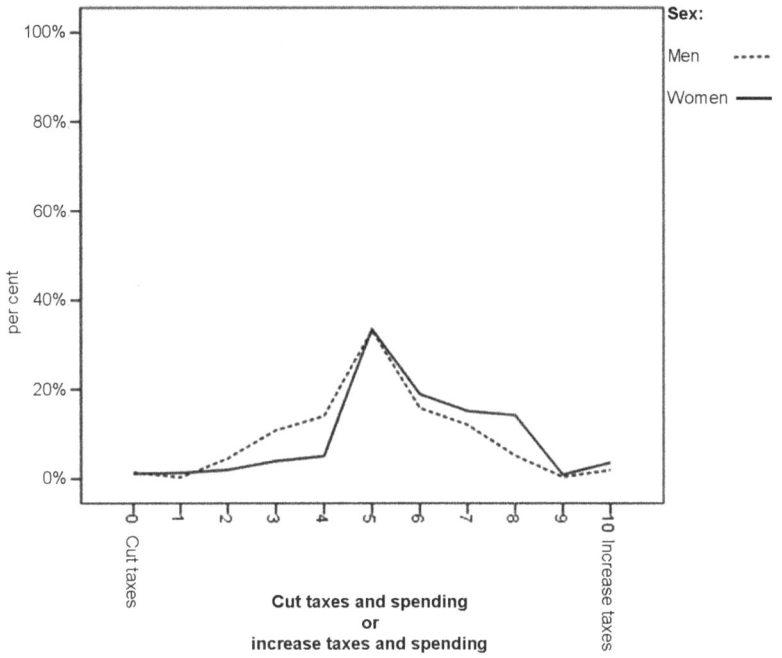

Notes: N = 827; sex difference significant at the 0.001 level.

The mail-back component of the 2010 face-to-face BES also includes items designed to measure socialist/laissez-faire and liberal/authoritarian positions (Evans *et al*. 1996; Heath *et al*. 1993; Tilley 2005). Whilst the list of items is not identical to those used by Childs and Webb (2012) in the party member survey there is some overlap, and the items are designed to measure the same latent variables (authoritarianism and socialism). The responses to the items are presented in Tables 12.1 and 12.2.

Starting with Table 12.1, of the four items that make up the socialist/*laissez-faire* scale in the 2010 BES there is a statistically significant sex difference in responses to three of the four items.[15] But crucially most of this difference is

---

15. The Cronbach's alpha for the scale was 0.526. A principle components factor analysis with varimax rotation indicated that there were two factors with eigenvalues above 1. The first factor explained 41 per cent of the variation in the items and the second 25 per cent. Examination of the factor loadings for the rotated solution suggested that the two items, 'ordinary people get their fair share' and 'there is one law for the rich' contributed most to the first factor and the items

Figure 12.3: Conservative supporters' self-placement on the left-right scale by sex, 2010 (post-election mail-back BES)

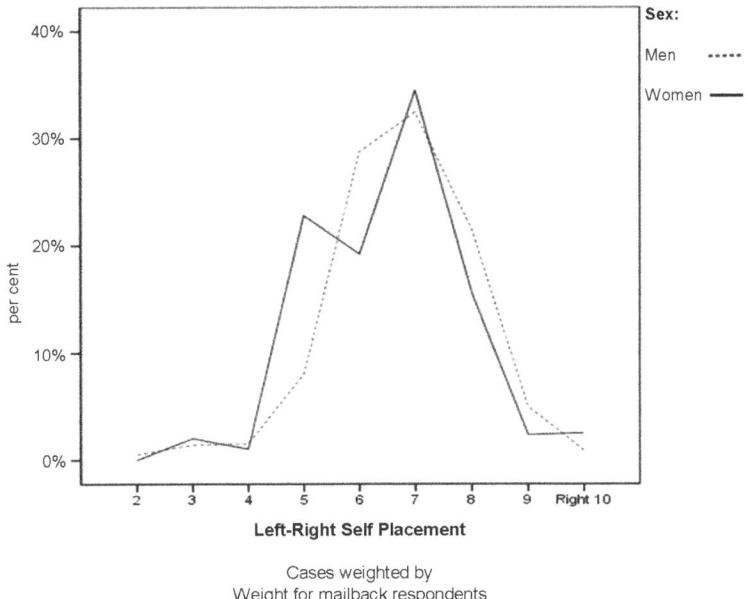

Cases weighted by
Weight for mailback respondents

Notes: N = 170; the difference between the sexes' responses is not statistically significant. Cases weighted by weight for mail-back respondents.

accounted for by women placing themselves more often in the neutral category. When asked whether 'Private enterprise is the best way to solve Britain's economic problems', 20 per cent more men than women Conservative supporters agreed strongly or agreed with the statement. However, only 8 per cent more women than men are to be found in the 'disagree' categories. Instead, women more often placed themselves in the 'neither' category than men (by 13 per cent). In response to the statement 'There is one law for the rich and one for the poor', women were also more often found in the 'neither' category than men; 6 per cent more women than men selected 'neither' and roughly 6 per cent more men than women disagreed strongly with the statement. There is no statistically significant sex difference in the way men and women Conservative supporters responded to the

---

relating to trade unions and private enterprise contributed most to the second factor. The items were nonetheless used in one cumulative scale due to the relatively high Cronbach's alpha and the fact that the scale is well established in the academic literature.

Table 12.1: Socialist/laissez-faire scale items by sex, 2010 (post-election mail-back BES)

	Sex	Strongly Agree	Agree	Neither Agree no Disagree	Disagree	Strongly Disagree	Total	n
		%	%	%	%	%	%	%
Private enterprise is the best way to solve Britain's economic problems***	Men	19.0	50.9	23.3	4.9	1.8	100	163
	Women	7.0	43.0	36.0	13.4	0.5	100	186
There is one law for the rich and one for the poor*	Men	9.1	37.8	15.9	29.3	7.9	100	164
	Women	9.2	35.1	22.2	31.9	1.6	100	185
Ordinary working people get their fair share of the nation's wealth**	Men	4.4	26.3	15.6	49.4	4.4	100	160
	Women	1.1	14.0	21.5	56.5	7.0	100	186
There is no need for strong trade unions to protect employees' working conditions and wages	Men	4.9	25.8	30.7	35.6	3.1	100	163
	Women	4.4	16.5	35.7	40.7	2.7	100	182

Notes: ***Sex difference significant at the 0.001 level chi-squared test. **Sex difference significant at the 0.01 level chi-squared test. *Sex difference significant at the 0.05 level chi-squared test. Discrepancies are due to rounding.

Table 12.2: *Liberal/authoritarian scale items by sex, 2010 (post-election mail-back BES)*

	Sex	Strongly Agree	Agree	Neither Agree no Disagree	Disagree	Strongly Disagree	Total	n
		%	%	%	%	%	%	%
Young people today don't have enough respect for traditional British values**	Men	31.3	49.1	8.0	11.7	0.0	100	163
	Women	19.8	58.8	12.8	6.4	2.1	100	187
Censorship of films and magazines is necessary to uphold moral values***	Men	9.7	43.0	20.6	22.4	4.2	100	163
	Women	20.0	53.0	16.2	10.8	0.0	100	185
People should be allowed to organise public meetings to protest against the government***	Men	11.7	66.9	16.6	4.3	0.6	100	163
	Women	9.1	50.8	29.4	10.7	0.0	100	187
People in Britain should be more tolerant of those who lead unconventional lifestyles	Men	3.7	34.6	37.0	22.8	1.9	100	162
	Women	2.2	33.0	44.9	18.9	1.1	100	185
Political parties that wish to overthrow democracy should be allowed to stand in general elections***	Men	2.5	17.4	9.9	46.6	23.6	100	161
	Women	0.5	15.8	25.1	39.9	18.6	100	183
The government has the right to put people suspected of terrorism in prison without trial	Men	13.4	37.8	18.9	26.8	3.0	100	164
	Women	14.4	41.7	16.6	21.4	5.9	100	187

Notes: ***Sex difference significant at the 0.001 level chi-squared test. **Sex difference significant at the 0.01 level chi-squared test. *Sex difference significant at the 0.05 level chi-squared test. Discrepancies are due to rounding.

statement 'There is no need for strong trade unions to protect employees' working conditions and wages'. Finally, with regard to the statement 'Ordinary working people get their fair share of the nation's wealth' there is a statistically significant sex difference, with 15 per cent more men than women agreeing strongly or agreeing with the statement, 6 per cent more women than men giving a 'neither' response and approximately 10 per cent more women disagreeing or disagreeing strongly with the statement. Thus, overall there is evidence of a small sex gap among Conservative party supporters, with women responding to the ideological left of men on the socialist/*laissez-faire* scale, but the substantive difference largely relates to just one item – 'ordinary people'. When the responses to the four items are added together to create a cumulative socialist/*laissez-faire* scale there is no significant sex difference among Conservative supporters.

Moving to consider Table 12.2, we consider liberal/authoritarian position.[16] There are statistically significant sex gaps among Conservative supporters in four out of the six items. Again much of the variation in responses between the sexes results from more women placing themselves in the neutral category. In response to the statement 'Young people today don't have enough respect for traditional British values', the sex difference is in strength of feeling rather than direction – with 11 per cent more men than women agreeing strongly with the statement, and 10 per cent more women than men agreeing. Women more often placed themselves in the 'neither' category in response to two of the items, 'People should be allowed to organise public meetings to protest against the government' and 'Political parties that wish to overthrow democracy should be allowed to stand in general elections', with 13 per cent and 15 per cent more women than men selecting the neutral response respectively. There is, however, a large sex difference in the censorship item: 20 per cent more women than men agreed strongly, or agreed with the statement 'Censorship of films and magazines is necessary to uphold moral values'. Women clearly hold strong opinions on censorship, 4 per cent fewer women than men selected the 'neither' response in this case. Added together, the items do not suggest that women hold more authoritarian attitudes than men, with the exception of the sizeable difference in responses to the censorship question, which are well documented elsewhere. When the items are added together to create a cumulative liberal/authoritarian scale there is no significant sex difference in the mean position of Conservative supporters. This finding suggests that hypothesis four, that the Conservative sex gap in left/right economic attitudes results from women's greater authoritarianism, is unlikely to have much purchase, as overall Conservative-supporting women are not more significantly more authoritarian in their attitudes than Conservative-supporting men.

---

16. The Cronbach's alpha for the scale is 0.346 and a principal components factor analysis with varimax rotation indicated that there were two factors with eigenvalues above 1. The first explained 30 per cent of the variance in the items and the second 20 per cent. Examination of the rotated factor solution suggests that the items related to tolerance of unconventional life styles and permitting protest made the greatest contribution to the second factor and the remaining items to the first.

Thus, as there is no statistically significant sex difference in Conservative supporters' liberal/authoritarian, socialist/*laissez-faire* or left/right positions there seems to be consistent evidence of a left/right sex gap only in regard to attitudes towards taxation/expenditure. In order to test the strength of this sex gap further we ran a series of OLS regressions with tax/spend as the dependent variable.

In Model 1 (Table 12.3) sex is the only dependent variable, and we can see that Conservative-supporting women were on average 0.74 points further towards the increase-taxes-and-spending pole of the scale than men, and the relationship is highly statistically significant.[17]

In Model 2 employment in the private sector is added as a control variable. Men Conservative party supporters are more often employed in the private sector than women, as we expected (78 per cent men, 64 per cent women), and the employment gap is larger among Conservative supporters than Labour (70 per cent men, 60 per cent women) or Liberal Democrat (66 per cent men, 59 per cent women) supporters. Nevertheless, examination of Model 2 shows that there is no apparent effect of private sector employment on tax/spend attitudes, although the variable has a large number of missing responses – this has the effect of reducing sample size and statistical power, making significant effects more difficult to pick up. It would seem, nonetheless, that Conservative-supporting women do not favour increased taxation and spending more often than men simply because they are more often employed in the public sector, a finding which refutes hypothesis five.

Private sector employment is excluded from Model 3 in order to preserve sample size.[18] Added to the model are: interest in politics, age, caring for children under five and under fifteen, household income and holding a degree. Including these items did not remove the gender effect and thus we have evidence to refute hypotheses two and three. Both age and household income did have a significant effect on responses to the tax/spend question. For every increase of one point on the household income scale there is a reduction in support for increasing taxes and public spending by 0.06 points, and for every increase of one year in age there is an increase in support for greater taxation and public spending of 0.02 points. However, neither women's greater longevity nor their greater representation in lower-income households can account for the sex gap in Conservative supporters responses to the tax/spend measure: their inclusion reduces the mean difference between men and women on the tax/spend item by 0.21 points from 0.74 to 0.53 but the effect remains and is significant at the 0.01 level. Furthermore, examination of the standardised coefficients demonstrates that age, household income and sex

---

17. The adjusted R^2s are low. However, we are not seeking to maximise model fit, as we are interested in the sex effect, not in providing a complete explanation of attitudes.

18. When Model 3 was run with the private sector employment variable included, none of the independent variables reached statistical significance, this is not surprising given the reduction in sample size. The variable that was closest to having a statistically significant effect on the dependent variable was the respondent's sex with a t value of 1.83. The coefficient for the sex variable was 0.45 and the standardised coefficient for the sex variable was 0.132 (the largest of the standardised coefficients).

Table 12.3: OLS regression on tax/spend, BES 2010 (post-election face-to-face survey)

Independent variables	Model 1		Model 2		Model 3	
	B (SE)	Beta	B (SE)	Beta	B (SE)	Beta
Women	.74***(.15)	.20	.82***(.22)	.23	.53 **(.17)	.15
Private sector employment			-.08 (.24)	-.02		
Interest in politics					.10 (10)	.05
Cares for children<5					.11 (.27)	.02
Cares for children<15					.26 (22)	.06
Degree holder					-.46 (.28)	-.08
Age					.02** (.01)	.14
Household income					-.06* (02)	-.13
n	583		271		449	
Adjusted R^2	.04		.05		.07	

Notes: ***Sex difference significant at the 0.001 level. **Sex difference significant at the 0.01 level. *Sex difference significant at the 0.05 level.

Table 12.4: Attitudes to public sector cuts, Conservative identifiers by sex (BES 2010 CMS)

Spending item	Percentage supporting cuts to the item of government spending	
	Men	Women
	%	%
Freeze welfare benefits**	71	62
Raise retirement age***	59	45
Reduce NHS 5%***	21	11
Freeze public sector pay***	65	57
Reduce child tax credit***	56	45
Reduce unemployment benefits	49	51
Reduce student loan subsidies*	31	26
Reduce Winter Fuel Allowance*	23	19
Scrap Trident missiles	32	31
Reduce top public sector pay	77	76
Abolish regional dev agencies***	57	51
Freeze overseas aid budget**	71	67

*Notes:***Sex difference signficant at the 0.001 level chi-squared test. **Sex difference significant at the 0.01 level chi-squared test. *Sex difference significant at the 0.05 level chi-squared test. N = 1198.

all have roughly similar impacts on tax/spend attitudes with sex achieving the largest standardised coefficient of 0.15, followed by 0.14 for age and -0.13 for household income. Clearly Conservative-supporting women are more inclined to support increased taxation and spending than Conservative-supporting men and the effect does not seem to be an artefact of variations in men and women's personal circumstances. It is clear from this analysis that the resilient sex gap in tax/spend attitudes identified by Childs and Webb among Conservative party members is also evident among Conservative party supporters. The interest in politics variable does not have a statistically significant effect on responses to the tax/spend measure and does not diminish the sex effect. Thus, we have further evidence (alongside the fact that women did not disproportionately place themselves in the middle of the tax/spend scale) to refute hypothesis six that the left/right sex gap in Conservative supporters' economic attitudes is an artefact of lower levels of interest in politics.[19]

Conservative identifiers

Alongside the standard face-to-face surveys the BES team has developed an Internet continuous monitoring survey (CMS). The CMS, whilst not including a party supporter variable, does have a party identifier item, enabling us to undertake analysis on Conservative identifiers. The survey does not contain the tax/spend measure but does include a series of questions relating to public expenditure cuts (Table 12.4).[20] Examination of Table 12.4 shows fairly sizeable sex gaps in support of a number of potential cuts to public expenditure, with the most sizeable sex gaps of in support for raising the pension age (12 per cent), reducing child tax credit (11 per cent) and reducing the NHS by 5 per cent (10 per cent).

Whilst there were negligible sex differences in support for reducing unemployment benefit, scrapping Trident (the UK's nuclear missile), and in support of reducing top public sector pay, overall quite an array of measures designed to reduce public expenditure receive more support from Conservative-identifying men than women. This suggests that there are fairly stark sex divisions among Conservative identifiers in respect of spending cuts. The responses to the items were added together to create a cumulative scale, with responses ranging from zero (supports none of the cuts to public spending list) to 12 (supports all of the public spending cuts listed). The mean response for men Conservative identifiers was 6.10 and for women the mean was 5.41. The difference in the mean scores of men and women was significant at the 0.001 level. This sex gap of 0.69 points among Conservative supporters outstrips the 0.33-point sex gap among Labour

19. Model 3 was run again with socialist/*laissez-faire* and liberal/authoritarian position included. These items are included in the mail-back part of the survey and have a reduced sample size. The household income variable was removed from the rerun model, as this also has a low sample size and it was impossible to include this item and the scales in the same model. Neither scale had a statistically significant effect on the tax/spend item when included in Model 3 and the coefficient for the sex variable was 0.64**.

20. The items were included in the BES CMS between June and September 2011.

Table 12.5: OLS regression on Conservative identifiers' attitudes to cuts by sex (BES CMS)

Independent variable	Model 1		Model 2	
	B (SE)	Beta	B (SE)	Beta
Women	0.93*** (0.14)	0.19	0.66*** (0.14)	0.13
Year born			-0.04*** (0.01)	-0.23
Has school age children			-0.01 (0.14)	-0.02
Age completed education			0.08 (0.05)	0.05
Household income			-0.01 (0.02)	0.02
Attention to politics			0.24*** (0.03)	0.21
Adjusted R2	0.04	0.14		
N	1,198	1,135		

Note: The coefficients are Pearson correlation coefficients (***$p < 0.001$).

supporters, and is further evidence that the Conservative party faces a particularly stark sex gap in left/right economic attitudes.

We conducted an OLS regression on the cuts scale (Table 12.5) and added year of birth, having school age children, terminal educational age, household income and attention to politics as independent variables (Model 2). Note that there is no measure of public sector employment in the CMS and therefore we cannot test hypothesis five on attitudes to spending cuts. The sex effect remains, even after the addition of the controls (although the size of the coefficient is reduced by about one-third – from 0.93 to 0.66). Younger Conservative-identifying respondents and those who paid less attention to politics were less supportive of the cuts listed than the other respondents. However, the sex gap in support of the cuts remains and cannot be accounted for by women's lower levels of interest/attention in politics, nor by their greater longevity.[21] Thus there is little evidence to support any of the hypotheses: the sex gap is surprisingly robust to the addition of statistical controls.

Conclusion

Childs and Webbs' observation that women Conservative party members are to the left of men on economic issues extends beyond party members: to Conservative party supporters and identifiers. This is an important finding in and of itself.

---

21. When the regression was repeated for Labour identifiers the sex gap was statistically significant but the coefficients were smaller (the unstandardised coefficient for women Labour identifiers was 0.35 in Model 2, roughly half the size of the effect among Conservative identifiers). Overall, then, there is a significant sex difference in support of public expenditure cuts among Conservative identifiers.

Hitherto sex differences in voting behaviour in the UK have been of a smaller magnitude than those found elsewhere. Studies of voting behaviour and gender in the UK have failed to show a realignment of women – which would require a shift from the traditional to the modern gender gap. Here, though, on tax/spend issues, we find clear and large differences among Conservative women and men.

Establishing that within the UK's rightist party, women and men – at the level of members, identifiers, and supporters – are divided over tax/spend has the potential, as Childs and Webb suggested, to become significant for the Conservative party (and the Coalition) if and when tax/spend comes to dominate the political agenda. We suggest that this time is now. There are three main possible effects. First, the party cannot afford electorally to forget about women voters, particularly Conservative women supporters. Against the backdrop of critical media coverage of the party and the government's policies' effects on women, Cameron should be minded that Conservative women supporters are simply less in favour of his cuts programme than Conservative men. If he ignores this difference, it is likely that he will lose Conservative women's votes at the next election. Second, there are issues of intra-party management with the likelihood that women and men party members – and the party's organisations 'for women' (if we presume they are in line with women Conservative supporters and party members) are likely to be in conflict over the party's priorities in respect of tax and spend.

Third, our findings have implications for the political representation of right-wing women in terms of descriptive representation. Elsewhere researchers have argued for greater representation of women in politics on the basis of greater attitudinal congruency between elite women and women in society over gender issues, arguing that whilst the latter may not want women representatives, they nonetheless need them so that their interests are (or rather have a greater chance of being) better represented substantively (Campbell *et al.* 2010). This research strongly reinforces the earlier claim, and does so in our view at a time when the descriptive representation of sex appears to be increasingly questioned within the academy – calls for the representation of class are sometimes presented as a zero sum game, and seem to forget that women are members of the working class too (Childs and Cowley 2011; Kenny 2012).[22] Yet, if the sex gap evident among Conservative party members is also apparent among its supporters and identifiers then the party may well face a strong backlash along sex lines if it fails to address these issues. In turn, this raises questions of intra-party management, electoral competition, and electoral strategy. To extend the phrase: the Conservative party on the ground may not want women MPs but it might well need them to ensure that the party's platform represents Conservative women supporters' views. More conceptually speaking, we might question how a disproportionately male Conservative party can substantively represent Conservative women when their attitudes (perceived interests) appear to diverge so significantly.

---

22. *See* http://www.telegraph.co.uk/news/politics/conservative/9173646/David-Cameron-needs-friends-in-the-North-heres-how-to-win-them.html (accessed 5 May 2014).

References

Alvarez, R. M. and McCaffery, E. (1999) 'Gender and Tax', in Tolleson Rinehart, S. and Josephson, J. J. *Gender and American Politics: Women, Men and the Political Process*, New York: M. E. Sharpe, Inc.

Andersen, K. (1975) 'Working women and political participation, 1952–1972', *American Journal of Political Science*, 19: 439–53.

— (1999) 'The gender gap and experiences with the welfare state', *P.S. Political Science and Politics*, 32, 17–19.

Bale, T. (2010) *The Conservative Party: From Thatcher to Cameron*, Cambridge: Polity.

Box-Steffensmeir, J., DeBoef, S. and Lin, T.-M. (1997) 'Microideology, macropartisanship and the gender gap', paper presented at *American Political Science Association*, 13 August, available at http://www.polmeth.wustl.edu/media/Paper/boxst97c.pdf (accessed 22 May 2014).

Burden, B. (2008) 'The social roots of the partisan gender gap', *Public Opinion Quarterly*, 72 (1): 55–75.

Burns, N. (2001) 'Gender: public opinion and political action', in Katznelson, I. and Milner, H. (eds) *Political Science: The State of the Discipline*, Washington, DC: APSA, pp. 462–87.

Campbell, R. (2006) *Gender and the Vote in Britain*, Colchester, Essex: ECPR Press.

— (2011) 'The politics of diversity', Chapter 9 in Heffernan, R., Cowley, P. and Hay, C. (eds) *Developments in British Politics 9*, London: Palgrave Macmillan.

— (2012) 'What do we really know about women voters? Gender, elections and public opinion', *Political Quarterly*, 83 (4): 703–10.

Campbell, R. and Childs, S. (2010) '"Wags", "wives" and "mothers" … but what about women politicians?', in Geddes, A. and Tonge, J. (eds) *The UK Votes: The 2010 General Election*, Oxford: Oxford University Press.

Campbell, R. and Winters, K. (2008) 'Understanding men and women's political interests: evidence from a study of gendered political attitudes', *Journal of Elections, Public Opinion and Parties*, 18: 53–74.

Campbell, R., Childs, S. and Lovenduski, J. (2010) 'Do women need women MPs?', *British Journal of Political Science*, 40 (1): 171–94.

Carroll, S. (1988) 'Women's autonomy and the gender gap: 1980 and 1982', in Mueller, C. (ed.) *The Politics of the Gender Gap*, California: Sage.

— (1999) 'The disempowerment of the gender gap: soccer moms and the 1996 elections', *P.S.: Political Science and Politics*, 32 (1): 7–11.

Celis, K. and Childs, S. (2011) 'The substantive representation of women: what to do with conservative claims?', *Political Studies*, 60 (1): 213–25.

Chaney, C., Alvarez, M. R. and Nagler, J. (1998) 'Explaining the gender gap in US Presidential elections', *Political Research Quarterly*, 51 (2) 311–39.

Childs, S. and Cowley, P. (2011) 'The politics of local presence: is there a case for descriptive representation?', *Political Studies*, 59 (1): 1–19.

Childs, S. and Webb, P. (2009) 'The feminisation of the conservative parliamentary party: party members' attitudes', *Political Quarterly*, 80: 204–13.

— (2012) *Sex, Gender and the Conservative Party*, London: Palgrave Macmillan.

Conover, P. (1988) 'Feminists and the gender gap', *Journal of Politics*, 50: 985–1010.

Converse, P. E. (1964) 'The nature of belief systems in mass publics', in Apter, D. (ed.) *Ideology and Discontent*, New York: Free Press, pp. 206–61.

Dolan, K. (2010) 'The impact of gender stereotyped evaluations on support for women candidates', *Political Behavior*, 32: 69–88.

Duke Whitaker, L. (2008) *Voting the Gender Gap*, Urbana and Chicago, IL: University of Illinois Press.

Edlund, L. and Pande, R. (2002) 'Why have women become left-wing? The political gender gap and the decline in marriage', *Quarterly Journal of Economics*, 117 (3): 917–61.

Evans, E. (2011) *Gender and the Liberal Democrats: Representing Women?* Manchester: Manchester University Press.

Evans, G., Heath, A. and Lalljee, M. (1996) 'Measuring left-right and libertarian–authoritarian values in the British electorate', *British Journal of Political Science*, 47 (1): 94–112.

Fleishman, J. (1988) 'Attitude organisation in the general public: evidence for a biodimensional structure', *Social Forces*, 67: 159–83.

Ford, R. (2008) 'Is racial prejudice declining in Britain?', *British Journal of Sociology*, 59 (4): 609–36.

Frazer, E. and MacDonald, K. (2003) 'Sex differences in political knowledge in Britain', *Political Studies*, 51 (1): 76–83.

Gidengil, E. and Harell, A. (2007) 'Network diversity and vote choice: women's social ties and left voting in Canada', *Politics and Gender*, 3 (2): 151–77.

Greenberg, A. (2001) 'Race, religiosity and the women's vote', *Women and Politics*, 22 (3): 59–82.

Harmen, H. and Mattinson, D. (2000) *Winning for Women*, London: Fabian Society.

Hayes, B. (1997) 'Gender, feminism and electoral behaviour in Britain', *Electoral Studies*, 16 (2): 203–16.

Heath, A., Evans, G. and Martin, J. (1993) 'The measurement of core beliefs and values: the development of balanced socialist/laissez faire and libertarian/authoritarian scales', *British Journal of Political Science*, 24: 115–58.

Inglehart, R. and Norris, P. (2000) 'The developmental theory of the gender gap: women and men's voting behaviour in global perspective', *International Political Science Review*, 21 (4): 441–62.

Jennings, K. M. (1992) 'Ideological thinking among mass publics and political elites', *Public Opinion Quarterly*, 56 (4): 419–41.

Kenny, M. (2012) 'The political theory of recognition: the case of the "white working class"', *British Journal of Politics and International Relations*, 14: 19–38.

Lehman, K., Burns, N., Verba, S. and Donohue, J. (1995) 'Gender and citizenship participation: is there a different voice', *American Journal of Political Science*, 39: 267–93.

Mondak, J. and Anderson, M. (2004) 'The knowledge gap: a reexamination of gender based differences in political knowledge', *Journal of Politics*, 66 (2): 492–512.

Mueller, C. (1988) 'The politics of the gender gap', *Sage Yearbooks in Women's Policy Studies*, Beverly Hills, CA: Sage, p. 316.

Nie, N. and Andersen, K. (1974) 'Mass belief systems revisited', *Journal of Politics*, 36, 540–91.

Norris, P. (1999) 'Gender: a gender-generation gap?' in Evans, G. and Norris, P. (eds) *Critical Elections: British Parties and Voters in Long-Term Perspective*, London: Sage, pp. 146–63.

— (2001) 'The gender gap: old challenges, new approaches', in Carroll, S. (ed.) *Women and American Politics: Agenda Setting for the 21st Century*, Oxford: Oxford University Press.

Ruddick, S. (1989) *Maternal Thinking*, Boston, MA: Beacon Press.

Steel, G. (2003) 'Class and gender in British general elections', paper prepared for the presentation at the Midwest Political Science Association Annual Meeting, Chicago.

Tilley, J. (2005) 'Libertarian–authoritarian value change in Britain, 1974–2001', *Political Studies*, 53, 442–53.

Wängnerud, L. (2000) 'Testing the politics of presence: women's representation in the Swedish Riksdag', *Scandinavian Political Studies*, 23 (1): 67–91.

Webb, P. and Childs, S. (2012) 'Gender politics and conservatism: the view from the British Conservative Party grassroots', Government and Opposition, 47: 21–48.

Chapter Thirteen

Are Conservatism and Feminism Mutually Exclusive? A Study of 'Feminist Conservative' Voters in Belgium

Silvia Erzeel, Karen Celis and Didier Caluwaerts

Introduction

Research on gender and politics has long supported the idea that conservatism and feminism do not sit comfortably together. Conservative ideologies often include strong elements of traditionalism and/or liberalism. These do not fit well with feminist ideologies, since the latter usually accept a structural analysis of group discrimination and favour a strong government role in economic, social and welfare matters (Girvin 1988; Hyde 1995; Bryson and Heppell 2010). In Western democracies, conservative parties, as a result, are frequently found to make more non-feminist and anti-feminist claims than left-wing parties (Celis 2006; Lovenduski and Norris 1993; Wängnerud 2000; Tremblay and Pelletier 2000; Erzeel 2012). They are also more likely to oppose feminist policy change and are less likely to support the activities of (feminist) women's movements and women policy agencies (Banaszak *et al.* 2003; Bashevkin 1994).

Although conservatism and feminism seem on first blush less than compatible, Bryson and Heppell (2010) argue that at the theoretical level at least, they are sometimes able to find some common ground. The Conservative Party in the UK in particular, in their study, incorporates some basic liberal feminist ideas arguing in favour of equal rights (and opportunities) for men and women. Furthermore, recent studies on some Western political parties report that conservative and right-wing parties claim increasingly to represent women (Celis and Erzeel forthcoming). Conservative parties are even found to engage in feminist reforms in order to improve women's descriptive and substantive representation (Kittilson 2006; Childs and Webb 2012a).

These (feminist) claims should not be denounced as 'false consciousness', Celis and Childs (2012: 214) argue. For instance, conservative parties in the UK and Germany quite consciously participate in feminist or 'gendered' political debates and reforms (Childs and Webb 2012a, 2012b; Wiliarty 2010). Their main driving force is, arguably, ideological renewal and party modernisation, as they aim ultimately to broaden their electoral support (Childs and Webb 2012a; Wiliarty 2010). Yet, these findings demonstrate that it is important for scholars to reconsider the relationship between these two ideological stands and to assess to what extent – and how – the combination of feminism and conservatism influences political behaviour.

Much of the research on the relationship between conservatism and feminism so far has adopted an *elite perspective* by looking at the activities of conservative parties and MPs in parliament and in government (Wiliarty 2010; Celis and Erzeel forthcoming, but *see* Childs and Webb 2012b), but much less is known about how *citizens* reconcile conservatism and feminism. In sum, whilst parties combine conservative and feminist claims aiming to increase their electoral basis, very little research has hitherto shown whether there is such a basis among the public. Is there a potential voter out there who is both conservative and feminist?

This puzzle merits further exploration, and our general research question is as follows: to what extent does reconciliation between conservatism and feminism appear at the mass level? Do some citizens hold both feminist and conservative attitudes? Furthermore, if conservative parties are increasingly making feminist or gendered claims hoping to receive votes in return, the question is whether the combination of feminist and conservative attitudes also steers citizens' voting behaviour. Are citizens combining feminist and conservative attitudes electorally attracted to one particular party? In short, the answer to these questions will show whether there is an electoral market of voters who combine feminist and conservative traits, and whether conservative parties should bother making feminist claims if their goal is to maximise electoral support.

In what follows, we first clarify what we understand by conservatism and feminism, and show how they relate at the theoretical level. We then present an overview of how right-wing parties in Flanders (one of the Belgian regions) integrate feminist ideological positions. Then we elaborate on the methodological framework and the 2009 PARTIREP election survey in the region of Flanders, which provides the data for this chapter. Finally, we present the empirical findings. The results show that a rather large segment of the electorate in Flanders does claim to be conservative and feminist. Moreover, this set of attitudinal characteristics steers citizens' electoral behaviour: the combination of feminism and social conservatism leads voters more to the right hand side of the political party landscape.

Conservatism and feminism: Conceptual clarifications

In order to fully grasp the complex relationship between conservatism and feminism, we need to take into account the varieties of conservatism and feminism. In terms of conservatism, a distinction should be made between *laissez-faire* or liberal economic conservatism, on the one hand, and social or moral conservatism, on the other hand (Klatch 1988; Schreiber 2008; Bryson and Heppell 2010). *Laissez-faire* conservatives position themselves on the right of the socio-economic left-right scale. Their main aim is to downsize government intervention in the economic as well as private realm. Individuals are conceptualised as self-interested and rational actors, encouraged to make their own choices with as little government control as possible (Klatch 1988).

Bryson and Heppell (2010) argue that the argument of 'equal rights' that fosters liberal and *laissez-faire* conservatism has sometimes proven to be a useful tool in the hands of feminists claiming equal rights for men and women. *Laissez-faire* conservatives are, according to Klatch (1988: 34), for instance 'prochoice and support day care, as long as it remains in private hands' (Klatch 1988: 34). As such, this type of *laissez-faire* conservatism sits rather well with 'liberal feminism' (Childs and Webb 2012b) and with 'individualist feminism' (Offen 2000; Celis 2006). These types of feminism strive for individual rights and equal opportunities between women and men. They highlight women's pursuit of 'personal independence' or autonomy (Offen 2000: 136).

Social conservatives or moral traditionalists, in contrast, do not necessarily reject government intervention in the economic or private sphere. Their ideological goals directly target the private realm: their focus of attention is the promotion of conventional family structures, the protection of traditional values and morality, and the conservation of traditional gender roles (Klatch 1988; Girvin 1988; Bryson and Heppell 2010). In order to preserve traditional values and conventional structures, government control of the economic and private sphere is sometimes considered to be necessary. Typical examples of government actions relate to the promotion of 'family-friendly' working conditions for women and government (financial) support for married couples and male-breadwinning households (Bryson and Heppell 2010).

Social conservatism might appear to be more difficult to combine with liberal or individualist types of feminism, but it might more easily join together with a 'relational feminism' (Offen 2000). Offen (2000) distinguishes 'relational feminism' from 'individualist feminism', and argues that the former stresses the specificity of women (for instance with regard to their nurturing capacities) together with equal worth of women and men, and the complementarity and partnership between the sexes. Unlike individualist feminism, relational feminism does not stress women's autonomy, but rather maintains a 'couple-centred vision' on gender relations (Offen 2000: 136, 138).

If recognising differences within conservative thought bears on questions of feminism and conservatism, it is also the case that several studies have revealed the development of a 'conservative feminism' in neoliberal democracies (Dillard 2005; Bryson and Heppell 2010). This 'conservative feminism' arguably results from conservative women's rejection of anti-feminist counter-movements on the one hand and a rejection of the 'liberal' or 'progressive' character of contemporary women's movements on the other hand (Dillard 2005; Bryson and Heppell 2010; Schreiber 2002). As the study of Schreiber (2002, 2008) shows, conservative women's or feminist organisations are not always happy to receive the 'feminist label'. The organisations in Schreiber's study rather claim a 'gender consciousness' and aim at 'bringing a women's perspective to policy issues' (Schreiber 2002: 331). This gender consciousness serves, much in the same way as feminist attitudes, as a link between gender identity and political action (Schreiber 2002, 2008).

Conservative feminism has a 'feminist core' in the sense that it accepts that 'uniform standards of equality and justice must apply to both sexes [...] [and] that women have suffered and continue to suffer from historical injustice' (Dillard

2005: 26). Indeed, conservative feminists recognise that women's disadvantaged position has an historical – and thus structural – grounding (*see also* Bryson and Heppell 2010). They also argue that the principle of equality and justice between the sexes needs to be secured (Dillard 2005; Bryson and Heppell 2010). The 'conservative core' of conservative feminism, on the other hand, results from its focus on 'prudence' as a key element (Dillard 2005: 26): 'societal reform must be conducted in a slow and cautious manner [...], perfect justice and perfect equality are beyond the realm of possibility for limited and fallible human beings'.

The case of Flanders

Studies focusing on the relationship between conservatism and feminism often concentrate on two specific countries: the UK (*see* Bryson and Heppell 2010; Childs and Webb 2012) and the US (Schreiber 2008; Klatch 1988). Both countries are specific and similar in the sense that they represent majoritarian (as opposed to consociational) democracies whose institutional infrastructure is not primarily aimed at representing diversity. The proportion of women in the national parliaments is on average rather low – and especially so among right-wing parties. Parties in the US reject the use of gender quotas to improve women's representation. The Labour Party in the UK has adopted gender party quotas, but the Conservative Party eschews them. Both countries also have a party system with one or at most two right-wing parties. These conservative parties are proto-typical 'New Right' parties where neoliberal and social conservative tendencies coexist *within one party*. The mere coexistence of different conservative ideologies within one party sometimes creates internal ideological tensions for parties, leading parties to adopt contradictory positions on gender-related issues (Bryson and Heppell 2010).

In this contribution, we focus on a different case, namely the region of Flanders in Belgium. Flanders is an important counter-case. With a proportional list system and a history of multipartism and grand coalitions (Deschouwer and Lucardie 2003), Belgium constitutes a consensus democracy. The consociational logic of accommodating differences and diversity in society has furthered the inclusion of social groups (including women) in politics and policies (Meier 2000; Celis *et al.* 2012). Belgium was also one of the first countries in Europe to adopt legally binding gender quotas in 1994 and 2002. Due to these quotas, all Flemish parties – including right-wing ones – now have 50 per cent female candidates on their electoral lists and at least 30 per cent female representatives. The Flemish multiparty landscape is different from that of the UK or the US in that multiple strong right-wing parties exist. Four individual parties promote distinct conservative ideologies, as described below.

The Christian Democratic Party (CD&V) is socially conservative and morally traditionalist, but takes a more left-leaning stance on socio-economic issues. On the one hand the party favours state intervention in socio-economic and welfare issues, and is quite active in the feminist representation of these issues (Celis 2006; Erzeel 2012). It also has a strong women's ancillary organisation and has implemented gender quotas since the 1970s. On the other hand, the party does not adopt a progressive feminist position on moral–ethical issues (Celis 2006). Feminist claims made by the Christian democrats are often concerned with the appreciation of the specific role of women in the family and society – what Offen (2000) would term 'relational feminism'.

The liberal party Open VLD (*Open Vlaamse Liberalen en Democraten*), in contrast, adheres to a neoliberal, *laissez-faire* ideology on economic issues and a progressive stance on moral-ethical issues. As a result, the party often does not actively support group representation: it is the traditional opponent of gender quotas (although they temporarily applied quotas in the 1980s) and has only a very weakly formalised women's ancillary organisation. On the moral–ethical side, the party has contributed to the development of some progressive feminist legislation (cf. 'individualist feminism', Offen 2000) such as gay marriage and gay adoption rights. Overall, however, the liberal party was only marginally present in the pursuit of improving the situation of the female citizen throughout the twentieth century (Celis 2006; Erzeel 2012).

The two other right-wing parties, the regionalist party N-VA and the extreme right Vlaams Belang, adopt conservative standpoints on socio-economic and moral–traditionalist issues. They have no record of supporting feminist laws, no women's sections and no gender quotas. The Vlaams Belang had, in the 1990s, a more outspoken traditional (and even anti-feminist) view on the public and private role of women and on issues like abortion (Van Molle and Gubin 1998), but these explicit anti-feminist standpoints are no longer formulated (Erzeel 2012).

The PARTIREP survey

In order to study the conservative and feminist attitudes and behaviour of voters in Flanders, the empirical analyses make use of data gathered by the 2009 PARTIREP voter survey in Belgium (Flanders).[1] This survey was organised for the 2009 regional elections among 1,009 Flemish voters.

Based on our review of existing theoretical analysis of conservatism and feminism we distinguish between two types (and measures) of conservatism: 'social conservatism' refers to a conservative stance on moral–ethical issues,

---

1. PARTIREP is an inter-university attraction pole financed by Belgian Science Policy (BELSPO). More information regarding the PARTIREP project can be found on: http://www.partirep.eu/ (accessed 5 May 2014). The 2009 voter survey consisted of a three-wave panel study. The first wave was organised shortly before the start of the 2009 election campaign, the second wave took place during the election campaign and the third wave was conducted shortly after the 2009 elections. Wave 1 included a random sample of 2,331 voters. The 1,698 voters in wave 3 formed a subsample of the voters in wave 1. Employees of TNS Dimarso interviewed the voters face-to-face. In order to correct for biases in the dataset, we weigh the data according to sex, age, province, level of education, professional occupation and voting behaviour. Because we focus on actual voting behaviour in the 2009 elections, we can only use wave 3 of the data (recorded after the elections). Moreover, we limited our analysis to the Flemish voters (N = 1,009) for theoretical reasons (*see* above) and because the conservative and feminist scales (*see* below) only passed the test of reliability in Flanders.

whereas '*laissez-faire* conservatism' points at a liberal (conservative) stance on socio-economic issues. Social conservatism was measured on a one-dimensional scale consisting of five survey items: (1) 'It is normal that gay and lesbian couples have the right to adopt children'; (2) 'The use of cannabis should be severely punished'; (3) 'To what extent is abortion acceptable to you';[2] (4) 'To what extent is homosexuality acceptable to you?'; and (5) 'To what extent is euthanasia acceptable to you?'. Each of these items had a 5-point Likert scale answering category, ranging from 'completely agree/acceptable' to 'completely disagree/ unacceptable'. We construed a standardised additive scale measuring social conservatism, ranging from 1 to 5.[3] A low score on this scale indicates a socially progressive stance, whereas a high score indicates a social conservative attitude.

The survey item for the second conservative dimension, i.e. *laissez-faire* conservatism, was: 'the government should play a smaller role in managing the economy'. Respondents could again indicate on a five-point scale to what extent they 'completely agree' or 'completely disagree' with the statement.[4]

Measuring feminism is not easy, not the least because the varieties of feminism that exist are enormous. Generally, there are two ways to identify feminists. One is by asking a question of 'self-identification', e.g. 'to what extent do you call yourself a feminist?' The problem with this kind of question is that people are sometimes reluctant to call themselves a feminist although they might subscribe to feminist principles (Williams and Wittig 1997). This is even more problematic when we consider the fact that conservative feminism constitutes a reaction against second wave and liberal feminism, against the label of 'feminism' itself. It is also remains difficult for men to identify themselves as being a 'feminist'.

For all of these reasons, we identify feminists based on their position on a number of attitude questions. We construed a feminist scale based on the following – inversely coded – items: (1) 'In the current society, there is generally a genuine equality between men and women'; (2) 'Women's organisations are no longer necessary nowadays'; (3) 'When employment is scarce, men have more right to a job than women'; and (4) 'A woman should be willing to quit her job in the interest of her family'. These items all touch upon a core element that is central to all types of feminism: they relate to 'the collective, structural and socially produced nature of men's domination and women's disadvantage and [...] the promotion of greater gender equality and justice as a political priority' (Bryson and Heppell 2010: 38).[5]

---

2. The item on abortion was included in this scale on social conservatism, and not in the feminist scale because, empirically, the abortion item did not load onto the feminist scale. The factor analysis indicated, however, that abortion was strongly related to the other conservative items.

3. Factor analysis indicated that these five items formed a one-dimensional scale. A reliability analysis showed that the scale was high on construct validity (Cronbach's alpha = 0.700).

4. Even though the PARTIREP survey included several items that theoretically pertained to *laissez-faire* conservatism, these items were empirically unrelated because they did not form a reliable scale. We therefore chose to include one single survey item that showed the strongest factor loading (and thus the highest eigenvalue), namely: 'the government should play a smaller role in managing the economy'. This item was not only empirically the strongest one, but theoretically it goes to the core of the conservative critique that government plays too big a role in the economy.

5. Moreover, a factor analysis also showed that these items are empirically related and that they all load on a single dimension (Cronbach's alpha = 0.507).

Table 13.1: Correlation between conservatism and feminism

	Feminism
Laissez-faire conservatism	−0.130***
Social conservatism	−0.336***

Note: the coefficients are Pearson correlation coefficients.

Besides the variables of interest, i.e. feminism, social conservatism and *laissez-faire* conservatism, we employ a number of control variables. Left-right self-placement is traditionally an important predictor for party choice and was measured by asking the participants the following question: could you position your own opinions on a scale reaching from 0 (left) to 10 (right)? Moreover, we included the traditional socio-demographic variables, namely voters' sex, age (as a continuous variable) and educational attainment (as a categorical variable)[6] in the analysis.

Explorative data analysis: Identifying feminist conservative voters in Flanders

The relationship between feminism and conservatism is, as we have stated already, an uneasy one, both theoretically and in practice. We start our analysis by calculating the correlation between the feminist scale and both of the conservative scales. The results in Table 13.1 confirm that there is a trade-off between feminism and conservatism: both social conservatism and *laissez-faire* conservatism are negatively related to the feminist scale. In particular, the correlation between feminism and social conservatism is strong and significant ($r = -0.336$***). Voters who display a high score on the feminist scale are very likely to have a low score on the social conservative scale (and vice versa). In everyday parlance, feminism and social conservatism are indeed an 'odd' couple.

However, even though the data show that combining high scores on both the feminist and the conservative scales is not obvious, the fact that the correlation is not perfect suggests that voters *possibly* combine elements of both. In order to identify a group of 'feminist conservatives' among the voters, we divide each scale into two categories. Voters who score lower than the mean voter have a 'low' score, whereas voters who score higher than the mean voter display a 'high' score. Tables 13.2 and 13.3 present the association between feminism and *laissez-faire* or social conservatism respectively. The results in the two tables confirm that feminism is somewhat more difficult to rime with social conservatism than with *laissez-faire* conservatism. They also indicate, however, that approximately one-quarter of Flemish voters combine feminist and *laissez-faire* conservative traits,

6.   The education variable reflects the highest level of education of voters. Three levels are distinguished: lower secondary education, higher secondary education and higher education (including university and university college).

Table 13.2: Association between feminism and laissez-faire *conservatism (N=1003)*

		Feminism Low	Feminism High
Laissez-faire conservatism	Low	176	246
		17.5%	24.5%
	High	331	250
		33%	24.9%

Note: The percentages are 'total percentages' and they are calculated on the total number of voters.

Table 13.3: Association between feminism and social conservatism (N=1008)

		Feminism Low	Feminism High
Social conservatism	Low	174	302
		17.3%	30%
	High	337	195
		33.4%	19.3%

Note: The percentages are 'total percentages' and they are calculated on the total number of voters.

and that one-fifth of them combine feminist and socially conservative attitudes. These findings suggest that there might well be an important electoral market for parties that combine feminist and conservative claims.

This particular electoral market of voters is defined partly by voters' sex and age. The group of voters bringing together feminism and *laissez-faire* conservatism is significantly larger among women than among men: 29.7 per cent of the female voters compared to 20 per cent of the male voters combine feminist and *laissez-faire* conservative attitudes (Cramer's $V = 0.112$, $p < 0.001$). This sex difference is not present for voters combining feminist and socially conservative attitudes. The group of 'feminist *laissez-faire* conservatives' is, in addition, significantly smaller among older generations of voters born before 1950 than among voters born after 1950 (Cramer's $V = 0.137$, $p < 0.001$). The latter are, in general, more likely to present feminist attitudes (*see also* Inglehart and Norris 2003), and this *regardless* of their attitudes on economic issues. Finally, the youngest generation of voters (born after 1970) seems particularly unlikely to unite feminism and social conservatism (Cramer's $V = 0.083$, $p < 0.05$). This group of voters combines a feminist position with a more progressive stance on moral issues.

The explanatory power of 'feminist conservatism' in party choice

Now that we have identified a section of the electorate that is both feminist and conservative, we can determine whether, and to what extent, these attitudes direct voters' electoral behaviour. In order to do so, we ran a multinomial logistic regression analysis explaining the party choice of the respondents at the 2009 Flemish regional elections.[7] Table 13.4 presents the results for the multinomial logistic regression including only the main effects. In Table 13.5, we add the interaction term combining feminism and conservatism. Because our interest lies with conservative attitudes, we set the largest left-wing party in Flanders, the socialist party SP.A, as the reference category in both tables so that the effect of the right to far-right parties can be more easily determined.

Despite the fact that we have only included seven variables, the first notable finding in Table 13.4 is that the predictive power of the model is quite high. About 28 per cent of the variance in party choice can be explained by the variables that were taken up in the model.[8]

What can we now conclude with regard to the impact of the independent variables? We first of all find that feminism is not significantly related to party choice. This means that, perhaps counter-intuitively, feminist voters are not more likely to choose the left-wing socialist party SP.A over any of the centre or right-wing parties (CD&V, Open VLD, N-VA and Vlaams Belang). Voters' attitudes on gender issues do not steer their voting behaviour, at least not when we control for other ideological positions. Social conservatism does however affect party choice. With every increase on the social conservatism scale, Flemish voters are *less* likely to vote for the Green Party Groen!, and *more* likely to cast a vote for the Christian Democratic Party (CD&V) and for the far-right party Vlaams Belang. CD&V and Vlaams Belang adopt a more conservative viewpoint on moral issues (such as abortion and euthanasia), and as a result attract voters who share these more conservative views. The results for the *laissez-faire* items are also in line with the expectations. Voters who are in favour of a smaller role for government in managing the economy are more likely to vote for right-wing parties (Open VLD, N-VA or Vlaams Belang). The left-right self-placement of voters does not significantly affect their vote choice. The effect of this variable is largely absorbed by the effect of the other three ideological scales.

The party choice of voters is in addition influenced by their socio-demographic profile. The odds of voting for the Green Party or for the far-right party *decreases* with the voter's age, whereas the odds of voting for the Christian Democratic Party *increases* with age. The Green Party is furthermore more likely to attract votes from the higher educated, whereas the lower educated are more likely to turn

---

7.   Because we use a multinomial regression model, we keep the number of explanatory and control variables relatively limited. Multinomial logistic regressions are after all very vulnerable to skewing in the data and to a low number of respondents.

8.   Tests have moreover pointed out that this is the effective R^2, and is not due to problems of multi-collinearity (*see* Appendix 1 for an overview of correlations between the ideological variables).

Table 13.4: Multinomial logistic regression explaining party choice (N=812; without interaction)

	Groen!	CD&V	Open VLD	N-VA	Vlaams Belang
	Exp. ß	Exp. ß	Exp. ß	Exp. ß	Exp. ß
Feminism	n.s.	n.s.	n.s.	n.s.	n.s.
Social conservatism	0.618+	1.518*	n.s.	n.s.	2.562***
Laissez-faire conservatism	n.s.	n.s.	1.227+	1.354*	1.338*
Left-right self-placement	n.s.	n.s.	n.s.	n.s.	n.s.
Sex Man Woman (ref.)	n.s.	n.s.	n.s.	3.076***	n.s.
Education					
Lower secondary	0.121**	n.s.	n.s.	0.450*	4.041***
Higher secondary	0.494*	n.s.	0.546*	n.s.	n.s.
Higher (ref.)					
Age	0.971*	1.013+	n.s.	n.s.	0.959***
	Nagelkerke R^2 = 0.281; reference category = SP.A				

Note: ***p<0.001; ** p<0.01; * p<0.05; p<0.10

Table 13.5: Multinomial logistic regression explaining party choice (N=812; with interaction)

	Groen!	CD&V	Open VLD	N-VA	Vlaams Belang
	Exp. ß	Exp. ß	Exp. ß	Exp. ß	Exp. ß
Feminism	n.s.	0.291*	0.281*	0.183**	0.154**
Social conservatism	n.s.	0.240*	n.s.	0.114*	0.257+
Feminism* social conservatism	n.s.	1.686**	1.510*	1.943**	1.938**
Left-right self-placement	n.s.	n.s.	n.s.	n.s.	n.s.
Sex Man Woman (ref.)	n.s.	n.s.	n.s.	2.846***	n.s.
Education					
Lower secondary	0.119**	n.s.	n.s.	0.429*	3.962***
Higher secondary	0.478*	n.s.	0.532*	n.s.	n.s.
Higher (ref.)					
Age	0.970**	1.014+	n.s.	n.s.	0.960***
	Nagelkerke R^2 = 0.294; reference category = SP.A				

Note: ***p<0.001; ** p<0.01; * p<0.05; p<0.10

to the far-right party. Sex gaps, finally, remain mostly absent, with the exception of the regionalist party N-VA. This party is significantly less likely to receive votes from female voters. Noteworthy also is the fact that the Flemish voters do not present a sex gap in far-right voting. Contrary to other studies (*see* Givens 2004), our results indicate that male voters are as likely as female voters to vote for the Vlaams Belang.

Our central concern, however, is the interaction between feminism and conservatism: does the combination of feminist and conservative attitudes determine voting behaviour or not? In order to answer this question, we turn to the results in Table 13.5. Table 13.5 shows the interaction between feminism and the two types of conservative attitudes. Our results are somewhat mixed. On the one hand, we do not find any significant interaction between feminism and *laissez-faire* conservatism (the interaction term is therefore not displayed in the table). Feminist *laissez-faire* conservatives do not systematically tend to vote for one party or another. On the other hand, we do notice that the interaction term between feminism and social conservatism is significant. This means that the *combination* of feminist and social conservative attitudes affects vote choice. More precisely: the impact of feminism on vote choice is dependent upon the score of voters on the social conservatism scale. The 'feminism' variable in Table 13.5 gives the results for voters who have a *low* score on the social conservatism scale. The odds that socially progressive voters prefer a right-wing party (CD&V, Open VLD, N-VA or Vlaams Belang) to the socialist party SP.A decrease significantly as these voters are more feminists. This means that, among progressive voters, an increase in feminist attitudes leads to a vote for left-wing parties. The interaction effect ('feminism*social conservatism'), then, should be interpreted as a 'correction' on the effect of the 'feminism' variable. Whereas socially progressive feminist voters are likely to prefer the socialist party SP.A to right-wing parties, the significant interaction effect indicates that this preference is *weakened* when voters combine feminist and social conservative attitudes. The combination of feminism and social conservatism leads voters more to the right hand side of the political party landscape. Based on these results, we might conclude that the Christian Democrats (CD&V), the liberals (Open VLD), the regionalists (N-VA) and the far right (Vlaams Belang) all appeal, to some extent, to voters who combine a more feminist viewpoint on gender issues and a more conservative viewpoint on the social conservative scale.

Conclusion

This chapter has addressed two research questions: Do voters combine feminist and conservative attitudes? And is feminism and conservatism steering citizen's voting behaviour? Given that the case of Flanders features a multiparty system in which parties on the right embody different kinds of conservatism, our analysis could, unlike existing UK and US scholarship, differentiate between combinations of feminism with social conservatism and with *laissez-faire* conservatism. In line with theoretical expectations, the answer to the first question is that feminism and conservatism are negatively correlated. High levels of feminist awareness tend to go together with low levels of conservatism (either *laissez-faire* or social conservatism) among Flemish voters. Regarding the second question, the dominant finding is that ideological preference and socio-demographic variables, and not feminism, determine party choice.

Nevertheless, our results do indicate that feminism and conservatism are not mutually exclusive. Approximately one-fifth to one-quarter of Flemish voters combine a high score on the feminist scale with a high score on one of the two conservative scales. The relatively high number of such citizens furthermore constitutes a potentially important electoral pool for parties on the right. In particular, the combination of feminist attitudes and social conservatism affects vote choice in that it decreases the tendency to vote left, and it increases the tendency to vote for (centre-)right parties in Flanders. From that perspective, a vote for the Christian Democratic Party (CD&V) would be the rational choice because, in contrast to all the other right-wing parties, the party has a women's branch and a strong record in gendered and feminist policies. However, we see that other right-wing parties also attract votes based on the combination of feminism and conservatism, even when these parties cannot present the same track record. Overall, our findings suggest that a feminist (social) conservative profile might be electorally rewarding for right-wing parties, because there is an electoral market for these types of ideas and attitudes. The combination of feminist attitudes with *laissez-faire* conservative preferences on the other hand does not impact upon vote choice at all, and thus does not lead the voter to the liberal party Open VLD, which would be the logical choice given the party's *laissez-faire* ideas.

At a more general level the presence of a significant group of voters that combine feminist and *laissez-faire* or socially conservative views supports the idea that the substantive representation of women should not be elided with leftist–feminist substantive representation of women (Celis and Childs 2012). Our results confirm that, indeed, there exist plural views on what women want and need, and this not only seems to differ between left-wing and right-wing ideologies, but even within the group of conservative ideologies (i.e. *laissez-faire* and social conservatives). This in turn implies that responsive substantive representation of women cannot but require political debate about what is in the interest of women (Celis and Childs, Introduction, this volume) including classic left-right debates about women's issues and interests, as well as views formed by the intersections of a variety of feminisms and conservatisms.

Appendix

Table 13.A.1: Pearson correlations between ideological scales

	Feminism	Social conservatism	*Laissez-faire* conservatism	Left-right placement
Feminism	1	-0.336**	-0.130**	-0.078*
Social conservatism	-0.336**	1	0.065*	0.133**
Laissez-faire conservatism	-0.130**	0.065*	1	-0.090**
Left-right placement	-0.078*	0.133**	-0.090**	1

References

Banazsak, L. A., Beckwith, K. and Rucht, D. (eds) (2003) *Women's Movements Face the Reconfigured State*, Cambridge: Cambridge University Press.

Bashevkin, S. (1994) 'Confronting neo-conservatism: Anglo-American women's movements under Thatcher, Reagan and Mulroney', *International Political Science Review*, 13 (3): 275–96.

Bryson, V, and Heppell, T. (2010) 'Conservatism and feminism: the case of the British Conservative Party', *Journal of Political Ideologies*, 15 (1): 31–50.

Celis, K. (2006) 'Substantive representation of women and the impact of descriptive representation. Case: the Belgian Lower House 1900–1979', *Journal of Women, Politics and Policy*, 28 (2): 85–114.

Celis, K. and Childs, S. (2012) 'The substantive representation of women: what to do with Conservative's claims?', *Political Studies*, 60 (2): 213–25.

Celis, K. and Erzeel, S. (forthcoming) 'Beyond the usual suspects: non-left, male and non-feminist MPs and the substantive representation of women', *Government and Opposition*.

Celis, K., Outshoorn, J., Meier, P. and Motmans, J. (2012). 'Institutionalizing intersectionality in the Low Countries: Belgium and the Netherlands', in Krizsan, A., Skjeie, H. and Squires, J. (eds), *Institutionalizing Intersectionality: The Changing Nature of European Equality Regimes*, New York: Palgrave, pp. 119–47.

Childs, S. and Webb, P. (2012a) *Sex, Gender and the Conservative Party: From Iron Lady to Kitten Heels*, Basingstoke: Palgrave Macmillan.

—   (2012b) 'Gender politics and conservatism: the view from the British Conservative Party grassroots', *Government and Opposition*, 47 (1): 21–48.

Deschouwer, K. and Lucardie, P. (2003) 'Partijen en partijsystemen in Nederland en Vlaanderen', *Sociologische Gids*, 50 (2): 131–55.

Dillard, A. D. (2005) 'Adventures in conservative feminism', *Society*, 42 (3): 25–7.

Erzeel, S. (2012) 'Women's substantive representation in the Belgian Chamber of Representatives: testing the added value of a claims-making approach', *World Political Science Review*, 8 (1): 28–47.

Girvin, B. (ed.) (1988) *The Transformation of Contemporary Conservatism*, London: Sage.

Givens, T. E. (2004) 'The radical right gender gap', *Comparative Political Studies*, 37 (1): 30–54.

Hyde, C. (1995) 'Feminist social movement organizations survive the new right', in Ferree, M. M. and Martin, P. Y. (eds), *Feminist Organizations: Harvest of the New Women's Movement*, Philadelphia, PA: Temple University Press, pp. 306–22.

Inglehart, R. and Norris, P. (2003) *Rising Tide: Gender Equality and Cultural Change Around the World*, Cambridge: Cambridge University Press.

Kittilson, M. C. (2006) *Challenging Parties, Changing Parliaments*, Columbus, OH: Ohio State University Press.

Klatch, R. E. (1988) 'The New Right and its women', *Society*, 25 (3): 30–8.

Lovenduski, J. and Norris, P. (1993) *Gender and Party Politics*, London: Sage.

Meier, P. (2000) 'The evidence of being present: guarantees of representation and the example of the Belgian case', *Acta Politica*, 35 (1): 64–85.

Offen, K. (2000) *European Feminisms 1700–1950: A Political History*, Stanford, CA: Stanford University Press.

Schreiber, R. (2002) 'Injecting a woman's voice: conservative women's organizations, gender consciousness, and the expression of women's policy preferences', *Sex Roles*, 47 (7/8): 331–42.

— (2008) *Righting Feminism*, Oxford: Oxford University Press.

Tremblay, M. and Pelletier, R. (2000) 'More feminists or more women? Descriptive and substantive representations of women in the 1997 Canadian federal elections', *International Political Science Review*, 21 (4): 381–405.

Van Molle, L. and Gubin, E. (1998) *Vrouw en Politiek in België*. Tielt: Lannoo.

Wängnerud, L. (2000) 'Testing the politics of presence: women's representation in the Swedish Riksdag', *Scandinavian Political Studies*, 23 (1): 67–91.

Wiliarty, S. (2010) *The CDU and the Politics of Gender in Germany: Bringing Women to the Party*, New York: Cambridge University Press.

Williams, R. and Wittig, M. A. (1997) '"I'm not a feminist, but…": factors contributing to the discrepancy between pro-feminist orientation and feminist social identity', *Sex Roles*, 37 (11/12): 885–903.

Chapter Fourteen

Islamist Women's Leadership in Morocco

Emanuela Dalmasso and Francesco Cavatorta

Introduction

A number of surprising political and social dynamics have emerged, since the beginning of the Arab Uprisings, that have led to the contestation of authoritarian power in the Middle East and North Africa. These include the anti-neoliberal nature of the revolts, the demands for democratic rule and individual rights seemingly clashing with Orientalist assumptions, and the widespread politicisation of societies contradicting previous assumptions of apathy. While it is certainly too early to draw conclusions about its outcome, such dynamics have problematised received wisdoms about Arab politics. Among them is the role of women in Arab societies. The presence of women, and in particular young women, among the demonstrations and the violent confrontations with the security services was notable during the Arab Uprisings (Arshad 2013). Such presence undermined – for a time – the Western myth of the perpetual subjugation of Arab women and their invisibility on the public scene. Thus, 'the "empowered revolutionary woman," protesting in Tahrir Square, was a regular feature of images of the 25 January uprising [in Egypt]' (Pratt 2013).

However, this phenomenon should not have been as surprising as it was held to be because women have often played a significant role in Arab politics, albeit one not usually recognised. During the anti-colonisation struggle across North Africa, for instance, many women became prominent members in nationalist movements in different capacities, holding at times very important political roles (Amrane 1991; Benadada 1999). From the 1940s until the 1960s, moreover, women in North Africa, Egypt, Syria, Jordan, and Iraq created independent civil society organisations. The newly emerging states, subsequently, neutralised those independent women's organisations either by banning them, as in Egypt and Jordan, or by coopting them into state-run associations (Jad 2007). Women's subsequent political and social marginalisation following independence was partially offset, however, by their progressive inclusion into the education system and the workforce, although to different degrees across the region (Pratt 2007). In the socially progressive republics such as Tunisia, Algeria, Syria, Egypt and Iraq, the wider goals of national modernisation and anti-imperialism relegated women's rights to the sidelines, with women's associations and groups mobilising around the achievement of those wider goals (Pratt 2007), although an effort to improve the conditions of women was made. In conservative monarchies such as Jordan, Morocco and, more intensely, the Gulf States, very little initially changed for women's rights because ruling monarchies were able to remain in power due to an unwritten pact with traditional sectors of society, whereby political support was provided to the monarch in exchange for maintaining patriarchal practices (Charrad 2001). Yet, despite the widespread deprivation of the liberal principles of gender equality, many women still remained politically and socially engaged. For example, increased access to education led many women to become student activists during the 1970s when third-level education expanded massively across the region, in particular in the socialist republics. At that time, being politically engaged meant adopting an ideological frame of reference that was influenced mainly by Western political thinking (Ahmed 1982).

Arab women's engagement in political activities and in society more broadly was also influenced by state policies towards women and how different countries conceived the role of women in society. In countries like Tunisia, for example, gender equality as a complement to the Western-style modernisation of society was encouraged and driven by the ruling elites, leading to legislative 'liberal successes', such as the egalitarian personal status legislation (henceforth PSL).[1] Where, on the contrary, such an engagement was opposed by the regime as in countries like Jordan, Morocco or Saudi Arabia on the grounds that it undermined traditional support from conservative sectors of society, 'liberal successes' have been limited. In any case, as stated above, whether in 'progressive' republics or conservative monarchies, women's activism has tended to be framed within a Western-derived secular and liberal intellectual framework.

In the last decades, in contrast, an increasing number of women who decided to become politically active chose to do so not from a secular intellectual perspective, but rather via Islamist movements and political parties. When examined from a liberal perspective that privileges individual rights, the militancy of women in Islamist parties and movements constitutes a puzzle: not only do such parties and movements have a history of opposing what are considered basic women's rights but they also have a strict conservative social agenda based on privileging collective rights to the detriment, at times, of individual ones. In the Arab world such a conservative vision of society is additionally bound up with a type of cultural specificity that finds its roots in religion.

The activism of women in Islamist parties and movements has been examined in the past, but it was never genuinely central to scholarship and had little interest for policy-makers because such movements did not control political power. In the aftermath of the Arab Uprisings, this is no longer the case, with Islamist parties now in power in Tunisia and Morocco and doing well in other liberalising Arab countries such as Egypt and – until the summer of 2013 – Yemen and Libya (Hamid

---

1. Personal status legislation regulates matters concerning gender relations and specifically the rights and duties of women when it comes to citizenship, divorce, inheritance, custody of children and marriage.

2011). Winning state power has, then, brought the issue of the relationship between Islamism and women's rights centre-stage, not least because of widespread fears that their coming to power would be detrimental to women's rights as conceived in the liberal feminist tradition.

It is precisely this reconfiguration of state power in favour of Islamism that has once again placed the issue of women's rights on the agenda, leading to both domestic and international debates about the progress of women's rights in countries where Islamists come to power. These debates however tend to be extremely normative and politically biased in so far as there is a widespread assumption that Islamism is necessarily, and almost naturally, inimical to women. This assumption largely neglects the dimension of women's activism in Islamist parties. While it can be legitimately argued that some Islamist actors promote a very conservative view of gender relations and social roles, this should not lead to a conflation of conservatism with an anti-women's rights agenda. Indeed, it is precisely at this juncture that an examination of how Islamist women explain and conceive of their political activism is necessary.

This chapter examines this under-explored question and analyses the militancy of women in Islamist movements, in so far as these women clearly operate against the liberal feminist framework and expectations. In particular, we contextualise women's engagement in Islamist movements in the broader global trend that sees a significant amount of women joining conservative parties (Celis and Childs 2012). Thus, conservative parties across the globe have seen more of their female members come to prominence. In addition, conservative parties and movements can rely on the support of many ordinary women who find conservative political programmes to be in line with their material and identity expectations. Finally, and offering new insights, we analyse how women engaged in Islamist movements make sense of their activism once they are in prominent political positions. Following the Arab Uprisings, a number of Islamist parties and therefore Islamist women are effectively in power and this provides an opportunity to examine how their political engagement is translated into everyday practices of governance (Schwedler 2011).

Our case study is Morocco, where an Islamist party is presently in power – the Party for Justice and Development (PJD). Our data are interviews with high-ranking women activists and their public statements regarding their political engagement. While a focus on Islamists' female leadership prevents us from systematising the findings across the entire movement, we adopted this methodology for two reasons. First, it allows us to identify at least some trends related to the way in which Islamist women engage in conservative politics, and how they think about their involvement therein. Second, it permits us to examine over the longer term the development of these parties and by extension the role of women within them during the journey from opposition to government. The case of Morocco, and the PJD in particular, serves to illustrate a more general regional trend, and it allows for a clearer understanding of how women's political participation might develop in the aftermath of the Arab Uprisings.

Women in Islamist movements

In the past, much of the scholarship and the policy-making community looked with a degree of suspicion on the role of women in Islamist parties and movements because of their socially conservative attitudes (Grami 2008). For critics, there is an inherent contradiction in the decision of a woman to join a political or social movement whose ethos is based on a discriminatory reading of religious precepts that confine women to traditional gender roles, reaffirming strong patriarchal practices in the process. Discussing the problems that the Moroccan women's movement – traditionally the domain of secular leftist women – is currently experiencing due to its inability to attract a new generation of militants, Skalli (2011) talks about the paradox of a younger generation of women that has more freedom, more access to information, and can enjoy greater democratic openings, and yet chooses to be disengaged from a political activism that favours gender equality, preferring instead to join the ranks of Islamism. In her analysis, there is an obvious and unsolvable contradiction between gender equality and Islamism.

The scepticism of the secular and liberal sectors of Arab society *vis-à-vis* women who join Islamist movements appears legitimate when one examines the way in which the role of women has been traditionally conceived within Islamist movements. Clark and Schwedler (2003: 293) relate that 'at the onset of political liberalisation in Jordan and Yemen in 1989 and 1990, respectively, the largest Islamist group in each country expressed strong views opposing women's full and equal political participation'. These views were not confined to Jordanian or Yemeni Islamists, but were widespread within Islamist parties across the region. For instance, as recently as the early 2000s the PJD in Morocco opposed changes to personal status legislation that were meant to guarantee a stronger degree of equality to women when it came to marriage, divorce, or the custody of children (Dalmasso and Cavatorta 2009). The party eventually came around to accepting the changes the King intended to push through, but this seemed to reflect political expediency rather than genuine conversion to the idea of equality.

Such stances taken by various Islamist political actors provoke a heated debate about their commitment to democracy and equality. Post-revolutionary Tunisia provides a perfect example of this debate in so far as the electoral victory of the Islamist Ennahda party, and its role in government, are perceived to pose a threat to women's equality (Tchaicha and Arfaoui 2012). What follows from this is a political debate as to whether the Islamists are genuinely democratic and in favour of women's rights or whether they are simply using the mechanisms of democracy to get to power and set up theocratic institutions that would fundamentally undermine individual rights, including women's rights.

Whether democratic and genuinely committed to women's rights or not, political Islam is *de facto* composed by an important female constituency. In order to provide an explanation for what can be perceived as a paradox, three sets of explanation are provided in the literature. The first deals with the sociological profile of women. In this context, some scholars focus on the rising levels of education among women and link their increased education with political activism

(Göle 1997; Jad 2010). Others concentrate their attention on sociological issues, ranging from interpreting women's participation in Islamist organisations as the result of family ties, to considering women's engagement as a signal on the marriage market that the woman in question is a 'good Muslim' (Blaydes and Linzer 2008).

These explanations are only valid to a limited extent. For its part, focusing on increased education might explain why women become more politicised in the sense that they wish to take on a greater role in contributing to shape society, but it still does not tell us why they specifically join Islamist movements, particularly when the latter tend to see women in traditional roles. Emphasising family ties is certainly important too, because there is some evidence that having male family members in Islamist movements might have an impact on the decision to join. The cases of Rachid Ghannouchi's daughter in Tunisia or Sheikh Yassine's in Morocco demonstrate such a dynamic. However, given the number of women activists, it is certainly difficult to argue that this explanation constitutes the main reason for women joining Islamist movements and parties. It should also be underlined that men and women might meet when they become activists and might, therefore, form families following their decision to join.

Another set of explanations for women's political participation in Islamist movements emphasises internal party dynamics. Four different reasons are given in the 2003 study by Clark and Schwedler. First, they argue that the increased presence of women in Islamist movements is due to the realisation on the part of the leadership that women's participation will facilitate women's vote, once suffrage is made universal. Accordingly, Islamist parties and movements actively recruit women so that they can then attract other women to support the party. Second, Clark and Schwedler argue that increased women's participation is due to the necessity of presenting a more moderate and modern image for external actors. Third, they make the argument that different factions coexist within Islamist parties, and once the more progressive one controls the party then women will become more visible ,as they fit the ideological framework of the progressive elements. Finally, there is the focus on 'changing opportunity structures: women within these parties have seized windows of opportunity unrelated to shifts in strategy and/or ideology' (Clark and Schwedler 2003: 294). For instance, the jailing of male members of the party can favour the arrival of women to replace them in party structures, as the case of the Palestinian Hamas demonstrates (Milton-Edwards and Farrell, 2010). Despite being a fascinating analysis of Islamist women's political participation, Clark and Schwedler's study does not deal with the motivations that lead to such engagement.

Another line of inquiry as to why Islamist movements have become attractive to women who want to be politically and/or socially engaged, is offered in the broad discussion about Islamic feminism (Latte Abdallah 2010). A history of this phenomenon, and the acceptance of its validity on the part of traditional feminism are beyond the scope of this chapter. Here it suffices to say that over the last three decades dissatisfaction with traditional liberal feminism, whose intellectual framework is influenced by the West, has given rise to an attempt to construct an Islam-specific alternative. Focusing their criticism on pre-Islamic patriarchal structures rather than on the religion of Islam, women activists began to make the argument that Islam was an egalitarian religion and that it was by returning to the concept of gender equality specific to Islam that women's rights could be advanced (Ahmed 1992). This intellectual intuition spurned a significant amount of work on how traditional feminist goals and concerns could be claimed through a reinterpretation of key Islamic texts (Wadud 2006). A new feminist discourse began, then, to emerge in the late 1980s and early 1990s that saw itself as alternative to the one promoted by secular activists, who were accused of undermining Arab societies through the adoption of values and traditions from the West.

Within what is broadly called Islamic feminism, are different understandings and practices. They include, for instance, secular activists who have understood that promoting policies aimed at addressing gender equality has a better chance of success when couched and justified in religious language. They include Muslim women intellectuals who strive to combine the goal of gender equality without falling into the trap of assuming the necessity of secularisation to achieve it. They also include Islamist activists claiming that there is no need to actually link feminism and Islam because Islam on its own provides for gender equality (Badran 1995, 2009). These lines of inquiry have led to empirical studies about the nature of the choice of Islamist women and their social or political engagement. Yet, the objective of these studies has been more to demonstrate the practical application of Islamic feminism than to analyse the motivations of women who join Islamist movements (Karam 1998).

Thus, Islamic feminism in itself does not offer an answer to the question of what makes women join Islamist movements and what kind of representation these women provide; it simply offers a way to understand the choice *ex post*. Here we look for specific motivations, which may be decoupled from any attempt to promote gender equality, that might explain the choice of joining an Islamist movement. We argue that it is the policy positions on an array of issues that drive women to support and become active in Islamist parties. Importantly, such policy positions do not necessarily have to do with gender-related questions. In other words, Islamist movements attract members and command considerable support from the population because of what they stand for and represent, not least their promotion of social justice through the provision of services (education, health, childcare) that many ordinary Arab women see as fundamental to the life of the family. Conversely, political projects that are secular and liberal in nature are no longer as convincing or appealing as they used to be in the past when leftist thinking was dominant across the region from Iraq to Tunisia.

Moreover, in our analysis we avoid focusing on women's participation in Islamist movements as an exclusive and problematic issue for the Arab world. This tendency to look at the Arab world as if it is 'exceptional' ignores the similar phenomenon – the rise of women in conservative parties across the globe – within which the specific case of the Arab world can be better understood. Building on the wider discussion about the necessity to analyse conservative women's claims without normative bias – i.e. dismissing them as the product of 'false consciousness' – a number of works (Celis and Childs 2012; Webb and Childs 2012) have emerged examining the role of women's agency irrespective of the movement or party within which they are involved. Accordingly, we analyse Islamist women's participation within the framework of the global context of the crisis of liberalism, and the subsequent affirmation, usually based in identity politics, of the pre-eminence of collective rights as opposed to individual ones.

The point of departure is the acknowledgement that claims based on collective rights have become an instrument through which the dominant discourse of individual rights, inextricably linked to issues of Western cultural and economic domination in developing countries, is challenged. From this, the engagement of women in Islamist parties is part of this broader phenomenon. Identity-based conservatism allows for the articulation of policy positions that tend to converge with dominant values in society where the contestation of liberalism-based individualism is perceived to be detrimental to the stability and coherence of the polity. The neoliberal economic reforms and the partial liberalising reforms of the last two decades across the developing world have been based on the assertion of the primacy of individual rights as not only the natural state of individuals in society, but, crucially, as the engine for economic development. The problem is that this mythical development did not materialise for the whole of society, and has in fact increased the unequal distribution of wealth and unequal provision of social opportunities (Dillman 2001). In addition, it has included the import of social modes of behaviour that are out of kilter with the conservative values of the majority of citizens in many developing societies (Moghadam 1994). If we add to the mix the imperialistic and war-prone policies of a dominant West, a reaction to all of this could be expected and as Barber (1992) has argued in the past, this resistance has taken on forms of political conservatism, where identity-based politics and a return to the pre-eminence of collective rights are dominant. On closer inspection, furthermore, this resistance has occurred in developed and democratic societies as well, where the toll of the social, political and economic crisis is leading conservative movements to political success.

Against this backdrop, it could be hypothesised that a number of Arab women react to the social displacement and the economic marginalisation that they experience much in the same way as Arab men do, leading them to embrace what they feel is the only indigenous form of political resistance: Islam. In this wider context of resistance, becoming involved in politics – for women and men – derives from a perceived necessity to counter the changes that seemingly undermine a type of social stability that, rightly or wrongly, does not rest on a liberal individual conception of human rights, but on a collectivist one. The return to tradition offered by Islamism encompasses the promotion of traditional family structures with women's rights being fulfilled completely within what liberal feminists would identify as patriarchal forms of domination. At the same time, and possibly as an unintended consequence, this political engagement contributes to transforming women's roles in so far as by defending a conservative order they come to partially undermine it through their public presence. In addition, as it will be later established, this political engagement contributes to change both in the discourses about, and the practices of Islamist women's engagement itself, because through participation women gain greater agency. This might in turn have political consequences both for the movement in which they are active, and for the political system as a whole, which was accustomed to seeing only secular women becoming prominent political leaders.

Islamist women in Morocco

One of the most contentious terrains in Morocco, as in other Arab countries, in terms of gender equality is represented by PSL. As Charrad (2001) demonstrates in his study on Tunisia, Algeria and Morocco, the recognition of a higher degree of gender equality in the aftermath of independence in the three countries was highly influenced by the power relations between different political and social actors. In Morocco the monarchy needed tribal support in order to counterbalance the political parties that had emerged in the nationalist camp, which had stronger support in urban areas. As a consequence individual rights were subordinated to the collective ones that were necessary to maintain tribal ties. The monarchy subsequently abandoned any attempt to modernise the legal system, and did not then introduce progressive reforms for women in order to secure its power. It was only in 2004 that the monarchy, for self-serving reasons explored elsewhere (Dalmasso and Cavatorta 2009), promoted sweeping changes to the PSL and saw the introduction of gender equality-oriented reforms. These reforms have been profoundly divisive, but the authoritarianism of the system guaranteed that a lid was kept on such profound divisions so that the ruling elites could utilise the issue of gender equality to strengthen their power. The situation has now changed quite dramatically and the broader issue of women's rights is once again a terrain of intense public and political debate with an Islamist party now in office, albeit alongside a monarch who still wields considerable power.

In this context women's rights have become one of the preferred issues through which Islamists are attacked on the grounds of their perceived illiberal and anti-democratic views. Conversely, it is also one of the issues Islamists like to use to deflect such accusations. For instance, women within Islamist movements underline that obtaining degrees and diplomas is highly encouraged within Islamist parties because they want to be able to provide capable and well-educated cadres, suggesting that therefore educated women are a priority (Beau and Graciet 2006). This discussion tends to be never-ending because it is based on fundamentally opposite premises. Those who criticise Islamists positions towards women's rights do so through the categories of liberalism. Hence they talk about individual rights. Islamists however, and Islamist women in particular, counter-argue that they favour women's rights because they constitute and assert them as collective rights. This results in a focus on the favourite conservative theme of 'defending' and promoting the traditional family unit within which equality is defined as complementarity. Thus, when examining the role of Islamist women in conservative movements it is more fruitful to frame the analysis within the categories that they utilise if one wants to better capture and account for the perspective these women are coming from.

Before focusing specifically on how women come to decide to engage politically in Islamist movements, it is important to establish the bases of Islamist groups overall. According to Pellicer and Wegner (2012), there are two dominant profiles of Islamist party supporters: clientelistic and grievance-driven. 'The clientelist profile of an Islamist activist or supporter is generally placed in the context of the inability of Arab states to provide public goods' (Pellicer and Wegner 2012: 5). Islamist groups fill that specific vacuum, turning the provision of services into vote-gathering machines, whereby those benefiting from the services vote or support the party (Woltering 2002). This profile does not really fit with the one of an activist (man or woman) who becomes a full-time member and rises through the ranks. Rather, it is the profile of a passive supporter enticed by material benefits due to his/her poor personal socio-economic situation. The second profile is the grievance-driven supporter whereby 'grievances are mainly seen as relative deprivation suffered by recently educated citizens. Lacking employment opportunities, the unfulfilled aspirations of potentially upwardly mobile individuals transform into a demand for change' (Pellicer and Wegner 2012: 5). It is within this second profile that 'active party activists' emerge. Here the primary motivation for engaging in a political or socially oriented Islamist movement stems from the desire to contribute to the construction of a new society where grievances can be addressed both personally and for the citizenry at large. There is widespread academic and political consensus that the Arab world has been in crisis for quite some time and while profound differences exist as to the main reasons for the crisis, a number of scholars point to neoliberal globalisation as the culprit (Guazzone and Pioppi 2009). In many ways, the Arab Uprisings are the culmination of a long-running process of contestation of the imposition of a neoliberal economic system (Chomiak and Entelis 2011), which undermines possibilities for economic and social advancement for large sectors of the population, and it is not surprising that the first political experiences of leading Islamist women are in the charitable associational sector. This participation, usually after women have completed their studies, offers them the potential to begin to change the reality they see, and place themselves at the service of others. This non-state, religiously oriented, service sector is very much the refuge of a middle class that is both educated and professional, but unable to enter and benefit from the system of state patronage (Clark 2004).

The Islamist project of transforming society is appealing to many women because there is profound dissatisfaction with the secular and liberal model that the West has adopted, and that modernising elites 'live' every day and attempt to impose on others. From a very practical point of view for instance, economic liberalisation might have increased opportunities for women in the workplace, but, at the same time, the inability to provide modern welfare services is put down to the idea that the individual must be 'sovereign', which Islamists usually translate as 'left to his/her own devices'. As Soumaya Ben Khaldoun, one of the four female members of the general Secretariat of the PJD, states:

[W]omen's problems [in Morocco] are that there are no real public policies [in favour of women] and that all family responsibilities are placed on women [...] there are no crèches, there is no part-time work for either men nor women, there is short maternity leave and no parental leave.

This suggests that the critique is one based on the inability or unwillingness of the state to fill the vacuum that the privatisation and liberalisation of the economy have created. Ben Khaldoun added that 'in the past, we had an extended family, now it is no longer the case and therefore women are unable to enjoy the greatest pleasure of all, namely maternity' (Soumaya Ben Khaldoun: interview with Emanuela Dalmasso, March 2013), because of economic necessities and absence of pro-family welfare. Another example of this trend is provided by Khadija Moufid, a former PJD member now active in the civil society sphere who created the al-Hidn association. The primary objective of this association is to promote women's empowerment as a part of a wider effort that aims at strengthening the family as a whole in order to counter 'the effects of globalisation on the poorest by supporting childhood and offering to women the tools for an ongoing development' (association's manifesto, quoted in Belal 2012: 252).

In Islamist circles the crisis of the Arab state is also interpreted in light of foreign ideologies and values that have, seemingly, corrupted Arab Muslim identity. The notion that the individual is 'king' is only partly appealing to Islamists in so far as an excessive emphasis on individual rights is perceived to be incompatible with notions of social stability and common good (Fuller 2004). It is for this reason that gender issues are a privileged terrain of contestation between Islamists and secular sectors of Arab societies. Part of the motivation of women in Islamist parties therefore is to preserve the Arab Muslim identity, which passes through the rediscovery of 'family values'. Thus, it is not surprising that when she was the president of a Moroccan Islamist civil society women's organisation Bassima Hakkaoui, now a minister in the PJD-led government, declared that the work of the association was about protecting family values against the encroachment that can derive from international conventions on human rights (Bassima Hakkaoui: interview with Emanuela Dalmasso 2008). This does not indicate a negative attitude towards human rights per se, but suggests that human rights based on individualistic notions should not be applied universally because non-Western cultures tend to look at rights and equality in the context of collectivity. This obviously speaks to a classic debate about the universal nature of human rights, which still has to be settled in the Arab world. In similar fashion, Khadija Moufid argued that her primary interest is in exploring how legislation can protect family values (Khadija Moufid: interview with Emanuela Dalmasso 2013). In short, this seems to be the Islamist answer to the crisis of the Arab state, in so far as it is a specific expression of the necessity to protect the family and privilege collective rights over individual ones to the detriment, therefore, of what liberals term 'women's rights'.

A number of interesting developments that highlight, in practice, how women's activism both transforms and is transformed by external constraints and opportunities, emerge through the analysis of women activists' stances. First, the reconciliation of family and work mentioned earlier has moved from the general to the particular, with women in the party demanding – albeit ultimately failing to ensure – that important party meetings are not held late in the evening. Boutaina Karouri, a prominent PJD's member, declared, 'when meetings are in the evening women arrive at 8 but leave by 9:30 pm, thus missing most of the debate [...] and therefore we informally asked the party, back in 2009, to limit evening meetings [...] so far without success' (Boutaina Karouri: interview with Emanuela Dalmasso 2013). This indicates that the preoccupations of working women tend to coincide, despite their ideological differences. This is a significant development on which cross-ideological alliances and shared policies could potentially be built on, if less 'ideologised' animosity existed.

This observation leads to the second point relating to the transformatory potential of Islamist women political engagement, namely the inability to build common positions with women in politics who have a different ideological frame of reference, be it liberal and/or secular. Although women managed to collaborate across ideological lines on gender quotas for parliament (Nehza El Ouafi: interview with Emanuela Dalmasso, March 2013), they largely remain divided due to the inability of both sides to frame women's rights according to a common definition. Again, there is the return to the broader debate between collective rights, within which women's rights are subsumed for Islamists, and individual rights that are equated with women's rights.

A further development worth noting goes in parallel with the increasing amount of time Islamist women spend in active politics and their upward career trajectories as political actors. Much like their leftist counterparts in the past, Islamist women, although promoting conservative public policies on matters related to abortion or divorce for instance, have begun complaining about the existence of a glass ceiling within the party that prevents many of them from reaching the top echelons of the party/parliament. Some, such as Khadija Moufid, ultimately resigned from the party in protest and went on to create a conservative association first, and then a conservative research institute. She claimed that 'women who develop leadership skills do so in associations' (Khadija Moufid: interview with Emanuela Dalmasso 2013), explicitly accusing the party of not doing enough internally to promote women's leadership. This complaint is very similar to the one that leftist Moroccan women had about the left-wing parties of which they were members in the 1980s and 1990s (Dalmasso 2011).

Finally, typically conservative claims such as complaining about the high numbers of divorces – which are felt to undermine the social stability of Moroccan society – are made through an innovative assumption: that PSL is a piece of legislation like any other and can therefore be changed (Soumaya Ben Khaldoun: interview with Emanuela Dalmasso, March 2013). This means that Islamist women are no longer claiming that anything that has to do with PSL is derived from the sacred texts and therefore untouchable; the argument is that it is ordinary legislation that can be modified to fulfil conservative goals and expectations. In many ways, then, the female Islamist leadership of the PJD is a traditional conservative group in respect of specific and, to many feminists, crucial issues, but at the same time its engagement in pluralistic politics demonstrates that there are changes taking place that problematise the simplistic assumption of what a conservative woman in politics means.

Conclusion

There are two main conclusions that can be drawn from this initial study of women's activism in Islamist parties. First, the motives for women joining Islamist parties are very similar to the ones that men have and evolve around two factors: socio-economic grievances and Arab Muslim identity. These are not easily disentangled, but together they produce a type of women's activism that tends to focus on the family as the unit that policy-makers should favour, in preference to the individual. The second point is that, paradoxically, the role and stances of women in Islamist parties represent a form of women's empowerment that is extremely attractive for a younger cohort of educated Arab women. Rather than joining secular and liberal parties, women who become active in politics join and/ or support Islamist parties in part because they can remain true to the traditional values they hold even while challenging traditional gender roles, given that the women they look up to have a family life, a career and are politically and publicly engaged. Moreover, the demands that leading Moroccan PJD women members are beginning to make, and the criticism they level at their party in some instances, is indicative of this. What is more, the internal politics of Islamist parties is today playing out in public. Whereas in the past internal divisions did not necessarily become public because the parties needed to demonstrate internal unity in order to withstand regimes' pressure and repression, this is frequently no longer the case. This means that Islamist women have the potential today to increase their internal room for manoeuvre. It is apparent that a good number have very clear ideas about the necessity to increase women's participation in politics and in public institutions, even as they carry very conservative stances on specific gender-related issues.

Acknowledgements

The authors are grateful to the editors of this volume for comments and inputs. We also acknowledge the financial support of the Germany-based Gerda Henkel Foundation in the context of the project, 'From over-estimation to under-estimation: the trajectory of Political Islam in five MENA countries'.

Interviews

Ben Khaldoun, Soumaya. Member of the general Secretariat of the PJD, Rabat, 14 March 2013.

El Ouafi, Nehza. Member of the general Secretariat of the PJD, Rabat, 6 March 2013.

Hakkaoui, Bassima. Member of the general Secretariat of the PJD and current Minister for Solidarity, Women, Family and Social Development, Rabat, 11 November 2008.

Karouri, Boutaina. Member of the PJD, Rabat, 13 March 2013.

Moufid, Khadija. Former member of the PJD and president of al-Hidhn association, Rabat, 13 March 2013.

References

Ahmed, L. (1982) 'Feminism and feminist movements in the Middle East, a preliminary exploration: Turkey, Egypt, Algeria, People's Democratic Republic of Yemen', *Women's Studies International Forum*, 5 (2): 153–68.

— (1992) *Politics and Gender in Islam*, New Haven, CT: Yale University Press.

Amrane, D. (1991) *Les femmes algériennes dans la guerre*, Paris: PLON.

Arshad, S. (2013) 'The Arab Uprisings: what did it do for women?', *Middle East Monitor*, 23 March, available at: http://www.middleeastmonitor.com/articles/middle-east/5584-the-arab-spring-what-did-it-do-for-women (accessed 19 July 2013).

Badran, M. (1995) *Feminism, Islam and Nation: Gender and the Making of Modern Egypt*, New Jersey: Princeton University Press.

— (2009) *Feminism in Islam*, Oxford: Oneworld Publications.

Barber, B. (1992) 'Jihad vs. McWorld', *The Atlantic*, 1 March, available at: http://www.theatlantic.com/magazine/archive/1992/03/jihad-vs-mcworld/303882/ (accessed on 19 March 2013).

Beau, N. and Graciet, C. (2006) *Quand le Maroc sera Islamiste*, Paris: La Découverte.

Belal, Y. (2012) *Le cheikh et le calife, sociologie religieuse de l'islam politique.au Maroc*, Casablanca: Tarik Éditions.

Benadada, A. (1999), 'Les femmes dans le mouvement nationaliste marocain', *Clio, Histoire, Femmes et Société*, Toulouse: Clio et Presses Universitaires du Mirail.

Blaydes L. and Linzer, D. (2008) 'The political economy of women's support for fundamentalist Islam', *World Politics*, 60 (4): 576–609.

Celis, K. and Childs, S. (2012) 'The substantive representation of women: what to do with conservative claims?', *Political Studies*, 60 (1): 213–25.

Charrad, M. (2001) *States and Women's Rights: The Making of Postcolonial Tunisia, Algeria and Morocco*, Berkeley, CA: University of California Press.

Chomiak, L. and Entelis, J. (2011) 'The making of North Africa's intifadas', *Middle East Report*, 259: 8–15.

Clark, J. (2004) *Islam, Charity and Activism: Middle Class Networks and Social Welfare in Egypt, Jordan and Yemen*, Bloomington, IN: Indiana University Press.

Clark, J. and Schwedler, J. (2003) 'Who opened the window? Women's activism in Islamist parties', *Comparative Politics*, 35 (3): 293–312.

Dalmasso, E. (2011) 'On fait du lobbying. Transizione democratica e movimento delle donne in Marocco', PhD dissertation, Department of Political Studies, University of Turin, Italy.

Dalmasso, E. and Cavatorta, F. (2009) 'Liberal outcomes through undemocratic means: the reform of the *Code du Statut Personnel* in Morocco', *Journal of Modern African Studies*, 47 (4): 487–506.

Dillman, B. (2001) 'Facing the market in North Africa', *Middle East Journal*, 55 (2): 198–215.

Fuller, G. (2004) *The Future of Political Islam*, London: Palgrave Macmillan.

Göle, N (1997) 'Secularism and Islamism in Turkey: the making of elites and counter-elites', *Middle East Journal*, 51 (1): 46–58.

Grami, A. (2008) 'Gender equality in Tunisia', *British Journal of Middle Eastern Studies*, 35 (3): 349–61.

Guazzone, L. and Pioppi, D. (eds) (2009) *The Arab State and Neo-Liberal Globalization*, Ithaca Press.

Hamid, S. (2011) 'The rise of the Islamists', *Foreign Affairs*, 90 (5): 40–8.

Jad, I. (2007) 'The NGO-ization of Arab women's movements', in Cornwall, A., Harrison, E. and Whitehead, A. (eds), *Feminisms in Development: Contradictions, Contestations and Challenges*, London: Zed Books.

—— (2010) 'Islamist Women of Hamas: between feminism and nationalism', *Revue des mondes musulmans et de la Méditerranée*, 128, available at: http://remmm.revues.org/6971 (accessed 30 August 2013).

Karam, A. (1998) *Women, Islamism and the State: Contemporary Feminism in Egypt*, New York: Macmillan Publishers.

Latte Abdallah, S. (2010) 'Le féminisme islamique vingt après: économie d'un débat et nouveaux chantiers de recherche', *Critique Internationale*, 46 (1): 9–23.

Milton-Edwards, B. and Farrell, S. (2010) *Hamas: The Islamic Resistance Movement*, Cambridge: Polity Press.

Moghadam, V. (ed.) (1994) *Identity, Politics and Women: Cultural Reassertions and Feminism in International Perspectives*, Boulder CO: Westview Press.

Pellicer, M. and Wegner, E. (2012) 'Socio-economic voter profile and motives for Islamist support in Morocco', *Party Politics*, on-line preview available at http://ppq.sagepub.com.remote.library.dcu.ie/content/early/2012/03/14/1354068811436043 (accessed 5 May 2014).

Pratt, N. (2007) *Democracy and Authoritarianism in the Arab World*, Boulder, CO: Lynne Rienner Publishers.

— (2013) 'Egyptian women: between revolution, counter-revolution, Orientalism and "authenticity"' *Jadaliyya*, 6 May, available at: http://www.jadaliyya.com/pages/index/11559/egyptian-women_between-revolution-counter-revoluti (accessed 5 May 2014).

Schwedler, J. (2011) Can Islamists become moderates?', *World Politics*, 63 (2): 347–76.

Skalli, L. (2011) 'Generational politics and renewal of leadership in the Moroccan women's movement', *International Feminist Journal of Politics*, 13 (3): 329–48.

Tchaicha, J. and Arfaoui, K. (2012) 'Tunisian women in the twenty-first century: past achievements and present uncertainties in the wake of the Jasmine Revolution', *Journal of North African Studies*, 17 (2): 215–38.

Wadud, A. (2006) *Inside Gender Jihad: Women's Reform in Islam*, Oxford: Oneworld Publications.

Webb, P. and Childs, S. (2012) 'Gender politics and conservatism: the view from the British Conservative Party grassroots', *Government and Opposition*, 47 (1): 21–48.

Woltering, R. (2002) 'The roots of Islamist popularity', *Third World Quarterly*, 23 (6): 1133–43.

Index

Entries in italics refer to tables and figures.

Lightning Source UK Ltd.
Milton Keynes UK
UKOW07n1144101114

241350UK00002B/109/P